zinester's guide to
NYC

edited by

AYUN HALLIDAY

ISBN 978-1-934620-46-5
This is Microcosm #76084

First Edition - 5,000 copies - Jan 2011

Distributed in the booktrade by AK PRESS
674 A 23rd St.
Oakland, CA 94612
www.akpress.org
sales@akpress.org
510.208.1700

GRAPHIC DESIGN : JOE BIEL
FONTS: IAN LYNAM | IANLYNAM.COM
COVER ILLUSTRATION & LETTERING: NATE BEATY | NATEBEATY.COM

Microcosm Publishing
222 S. Rogers St.
Bloomington, IN 47404
(812)323-7395

Microcosm hQ Store
636 11th Ave.
Portland, OR 97214
(503)232-3666

WWW.MICROCOSMPUBLISHING.COM

INTRODUCTION

Welcome to New York! Contrary to what you may have heard, we're glad you're here, and even gladder that you're keen on deviating from paths well worn by other visitors.

NYC has five boroughs, all seamlessly connected by subway...uh, except Staten Island. It's no longer chic for Manhattanites to claim they've never been to Brooklyn except for Coney Island. Queens is a chowhound mecca. The Bronx is up, and all of NYC is your oyster.

We decided to organize this guidebook by category, rather than neighborhood. If we'd gone by neighborhood, you might notice how Bushwick gets much more ink than, say, the Upper East Side. What can we say? That's where we go, and if you're crashing on the couch of cash-strapped artist friends it may well be where you're staying.

Some of our listings are here because they'd be awesome anywhere. Others will help you navigate neighborhoods whose charms may not be as readily apparent as those of such popular destinations as the East Village or Williamsburg.

The one thing contributors have in common is we all make zines—self-published labors of love. It's not exactly what you'd call a mainstream activity, and that is reflected in our choices (it's also why we've devoted an entire category to photocopying).

If you're so inclined, make a one-shot zine about your experiences here and send it to us when you get home. It could be a lot of fun.

There are sushi bars that don't have websites, and holes in the wall that do. It's usually safe to assume that a restaurant will be open by noon. Be forewarned that stores selling the sorts of things you technically can live without may not open until the employees have had brunch. On the flipside, it's always possible to buy tampons, chips, cough medicine, condoms, and green tea ice cream, because the graveyard shift at the corner bodega are NYC's true 24 Hour Party People.

There are invariably several choices of subway stops near your destination, particularly if we're talking about a Manhattan address. We've chosen to go with the station that's nearest. For convenience's sake, you may want to check out the alternatives before embarking on your journey.

Outside of the Corporate Behemoth section, there are very few national chains listed, though some did sneak in. Contributors who've spent their whole lives in NYC may well find them exotic. Perhaps they remind the others of home.

Speaking of chains, some local businesses have multiple locations. Having agonized over the convenience vs. authenticity issue, we've led with the Manhattan branches, though rest assured that if those locations are but pale imitations of the Jackson Heights or Flushing flagship, you'll hear about it within the listing.

In terms of restaurants, we wound up with one giant mutant category that's been given the handle General Eats. Most of these places are open for lunch and dinner. Sometimes they're open for breakfast. Sometimes they're open 'til 4 in the morning. If you need to know for sure, call ahead.

The giant mutant category approach is not without its quirks. For instance, anyone who has gotten off the L train at Bedford Avenue can vouch that Williamsburg is chock full of places to eat. And yet the ZG2NYC chooses to list none of them? Check again! Exploding out the ass end of General Eats you'll find specialty categories ranging from breakfast to sweets, and enough Williamsburg listings to choke any number of indie rockers. While some of these restaurants may indeed specialize in the category in which they appear, others are there because that's the way the contributor who wrote the listing thinks of the place. One man's bar is another man's (or transman's or woman's) café.

And that applies throughout. That's why we've got a cheese store listed in the art supplies section.

If we had our way, none of these places would close, ever. The events would always go on in perpetuity. Real estate developers would keep their mitts off Coney Island, black box theaters, and beloved neighborhood dive bars. But change is a part of life in NYC, so cover your heiner with a little research, and remember that no matter what happens, it's an adventure.

Don't forget to send us a postcard! Or an email. Or your zine. We'd love to leverage your expertise and experience in the next edition of the ZG2NYC.

Ayun Halliday
PO Box 22754 Brooklyn NY 11202

Zinester's guide to NYC

edited by
Ayun Halliday

MICROCOSM PUBLISHING

Table of Contents

TRANSPORTATION

Public Transportation
www.mta.info
The Metropolitan Transit Authority governs all recommended ways of getting around town except those on water, or directly powered by our own legs. Below is some practical advice for riding the MTA.

Metrocard
This is the yellow card you swipe at subway turnstiles, or dip when boarding the bus. You can buy a Metrocard with cash, a debit card, or a credit card from vending machines by the turnstiles. You can also add money to an existing card.

Metrocard vending machines are as cranky as token booth attendants used to be. They're famous for rejecting dog-eared bills and worn credit cards, especially when I'm running late and my train is pulling into the station. Many stations retain their human staffers, but the only thing they can sell you is a single ride card, and even that's iffy. They may not have change. Their primary functions these days are to dispense information, bust would-be fare jumpers, and be available in case of an emergency.

The first swipe deducts $2.25; the second is free, provided it occurs on a different line within two hours of the first swipe. If you are treating a friend or friends, go first and dip or swipe the same number of times as there are riders,

then proceed through the turnstile one after the other. This will ensure that you get all the transfers you've got coming on the second round, when a single dip or swipe will suffice for the lot of you.

You can transfer from subway to bus, bus to subway, bus to bus, but you can't pop up out of the subway, have lunch, walk a few blocks, and then use your transfer to get on the subway again. No subway to subway transfers, nor can you reboard the same bus line, even if it's going in the opposite direction.

Route Planning
The MTA's website has a plan-your-ride feature on its homepage.

A lot of people like a website called HopStop, but I have found that its zeal for navigational minutiae rivals my late grandfather's in making things unnecessarily complex. It would have you take a 45-minute bus ride in order to begin your journey at the subway station on the corner, rather than have you walk the five blocks on either end to the subway line that would be a much straighter, and shorter shot. Don't let me stop you though: www.hopstop.com/?city=newyork

If you've got a tight schedule, be sure to go online to check if your travel plans will be affected by service advisories: www.tripplanner.mta.info/serviceadvisory

Maps
My advice is to do like Magellan, and use a map! This will not only give you some spatial understanding of how the city's laid out, you'll get a sense for what's right next to where, so you won't end up thinking like HopStop.

Subway maps are displayed on the wall near the main entrance's token booth, and should also be posted near the doors in every subway car. In bigger stations like the one on West 4th Street, where four lines stop on the downstairs platform and another three upstairs, there are giant subway maps with schedules in freestanding glass frames.

You can also get a free subway map from the token booth operator. Get one every day! They make nice wrapping paper.

Don't feel shy about asking your fellow riders if you're waiting on the right platform, or boarding the right train. It's not even a tourist question! There are plenty of lines I take infrequently and would much rather seek help than find I'm heading toward a connection that only works on weekdays.

Zinester's Favorite Books About NYC: Extremely

You'll also find some basic maps in the back of this book.

Etiquette

Whenever you are about to use public transportation, if there is even one person about to get off, stand to the side of the door until the passengers have exited. This is very important: Then and only then should you get in the subway or on the bus. This is a matter of courtesy. Everything will move along quickly and easily if you let everyone off first. – Josh Saitz

Gentlemen, we know your balls are smokin', but please find some other way to air them besides sitting with your thighs akimbo, taking up more space than the single passenger allotment. And don't be like Principal Skinner's mother and give your change purse a seat all to itself when others are standing.

Even if it means your friend will spend a few stops sitting next to a stranger, offer your seat to those who really need it—elderly people, disabled people, people traveling with small children, pregnant women and pregnant transmen...maybe even someone encumbered with luggage or heavy looking parcels.

The MTA doesn't want you holding the doors for people, but my feeling is that if someone's hauling ass through the turnstiles with a wild look of anxiety, it's discourteous not to. – AH

Getting Out of Airports

There are many ways to get to and from the various airports, in addition to cadging a ride from a friend. (And please be advised that even those with cars in NYC may be hesitant about picking you up, if it means battling rush hour traffic and losing their parking spaces.) I have never been one to leap in a cab. I'd rather put the money toward something tastier.

JFK
www.mta.info/mta/airtrain.htm 1-877-JFK-AIRT
The Air Train - subway combo is a highly civilized way to get all the way to your destination from JFK for about the same price as getting to the nearest airport hotel in a cab. From the airport, follow the signs to the Air Train. You won't have to wait long. Those light rail suckers pride themselves on going very few places but the Howard Beach A train station, which is where you're likely heading, unless you're crashing with a friend in Long Island or deepest Queens, in which case you may prefer the Air Train bound for Jamaica Station, where you can catch the Long Island Rail Road, the E, Z, and J trains, and a bunch of Queens-y buses.

No need to dig for your wallet until arriving at Howard Beach or Jamaica, where there are the same Metro Card vending machines you'll find in any subway station, except these ones are tended by actual humans whose job it is to help the hopelessly corn-fused. You'll want to load that card up with a minimum of $7.50, $5 of which will be deducted as soon as you pass into the subway station proper. Make it $9.75 and you'll be fixed for your next ride, too. Maps in the subway station will help you figure out how to make the necessary connections to your ultimate destination.

LaGuardia
www.mta.info/nyct/service/airport.htm
If you like Indian food, hate unnecessary expense, and aren't racing to make a departing flight, you're going to love the Q33 bus between LaGuardia and the 74th St-Broadway/Roosevelt Ave stop in Jackson Heights. Upon landing, follow the ground transit signs to the bus stop. You shouldn't have to wait more than 20 minutes. Have a few singles and some change because there's no Metrocard vending in the airport, and you have to pay for the bus with exact change.

Don't worry about missing your stop. It's the last one and the driver will announce it loud and proud. Should your tank be in need of filling before you continue on your journey, ask a friendly local to give you a nudge toward 74th St, where a host of Indian restaurants, groceries, and sari stores await. Alternately, walk east along Roosevelt Ave, under the elevated tracks, and you'll come to Little Columbia (the country, not the University). Whenever you're ready you can get back on the subway and board the E/F/M/R or 7 toward your destination.

Newark
www.panynj.gov/airports/ewr-airtrain.html
www.njtransit.com
Oh shit, you let 'em book you into Newark? Just kidding, they've got an Air Train now too. It'll connect you with an Amtrak train or a New Jersey Transit bus, getting you to Penn Station for under 12 bucks. From thence you can get the A/C/E.

Islip
Do not let anyone book you into NYC via Islip.

Bridges

New York City has so many beautiful bridges, the best, of course, being the Brooklyn Bridge.

Walk over them. Bike over them. The bridges ranked highest as ZG2NYC correspondents' favorite places to ride their bikes.

If you want company, direct action environmental group Times Up! sponsors two beautiful Bridges by Night rides, one uptown, the other crossing the Queensboro, Pulaski, Williamsburg, Manhattan, and Brooklyn bridges.

Every New Year's Eve a tour guide named Dr. Phil leads a group across the Brooklyn Bridge, but at 60 bucks a head, I'd advise doing it yourself for free.

Or enjoy them by transit. The B/D/N/Q trains offer glam views as they cross the Manhattan Bridge.

The artist Barton Lidice Benes' Curiosa collection includes a severed human toe someone found on the Williamsburg Bridge.

The billy goats're up, and the hungry troll's down, New York, New York! It's a helluva town!

Boats

Gondola in Central Park
Loeb Boathouse (near 72nd & 5th Ave)
212-517-2233
www.thecentralparkboathouse.com/sections/gondola.htm

I have never done this because $30 per half hour makes it seem like a water-born limo to nowhere, but split between six friends that could be okay. Turning a blind eye for the moment to the striped shirt and straw hat the gondolier is forced to wear, this is a far more humane tourist trip-trap than a horse drawn carriage.

Staten Island Ferry
Whitehall Terminal
1 Whitehall St (@South St) 718-876-8441
www.nyc.gov/html/dot/html/ferrybus/statfery.shtml (1 to South Ferry)
Those taking the Staten Island Ferry are under no obligation to get off in Staten Island. One of our correspondents lives there, but the others mainly use the ferry as a conduit to romance. It's also free, and the views are spectacular!

Ikea Water Taxi

from Wall Street to Red Hook, Brooklyn
Pier 11
Wall St @ South St, phone
Financial District: subway
www.nywatertaxi.com/commuters/ikeawww.nywatertaxi.com/commuters/ikea
Monday-Friday, noon – 9pm
Saturday & Sunday 11:40am – 8pm
The yellow and black water taxis are one of the cuter ways to destroy your hairdo, but they ain't cheap. I guess there are those who actually use them to commute to their jobs, but many New Yorkers regard these as more for holiday pleasure seekers.

Ride free on the weekend, or all the time if you're under 12. On weekdays, Ikea will subsidize $5 of the non-kid water taxi fare (i.e. the return trip) if you drop at least $10 in-store. You pass by the Statue of Liberty and can wander Red Hook, which has great key lime pie at Steve's and boasts one of my favorite bars, Sonny's.

Tram

Roosevelt Island Tramway
TramPlaza
59th St & 2nd Ave, 212-832-4543, x-1
www.rioc.com/transportation.htm
The Roosevelt Island Tram costs the same as taking the subway. It's a bright red bit of a thrill, and a very popular field trip destination for 2ndgraders. Once you're on Roosevelt Island, you can catch a bus—also red—for 25¢!

Driving & Parking

Do not drive or rent a car if you're staying in the city.

If you bring your car, odds are it will be stolen, damaged, towed, or dented.

If you rent a car, you'll get ripped off by the rental agency, you'll go insane trying to park, you'll get run off the road by crazed cab drivers, and you'll probably end up wishing you'd never been born.

New York City, as a whole, hates cars, and to show you how much, it imposes confusing and ridiculous regulations and offers few public places to park. Most private garages will charge you about $8 per half hour to park, before any surcharges—and before the 18.25% parking tax.

The city has done everything it possibly can to discourage you from bringing a car. Take the hint. The city has cheap,

Love You More Than You Know • Peops- Fly •

(THE CROSS BRONX / MAJOR DEEGAN INTERCHANGE)

simple, and efficient public transportation and more cabs than most other cities have cars. It's safer, smarter, and easier to not have a car, trust me. – Josh Saitz

I know some of you are on tour, and need to park, refuel and possibly sleep in the van. Most of the people who seem like they've got it together automotively figure out a way to ditch their cars across the river in New Jersey or Queens and take transit into the city.

There's a website called Primospot (www.primospot.com) that can help you out with interactive dirt on parking regulations, parking garages, and (yay!) bike racks. The site covers NYC as well as relatively headache-free locations like Weehawken and Hoboken. - AH

Taxis
Cabs are expensive and prone to hitting bicyclists. Avoid them.

Chinatown Buses
www.staticleap.com/chinatownbus
If you want to go to another big city on the northern part of the eastern seaboard, Chinatown buses are the way to go. They literally take you from one Chinatown to another

Chinatown (Boston, Philly, DC, etc.) They were originally started in 1998 to transport restaurant workers. Today they are populated by anyone who doesn't want to splurge for a train ticket.

Chinatown buses are much cheaper and faster than Greyhound or other traditional bus companies. They tend to be old buses (make sure your seat does not have a major malfunction), and the operations have little overhead—most do not have a waiting room or even a ticket counter. They don't make a bunch of stops like other regional buses. And they speed a lot.

Most companies are pretty interchangeable. Some even have free wifi.

Typical Chinatown Bus prices:

NYC to Philly	$12 one-way, $20 roundtrip
NYC to Boston	$15 one-way, $30 roundtrip
NYC to DC	$20 one-way, $35 roundtrip

You can buy tickets online, but I prefer just to go down there and buy them in person. I like the flexibility of not committing to a departure time and I don't trust that they have a secure website.

Buses to different cities leave from different places, so it's best to look them up online before heading out. Once you are in the right area, women will shout at you asking where you want to go and aggressively usher you to the bus of the company they work for. You'll end up in the right city, but you could end up on the 8pm bus for one company, even though there is a 7:30 bus for another company right there. Buses leave frequently, either on the hour or half hour. If you have a few minutes to kill, pick up some snacks for your trip. I suggest a veggie steam bun.

Some newer companies, like MegaBus and BoltBus, offer cheaper tickets if you buy them online way ahead of time. The ticket prices the week of tend to be about the same as a Chinatown bus. – Amanda Plumb

HOUSING

Where you stay depends on what you're into, who you're with, how uptight you are, and how much you're willing to pay.

While you're researching accommodations, don't forget to check out creative (and more up-to-date) options). If you don't have friends or friend-of-friends to stay with, try couch surfing (www.couchsurfing.org) or Book Your Own Fuckin' Life (www.byofl.org).

Or check out craigslist, where you'll find people looking to sublet their apartment for like three days. (www.newyork.craigslist.org/sub)

Other up-to-the-minute budget lodging tips can be found on the Lonely Planet's Thorn Tree discussion boards. (www.lonelyplanet.com/thorntree/forum)

My dad's friend has good luck with Priceline.com. He usually ends up paying $80 to stay in the New Yorker, a giant old hotel that's nothing special, and neither is the neighborhood, but it's centrally located and the subway's right there.

Most locals are clueless about lodging and your authors are no exception. We did some looking around, but take the listings below with a grain of salt.

East Village Bed & Coffee
110 Ave C (btwn 7th & 8th St) 917-816-0071
www.bedandcoffee.com (East Village: 6 to Astor Pl)

Any time I have the option to stay in a place where every room has its own distinct personality and name, I end up falling in love with the most expensive one, and booking the cheapest. This one is the exception—the Dutch Room totally sucked me in with its bright orange walls! At $115 a night, it's also the cheapest. My kind of place! Shared bathrooms! Meet the neighbors. Bring walking shoes because it's a hike to the subway.

St. Mark's Hotel
2 St. Mark's Pl (btwn 2nd Ave & 3rd Ave) 212-674-0100
www.stmarkshotel.net (East Village: 6 to Astor Pl)
I remember when this one rented by the hour. I can't imagine that it had Pottery Barn-looking headboards back then. There will be plenty of yahoos out your front door, but you'll have a private bathroom.

Bowery's Whitehouse Hotel of New York
340 Bowery (btwn Great Jones and Bond) 212-477-5623
www.whitehousehotelofny.com (NoHo: F to 2nd Ave)
In a not-so-distant past incarnation this hotel was chronicled in David Isay's Flophouse: Life on the Bowery. Latticework separates the tops of the walls from the ceilings in tiny, windowless rooms, and bedbugs are rumored to remain. Trust me, despite the photo on the website, Bill Clinton did not sleep here. Potentially a perfect choice for intrepid urban history freaks who relish every fart and squeak.

Jazz on the Town Hostel
307 E. 14th St (btwn 1st & 2nd Ave) 212-228-2780
www.jazzhostels.com (East Village: L to 1st Ave)
Don't expect that official AYHA Boy Scout feel. There are a bunch of Jazz variations for uptown boys and girls, mostly around Harlem and Morningside Heights. Stay in any of them for two nights, and you can stay for a week on the Ronnybrook Farm in the Hudson River Valley for $99! For a week! You contribute about 35 hours of volunteer labor to the farm in return for round trip transport from the Union Square Greenmarket, veggie meals, and accommodations in the farmhouse! Dang!

Larchmont Hotel
27 W. 11th St (btwn 5th and 6th Ave) 212-989-9333
www.larchmonthotel.com
(Greenwich Village: L/N/Q /R/4/5/6 to Union Sq)
This European hotel seems like it could be a romantic place for new couples to stay, unless you were hoping to get it on in the bathtub. (Shower and toilet are down the hall, mon frere.) Breakfast's included.

Reverend Jen • Up At the Old Hotel – Joseph

Chelsea International Hostel
251 W. 20th St (btwn 7th and 8th Ave) 212-647-0010
www.chelseahostel.com (Chelsea: 1 to 18th St)
They're doing their bit to keep NYC's scary reputation
alive by emphasizing their 24-hour-security staff, Chelsea's low crime rate, and a "highly motivated maintenance and maid staff." Hmm.

New York International HI-AYH Hostel
891 Amsterdam Ave (@ 103rd St) 212-932-2300
www.hinewyork.org (Morningside Hts: 1 to 103rd St)
A beautiful, big old brick pile, the kind of place Miss
Clavel might have taken her charges if Madeline had ever
made it to New York. It's also way the hell uptown, which
could be a drag if your nightly activities transpire, as
mine often do, on the Lower East Side and in Brooklyn.

Awesome Bed & Breakfast
136 Lawrence St (btwn Fulton & Willoughby, Downtown
Bklyn) 718-858-4859
www.awesome-bed-and-breakfast.com
(Downtown Bklyn: M/R to Lawrence)
When my old friend Tom was looking for recommendations for places to stay on a holiday weekend with his
wife, this is one of the places I threw at them, and he
reported that they had a swell time. Brooklyn-wise, you're
walking distance to Boerum Hill and Fort Greene, and like
seven minutes by subway to the Lower East Side.

The New York Loft Hostel
249 Varet St (btwn Bogart & White, Bushwick, Bklyn)
718-366-1351
www.nylofthostel.com (Bushwick: L to Morgan Ave)
I'm fixated on the idea of a pair of nice, not-yet-worldly,
European backpackers arriving here from some fresh
mountainous land, seeing the Boar's Head plant and the
desolate streets and wondering what the hell they've gotten themselves into. Actually, I think staying here would
make you feel pretty in-the-know. And that short ride to
the attractions of Manhattan is even shorter if you get off
in Williamsburg!

WHY AM I HERE?
They are any number of ways to find out what's going on
at any given time...

Free
Nonsense New York
www.nonsensenyc.com
This is the greatest resource ever. Many of the events never appear in the weekly magazines and alternative papers.
Most are free or low budget, and the listing is emailed every Friday. There are always people looking to sublet their
rooms in a queer-friendly, vegan, bike-centric Bed-Stuy
or Bushwick communal housing situation. Others are

recruiting participants for pranks and festivals. Once a month, ongoing volunteer and learning opportunities are posted *en masse*. Email Jeff if you're putting on an event. – AH (Sign up for Jeff Stark's Nonsense list of things to do that are like, your roommate's girlfriend's bandmate's party. Everything on the list is something you would find out about if you had all of NY's coolest people as friends. I do not have those friends, therefore I rely on the list. It's free and old school and I couldn't live here without it. – Andria Alefi) (Online only)

Free NYC
www.freenyc.net
This daily email yields about four activities per day. Some events show up week after week, like a sketch comedy group with a Monday night gig in a downtown bar. Free NYC also brings to the fore strange one-offs, like a nou-veau weenie stand giving their bulgogi dogs out free on Christmas Day. If you're hosting a free event, this could be your best publicity outlet. (Online only)

Chowhound
www.chowhound.chow.com/boards
If there's an obscure foreign delicacy you're itching to sample, do a search of Chowhound's Outer Borough Dis-cussion Boards. Odds are good you'll stumble upon a pas-sionate debate as to which roving food cart or unmarked hole-in-the-wall makes it better. There are also articles, recipes, trip reports from fellow low budge epicures, and seasonal panic attacks centering on the best restaurants for Thanksgiving, Christmas, New Year's Eve, and im-pending marriage proposals. (Online only)

The Village Voice
www.villagevoice.com
Terminally skinnier, but still free every Wednesday. If nothing else, *The Voice* is still an acceptable source for finding out about Manhattan movie times and expert bodywork performed by discreet Russian ladies, Asian she-males, and large busted glamour pusses with handles like Domineek and Fantazia. I'm kind of a sucker for Michael Musto's local homo/theater dish and food critic Robert Sietsema's "Counter Culture" column. – AH

The Onion
www.avclub.com/newyork
Also free, also hitting the streets on Wednesdays, the print version of *The Onion* is a constant source of pleasure. Tragically, its NYC-specific "AV Club" listings section has been whittled down to a ghost of its former self. There's still at least one excellent interview a week, in which a

notable personage gets to sound like an actual human being—just the right amount of reading material for your average subway ride.

The L Magazine
www.thelmagazine.com
The digest-sized *L* is free, ubiquitous, listings-packed, and written by veritable infants. While it sometimes feels like their sex advice columnist and restaurant critics are leaning on the snark to cover up some behind-the-ears wetness, the man on the street type interviews with cab drivers (including where they were hailed, where they hail from, and their previous professions) are a down-to-earth pleasure. – AH

Edible Brooklyn
www.ediblebrooklyn.com
Don't pick this one up if you're allergic to the word "ar-tisanal." And don't pick up its Manhattan cousin expect-ing it to be free, because Whole Foods will think you're shoplifting. But if you get off on sustainable agriculture, home brewing, the slow food movement, and down-sized executives who realize their real life's work is raising bees or baking cookies, hit any upscale-ish gourmet store in Brooklyn for your copy of this lovingly photographed, non-glossy mag.

My Open Bar
www.myopenbar.com
My Open Bar keeps tabs on happy hours, drink specials, which restaurants give away a free glass of wine with pur-chase of entrée, and which bar justifies their weeknight cover with free PBR and tater tots. (Online only)

Sheckys
www.sheckys.com
If you want to find a good place to drink in NYC, make it easy on yourself and go to Shecky's. They review every bar in the city and organize them by crowd, price, location, etc. I am not saying this because the owner was my col-lege roommate, I am saying it because he actually sends people into every bar to write real human reviews. – Josh Saitz (Online only)

Art Cards
www.artcards.cc
Art Cards lists gallery and art museum events, openings, and ongoing shows in Manhattan, and to a lesser degree, the other boroughs and nearby New Jersey. You can sign up to get it as a free weekly email. One nice feature is a heads up for shows that are about to close soon. (Online only)

Donleavy • A New York Diary by Julie Doucet

Wag Mag
www.wagmag.org
Wag Mag, the Brooklyn Monthly Art Guide lists art exhibitions in Brooklyn. It's particularly helpful at ferreting out worthy looksees in frontiers like Bushwick and Bed-Stuy, where both the rents and advertising budgets are low. The digest-size print version can be pretty difficult to find outside of Williamsburg.

Paper Magazine
www.papermag.com
Paper, the self-described "Guide to New York Nightlife and Beyond," doesn't seem as glam as it once did, but their website is sz a good way to find out if say, Kenny Scharf's decking the interns out in day-glo body paint at some Cosmic Cavern party last week.

Showpaper
www.myspace.com/showpaper
A community-run, biweekly listings broadsheet that puts a ton of free and cheap all-ages shows above the radar. So egalitarian they list venues in Connecticut, New Jersey, and Westchester County! Who knows? It may be worth the trip. To scare up a copy of the terminally-in-danger-of-going-under print version, paw around Greenpoint, Williamsburg, and the Lower East Side.

Next
www.nextmagazine.net
Next is free, glossy, and gay, with an emphasis on drag events and ripped guys in slingshot undies. It's a good way to find out about nightlife. The print version is available in many gay-owned businesses, with a high concentration in Chelsea and the West Village.

Go City Kids
www.gocitykids.parentsconnect.com/region/new-york-ny-usa
This is where I turn on Saturday morning, when it's sleeting and no activities have been set up in advance. It's totally democratic (free-of-charge colonial craft demonstrations rub elbows with big ticket Disney Princesses on Ice) but it's bound to flush the children out of our apartment one way or another and that's what counts. Be sure to click the calendar on the left for the full menu, not just the handful the editors are choosing to feature. (Online only)

Gawker
www.gawker.com
Gawker serves up Manhattan celebrity sightings for the commenting pleasure of serpents who use their office jobs to spew great volumes of quick-witted venom. If you see a celebrity doing anything worth mentioning, you can tip them off with an email or by calling 646-214-8138. (Online only)

Gothamist
www.gothamist.com
The Gothamist is Gawker for lovers of NYC breaking news. If there's a night club to be shut down for smoking violations, a local politician making a fool of him or herself, a supermarket chain being picketed, or a celeb denouncing *The New York Post* for making mean comments about her weight, Gothamist covers it with the cynicism and humor of the insanely well-informed. (Online only)

Todd P's list
www.toddpnyc.com
Todd P is a promoter who books tons of all-ages shows, which he then lists on his website. He also maintains a pretty up-to-the-minute list of links to these oft-underground venues, so if you're a band looking for a place to play, he may well be your man. (Online only)

The Douglas Kelley Show List
www.dks.thing.net
The Douglas Kelley Show List is a component of the Douglas Kelley Show, viewable on YouTube, and is a good way to scare up a manageable dose of music and art listings simultaneously. (Online only)

Free & Pay-What-You-Can Schedules for NYC Museums
www.ny.com/museums/free.html
Except for MOMA being open on Monday when just about everything else is closed, I can't keep all the museums' schedules in my head. And now they're all leaping into bed with Target, whose great red dotted benevolence makes possible free hours at MOMA, the Brooklyn Museum, El Museo del Barrio, the New Museum, and the Museum of Chinese in America. (Online only)

Oh My Rockness
www.ohmyrockness.com
Oh My Rockness gives you lots of lead time to line up a posse or a date for indie rock shows in both all-ages and over-21 venues. Band interviews and free MP3s can help you decide. Sign up for the free weekly email and you may win free tickets. (Online only)

NYC Punks
www.myspace.com/nycpunks
&
Brooklyn Vegan
www.brooklynvegan.com
Reliable sources for finding out about all-ages venues and house shows in Brooklyn. (Online only)

AM New York
www.amny.com
AM New York, handed out free in the mornings to subway commuters, is good for short, bite-sized reviews and articles about happenings in the city. – Josh Medsker.

Possibly worth paying for
The New York Times
www.nytimes.com
Please buy a copy, then leave it neatly folded on the subway bench for the rest of us.

The New Yorker
www.newyorker.com
I get an undeniable thrill from reading the New Yorker in New York City, emitting a small yelp of acceptance and/or envy when they publish a humorous caricature of some performer or event in my actual orbit. Reading the listings reminds me that there are people here who care as much about dance as I do movies.

Time Out New York
www.newyork.timeout.com
If you're only in town for a week, it's definitely worth parting with a few bucks for a copy of this rag's comprehensive listing. They care about some of the same things I do, as well as many I don't, like speed dating, fitness promotions, and sample sales. It's a particularly good source for finding out about readings. Everyone with a toe in the NYC arts scene should be grateful to them for their color photographs and friendliness toward those of us who have yet to become critical darlings or household names.

Time Out Kids
www.newyorkkids.timeout.com
Family events used to occupy a full section of regular Time Out, but I guess all those sing-alongs and mask-making workshops were shrinking their childless readers' libidos or something, because now this information is ghetto-ized into a monthly magazine of its own.

New York Magazine
www.nymag.com
I like New York Magazine the best. What can I say, I am literate. I would avoid the NYPress because not only is it horrible and annoying, their opinions are worthless. – Josh Saitz

Blogs
Blogs aren't zines. You'll never find them in a basement or used bookstore. You can't hand one to a stranger on the subway. I had one for a year and it was a millstone around my neck. Fortunately, there are those who don't feel that way, and cafés that juice them up with free wifi, so they don't have to spend all their time hunched in their apartments, writing about how cool their neighborhoods are. If you're interested in a particular part of NYC, type that neighborhood's name plus the word "blog" into a search engine, and you'll come across some tech savvy,

Richard Price • The Air-Conditioned Nightmare

photographically skilled cyber-Pepys, exhaustively documenting his or her coordinates' openings, closings, deals, gossip and dust-ups.

Here are a few to give you a taste.

EV Grieve www.evgrieve.com
Greenwich Village Daily Photo
www.greenwichvillagenydailyphoto.blogspot.com
Bowery Boogie www.boweryboogie.com
Uptown Flavor www.uptownflavor.com
Free Williamsburg www.freewilliamsburg.com
Bushwick BK www.bushwickbk.com
Brooklyn Based www.brooklynbased.net
Joey in Astoria www.astorianyc.blogspot.com
Curbed www.curbed.com
Eater www.ny.eater.com
New York Shitty www.newyorkshitty.com
Streetsblog www.streetsblog.org

ANNUAL EVENTS

One of the things I love about NYC is all the things I end up missing. No matter how hard I try, something I'd love to go to will end up conflicting with something else I'd love to go to, and sometimes I find out about both of them after the fact. Fortunately, some events happen year after year, so you can perpetually look forward to them with excitement rather than a sigh of regret.

Try to do a little advance research, as many annual events' schedules get jimmied around from year to year.

You'll find more annual events like film festivals, music fests, food-related events, craft fairs, and free summer fun in their own sections.

January
New Years Day Coney Island Polar Bear Plunge
January 1
www.polarbearclub.org
Coney Island, Brooklyn
On New Year's Day, the ranks of the Coney Island Polar Bear Club swell with thrill-seeking once-in-a-lifetimers, who usually arrive in pairs. A few have camera-wielding, head-shaking supporters on the shore. Bring your warmies and some surf booties to protect your feet when you accidentally step on a broken beer bottle left over from last summer, when it was actually almost warm enough to get in the water.

No Pants Subway Ride
Early to Mid January
www.improveverywhere.com/missions/the-no-pants-subway-ride
Various subway lines throughout NYC
A liberating tradition, courtesy of Improv Everywhere's master prank-builders. Monitor the website for the date and starting locations. Join the throngs at the meet-up spot, where your instructions will be doled-out via bullhorn. You'll be given a line to ride and a prearranged stop before which you must shuck your trousers prior to disembarking. Then you hang out on the platform in your coat and skivvies until the next train arrives. The pantsless hordes will continue to multiply until mysteriously, as if by secret signal, you all get off together, and cross the platform to await the next train en masse. Bring a friend, your best poker face, and some underwear that looks like underwear.

Idiotarod
Last Saturday in January
www.cartsofbrooklyn.com
Those Alaskans think they're so big with their sled dogs and their Iditarod. Yeah, well we've got shopping carts

and teams of 20-somethings too liquored-up to feel the cold. Mush! Mush! The website is necessarily vague about the route in the days leading up to the race. Williamsburg is a good bet. If you're feeling husky, you might be able to join Kostume Kult's team, provided you can pull together a non-lame, last-minute costume that fits within the parameters of their theme this year. (Put yourself on the notification list at www.kostumekult.com)

February

Chinese New Year
Usually falls in mid February, beginning on the 1st day of the Chinese calendar's 1st month
www.betterchinatown.com
The celebration lasts longer than a week, with events in Manhattan, Flushing, Sunset Park, and dozens of cultural institutions. What I like best is the culmination of the final Sunday's Lunar New Year Parade, when marauding *papier-mache* lions trick or treat door to door, shaking shopkeepers down for strings of cabbage and cash-filled red envelopes. Listen for drums west of Bowery and south of Canal, and you'll no doubt run into a few. I also like hanging out on Bayard west of Bowery as my fellow celebrants shoot off tissue paper cannons (which are, like the sawdust-packed poppers the kiddies love hurling into the street long after the party is over, much cheaper from vendors in the less touristic area further east). Claustrophobes should steer clear of any sidewalk where police barriers are creating gridlock, or at least attach themselves to a take-no-prisoners Chinatown granny, the only customers tough enough to bust through those stubborn clogs.

March

The Independent and Small Press Book Fair
A weekend in early March
The General Society of the Mechanics and Tradesmen
20 W. 44th St
www.nycip.org
A chance to mix it up in the world of independent publishing, though the high price of tabling and the nosebleed seats assigned to the smallest of the small fish don't exactly qualify as a participant bargain. Lots of good workshops and panels make it worth attending, as does getting a look at the venue, a grand old wood-paneled relic.

Phagwah Parade/Holi celebration
Usually falls in Mid-March, the Sunday after the first full moon of the Hindu calendar
www.queens.about.com/od/holidays/p/phagwah.htm
This is a good annual spring event, though it's a trek out to Queens' Richmond Hill neighborhood. It's the "festival of colors"—you'll be doused from head to foot with multicolor baby powders, so dress accordingly. Seriously great food, especially sweets, is all over the place—mostly for free, as people will come up to you, douse you with colors, and then give you snacks! It will totally rock your world! – Jerry the Mouse

LepreCon
The Saturday before St. Patrick's Day
To the best of my knowledge, referring to yourself as Patty O'Furniture as you lurch from pub to pub in buckled shoes is not going to sully anyone's faith in leprechauns (or short skirted leprachaunettes). You will, however, earn the enmity of your fellow revelers if you show up in some lame-ass plastic derby from Party City, so liven the airport security bag screeners' day by coming prepared. Count on Nonsense New York and Time Out New York for event details at least a week in advance.

St Patrick's Day Parade
March 17, 5th Avenue from 44th to 86th St, 718-231-4400
www.nyc-st-patrick-day-parade.org
Once the frat rats start barfing green, it's time to get the hell out of this colorful, officially sanctioned event. Seek refuge in the National Jewelers Exchange on 47th St, where it'll just be you and the Orthodox Jewish jewelry vendors, glumly riding out their slowest day of their year.

The NYC Beard and Moustache Championships
Mid March
www.nycbmc.com
This isn't one of those pledge-driven see-how-long-you-can-go-without-shaving charity events. This is for fame and profit! There are eight categories so even unbearded ladies and scrub grassed menfolk can run for the roses.

Elephant Walk
Midnight, usually two nights before Ringling Brothers opens at Madison Square Garden, from 34th St from the Midtown Tunnel to Madison Square Garden
www.ringling.com/TourSchedule.aspx
A surreal annual sight, and you won't be alone if you decide to take it in with protest banner in hand. Call Ringling Brothers to see when the Walk will take place this year. (A tip: They won't tell you if you start haranguing the operator. Just say you've heard they do this, and you want to know when it is because you love elephants.)

Nick Courage • The Fearless series —

April

MOCCA fest
One weekend, early to mid April
www.moccany.com/mocca_festival.html
Dumpster your dinner and get behind on your rent to help you amass a nice thick wad to blow on indie comics at the Museum of Comic and Cartoon Art's annual clam-bake. If you put out your own comics, you should definitely splurge on a half-booth. Used to be the tragedy of this event was that it never failed to conflict with the Coney Island Mermaid Parade. Three cheers (non-Bronx variety) to whoever had the bright idea to move it to April!

Greek Independence Day Parade
www.paradeonfifth.org
&
Tartan Week
www.tartanweek.com
Early to Mid April
A couple of years back, I discovered the Greek Pride Parade along the eastern side of Central Park as well as Tartan Week in Grand Central Terminal on the same day, and I daresay it was lovely. – Marguerite Dabaie

Easter Parade
Easter Sunday, 5th Avenue from 49th to 57th, 10am – 4pm
www.ny.com/holiday/easter
A benign, directionless, drop-in promenade up and down 5th Avenue. Show up to show off your most over-the-top bonnet. For another, less benign sort of Easter Parade, position yourself on Park Avenue just as church lets out. Those conservatively dressed wealthy dowagers can sniff an outsider from half a block away. Watch the way they clutch their single daffodils to their bony chests as they refuse to return your smile! God bless us every one!

New York City Anarchist Bookfair
Judson Memorial Church, 55 Washington Square South (at University Place)
anarchistbookfair.net
(Greenwich Village: A/B/C/D/E/F/M to W 4th St)
Manhattan hosts its own version of the Anarchist Bookfair. Featuring vendors, talks, skillshares, videos, and discussions from folks from all over the country, the bookfair and workshops provide a broader access to anarchist ideas, practices, and thought for committed idealists and the anarcho-curious alike. –Joe Biel

* Left your calendar at home? If the sidewalks of Park Ave are blocked by imperious looking ladies clutching the daffodils they were given in church, it's Easter Sunday on the upper East Side. For fun, you can whisper 'electrified up the anus' to your companion every time you pass one in a fur coat. Act like rabble!

May

Annual May Day Demonstration in Union Square
Union Square Park
www.leftshift.org/may1/index.shtml
They don't call it Union Square for nuthin'. Since the early 20th century, 14th St. has been a hub of radical ideas and action, including the annual celebration of International Workers Day on May 1. The day-long event features cultural performances, speakers, and a spirited march to the downtown Federal Building. There's no better place to see the incredible diversity of New York's activist movements. –redguard

Free Comic Book Day
First Saturday in May – various venues
www.freecomicbookday.com
Who doesn't love a hand out? Lots of NYC comic vendors participate. Past years' booty has included a vintage Peanuts reissue, a sneak preview of Lynda Barry's *What It Is*,

and more superfriends than there is seating in the Hall of Justice.

Dance Parade
Mid May Down Broadway from 28th St, then across St. Mark's Pl to Tompkins Square
www.danceparade.org
None of that Bob Fosse uh-5-6-7-8 nonsense here. As long as you register for free in advance, you can dance down 5th Avenue with the best *and* the rest. You even get to state your preferred genre off a huge hooftastic menu, featuring such delicacies as Whirling Dervish, Bunny Hop, Roller Disco and Ecstatic.

June
Egg Rolls and Egg Creams
Early June, Eldridge Street btwn Canal & East Broadway
www.eldridgestreet.org/programs_c.htm
Having long celebrated Christmas together, the Jews and the Chinese team up on a bit of jointly controlled turf, inviting the public to sample their contributions to NYC's cultural mash. Tour the historic Eldridge Street synagogue, decorate a yarmulke, crowd around for free Chinese opera performances, and take multiple elbows to the kidneys, courtesy of pushy old ladies of both stripes determined to cut to the front of the dirt cheap egg cream line.

Earth Celebrations' Hudson River Pageant
Mid to late May
www.earthcelebrations.com/arts-pageants/hudson-river-pageant
The successor to Earth Celebrations' Rites of Spring Procession, a 15-year freaks' crusade to save the Lower East Side community gardens from real-estate-related destruction. The damage was done, some battles were won, and in time, the focus of this grand jamboree shifted toward climate change and the health of the Hudson River. The culmination of three months of community costume and puppet making workshops, this is a favorite of groovy children and adults whose love of Mother Earth finds an outlet in patchouli, gauze, and ankle bells.

Fleet Week
Usually the week before Memorial Day, NY Passenger Ship Terminal, Hudson River btwn 46th & 54th
www.cnic.navy.mil/cnrma/Programs/FWNY/index.htm
877-957-SHIP
Ever seen *On The Town*, you know the one, where Gene Kelly, Frank Sinatra, and Jules Munshin are sailors on 24-hour leave in New York City? Fleet Week's like that, but longer and multiplied by many thousands. You literally

will not be able to swing a cat in Times Square without bopping a stubble headed, middy blouse wearing boy (or girl, with longer hair and vastly less cool hat.) The public is invited to tour their ships, and the *Intrepid* hosts several events, including a parade of military craft down the Hudson.

Museum Mile
Usually first Tuesday in June, 5th Ave from 82nd to 105th
www.museummilefestival.org
A glorious time to go museum-hopping, when even "suggested" admissions are no longer suggested. This is the one night of the year they're all free, though only sprinters with attention deficit disorder should try hitting them all. The high concentration on the northern end makes it easy to zip out of El Museo del Barrio into the Museum of the City of New York, then back out again to the Jewish Museum. Or, you can stick it to the man all night long at the Guggenheim. Or just loiter on a car-free 5th Avenue, taking in the scene, listening to the bands, and join the chalk-drawing activities ostensibly aimed at children.

Figment NYC
Early June, Governors Island
www.figmentproject.org
For one weekend, Governors Island transforms itself into a tiny, mind-altering, (officially) substance-free, non-residential Burning Man, with sound installations, costumed bicycles, hula hoop-a-thons, giant puppets, roving performance, artist-designed mini golf, and other al fresco surprises. My only regret from 2009 is that I never did find the Gnome Village. If you're bursting with crazy ideas for portable sculptures, temporary structures, and creative mini golf holes, you should submit some designs for next year's festival!

National Puerto Rican Day Parade
2nd Sunday in June, 5th Avenue from 44th St to 86th St
www.nationalpuertoricandayparade.org
I've yet to meet a nation that doesn't throw down with an independence parade or heritage festival at some point on the NYC calendar, but here's one you can feel like you've participated in even if you don't actually get a chance to attend, thanks to the many giant Boricua-pride flags flapping out celebrants' car windows in the days leading up to the main event. Apparently there was a *Seinfeld* episode devoted to this, but I think I'd rather watch Rosie Perez's documentary, *Yo Soy Boricua, Pa'que tu lo Sepas!*

Playlist - Rachel Cohn & David Levithan

Make Music New York
Saturday or Sunday close to the the first day of summer, all over NYC
www.makemusicny.org
Don't you dare pay a cover charge today when hundreds of bands are playing for free in all five boroughs (and on Punk Island, better known the rest of the year as Governors Island). Indoors, outdoors, hip-hop, opera, salsa, jazz, big band, blues, shoegazers, and every kind of folk music known to man—just the Q-tip of this iceberg, baby. The festival's Mass Appeal program unites single players of a given instrument with others of their species in pre-specified locations. Dust off that bagpipe and play along!

Lesbian and Gay Pride Week and March
Mid to Late June, all over NYC (March runs down 5th Ave from 52nd, then west on 8th St)
www.hopinc.org
Come, come, Aunt Fanny, surely you must know that *every* week is Pride Week in NYC, but Sunday's parade is something not to miss (and for the length of its marathon duration, Seventh Avenue is something not to cross). I like to station myself towards the end of the route, to see which of the boa-flinging, panty-clad float riders are still workin' it after several hours of full-sun broiling beside refrigerator-sized speakers blaring Gloria Gaynor and Ru-Paul. Many ladies find the Rapture on the River women's dance gets rid of the nasty aftertaste they've been trying to free their mouths of ever since junior prom. – AH (I have never in my life seen so many trannies, well spandexed "packages," and just all-over people glory in one place. – Matana Roberts) (Though it has grown increasingly commercial, I never tire of the Pride festivities each June, particularly the Dyke March. – Jessica Max Stein)

Coney Island Mermaid Parade
Saturday closest to the 1st Day of Summer, Coney Island Boardwalk & Surf Ave, Brooklyn
www.coneyisland.com/mermaid.shtml
The East Village Inky's High Holy Day. Rain or shine, I'll be jiggling on up the boardwalk in a tail and kelp bra. You can too! Bring sunscreen, water, toilet paper, bribes for the judges, trinkets for the crowds, and a camera to take pictures of everyone else's fabulous costumes. Arrange to meet your friends in front of Cha-Cha's or something, because the poor cell phone reception all-but guarantees you'll never find them otherwise. Free to watch, and only $10 (and much more fun) to march.

July

Macy's 4th of July Fireworks
www.macys.com/campaign/sitelets/fireworks/index.jsp, 212-494-4495
This is but one opportunity to see fireworks in New York City. They shoot 'em off on New Year's Eve, Diwali, and every warm Coney Island Friday, but if you're homesick for your hometown display come Independence Day, you can take in the display from pretty much any rooftop, particularly one situated across the river from Manhattan. Also good from a kayak (Call 212-494-5243 for water-related restrictions).

Nathan's Famous Hot Dogs Hot Dog Eating Contest
July 4, 1310 Surf Ave, Coney Island, Brooklyn
www.nathansfamous.com
According to legend (Wikipedia) on July 4, 1916, four European immigrants held an impromptu hot dog eating contest to decide who was the most patriotic. Irishman James Mullen won the first contest, downing 13 dogs in 12 minutes. Recently, my friend Kim took her 12-year-old son Alex to watch the contest. In his words: "They eat so fast it's like a blur. It's like watching NASCAR, but they are eating." My friend AJ was there, too—protesting for animal rights. Sign up is online. – Amanda Plumb

The Big Draw
Saturday in mid July, at venues around Lower Manhattan
www.drawingcenter.org/events_bigdraw.cfm
You don't have to bother yourself about a sketchpad or a model or nothing. It's all provided for you. You may be hunched over, but you're not solitary, as artists and people who like to draw come together for one glorious day of communal sketching.

Missing Angel Juan – Francesca Lia Block

August

The Hong Kong Dragon Boat Festival
First Week in August, Flushing Meadows Park, Queens
www.hkdbf-ny.org
Rowing teams race long boats decorated with dragon heads at the prow through Meadow Lake to the beat of the drummer at the head of each boat. It's a great afternoon of cheering for the rowers with other performances throughout the day, such as live music and kung fu demonstrations by Shaolin monks. – Alisa Harris

Traditionally, Chinese Dragon Boat Festivals are held on the fifth day of the fifth month of the lunar calendar, but here in the US, they're always on the weekend. The boats are beautiful—the colors on the water in the summer sun are blinding, but in the best way. These are serious races in which teams compete for a major monetary prize, as well as the usual prestige that accompanies placing positions. Races run from morning to early evening. It's definitely a family affair, so bring the kids. – Melissa Bastian

Harlem Week
All summer long, but especially in August, Harlem
www.harlemweek.com, 212-862-7200
What started in 1974 as Harlem Day has mushroomed into a banquet of events running from June through October, still quaintly referred to as Harlem Week. August is when it kicks into high gear with concerts, vendors, the Uptown Saturday Night street fair, an auto show, the National Historic Black College Fair & Expo, a kid fest, and plenty of opportunities for senior citizens to strut their stuff. Head to the Hansborough Swimming Pool for a live demo by the Harlem Honeys and Bears, Manhattan's only synchronized swimming group for adults over age 50.

Dominican Independence Day Parade
August, Washington Heights
212-740-6806
Immigrants from the Dominican Republic are the largest (and growing) recent group of New Yorkers born outside the US. If you visit Washington Heights, you will be introduced to an amazing Dominican universe you may not have known existed. Now, it's true that February 27th is the official Dominican Independence Day, celebrating independence from Haiti in 1844, after a 22-year occupation. But August is when the Dominican Day Parade happens, on Pablo Duarte Boulevard (aka St. Nicholas Ave) from around 188th Street down to around 160th Street. Go for the food, the live music, the dancing, just go. If you're here in July, you can also check out the amazing Dominican *Carnaval* parade. – Jerry the Mouse

September

HOWL! Festival
Labor Day weekend, Tompkins Square, and venues around the East Village
www.howlfestival.com
Count on enough spoken word hollerin' to wake a dead poet, plenty of live music and performance, some well meaning but discombobulated kids' activities (Can we go to the playground *now*? I'm *hungry!*) and Art Around the Park, where artists with varying degrees of ability share their vision on plywood panels ringing the park. – AH

West Indian Parade
Labor Day, Eastern Parkway, Brooklyn
www.wiadca.com
Just pray it's not an election year, when khaki-butt politicians and their t-shirted supporters hog the front of the line. Don't they know we're there for the beaded bikinis, eye-popping feathered headdresses, and deafening island music? If you plan to feast on curried goat or an Ital veggie roti, get there before the parade starts or you'll have a long wait. Those who like steel drums, late nights, blowing whistles, and getting pelted with powdered dye should check out J'Ouvert, a Trinidadian pre-carnival custom starting at 2am in Grand Army Plaza before before moving deeper into Brooklyn.

The September Concert
September 11, al over NYC
www.septemberconcert.org
This organization wants people to mark the events of September 11, 2001 with free, public concerts all over the world. The venues range from well-known halls to gardens to subway platforms. You're welcome to do more than just listen. The website provides a tool kit for anyone wanting to organize a concert. (Don't let a lack of NYC experience stop you from joining in. Try contacting any of the places in this book and asking if they'll let you play.)

Tribute in Light
Sunset September 11 – dawn September 12
www.tributeinlight.com
The two columns of white light that shoot into the night sky where the World Trade Center's twin towers once stood take my breath away every September 11. Thanks to artists Julian LaVerdiere and Paul Myoda for creating such an eloquent, dignified tribute. It's comprised of 88 searchlights, running on recycled biodiesel. I've heard that this tradition will end on the ten-year anniversary, but I hope not. It's beautiful.

• The Intuitionist – Colson Whitehead • The

Conflux Festival
A mid September weekend
www.confluxfestival.org
A philistine like me needs more than three days to wrap my head around the concept of psychogeography, otherwise known as the creative exploration of urban public space. Interactive text messages, iPhone apps, and MP3 downloads figure heavily, though there are enough unhinged walking tours, guerrilla gardening how-to's, and extremely-open-to-interpretation scavenger hunts to allow dedicated Luddites to participate 'round the clock as well. They accept proposals.

The Brooklyn Book Festival
A Sunday in Mid September
www.brooklynbookfestival.org
A cornucopia of literary pleasure in the most literary of boroughs. There are read-alouds on rickety stages set up in front of the post office and Borough Hall, kid-friendly workshops, and high profile panels requiring (free) tickets. If you like zines and such, your favorite part will no doubt be the tables where everyone from publishers who need no introducing to the most humble, self-distributed, in-your-face local authors pimp their wares. The brainchild of Akashic Books publisher and former Girls Against Boys bass player, Johnny Temple. Let's give him a hand!

The Feast of San Gennaro
Ten days, starting the 2nd Saturday in September, Mulberry between Canal and Houston
www.sangennaro.com
Yeah, it's a nightmare, but it's our nightmare and it was in The Godfather, so if you wind up walking through it, get yourself an Italian ice and shut up your goddamn complaining mouth.

PARK(ing) Day
One weekday in mid-September
www.parkingdaynyc.org
It's almost just like Brigadoon, all these parking space-sized parks materializing next to parking meters all over the city, then disappearing by day's end. If you're up for schlepping lawn chairs, pink flamingos, and other park-y attributes, keep an eye on the website for the summer application deadline. If you're just looking to sunbathe and toss a Frisbee in an extremely small public park, you can check the website closer to the big day, when a map of all the approved locations will be posted for the edification of the general public.

October

The New York Burlesque Festival
Usually the first weekend in October, at various bars in Manhattan & Brooklyn
www.thenewyorkburlesquefestival.com
Oh my, pass me my smelling salts and my peacock fan! Burlesque revivalists come from all over to show NYC what they've got and compete for the Golden Pasties in categories like Most Scandalous, Hottest Mess, Biggest Hair, and Most Likely to Wind up in Bangkok Missing a Kidney.

Atlantic Antic
The first Sunday in October, sometimes earlier, Atlantic Avenue, from 4th Avenue to Hicks St. Brooklyn,
www.atlanticave.org/specialevents.htm
Most of the higher profile New York City street fairs are forgettable affairs featuring the same old Mozzerepa stands, New York Times subscription shills, and World's Softest Socks booths, but this behemoth retains real neighborhood flavor. Come early to beat the crowds and get first dibs on the cheap, multicultural home cookin' offered outside the four churches between Hoyt and Nevins. Dive off the Avenue for a second and you'll find dozens of locals throwing date-savvy stoop sales. When you get claustrophobic, escape the crush on one of the hay bales set up outside Hank's Saloon or Last Exit bar, my Antic go-to's for live music and bigger cups.

Fort Tryon Medieval Festival
Sunday in early October (or late September!) Fort Tryon Park
www.whidc.org/home.html
Ah, New York. You can get Vietnamese sandwiches and a hot yoga class on every other corner, but if you want to

see live jousting, you have to haul it up to Inwood, where an alternate universe of goodly wenches, cowled Dungeons and Dragons masters, and, go figure, pirates gather for the huge yearly Medieval Festival. It's way more honky tonk and hammy than the usual hushed Cloisters scene, but that's what I like about it. I also like the *Simpson*ian wit evident in Master Bunting's House of Ye Fried Dough.

Blessing of the Animals
October 4
The Cathedral Church of St. John the Divine,
1047 Amsterdam Ave
www.stjohndivine.org/news.html, 212-316-7490
Could St. Francis of Assisi have foretold a day when tattooed non-believers of all sexual orientations would haul their pet ferrets a hundred blocks by subway to receive holy blessing next to a camel? The showiest place to take in the spectacle (see: camel) is the Cathedral of St. John the Divine, though if you keep an eye on neighborhood bulletin boards, you'll notice that other smaller churches also celebrate.

Open House New York Weekend
1st or 2nd weekend in October, all over NYC
www.ohny.org/weekend
The architectural equivalent of peeking into your host's closet and medicine chest, except that in this case, the hosts are the ones throwing open the doors. Many of the participating institutions are closed to the public for the rest of the year. The ones that aren't will allow you into areas that are normally off-limits. Check the website a week before the event for the full schedule, and RSVP to the events that require reservations. It's all about what you're into, but past favorites include sculptor Tom Otterness's studio, the little Red Lighthouse, the New York Marble Cemetery, and the spooky Angels and Accordions performance leading to the catacombs of Greenwood Cemetery.

Diwali Mela
One day street fair, determined by the lunar Hindu Calendar, usually in mid October or early November
South Street Seaport and Jackson Heights
www.deepavali.net/usa.php, 718-651-6971
Diwali (also called Dipavali) is the Festival of Lights celebrating the return of Lord Rama from his defeat of the Demon King Ravana. Throngs of happy, strolling Indians in gorgeous saris and salwar kameezes shop at the amazing Patel Brothers and nearby little DVD and music stores. Holiday lights go up on 74th Street, but the real lights for Diwali are the little clay lamps outside and inside the shops. The gadjrelela halva (carrot halvah) is so amazing

you just have to taste it to believe it. – Jerry the Mouse

Bike Kill Festival
Usually a Saturday in late October
www.myspace.com/bikekill
The Bike Kill event put on by Black Label is a full day and night of uninhibited bike/skateboard centered chaos, art, debauchery, and parades beyond description. Punks and bike freaks from all over the place gather at the dead end of Sanford and Willoughby Street in Bushwick for everything from jousting on tall bikes to racing their wheeled homemade contraptions, often in costumes and often near naked, all in the exaltation of pure anti-consumerist bike-lovin' beauty. It's my favorite holiday. - Caitlin Mcgurk

Zombie Con
Saturday before Halloween, the streets and bars of central and lower Manhattan
www.zombiecon.com
Like LepreCon, but with zombies. The organizers occasionally provide make-up artists for participants whose flesh isn't rotting of its own accord, but who needs help when all it really takes is some shredded bridal finery from Salvation army, a handful of bait, and a couple of likely-looking tubes from Rite-Aid's Halloween aisle? The undead learn the coordinates by email or text message the day before the event, so don't forget to sign up in advance!

Tompkins Square Dog Run Halloween Parade
The Saturday or Sunday before Halloween, Tompkins Square Dog Run
www.dogster.org
The folks who get up in arms about elephants marching through the Midtown Tunnel have yet to get too exercised about pet owners dressing their bull terriers and Irish setters up as fairies and firemen. This is rumored to be the biggest pet parade in the country, and folks go all out, building elaborate props—biplanes to pilot, sleighs to be pulled. I prefer the simple elegance of a greyhound in dragonfly wings. My all-time best in show goes to a regal, tutu'ed pug, sitting immobile in a baby stroller, her tiara, lipstick, and blue eyeshadow familiar to anyone who's witnessed the aging season ticket holders rolling up to the Met's Opening Gala.

Greenwich Village Halloween Parade
October 31 Avenue of the Americas, from Spring to 21st St
www.halloween-nyc.com
New York City offers so many other wonderful opportunities for dressing up, I'm content to spend this night tak-

Happiness - Nick Courage · Lipshitz Six, or

their t-shirts.

Grand Meeting of the Corduroy Appreciation Club
November 11 – a bar in Brooklyn
www.corduroyclub.com
We associate so many things with November 11. Stanley Tucci, Kurt Vonnegut, and Holy Roman Emperor Henry IV were born. Poland and Angola gained independence. And, most importantly, it is the date that most closely resembles corduroy: 11|11. (The other is January 1, but sadly, many members of the Corduroy Appreciation Club are occupied in sleeping off their hangovers from the night before, a day which in no way resembles corduroy.) Anyone is welcome to attend the meeting, provided they wear at least two swatches of the favored fabric, and know how to keep their tongues in their cheeks while performing strange rituals and enjoying musical entertainment and the annual keynote address. You may be hit for dues totaling $11.11.

Macy's Thanksgiving Day Parade
From the Museum of Natural History to Herald Square
www.macysparade.com
For most New Yorkers, the Thanksgiving Parade is less traditional than hauling it out in the freezing cold to see the balloons being blown up in front of the Museum of Natural History the night before. This is not the night to dress like a city slicker, by the way. A puffy coat and some serious fleece-lined boots might keep you from getting *too* frost bitten as you trundle past a flaccid rubber pancake that's still hours away from looking like a Saturday morning cartoon character you've probably never heard of.

December
Metro Metro Holiday Office Party
A Saturday night in December in a Manhattan bar
www.metrometroland.com/events.htm
You don't have to work in an office to come to this office party. Just dress like you could. Make up a job title to put on your nametag, one that honors the organizers' request to keep it semi-clean ("no *I'm the guy at the office who doesn't wear pants and likes to give back massages*") Since they're not withholding any taxes, you'll have to pay a small admission fee, but you get to drink free and after that, cheap. You can ride their Xerox machine if it isn't on the blinkie. You may even win Employee of the Year.

The Blip Festival
3 days in December, an all ages venue in Manhattan or Brooklyn
www.blipfestival.org

ing my children trick or treating in brownstone Brooklyn. But if you're up for withstanding enormous crowds, you'll see plenty of freak flags hoisted high, some public drunkenness, and a lot of straight-looking guys in policemen costumes. You can march solo or with your entire panty clad baseball team, provided you're patient enough to join the endless line-up between Spring and Canal—it takes two hours to get everybody through the chute. The organizers also need plenty of hands to help hoist their giant puppets, if you feel participatory, but not enough to schlep a costume of your own devising. There's a volunteer registration on their website. - AH

November
The New York Marathon
First Sunday in November – all five Boroughs
www.ingnycmarathon.org
This monster covers some serious ground, but for my money (uh, what money would that be again?) mile 8 in Brooklyn is the best place for a non-runner like me to view the race. The frontrunners blow past shortly after the starting pistol. (Dayumn!) By 9:30 or 10am the others start showing up, and then come the serious stragglers, wheezing like wall eyes. I like to throw them some love by standing at the intersection of 4th Avenue and Pacific, screaming the names they have helpfully scrawled on

The Blip Festival may be your last chance to prove to Mom and Dad that spending the ages of 11-16 playing video games in the rec room of their split-level ranch was a good use of your time. Geeking out on the chip music compositions and low-res video art of marginally reformed Atari/Nintendo/Gameboy obsessives can provide pleasant respite from the Christmas onslaught that begins the day after Halloween.

Phil Kline's Unsilent Night
A Night in Mid-December, from Washington Square to Tompkins Square
www.unsilentnight.com
An ethereal and pleasantly non-denominational take on holiday caroling. Back in the day, people would show up with boomboxes, and rush Composer Kline for one of his hotly desired cassette tapes. At his signal, everyone pressed play simultaneously, and processed *en masse* from the Washington Square Arch to that big elm in Tompkins Square. It sounded like a minimalist symphony played entirely on icicles. It's now possible to download MP3s in advance, but even played on iPhones, it's still a lovely, non-commercial way to get into something resembling the holiday spirit.

Santa Con
The 1st or 2nd Saturday before Xmas, the streets and bars of central and lower Manhattan
www.nycsantacon.com
The one that started it all. If you're naughty enough to join in the debauchery, you should come in full regalia. You don't have to be Santa—he has a wife you know, and a lot of sexy girlfriends, not to mention elves, reindeer, snowmen, snowwomen, snowtransmen, and snowtranswomen. Santa's open-minded as long as you remember the four Fs: don't fuck with kids, security, cops, and Santa. Bring a Metrocard, a good attitude, tips for the bartenders, and trinkets for the good little children (they're all good little children.)

New Year's Eve Concert for Peace
December 31, 7pm
The Cathedral of St. John the Divine
1047 Amsterdam Ave (@112th St) 212-316-7490
www.stjohndivine.org/news.html, (Morningside Hts: B/C to Cathedral Pkwy)
Just think, while other people are driving themselves nuts, getting drunk and/or laid, you can be passing around candles and singing This Little Light of Mine! The idea might embarrass you now, but not when you wake up on New Year's Day feeling totally purified and hopeful. (Though the concert's only 90 minutes, leaving you plenty of time afterward to tie one on and do something you'll regret.) Reserved seating is expensive but general admission is free—and hotly desired, so get there early.

Critical Mass New Year's Eve Ride
December 31, 10:30pm Washington Square to Central Park
www.times-up.org/index.php?page=new-years-ride
You know how little kids get super psyched about all New Year's Eve noisemakers, party hats, and those goofy glasses that should've gone out with the 'aughts? Indulge your inner child by strapping some of that silliness onto your bike helmet and honking at passersby the whole way up.

And then there are the simple things like
Watching holiday lights slowly appear around the city Watching plants come back to life and flowers burst into color in the spring (Okay. May.) Watching the leaves change in the fall – Melissa Bastian

Fix It
It's a bummer when your stuff breaks on holiday, but going to get it repaired can open your eyes to a whole new way of looking at the city.

Chrysler Camera Repair
367 W, 34th S, 2nd Floor (btwn 8th Ave & 9th Ave) 212-682-3547 (Hell's Kitchen: A/C/E to 34th St-8th Ave)
When a certain Mermaid of my acquaintance (me) dropped the family camera in the heat of the Coney Island Mermaid Parade, the folks at Chrysler were not only fast and cheap, their bedside manner was way warmer than I deserved. They brought my camera back from the dead (only to have someone steal it out of my bag in the subway).

Bellevue
462 1st Ave (Btwn 27th & 28th) 212-562-4141
www.nyc.gov/html/hhc/html/facilities/bellevue.shtml (Murray Hill: 6 to 28th St)
If it's good enough for Sylvia Plath, it's good enough for you! George Washington was four when Bellevue was founded. We aren't sure if he was ever treated there, but seriously, Bellevue will treat you, regardless of your insurance status and ability to pay. It's the oldest public hospital in the country, and their billing department is used to getting the old run around. If you're under 25, you can go to the pediatric ER, which is pretty good for weeding out the crazies.

Ely's No Kiss List – Rachel Cohn & David

Dr David Ores
15 Clinton St (btwn Houston & Stanton) 212 353-3020,
drdave666@gmail.com
Recommended by Fly for affordable healthcare.

The Icarus Project
www.theicarusproject.net
The Icarus Project is a network of people living with experiences often diagnosed and labeled as psychiatric conditions. Their goal is no less than to change the language
and culture of "mental illness" and to inspire transforma-
tion in an oppressive and damaged world based on the
principles of self-determination & mutual aid. Based in
NYC, these folks have a million things going on that you
can tap into, from art shows to groups that meet regularly
to a lively online forum. Check out the blog section on
their site for the latest.

Shoe Repair
There are cobblers all over, and most of them change
watch batteries too! Try a subterranean one in a massive
subway station complex. (A/C to Broadway-Nassau, B/D/
F/M to Rockefeller Center, N/Q /R/A/C/E to Times Square).
For extra adventure, visit one of the al fresco Chinese
cobblers who set up their benches around the Manhattan Bridge. Try Market, East Broadway, or the corner of
Elizabeth and Grand. If all else fails, just flip your shoe
over, pretend you're a cobbler-mime, and let someone
take you. It's strange how getting your shoes fixed can
make you feel like you belong somewhere, that you aren't
just a dumb tourist, hemorrhaging money and trying to
occupy your time.

New York Fountain Pen Hospital
10 Warren St, Front-A (btwn Church St & Broadway)
212-964-0580, www.fountainpenhospital.com
(Financial District: City Hall-Broadway (R, W)
There's no reason you can't take what I said about shoes
and apply it to your fountain pen, except there's really
only one place to go, the beautifully named New York
Fountain Pen Hospital. They sell some crazy pliers and
scissor-like things in case you, too, want to play doctor.
They also sell brand new pens, some priced to send you
into a swoon, some no higher than the school supply
aisle.

Tek-Serve
119 W 23rd St (btwn Avenue Of The Americas & 7th Ave)
212-929-3645, www.Tekserve.com (Chelsea: F/M to 23rd St)
Back when any subway passenger whose headphones
plugged into a Discman was considered cutting edge,
this was literally the only place to go when your Apple
computer started acting funny. Even with Apple Stores
out the wazoo, Tek-Serve's still a scene. It's a little cheaper
than the big guys, and a whole lot more indie-feeling.
You take a number, just like at the deli, then park it in a
waiting area filled with old theater seats and a groovy '70s
rec room pod. Keep your ears peeled and you will hear all
sorts of interesting tales about how people's laptops and
iPods came to their sorry states. Repairs take a few days.
They sell all sorts of accessories, software, and related
books, too.

City Acupuncture of New York
139 Fulton St #600 (btwn Broadway & Nassau) 551-574-1803
www.cityacuny.com
If you're acu-curious, City Acupuncture is an extremely cost effective way to check it out, since all treatments are performed on a sliding scale, from $25 to $50. Nor will it wipe out your purse to keep going. After you've filled out a lengthy intake form, with particular emphasis on bowel-and-mental-health, you'll be needled up, and allowed to zone out for some forty minutes under a Mylar blanket. The communal nature of the treatment room is a bonus in my book. I always feel like a drowsy little kid, struggling to stay awake as the grown ups murmur on the other side of the wall. Be sure to look out the window when you regain consciousness – the 6th floor view from their creaky office building is old-timey and grand.

Automotive High School
50 Bedford Avenue (@ Berry, Williamsburg, Bklyn)
718-218-9301, www.autohs.com
On a recent trip to Brooklyn with the old SVO greasetruck, we needed a mechanic and SVO pioneer Arrow pointed us in the direction of this place: an educating mechanic's garage. It's like when you need the cheap dentist, you go to the dental school. If you need your greasecar fixed (or even just your regular clunker sedan), this is the economical place to do it. Scheduling can be a bit of a pickle with school breaks and all, so plan your breakdowns in advance! – Joe Biel

FOOD

GENERAL EATS

All of these places are cheap. Some are even dirt cheap. In fact, our first listing represents one of several options where it's possible to fill your belly for under $3, though please don't forget to tip. If you're looking to stretch your dining dollar, make lunch your big meal, as many places offer specials whereby you'll either get more grub, or the same grub they serve at night but for a significantly cheaper price. Bon Appetit!

MANHATTAN

Chinatown
Vanessa's Dumpling House
118 Eldridge St (btwn Broome St & Grand St) 212-625-8008
(Chinatown: B/D to Grand St)
&
220 E 14th St (btwn 2nd & 3rd Ave) 212-529-1328

(East Village: L to 3rd Ave)
Best dumplings I've ever had, plus they are really cheap. The veggie dumplings are $3 for eight dumplings, and for 50 cents more you can get them in a soup. One order of dumplings is usually enough for me, but if I'm really hungry, or just gluttonous, I will also get a sesame pancake, fried in oil--which is probably why it tastes so good. It's just 75¢. You can also get it as a sandwich with veggies or meat, but that's a little more. In the old days, you went up to the window to order and all the orders were taken by hand. Then you went inside the tiny, hot restaurant, tried to squeeze into the counter and fought to claim your order. Now, there are tables so you can sit inside on a cold or rainy day, and you are given a little receipt with the number of your order. On a nice day, pick up a beer at the corner bodega and walk a block west to watch the bike polo in the park. – Amanda Plumb

New Green Bo
66 Bayard St (btwn Elizabeth & Mott) 212-625-2359
(Chinatown: J/Z/N/Q /R/6 to Canal)
If there's a wait here, I amuse myself by imagining the editors of *Bon Appetit* and *Vogue* actually eating at New Green Bo. Their rhapsodic pull-quotes, taped like patchwork to the windows and door, seem to indicate that they have. Still, I'd pay good money to see Anna Wintour perched on a tippy restaurant supply chair, squirting scalding soup dumpling juice onto the dingy honeydew-colored walls with the rest of us proles and being asked to share her table with people she doesn't know.

Prosperity Dumpling
46 Eldridge St (btwn Canal & Hester) 212-343-0683
(Chinatown: B/D to Grand)
FIVE fried pork dumplings for $1. They're not as good as Fried Dumpling (RIP) fare was, but you can't argue with five dumplings for $1. – Kate Black

Doyers Restaurant
11 Doyers St, basement level (btwn Bowery & Pell)
212-513-1527, www.doyersvietnamese.com
(Chinatown: J/M/Q /R/Z/ 6 to Canal)
Don't feel intimidated by Christmas decorations in July or the hundreds of Vietnamese dishes on the menu. Christmas will be here again before you know it, and if you really don't know what to order, tell the waiter to bring you an entrée-sized portion of shrimp paste grilled on sugar cane. To give the illusion that you know what you're doing, tear off a bit of the rubber-consistency paste, put it on a lettuce leaf off that plastic platter, sprinkle it with sauce, add a few leaves of mint and roll it up. Really,

New York City - Joanne Dugan • City of

though, it's no big deal. Don't neglect the specials board. I also have to say that the crooked little one block excuse for a street that it's on is one of my favorites in NYC.

Joe's Shanghai
9 Pell St. (btwn Bowery & Doyers) 212-233-8888
www.joeshanghairestaurants.com
(Chinatown: J/M/Q /R/Z/ 6 to Canal)
Xiao long bao are a spiritual experience, soup dumplings with crab and pork meat, and hearty broth inside the thin wrapper. Avail yourself of the delicious chili oil and vinegar soy concoctions on the table. A basket of eight is under $10. If you've got a little more scratch, I recommend the salt and pepper prawns, heads on. – Kate Black

Great New York Noodle Town
28 1/2 Bowery (@ Bayard) 212-349-0923
(Chinatown: J/M/Q /R/Z/ 6 to Canal)
If your appetite may be negatively impacted by the forceful decapitation of an already dead duck, sit with your back to the window, where all manner of tasty cadavers hang from hooks. You'll still hear the thwak every 30 seconds or so. My god, those cutting boards are sturdy. Noodletown's open until 4am, and its corner location feels cheery. You can get a bowl of noodle soup with roast pork for under six bucks.

New Wonton Garden
56 Mott St (btwn Bayard & Canal) 212-966-4886
(Chinatown: J/M/Q /R/Z/ 6 to Canal)
I have a thing for New Wonton Garden's bubbling cauldrons on blustery nights, when the windows are all fogged up, and the waiters appear even more disgruntled than usual to be sporting their ludicrous Hawaiian shirt uniforms. Cheap to the point of ridiculous. Even when you order beer. Take a hint from their name and order something with wontons because there ain't no garden.

Hong Kong Station
45 Bayard St (btwn Elizabeth & Bowery) 212-233-0288
(Chinatown: J/M/Q /R/Z/ 6 to Canal)
&
128 Hester St (btwn Bowery & Chrystie) 212-966-9382
(Chinatown: B/D to Grand)
&
45 Division St (btwn Catherine & Market) 212-966-9682
(Chinatown: F to East Broadway)
www.hongkongstation.us
The atmosphere is straight up fast food, but I love the approach. You buy a bowl of noodles for a buck-fifty, then add as many toppings as you want for a buck-fifty

a pop. Actually, I think Bed Bath & Beyond does salad the same way, but boring. I say bring on the curried fish balls, fried gluten, turnips, tofu skin, and tripe. Maybe not all at once, though, as the point is to get a good meal about which you can say, "Oh my god, it's so cheap!" in between scalding, eye-tearing-up mouthfuls. They also have pretty much every part of the pig except for the squeal. A great option for culinarily adventurous parents traveling with kids who require things unadorned and right now!

Dim Sum Go Go
5 E Broadway (btwn Catherine St and Chatham Sq) 212-732-0797 (Chinatown: J/M/Q /R/Z/6 to Canal)
The most Western feeling of the Chinatown dim sum options. If you want a recommendation, how about f-ing you up some Chinese parsley dumplings? If cilantro skeeves you out, substitute the snow pea leaf dumplings. Sit in the second-story window to watch the cheap Chinatown buses lumbering to and fro. The Go Go Hamburgers in steamed buns are close cousins to the Australian Pizza I was served once in Bali. Don't make the mistake of ordering them for your picky eater.

C&L Dumpling House
77 Chrystie St (btwn Canal and Hester) 212-219-8850
(Little Italy: B/D to Grand St)
You know those old movies where the big city swells wave away the menu, instructing the waitress to bring them

the most expensive thing on it? If you're going to do that, do it in this humble Chinese dumpling spot, where the biggest bank buster is the special fujianese wonton soup at $3.25. Even those with but a dollar to their names have enough of a nest egg to blow it on such filling fare as pork with bok choy pancakes, plain congee, or four fried pork and chive dumplings. There's plenty of better established, better known dumpling places, but let's give the freshman a boost. Hopefully, its aura of cleanliness and optimism will linger past the point when the lucky red ribbons on the grand opening potted plant fade.

Pho Bang
157 Mott St (btwn Grand & Broome) 212-966-3797
(Little Italy: B/D to Grand)
Is it just me, or is pho an effective jet lag cure? (I've already tried ginger and spinning counter-clockwise, and hope one day to test first-hand the proven effectiveness of receiving a massage from someone who's fully adjusted to the time zone in which I find my weary ass.) Whatever. That good ol' Vietnamese penicillin perks me right up. Must be the combination of lemongrass and steam. If you've never gotten your pho on before, the big side platter of leaves and sprouts isn't a passive-aggressive suggestion that you need more roughage in your diet. Tear it up and throw it in your bowl. Finish off with a few spurts of fish and chili sauce.

Lower East Side / East Village

Congee Village
100 Allen St (btwn Delancey & Broome) 212-941-1818
www.sunsungroup.com/congeevillage
(LES: F/J/M/Z to Delancey-Essex)
East of the West Village and south of the East Village lays Congee Village, a savory enclave identifiable only by the giant, flashing neon signs screaming CONGEE VILLAGE! This place never fails to put me in a festive, feasting mood, even when my friends aren't bullying me into ordering a ridiculous cocktail billed as Liquid Marijuana. If I can only pick one favorite restaurant, this might be it. The menu rambles on, offering about five million choices. I recommend them all, especially the Salt and Pepper Shrimp, Pea Shoots in Season, and the extremely cheap titular Rice Gruel with anything you don't normally eat, like fish intestines (sorry, don't mean to presume). If there's a wait for a table, ride it out in the bar. Lychee martinis are $5 a pop. – AH (The menu looks expensive at first, but keep turning pages 'til you get to the cheap stuff. Plenty for vegans here. – Jenna Freedman)

Tiny's Giant Sandwich Shop
127 Rivington St (btwn Essex St & Norfolk St) 212-982-1690
www.tinysgiant.com (LES: F/J/M/Z to Delancey-Essex)
Tiny's giant sandwiches are big enough to quiet a talking stomach and provide leftovers to snack on later that day. A nice little dining area, housing a large variety of patrons, is available for that mid-afternoon lunch-break/date. The only drawback is that there is no alcohol. – Heath Row (To which I would counter "BYOB, baby!" – AH)

Mama's Food Shop
200 E. 3rd St (btwn Ave A & B) 212-777-4425
www.mamasfoodshop.com
(LES: F/J/M/Z to Delancey-Essex)
Where I'm from, this kind of food is straight-up grandma. My Gran was one of those old-fashioned cooks who laid out every meal as if expecting half a dozen hungry farmhands. I'm not sure she would've known what to make of the thrift store mother portraits climbing the walls or the buff, out-and-proud men dishing fried chicken, mashed potatoes, candied yams, green beans, mac and cheese, meatloaf (all her greatest hits) cafeteria-style, but I know she would have approved of the portion sizes. If you and your big smile go there right before closing, portions get even bigger.

Nicky's Vietnamese Sandwiches
150 E. 2nd St (btwn 1st Ave & Avenue A) 212-388-1088
(East Village: F to 2nd Ave)
&
311 Atlantic Avenue (btwn Smith & Hoyt, Boerum Hill, Bklyn) 718-855-8838 (Boerum Hill: F/G to Bergen St)
www.nickyssandwiches.com
One of the harshest realities of my aquarium-tarian status a few years back was having to cold-shoulder Vietnamese sandwiches, which were even dearer to my heart than cubanos. This was before all those bao places started cropping up. When Nicky's opened, I noted with interest that they had a vegetarian version, although I didn't hold out much hope for it. Indeed, the first bite was disappointingly redolent of that fuck you substitute, the Portobello mushroom. The second and all subsequent tastes, however, were more Proustian, and I felt virtuous that the only creature who'd taken a bolt to the cap for my eating pleasure was a fungus. If the rumors are true, by the time you read this, there will be one in City Hall.

Bahn Mi Zon
443 E. 6th St. (btwn 1st Ave and Ave A) 646-524-6384
www.banhmizon.com (East Village: F to 2nd Ave)
This Vietnamese sandwich shop's vegetarian sandwich

Berry – Wallace Thurman • Bright Lights, Big

costs $5.50 and is 9" long. I had half a sandwich two hours ago and I'm still totally full. It's heavy on the mushrooms, so if you're not into that, you should go elsewhere. I liked it because I asked for no cilantro and no mayonnaise, and that wasn't a problem. They substituted peanut sauce, which is maybe why it was so filling. They also have vegetarian summer rolls for $4.50 and some vegetarian salads and intriguing-sounding beverages like Salted Lemonade and Soybean Drink, served hot or cold. The proprietors are super nice. – Jenna Freedman

Milon
93 1st Ave (btwn 5th & 6th St) 212-228-4896
(East Village: F to 2nd Ave)
This is the wonderful mess of Christmas lights, chili pepper lights, cellophane, and plastic fish that you see when you walk down 1st Avenue between 5th and 6th. The food is affordable and amazing, with tons of vegan options. I specifically recommend the malai kofta. You can't go wrong with dumplings and banana sauce. The interior decor is definitely one of my all-time favorites, strings of lights and shiny objects dangling low off the ceiling. And if it's your birthday, you will receive the most amazing light show of your life (and mango ice cream). – Cristy Road

Oh Taisho!
9 St Marks Pl (btwn 2nd Ave & 3rd Ave) 212-673-1300
www.yakitoritaisho.com (East Village: 6 to Astor Pl)
They have a huge picture menu and the place is super Japanese. It's good in a group or to go alone. They have a sushi bar, but you can also just get tiny skewer bites for like $1.50 each of meat or garlic, peppers, scallions, all grilled Yakitori style. - Andria Alefi

Kenka
25 Saint Marks Pl (btwn 2nd & 3rd Ave) 212-254-6363
(East Village: 6 to Astor Pl)
Sleazy izakaya fare, with particularly tasty takoyaki and $1.50 Sapporo and Kirin. Free cotton candy after you pay. (Let the machine warm up for 30-60 seconds before you pour in your sugar.) – Kate Black (It takes time to cook squid legs, so I don't let it bother me too much if the service is slow, and neither should you. It helps that pitchers are so cheap. And if you don't like cotton candy, you are a fool. – Heath Row) (Can't wait for squid legs? Order the Bull Penis. Thirding the cotton candy. – AH)

Café Mogador
101 St Marks Pl (btwn 1st Ave and Ave A) 212-677-2226
www.cafemogador.com (East Village: 6 to Astor Pl)
If you're hankering after some Paul Bowles, this romantic, thick-walled Moroccan place is your *Sheltering Sky*, particularly at lunch when a chicken tagine with soup or salad is only $9—five bucks less than at dinner. The merguez sausage may look like the bodily function my friend Little MoMo refers to oh so delicately as "growing a stinky tail," but it's ever so much spicier and more delicious! If you want to sleep like a baby, try some bastilla, a filo pastry squishy with shredded chicken, almonds, and cinnamon. If I've been there on belly dancing night, I blocked it out.

Sidewalk Cafe
94 Ave A (@ 6th St) 212-253-8080
www.sidewalkmusic.net (East Village: F to 2nd Ave)
Sidewalk has a great black bean burger and the wait staff is always pretty fun. – Megan Garrity (And let's not forget those cheap breakfasts served all day! – AH)

The Question Mark Cafe
135 1st Ave (btwn St Marks Pl & 9th St) 212-614-9800
(East Village: 6 to Astor Pl)
This may be premature, but I'm running with it because I can't have you leaving the East Village without meeting one of its nicest characters, Habib. To know him is to love him. He used to have his own place, right around the corner, and on summer evenings, he'd arrange for a jazz trio to set up on the sidewalk, there being no way for a stand-up base to squeeze in alongside three or four tables and the carryout throngs. He served wonderful, fat falafels, mint tea, and his sister's homemade pie (sorry, folks, she's back in Algeria now). Circumstance eventually forced him to shutter that location, but he popped back up on St. Mark's Place, then Avenue A, and a few weeks ago he turned up at this cheery little Serbian spot, which he's thinking of buying. The black and white jazz photos from the old place are on the walls, and Louis Armstrong's on the stereo. I'm taking that as a good omen.

City - Jay McInerney • Beebo Brinker – Ann

Life Café

343 E. 10th (@ Ave B) 212-477-8791
(East Village: L to 1st Ave)

&

983 Flushing Ave (@ Central Ave, Bushwick, Bklyn) 718-386-1133 (Bushwick: L to Morgan Ave)
www.lifecafe.com

When I used to feel homesick for Chicago, the big old vegan Life salad here, a Dispose-All assemblage of greens, tofu, steamed veggies, hijiki, brown rice, black beans, and tahini dressing filled the hole left by the mighty Heartland Café salads I'd so often enjoyed with my Chicago friends. Yes, this is the café where they dance on the tables in *Rent*, turning their dining companions into prisoners of performance art. Don't begrudge the little *Rent*-heads their pilgrimages. Prices remain within reach of modern day cash-strapped artists, especially at lunch and happy hour. If you have a memorable Life moment, you can submit it for publication on their website, earning yourself a $25 gift certificate for next time. – AH (Life has these vegan chili nachos that I've eaten two orders of in one sitting. – Caitlin McGurk)

Sapporo East

245 E 10th St (@ 1st Ave) 212-260-1330
(East Village: L to 1st Ave)

A party atmosphere holds sway here, with some of the Rising Sun's punkiest (and cutest) sushi chefs taking care of business on the other side of the counter. Pay attention to the handwritten specials signs slapped up on the walls. If you're grabbing a bite on your way somewhere else, keep in mind that this is a longtime East Village favorite and lines out the door are part of the allure. Even if you eat yourself silly on a well-named bowl of Special Udon, you'll feel healthy and non-overstuffed after. Magic!

Rai Rai Ken

214 E. 10th St (btwn 1st Ave and 2nd Ave) 212-477-7030
(East Village: L to First Ave)

I've sworn my shifting allegiance to nearly all the ramen joints that came pouring into the East Village a few years back. Now that things are calming down a bit in Ramen Land, I have decided my heart belongs to Rai Rai Ken, the smallest, and in some ways, most modest of their number. You're not going to get a private table here. It's a stools-only operation and very, very narrow. The steam from the eternally-boiling vat of noodle cooking water will wilt your hairdo, fog the windows, moisten the walls, and get you stripped down to your tank top on the coldest day of the year. Like all ramen restaurants, the menu

is not what you'd call expansive. My favorite, Mabo Tofu Ramen, is probably the weirdest thing on it, a large, soy-sauce-heavy bowl of ramen, tofu, ginger, chili, garlic, scallions, and ground pork.

Ramen Setagaya

141 First Ave (btwn 9th St & St Mark's Pl) 212-529-2740

&

34 St Mark's Pl (btwn 2nd and 3rd) 212-387-7959
www.setaga-ya.com (East Village: 6 to Astor Pl)

Ramen Setagaya was my boyfriend before Rai Rai Ken. I liked his shio ramen. I still do, it's just, I'm with Rai Rai Ken now. I think he's moved on too...he was making a lot of noise about his BiBimBar recently. It was always there in the back of the First Avenue place, but it's like he wants everybody to know now, or something. Anyway, carnivores may even want to try the St. Mark's Place appetizer of chopped and squishy fatty bacon atop rice. though not right before the noon class at Yoga For the People.

S'MAC (short for Sarita's Macaroni & Cheese)

345 East 12th St (btwn 1st and 2nd Ave) 212-358-7912
www.smacnyc.com (East Village: L to 1st)

My favorite mac and cheese at this all-mac and cheese spot is the Alpine, a carbonara-esque mix of Gruyère cheese and slab bacon. Mediterranean, Cajun, Parisian, La Mancha, Masala--you can travel the world in a skillet! As with other modes of travel, there's something for every budget, beginning with "nosh" and going all the way up through "partay!"

Tribeca / SoHo / Nolita

Pakistan Tea House

176 Church St (btwn Duane and Reade) 212-240-9800
(Tribeca: 2/3/A/C/E to Chambers St-Park Pl)

Pakistan Tea House has a real tandoori oven. I love their chicken tikka, chicken makhani, eggplant, cabbage, cauliflower, dal, and onion kulcha (though it takes them forever to make it). Their chai is good, though on the sweet side. They have authentic vegetarian food too, unlike most Chinatown restaurants where tofu dishes come with a little pork for flavor. One special is enough for two people. New Shezan Restaurant across the street has excellent vegetable dishes, but I don't like their meat as much. – Esther Smith (Open until 3am for all you kulcha-craving vampires! – AH)

Pinche Taqueria

227 Mott St (btwn Prince & Spring) 212-625-0090
(Nolita: 6 to Spring St)

&
333 Lafayette St (@ Bleecker) 212-343-9977
(NoHo: B/D/F/M to Broadway-Lafayette)
www.pinchetaqueria.us
The month after we moved from our bathtub in the kitch-
en tenement to a two-bedroom that still feels like we won
the lottery, a picture of the Chuck Close mural and our
building was in the Sunday New York Times real estate
section and the word NoLiTa (North of Little Italy) was
coined. Trust fund baby fashion stores sprouted up. Now
they shoot *Gossip Girl* there. The neighborhood had been a
mess, then it gentrified to something worse. Finally some
nice things happened. McNally Jackson Bookstore opened
on Prince Street. It felt like NoLiTa was getting a soul.
And a couple years ago, I was having a coffee in Gimme
Coffee and across the street was a taco place. The tacos are
cheap. On the menu they're fried, but the lovely people at
this location are willing to grill them, though it does take
longer. Excellent tamales, fish tacos, and shrimp tacos. –
Esther Smith

Emporio
231 Mott St (btwn Prince & Spring) 212-966-1234
auroroaristorante.com (Nolita: 6 to Spring St)
A few stores up from the Mott Street Pinche is Emporio.
Our daughter studied in Milan when the dollar was really,
really low. She discovered *aperitivo*, the tradition whereby
you pay for a drink and get a free meal. Some places in
NYC call themselves *aperitivo*, but they don't even know
what the word means. Emporio does. From 5-7pm, for
$6 you get wine or beer with a free refill. (Plus occasional
drink specials.) And they have little plates and cut-up
small pizzas and white beans and slivered sandwiches and
some cheese on the bar. Not a real meal, but the house
wine is nice and it's a pleasant place. – Esther Smith

Greenwich Village / Union Square

Peanut Butter & Co
240 Sullivan St (btwn Bleecker and W. 3rd St) 212-677-3995
www.ilovepeanutbutter.com
(Greenwich Village: A/B/C/D/E/F/M to W 4th)
This peanut butter–themed restaurant has all different
varieties of sandwiches including the classic Fluffernut-
ter. They make their own peanut butter that is sold in
stores (I highly recommend their dark chocolate version).
They also make shakes. – Josh Saitz

Cowgirl
519 Hudson (btwn 10th St & Charles) 212-633-1133
www.cowgirlnyc.com (Greenwich Village: 1 to Christopher St)
Hey, pardner, saddle on up to this theme-heavy West Village joint, formerly known as The Cowgirl Hall of Fame.
I'd boycott them for changing names except they're the
only place in town that serves ice cream made to look like
baked potatoes. It's also a great place to go with children,
if only to see the irritation they cause some of the more
flamboyant members of the wait staff. Too bad they can't
mellow down with a couple of their own beyond-fine
margaritas. Couple other things: There's a photo gallery
of singing cowboys and cowgirls to help pass the time
when the bathrooms are occupied; a lot of dishes have
Fritos in them; and there's a gift counter where you can
brass up with a tin sheriff's badge.

Republic
37 Union Sq W (btwn E 16th & E 17th St) 212-627-7172
www.thinknoodles.com (Union Sq: 4/5/6/L/N/Q/R to
Union Square)
I would say 90% of the amazing, bursting-with-fresh-fla-
vor food on the menu is $10 or less. It's Asian and largely
noodle-based, with plenty of vegetarian options. The por
tions are sizable, satiating without weighing you down.
My favorite dish is the Vietnamese Vegetable Noodles:
cold rice vermicelli with mint, broccoli, celery carrots,
tofu, egg, shallots, bean sprouts, and peanuts for $9. I al-
ways ask for no egg in it and they are happy to oblige.
– Genevieve Texiera

Chelsea / Garment District

Natural Tofu (also known as Seoul Garden)
34 West 32nd St, 2nd Fl (btwn 5th Ave & Broadway) 212-736-9002
(Garment District: B/D/F/M/N/Q/R to 34th St-6th Ave)
&
40-06 Queens Blvd (@ 40th St, Sunnyside, Queens) 718-706-0899
(Sunnyside: 7 to 40th St)
Looking to rid yourself of that pesky pink stuff lining

& Clay – Michael Chabon • A Tree Grows in

the roof of your mouth? Dig into a steaming crock of Daenge Jang Jigae or Vegetarian Soon Tofu before it's had five minutes to cool down. And wear low-slung pants because they're also going to hit you with a half-dozen banchan, those delicious appetizer-sized Korean freebies, an orange, and possibly an egg. Sit by the window of the second-story Manhattan location, pitying the fools who aren't you!

Mandoo Bar
2 W. 32nd St. (btwn Fifth Ave and Broadway) 212-279-3075
(Garment District: B, D, F, V, N, Q, R, W to 34th St/6th Ave)
I can never change zine printers because Wholesale Copies a) rocks and is b) just a couple of blocks from this Korean dumpling house. On a cold day, nothing beats the vegetarian green versions floating in a generously-mushroomed broth...especially spot-hitting if you're coming off a good scrubbing courtesy of one of the nice ladies at Yi-Pak Spa down the block.

Maui Tacos
330 5th Ave (btwn 32nd & 33rd) 212-868-9722
www.mauitacos.com
(Garment District: B/D/F/N/Q /R/M to 34th St)
Just around the corner from Jim Hanley's Universe, Maui Tacos is an island themed taco joint. A little weird, I know, but hey, its delicious. The prices are cheap and the food is fab! Look out for something called "Dumps".
– Lola Batling

Kashmir 9
478 9th Ave (@ 37th St) 212-714-0657
(Garment District: A/C/E to 34th St)
This is an amazing restaurant. There are steam trays of Indian and Pakistani food behind the counter and about $7 will get you two items, meat or vegetarian, with rice or naan. Be sure to get the mango juice; it's great. You can enjoy Indo-Pak pop music and news reports on the big-screen TV while you dine. The main sign outside reads Cuisine of Pakistan. – Heath Row

Curry in a Hurry
119 Lexington Ave (@ E 28th St), 212-683-0900
www.curryhurry.net (Murray Hill: subway)
Order your jumbo masala dosa downstairs, put it on a tray and haul it to the upper dining room where you'll find a chutney bar, cheesy, endearing paintings on the walls, and large windows through which you can have a New York moment watching the yellow cabs zooming down Lexington Avenue. Ruin a provincial companion's dessert by bringing them a treat from the case of fluores-

cent milk sweets, only to reveal that it is barfi.

Ali Baba
212 E 34th St (btwn 3rd Ave & Tunnel Exit St) 212-683-9206
www.alibabaturkishcuisine.com
Go with a mixed group, and you'll do well! They also have a back room under an awning that might be good for groups. I recommend the zucchini pancakes and the divine Turkish coffee, double sweet. – Heath Row

Hell's Kitchen / Midtown

Tehuitzingo Mexican Deli
695 10th Ave (btwn 47th and 48th)
(Hell's Kitchen: C/E to 50th St-8th Ave)
If someone in your party is ruining your reputation by taking you to a Broadway musical, insist that you dine at Tehuitzgo before and/or after as a matter of taste, budget, and pride. It's a bodega up front. In back are a couple of counters with seating of sorts. An extremely respectable place for someone of your sensibilities to hork down a few insanely good, insanely cheap tacos. Those papas con rajas are so fine, I'm surprised there's no contrarian posting to the Chowhound discussion boards about how they crawled here on their fucking knees from Sunset Park. Plenty of fire to go around, including my favorite, El Yucateca Chipotle Hot Sauce.

Menchanko-Tei
131 East 45th St (btwn Lexington and 3rd Ave) 212-986-6805
(Midtown: 4/5/6/7/S to Grand Central)
43-45 West 55th St (btwn 5th and 6th Ave) 212-247-1585
(Midtown: E/M to 5th Ave-53rd St)
&
there's one in Honolulu, but that's Hawaii, fool!
www.menchankotei.com
Eat like a salaryman who thinks he's a sumo wrestler! Heaping portions! Manly iron serving vessels! Every ingredient but the kitchen sink! Forget about that sissy sushi for a second and get some oden, a hearty Japanese stew that's going to put some hair on that scrawny chest. The West Side branch is an ace up the sleeve for MOMA visitors looking to do an end run around the mad-pricey in-house dining options with something more memorable than a dog or a slice. The East Side location makes a good feed in the culinary barrens surrounding Grand Central (as opposed to in Grand Central, where there's that famous oyster bar and a gourmet market with lots of stalls.)

Brooklyn - Betty Smith • Subwayland - Randy

Upper West Side

La Caridad
2199 Broadway (@ 78th St) 212-874-2780
(Upper West Side: 1 to 79th St)
It took moving to NYC to realize that "Cuban Chinese" is more than some crazy made-up Tom Waits lyric! Communism does make for strange bedfellows, but these turn out to be the Fred and Ginger of New York's low budget culinary dance. I recommend sticking to the Cuban end of the menu, served by grouchy Chinese waiters in a no-frills setting pulsing with the anxieties of the multitudes crowded by the entrance, eying your table. Wait until you get a load of the raw garlic smothering the fried pork chops!

Morningside Heights / Harlem

Ms. Mamie's Spoonbread 2
366 W 110th St (btwn Columbus and Manhattan Aves)
www.spoonbreadinc.com
(Morningside Hts: B/C to 110th-Cathedral Parkway)
As a Hoos-Yorker of semi-Southern descent, I was proud to make the acquaintance of Ms. Mamie's Spoonbread 2. Chicken and waffles, mason jars of sweetened ice tea, and smothered chicken...it's like Mama's with 20 times the praise Jesus and none of the oh Mary! Her white lace curtains and gracious, church lady manners make her a natural for visiting relatives. Reportedly everyone from Bill Clinton to Oprah have experienced nirvana in the form of Ms. M's red velvet cake. They've got a kid's menu. They've got a cookbook! Look for the white picket fence on an otherwise urban-looking sidewalk across from Morningside Park.

Taqueria y Fonda La Mexicana
968 Amsterdam Ave (btwn 107th & 108th) 212-531-0383
(Morningside Hts: B/C/1 to Cathedral Pkwy)
The best Mexican food I have had outside of California exists in this tiny hole-in-the-wall. I can assure you that no tourists can be found here. It's extremely small. You will bump into everything, but it's worth it. Their Giant Burrito is so huge it's almost head-sized. I have successfully eaten an entire one all by myself, but only once. They bring chips and three different amazing salsas to the table. The menu is mostly under $10 except for their Southwestern Mexican dishes which are $11–$13. – Genevieve Texiera

Amir's Falafel
2911 Broadway (btwn 112th & 113th) 212-749-7500
(Morningside Hts: 1 to 116th St-Columbia University)
They rock. They have the coolest t-shirts (you can buy one), and the best baba ganoush you will ever eat. The owners are Lebanese. The cooks, as in all NYC restaurants, are Mexican, and they do a mean falafel. You can stuff yourself for $6. Oh, and try the lentil soup...heavenly. They also have pastries—the kadaifi's great. - Jerry the Mouse

Washington Heights

El Malecon
4141 Broadway (btwn 175th & 176th) 212-927-3812
www.maleconrestaurants.com
(Washington Hts: A to 175th St)
Way uptown, like Washington Heights, there's a Dominican restaurant where they will do their best to be friendly. They might let you sit there for hours. You can people watch and work on your zine! – Lola Batling

Tacqueria Los Jarritos
1555 Saint Nicholas (btwn 187th & 188th) 212-740-2496
(Washington Hts: A to 190th St)
Greatest Mexican food EVER! Homestyle! Cheapest prices you have ever encountered, too. – Jerry the Mouse

Great Wall Chinese Food Corporation
800 W. 181st St (btwn Fort Washington & Pinehurst) 212-795-9373
(Washington Hts: A to 181st St)
Best vegetarian hot and sour soup! And darn good veggie steamed dumplings. - Jerry the Mouse

Coogan's
4015 Broadway (btwn 169th St & 170th St) 212-928-1234
www.coogans.com
(Washington Hts: A/C/1 to 168th St)

Used to be much better than now, but it's still pretty good; nice atmosphere, and they sponsor all sorts of great neighborhood events, like the Shamrock Run for MS, and other good causes. Famous people come here. Their signed pics are all over the walls, as are other neighborhood and NYC memorabilia items. Coogan's has great karaoke nights. - Jerry the Mouse

BROOKLYN

Mojito Loco
102 Meserole St (btwn Manhattan & Leonard, Williamsburg, Bklyn) 718-963-2960
www.mojitoloco.com
(Williamsburg: J/M to Lorimer)
Mojito Loco is a small, moderately priced eat-in Mexican restaurant with drink specials beyond compare (all you can drink sangria, cough) and one of the best veggie burritos I've ever had. Never too crowded and with excellent service, this place is equally satisfying to stop into for a drink as for a full meal. – Caitlin McGurk

Basia Restaurant
167 Nassau Ave (btwn Diamond & Jewel, Greenpoint, Bklyn) 718-383-0276
(Greenpoint: G to Nassau Ave)
Basia is one of the better Polish restaurants in Greenpoint. There's the usual process: Order at the counter off a board, pick up your silverware, and sit down until your food is ready. Basia is notable because it has Warsaw Bakery's rye bread free for the taking by the napkins. Besides the food, a highlight of the place is that they have a television tuned to a Polish-language station, so you can fully immerse yourself in the sights and sounds of the culture. – Heath Row

Superfine
126 Front St (btwn Pine & Wall St, DUMBO, Brooklyn) 718-243-9005 (DUMBO: F to York)
When was the last time you dined in a loading dock? Turns out it's the perfect place to find a killer Bloody Mary and a cute crowd. Good Southwestern eats, bluegrass Sunday brunches, and a basket of blocks for the spawn of parents apt to let their feral young go unsupervised on multiple concrete levels ringed with industrial metal railings. If you're aiming to go here after a show at St. Anne's Warehouse, you'd best run before your waitress gets slammed.

Fatoosh Pitza & Barbecue
330 Hicks St (btwn Atlantic Ave & State St, Brooklyn Heights, Bklyn) 718-243-0500
(Brooklyn Hts: 2/3/4/5/M/R to Court St-Borough Hall) &
437 5th Ave (btwn 6th Ave & 7th Ave, Park Slope, Bklyn) 718-369-0606 (Park Slope: F/M/R to 9th St-4th Ave)
Home of a great, cheap falafel sandwich! The spinach pie is like no other. More like a calzone. It's huge and tasty and $6 - Amy Burchenal

Ferdinando's Focacceria
151 Union St (btwn Columbia & Henry St, Carroll Gardens, Bklyn) 718-855-1545 (Carroll Gardens: F/G to Carroll)
Damn, why can't this be the dominant Italian cuisine? This unpretentious Sicilian place opened in 1905 and they're not going to let the tastes of a fickle American public start shoving them around now. Having spent most of my adult life running around telling anyone who will listen how much I dislike pasta, I was afraid of coming off as culturally insensitive, so I ordered the spleen sandwich. You heard me. Its proper name is Vastedda and it's a hot mess, melted ricotta squishing out all over a homemade bun. They've got celebrated rice balls (good band name) and tons of atmosphere without trying. They close at seven on weeknights.

Habana Outpost
757 Fulton St (@ S Portland Ave, Fort Greene Bklyn) 718-858-9500
www.habanaoutpost.com
(Fort Greene: C to Lafayette Ave)
This is an absolute MUST. Gorgeous people, cheap hot dogs and veggie dogs, affordable beer, outdoor beauty. Noteworthy bathrooms. At the forefront of eco-conscious restaurants; they educate and practice it in a really fun way. Get the Cuban Corn and skip the tempting/pricey frozen mojitos. – Robyn Jordan (If you're craving fresh juice and a good workout, go for weekend brunch when you can get a buck off by volunteering to pedal their human-powered bike blender. – AH) (They even have solar-powered chargers so you can charge your phone. You order inside and then take your receipt to the solar-powered truck outside. At this point it's kind of confusing--you have to hand your receipt to one of the busy cooks and then try to figure out which order is yours. Then you find a picnic table. On Sundays in the summer, they show outdoor movies. It's a good place to meet friends with kids because of the combination of alcohol and kid-friendly food and atmosphere. – Amanda Plumb)

Motherless Brooklyn - Jonathan Letham • I Am

Smith St waiters

Taro Sushi

446 Dean St (btwn 5th Ave & Flatbush, Park Slope, Bklyn) 718-398-0872

(Park Slope: B/D/M/N/Q /R/2/3/4/5/ to Atlantic Ave-Pacific St)

Its nothing special appearance and blah location near the crazy traffic and chain stores of Atlantic Center keep prices low, but that's all part of what makes this excellent sushi bar feel like such a find. The owner's hooked up with the guys who buy fish for his father's sushi bar in Japan, meaning the specials arrived today on a one-way ticket from Tokyo's famous Tsukiji Market. My Japanese friends were majorly psyched to find out that Taro Sushi roasts its own eel. If you're traveling with a raw fishaphobe, the udon noodles, teriyaki, and agedashi tofu are great too. (Not much for veg-heads, though, as bonito stock figures in just about everything.)

Song

295 5th Ave (btwn 4th Ave & 1st St, Park Slope Blyn) 718) 965-1108 (Park Slope: M/R to Union St)

Song is a great Thai place to meet friends, especially for a little birthday celebration. It's a really well-rounded restaurant with great atmosphere (including outside seating and a DJ on the weekends) and good food that's surprisingly cheap (vegetarian dishes are about $7). The folks that work there are really accommodating. – Amanda

Plumb

Tacos Matamoros

4508 5th Ave (btwn 45th & 46th St, Sunset Park, Bklyn) 718-871-7627 (Sunset Park: R to 45th St)

People claim that you can't get good Mexican food in New York, but they obviously haven't been to Sunset Park. Everyone who comes to Matamoros orders al pastor because their al pastor is freaking awesome. You can't peek into the kitchen as easily in its new location but, even so, go to Matamoros, order yourself some tacos al pastor, and try some other tacos too. At $1.50 a taco, you can't go wrong. And if you do, so what, you're only out $1.50. – Lauren Jade Martin

Gan Eden

4620 5th Ave (btwn 46th & 47th St, Sunset Park, Bklyn) 718-439-3399

www.ganedencafe.com (Sunset Park: R to 45th St)

A space with exposed brick walls and tiled floors that thankfully, instead of opening as a dreaded coffee shop/harbinger of gentrification, turned out to be yet another Mexican food joint. The name means Garden of Eden in Hebrew, but rather than falafel or challah bread, the fare is typical burritos, chilaquiles, tacos. The huaraches and quesadillas are outstanding. Vegetarian choices include mushrooms and pumpkin flowers. – Lauren Jade Martin

Ba Xuyen

4222 8th Ave (btwn 42nd & 43rd St, Sunset Park, Bklyn) 718-633-6601 (Sunset Park: D/M to 9th Ave)

Ba Xuyen is one of my favorites for incredible banh mi sandwiches on toasty baguettes filled with your choice of meat, cilantro, veggies, and jalapeños. My favorite is #5, barbecued pork. Try a lychee or avocado shake! – Lauren Jade Martin

Kai Feng Fu

4801 8th Ave (btwn 48th & 49th St, Sunset Park, Bklyn) 718-437-3542(Sunset Park: D to Ft. Hamilton Pkway)

Several years ago, I was shopping in Chinatown with my mother, when I saw a flyer for Kai Feng Fu Dumpling House. I could not believe the prices that were listed. I thought it was a misprint. Inflation has raised the price somewhat (now you "only" get four dumplings for $1, the nerve!) but it's still so worth it. If meat's not your thing, you can get eight vegetable dumplings for $2. – Lauren Jade Martin

a Woman - Ann Bannon • Low Life: The Lures

XSG Dumpling House
5301 8th Ave (@ 53rd St, Sunset Park, Bklyn) 718-633-1588
(Sunset Park: N to 8th Ave)
The best thing about this place, besides its cheap eats, is
the cook's sideburns. This guy has lovely, long sideburns
that end with a loop, kind of like spit curls, but literally
attached to his face. I come here at least once a week for
pork and chive dumplings (four for $1) and, my favorite,
the sesame pancake with egg, a round pancake sliced
in half and filled with a fried egg, cilantro, lettuce, and
cucumber. They wrap it up in cellophane, making it perfectly portable. Yum. – Lauren Jade Martin

Family Dumpling
5602 7th Ave (@ 56th St) Sunset Park, Bklyn) 718-492-0686
(Sunset Park: N to 8th Ave)
I once ran into an former student here, when I was wait
ing to pick up my order of dumplings and a scallion pancake
with fried egg on top. It caught me off guard; it felt like this
student had found out a deep dark secret about me. Well, the
secret's out: Your poorly-paid adjunct instructors feed themselves on $1 dumplings. – Lauren Jade Martin

Adelman's Deli
1906 Kings Hwy (btwn 19th St & Ocean Ave, Gravesend,
Bklyn) 718-336-4915 (Gravesend: B/Q to Kings Highway)
I get a bit gloomy contemplating the Remembrance of
Pastramis Past at long-gone Brooklyn Delicatessens like
Edna's, where Edna herself warned me that nobody would
be kissing me once I ate the garlicky salami sandwich I
ordered. When the gloom descends, I head for Adelman's
on Kings Highway in deep, immigrant-infused Brooklyn.
Though the décor has been blandly updated to that of a
sports bar, the old neon sign still swings overhead, and
the free seltzer (!) has bubbles sharp enough to bring
tears to your eyes. Once your order reaches $8.25, you can
partake of the all-you-can-eat salad bar. The stretch of
King's Highway between Ocean Avenue and Coney Island
Avenue is well worth exploring for the international mix
of stores, especially Russian and Turkish. A few doors up
from Adelman's is Meat Heaven, a toothsome Russian
grocery. – David Goren

The Roll-n-Roaster Restaurant
2901 Emmons Ave (@ Nostrand Ave) Sheepshead Bay,
Bklyn) 718-769-6000, www.rollnroaster.com
(Sheepshead Bay: B/Q to Sheepshead Bay)
Imagine you get a time machine and you accidentally set
the destination year dial to "Indistinguishable mash-up
of dates." When you get out you will probably be at Roll-
n-Roaster in Sheepshead Bay. (You could also ride your

bike there). The food is not that great, but the atmosphere
is *amazing*. It's all you would imagine a '50s (or '60s? or
'70s?) fast food joint to look like: a whole lot of brown,
a whole lot of yellow, a bizarrely-shaped dining room to
facilitate a once roller-skating staff, and a line exclusively
for roast beef orders. You can get cheese on anything and
you can order Moet champagne by the bottle. – Cecile
Dyer

QUEENS

Family Corner Restaurant
2102 31st St (@ 21st Ave, Astoria, Queens) 718-204-7915
(Astoria: N to Ditmars Blvd)
Family Corner has gyro on a pita for $5. Lots of veggies.
They also have iced coffee for a buck fifty and spinach
pie for super cheap if you can't spring for a whole meal. –
Josh Medsker

Afghan Kabob House
25-89 Steinway St (@ 28th St, Astoria, Queens)
718-777-7758 (Astoria: N to Ditmars)
We found this place when we couldn't find the place we
were looking for. Their side dish eggplant with yogurt
was divine. There's no translation on the menu - you have
to ask. The amazing lentil soup seemed to have almost
everything but lentils. Same with the non-ricey rice pudding - very rich! – Esther Smith

The Flushing Mall
133-31 39th Ave (btwn Union & Main, Flushing, Queens)
718-888-1234
www.888flushingmall.com (Flushing: 7 to Main St)
Flushing is a bursting-at-the-seams immigrant community filled with tiny shops packed into every possible
corner. It's a fantastic place to explore if you're willing to
poke around and see where your feet take you. On the upper floor of the Flushing Mall there is a Korean dumpling
stall which is not to be missed. It's right near the fountain. I could eat the fresh kimchee alone and be perfectly
content. Downstairs you'll find the main food court with
Taiwanese shaved ices and a Delimanjoo (tiny cakes with
custard filling) stand. On the weekends, the machine is
usually running and you'll get your cakes piping hot.
Beware of burning your tongue on custard! As is the case
all over Flushing, many vendors speak very little English.
Most folks are incredibly friendly, but you may have
trouble communicating about dietary restrictions. There
is wonderful food to be found in Flushing, but aside from
what can be found in the bakeries and supermarkets,
very little of it is vegetarian. – Sharon Furgason (Shaved

ice and stinky tofu? My heart beats so that I can barely speak! – AH)

STATEN ISLAND

Gourmet Dog
40 Richmond Terrace (by St George Terminal, Staten Island) 718-727-1234 (Staten Island: Ferry to Staten Island)
Staten Island is not a borough known for its convenience. I've lived here for seven months now and don't even know where the grocery store is. You need a car to get almost everywhere, so it's not like Brooklyn or Manhattan where you can fall off your fire escape and land face-first into a slice of pizza. Having grown tired of ordering delivery from the same place every other night, I took a walk around and discovered Gourmet Dog, a little shack located right across the street from where the ferry spits out. As far as I'm concerned there is only one item worth ordering, and that's the Crunchy Dog. The Crunchy Dog is a snappy hot dog in a lightly-toasted bun that is sprinkled with mashed-up potato chips. It's like a fat kid's dream. – Kelly McClure

Cargo Café
120 Bay St (near Slossen Terr, St George, Staten Island)
718-876-0539, www.cargocafe.com
(walk 2 blocks from the St. George Ferry Terminal)
The Cargo Café is the first place I ever ventured out to after moving to Staten Island. I was drawn there because one of the things I read online mentioned that it features a clock that counts down to the end of the world. Intense! Since discovering Cargo, I have yet to see this spooky clock, but I have seen their slender but cozy outside patio and have knocked back my fair share of $3 mini-Colt-45s. This place also hosts weirdo nightly events for the townies, such as "Grab Ass Tuesdays," which is a Twister tournament. – Kelly McClure

VEGETARIAN

MANHATTAN
Chinatown

Vegetarian Dim Sum House
24 Pell St (@ Doyers) 212-577-7176
(Chinatown: J/M/Z/N/Q /R/6 to Canal St)
No worries here about accidentally ending up with a plate of steamed chicken feet when you tick off the more mysteriously named dishes on the DIY order sheet. Treasure Balls with Assorted Flavor? Check! Half Moon Pockets? Check! Monk Dumplings? Check, check, check! Check

them all because everything here is outta sight and most items are less than $3. Do save room for the Mango Pudding. It may sound ordinary, and it comes in a disposable plastic cup, but it's the perfect ending.

Buddha Bodai
5 Mott St (btwn Chatham Sq & Mosco St) 212-566-8388
www.chinatownvegetarian.com
(Chinatown: J/M/Z/N/Q /R/6 to Canal St)
Go here if you're in Chinatown around lunch time. They have both lunch specials and veggie dim sum! – Victoria Law (For dim sum, I actually prefer Buddha Bodai to the Vegetarian Dim Sum House, despite their more traditional dim sum hours of weekend lunchtime. Arrive early. - Melissa Bastian)

Lower East Side/East Village

Tiengarden Vegan Restaurant
170 Allen St (btwn Stanton & Rivington) 212-388-1364
(LES: F to 2nd Ave)
Back when the Lower East Side's low budget arts scene was still somewhat lower and east of being "discovered", tiny Tiengarden provided the only healthy neighborhood alternative to the pizza and falafels we would race out for on our ten minute rehearsal breaks. How virtuous it felt to sit on that black painted floor, eating brown rice and unidentifiable greens! When Bluestockings Books opened

next door, Tiengarden was assured a steady source of customers. I can't promise that she'll still be working there, but Tiengarden has *the nicest* waitress in New York City, a gentle, galumphing soul in owl glasses and a doughty knit cap, who becomes enwreathed in great rainbows of gratitude any time a customer compliments the food.

Kate's Joint

58 Avenue B (btwn 4th St & 5th St) 212-777-7059
www.myspace.com/katesjoint
(East Village: F/J/M/Z to Delancey-Essex)
Kate's Joint is the old-school mama of the veggie standbys. You can stay just under the $10 mark if you don't get a drink and appetizers and the fun stuff. Or if you just drink their vegan white russian as your lunch! – Megan Garrity (I don't eat out much, but I have to say that Kate's Joint is great. My best times there have been with trav eling bands. Crusty or stinky as you may be as you sit crammed into a back table with your disco fries, they'll never bug you to leave. – Fly)

Atlas Café

73 2nd Avenue (btwn 4th and 5th) 212-539-0966
(East Village: F to 2nd Ave)
&
Little Atlas Café
6 W. 4th St. (btwn Broadway and Mercer) 212-253-5535
(Greenwich Village: R to 8th St)
I am a bad vegan: I love fake meat. I will eat tofu, seitan, or TVP mushed into the shape or consistency of a dead animal over a plate of steamed vegetables every time. So this is where I'm coming from when I tell you how yummy I think Atlas Café's vegan sandwiches are. I've tried a few of them, but I almost always order the Vegan Chicken Artichoke ($6.25). A carnivore friend enjoys the not vegan Chicken Artichoke just as much. Moroccan standbys like soup, pasta, and couscous also please. Atlas is also celebrated for its vegan pastries and the somewhat elusive-in-NYC vegan soft serve. The place is small and gets crowded, but the people are usually pleasant. There's outdoor seating when weather permits. – Jenna Freedman

Pukk

71 1st Ave (btwn 4th & 5th St) 212-253-2742
www.pukknyc.com (East Village: F to 2nd Ave)
Pukk is hella trendy but you'll have to get over that because it's also hella delicious and very reasonably priced. The appetizers are like four bucks apiece and could be your whole meal. I wholeheartedly recommend the Curry Thai Pancake. The curry dip is friggin' delicious and the tofu is chunky enough to balance out the fried carbitude

of the pancakes. The enormous entrées (also rice and noodle dishes) cost between $7 and $9, with a variety of vegetable and fake meat choices. Egg is optional, so it's easy to eat vegan. – Jenna Freedman (I recommend it for lunch, when their specials include vegetarian soup, appetizer, and main course for only $6.50. After 3:30pm, prices spike. – Victoria Law) (This is the only place I know of where one can obtain vegan Thai iced tea—yum! – Melissa Bastian)

Downtown Bakery

691st Ave (btwn 4th & 5th St) 212-254-1757
(East Village: F to 2nd Ave)
If you don't care for Thai food, try this Mexican bakery next door to Pukk. They have tamales, burritos, tortas, and all sorts of other mouthwatering foods for vegans, carnivores, and anyone who falls in between. – Victoria Law

Lan Café

342 E 6th St (btwn 1st Ave & 2nd Ave) 212-228-8325
(East Village: 6 to Astor Pl)
It's easy to have a cheap meal here, and where else are you going to find amazing all-vegan Vietnamese food?! Truly a blessing. Try the lemongrass seitan in any incarnation. The baguettes are a particularly good bargain. – Melissa Bastian (Their banh mi are pricy, but mock meat ain't cheap. – Kate Black)

Caracas Arepa Bar

93 1/2 E 7th St (btwn 1st Ave & Ave A) 212-529-2314
(East Village: F to 2nd Ave)
&
291 Grand St (btwn Havemeyer & Roebling, Williamsburg, Bklyn) 718-218-6050
(Williamsburg: L to Bedford Ave)
Can arepas stuffed with shredded beef and grilled chicken con chorizo be classified as vegan? Yes, when you find a kitchen staff as willing to replace everything save the vintage wallpaper and *jugos naturals* with baked tofu. (And all you wheat-freegans will be glad to hear that there's nothing red flaggy for you, either, in these Venezuelan corn cakes.) The Roneria rum bar inside the Brooklyn location takes the pain out of the long wait.

Quantum Leap

203 1st Ave (btwn 12th & 13th St) 212-673-9848
(East Village: L to 1st Ave)
&
226 Thompson St (btwn 3rd St & Bleecker)
212-677-8050
(Greenwich Village: A/B/C/D/E/F/M to W 4th St)

— Jonathan Letham • The Alcoholic – Jonathan Ames

www.quantumleaprestaurant.com
Whenever you're downtown, you know you're only a hop, a skip, and a jump way from the Leap. Featuring a surprisingly large, international menu, "the Leap" has got seafood dishes like broiled salmon and seafood scampi for the pescetarians, cheesy eggy yumminess like omelets and a million kinds of veggie cheeseburgers for the lacto-ovo vegetarians, and divine seasonally-flavored pancakes and savory tacos for pain-in-the-ass vegans like me. – Emily Rems

Curly's Vegetarian Lunch
328 E. 14th St (btwn 1st & 2nd Ave) 212-598-9998
www.curlyslunch.com (East Village: L to 1st Ave)
Curly's Vegetarian Lunch has a number of substantial options in their Small Plates and Appetizers listings. Of note are the Chili and Grain and the appetizer-sized quesadillas. The *entrées* are also under $10. Curly's will make anything on the menu vegan (including their Mexican chocolate milkshake!), so it's a great place for vegans and omnis to dine happily and cheaply together. And they have beer! Still one of the best brunches in town. – Melissa Bastian

SoHo

Wild Ginger Vegan Café
380 Broome St 212 966-1883
(SoHo: 6 to Spring St)
112 Smith St (btwn Dean & Pacific, Boerum Hill, Bklyn)
(Boerum Hill: F to Bergen St)
www.wildgingervegan.com
One order of Malaysian Curry Stew—a delicious mélange of potatoes, pumpkin, carrots, broccoli, soy protein and coconut milk—and I am ready for a nap in one of their rowboat sized booths. Go before 3:30, as the lunch specials not only come with miso soup and a spring roll, they're five bucks cheaper than these same dishes cost at night. The décor is high end Zenned out, which I appreciate, especially when the Smith St staff spices up the soundtrack with a little Kimya Dawson or Lou Reed. If you're sweet on a vegan, this'd be a nice place to take him or her on a date.

Souen
210 Sixth Ave (@ Prince Street) 212-807-7421
(SoHo: C to Prince St)
28 East 13th St (btwn University Pl and 5th Ave)
212-627-7150
(Greenwich Village: L/N/R/Q /4/5/6 to Union Sq)
www.souen.net
A time-honored macrobiotic spot, good for vegans, the

gluten-free, and anyone whose carcass is in need of purification (both internally and atmospherically.) The best offerings have an Asian feel. Maybe I'd feel differently about Deep-Fried Seitan Parmigiana cooked in no-tomato marinara sauce and topped with tofu cheese if dietary restrictions prevented me from tucking into the real Italian deal elsewhere. Non-veg friends will be reassured to know that there are a few fish swimming around the menu, too.

Greenwich Village

Dojo
14 W 4th St (btwn Mercer St & Broadway) 212-505-8934
(Greenwich Village: R to 8th St)
Dojo's Soy Burger Sandwich, served inside a whole wheat pita with mixed greens, tomato, cucumber, sprouts, and tahini dressing is just $3.95. – Jenna Freedman

Red Bamboo
140 W 4th St (btwn MacDougal & 6th Ave) 212-260-7049
www.redbamboo-nyc.com
(Greenwich Village: A/B/D/E/F/M to W 4th St)
This was the first vegan restaurant I went to in NYC. It was recommended for their killer panko-breaded soy nuggets and *boy*, were they *right*! The entire menu is great, a bit pricey, but hey... I tend to just go here on romantic dates. The menu is eclectic and includes a vast array of soul food for the Caribbean soul. – Cristy Road
(Delicious, creative eats for businessmen and street punks alike – Megan Garrity)

'sNice
45 8th Ave (@ 4th St) 212-645-0310
(Greenwich Village: A/C/E/L to 14th St)
&
315 5th Ave (btwn 2nd & 3rd St, Park Slope, Bklyn)
718-788-2121 (Park Slope: M/R to Union St)

& Dean Haspiel • Dreamland – Kevin Baker •

'sNice is an all-vegetarian café and coffee shop with counter service, dishing out some truly delish salads, sandwiches, pasta salads, and the like, alongside coffees, and teas. They frequently have fabulous vegan baked goods, and half of what's on the giant chalkboard menus is vegan. I'm addicted to their vegan panini and the vegan club. Both locations hang funky, affordable art by local artists. The Brooklyn location tends to be less crowded and is more sunny, but if you like nothing better on a Saturday night than to hang out in a coffee shop reading, the West Village location clears out as well. – Melissa Bastian ('sNice has THE most delicious cupcakes I've ever had, and they're vegan! You get a ton of food for your money. Their sandwiches are so thick you can't get them in your mouth in one bite. – Megan Garrity)

Mamoun's
119 MacDougal (@ W 3rd St) 212-674-8685
(Greenwich Village: A/C/E/B/D/F/M to W 4th St)
&
22 St Marks Pl (btwn 2nd & 3rd Ave) 212-387-7747
(East Village: 6 to Astor Pl)
www.mamounsfalafel.com
Everyone knows Mamoun's. It's cheap ($2.50), it's quick, it's open late, and it's surprisingly good. You can also ask for hummus or baba ganoush to be added to your falafel for 50 cents or an order of falafel (without the sandwich) for just $1. But the falafel joint across the street is the same price, and I think their falafel has more flavor. – Amanda Plumb (The East Village Mamoun's makes its own tamarind drink, along with fresh mango juice. - AH)

Temple in the Village
74 W. 3rd (btwn Laguardia Pl & Thompson St) 212-475-5670
(Greenwich Village: A/C/E/B/D/F/M to W 4th St)
This macrobiotic/vegan buffet is a little pricey but it's run by a really nice family. The food is tasty and next to the dosa cart guy on the south side of Washington Square and Mamoun's, this is the cheapest, most edible vegan food I know of on that side of town – Matana Roberts

Gramercy Park

Maoz
38 Union Sq E (btwn 16th & 17th) 212-260-1988
www.maozusa.com (Union Sq: L/N/Q /R/4/5/6 to Union Sq)
At Maoz you can get fried falafel in a pita, with hummus—and the best part is they have a bar with all these toppings, from beets to this cucumber sauce that's sooo good. It comes with giant fries. – Josh Medsker

Express Manna Kitchen
28 E 18th St (btwn Broadway & Park Ave) 212-228-1044
www.mannakitchen.com
(Gramercy Park: 4/5/6/L/N/Q /R to Union Square)
Express Manna Kitchen is this fast food Korean place that makes such a good tofu bowl! Eat it! – Dear Drunk Girl

Tiffin Wallah
127 E 28th St (@ Lexington) 212-685-7301
www.tiffinwallah.us (Gramercy Park: 6 to 28th St)
The tragedy of Tiffin Wallah's buffet lunch special is that my abdomen is physically incapable of holding "all I can eat." This alone keeps me from drinking the Kingfisher beers they keep on ice for degenerate businesspeople such as myself.

Hell's Kitchen/Midtown

Tanaka Sushi
222 51st St (btwn 2nd & 3rd Ave) 212-308-6976
(Midtown: 6/E/M to Lexington-3rd Ave-51st St)
Tanaka's two-roll lunch special is a mere $8.25 and comes with miso soup and a salad. They have some really fab veg offerings like the mango roll, the sweet potato tempura roll, and the peanut roll! – Melissa Bastian

Zen Palate
663 Ninth Ave (@ 46th St) 212-582-1669
(Hell's Kitchen: A/C/E/N/Q /R/S/1/2/3/7 to 42nd St-8th Ave)
&
115 E 18th St (btwn Park Ave & Irving Pl) 646-291-2613
(Flatiron: L/N/Q /R/4/5/6 to Union Sq)
www.zenpalate.com
Unless you're on an expense account, stick to the weekday lunch specials, when you can fill up on Eggplant Zentastic, Shredded Melody, and Rose Petals with your choice of tea for less than ten bucks. Come dinner time, the prices skyrocket and the names get much more florid: Tapestry Embrace, Celestial Tofu, Wheel of Dharma… zinester, *please!*) This is one of the more reliable vegetarian options in Times Square.

Harlem

Strictly Roots
2058 Adam Clayton Powell Blvd (btwn 122nd &123rd)
212-864-8699 (Harlem: 2/3/A/B/C/D to 125th St)
I love, love, love this Rastafarian restaurant and regularly make the epic trek from all-parts Brooklyn just to have a serving of their tasty, tasty greens and other vegan delicacies. There is absolutely nothing you could order

Scarlett Takes Manhattan - Molly Crabapple 8

from this menu that would taste suspect, as vegan fare sometimes can if you're not careful what you choose.
– Matana Roberts

Inwood

Indian Road Café
600 W 218th St (@ Indian Rd) 212- 942-7451
www.indianroadcafe.com (Inwood: 1 to 215th St)
Right next to Inwood Hill Park's eastern exit, and close to Columbia University stadium. It has the greatest vegan-friendly menu and friendly people. It's a real community space. Knitting on Mondays! – Jerry the Mouse

Upper East Side
Among your many choices....

Pita Grill
1570 1st Ave (btwn 81st St & 82nd St) 212-717-2005
(Upper East Side: 4/5/6 to 86th St)
&
1083 2nd Ave (btwn 57th St & 58th St) 212-750-1122
(N/Q/R to Lexington Ave-59th St)
&
441 3rd Ave (btwn 30th & 31st St) 212-683-3008
(Murray Hill: 6 to 33rd St)
&
790 9th Ave (btwn 51st & 52nd St) 212-765-1100
(Hell's Kitchen: C/E to 50th St)
&
291 7th Ave (btwn 26th & 27th St) 212-243-7482
(Chelsea: 1 to 28th St)
&
92 8th Ave (btwn 14th St & 15th St) 212-337-0300
(Chelsea: A/C/E/L to 14th St-8th Ave)
&
69 New St (btwn Beaver St & Exchange Pl)
(Financial District: 4/5 to Bowling Green)
www.orderpitagrill.com
Pita Grill has the most amazing sweet potato fries, lots of healthy vegetarian items, and plenty of salads. I like dining there, but every time I do, I think they're on the verge of going out of business. I have to assume they do most of their business in delivery because they are always opening new locations. – Josh Saitz

inside, two Japanese d.j.'s spin heavy dub.

BROOKLYN

Supercore
305 Bedford Ave (btwn 1st St & 2nd St, Williamsburg, Bklyn) 718-302-1629
www.supercore.tv (Williamsburg: L to Bedford Ave)
This Williamsburg café/bar's $3.50 Super Healthy Special Lunch Plate is a fiscally and planetarily responsible way to fill your tank with salad, rice and beans, and a bunless "Tofu Hamburg" that tastes 50,000 times better than it sounds.

Khao Sarn Thai
311 Bedford Ave (btwn 1st St & 2nd St, Williamsburg, Bklyn) 718-963-1238
khaosarnbrooklyn.com (Williamsburg: L to Bedford Ave)
Khao Sarn Thai makes a delicious mock duck! - Dear Drunk Girl

Foodswings
295 Grand Ave (btwn Roebling & Havemeyer) Williamsburg, Bklyn) 718-388-1919
www.foodswings.net
(Williamsburg: G/L to Metropolitan-Lorimer)
Cheap fast food with all the artery-clogging deliciousness you want. Oh, how I love your fake buffalo wings. Even though they just changed owners, it's STILL all vegan and delish. – Megan Garrity (It calls itself vegan fast food, but don't think greasy, sweaty burgers. Dine there for cheap, surrounded by awesome decor! – gracie janovie) (My mouth is watering just from thinking about them. Addictive like nothing else. This place is the polar opposite of healthy. – Kate Black)

Phoebe's
323 Graham Ave (btwn Ainslie & Devoe, Williamsburg, Bklyn) 718-599-3218
(Williamsburg: L to Graham Ave)
Phoebe's was one of the first veggie places in the neigh-

borhood and has a limited but very tasty and reasonable menu. Their brunch is delicious! There are a bunch of hipster coffee shops around there now, but Phoebe's was the first and is the coolest. Free internet and a comfy place to be. – Megan Garrity

Vegetarian Palate
258 Flatbush Ave (btwn Prospect Pl & St Marks Ave, Park Slope, Bklyn) 718-623-8808
(Park Slope: B/Q to 7th Ave)
Vegetarian Palate is cute and quiet in Park Slope. I remember walking here for the first time from the Brooklyn Museum, during a killer sinus infection that was taking over my body. I held in the pain because I wanted to go to this place so bad. I love the vast array of dishes from varying ethnic backgrounds. The majority of stuff seemed to be of Asian influence (orange beef, wonton soup, fried rice dishes), but *then*, all of a sudden, you will stumble upon items such as BBQ ribs, vegan *Cornish hen*, and turkey sandwiches. I definitely had the Cornish hen and it was definitely shaped like one. – Cristy Road

Food For Thought
445 Marcus Garvey Blvd (btwn Macon & McDonaugh, Bedford-Stuyvesant, Bklyn) 718-443-4160
www.myspace.com/food4thoughtcafe (Bed-Stuy: C to Kingston Ave-Throop Ave)
Bed-Stuy, do or die! This neighborhood is central for anyone not in the know. Cool vibe, interesting people, cheap grub... – Matana Roberts

QUEENS

Dosa Diner
3566 73rd St (btwn 35th & 37th Ave, Jackson Heights, Queens) 718-205-2218
(Jackson Heights: 7/E/F/M/R to 74th St-Roosevelt Ave)
I love Dosa Diner in Jackson Heights. It might be called Dosa Café or something now. It changes names often! It's South Indian. Totally veggie. – Jerry the Mouse

Seva
30-07 34th St (btwn 30th Ave & 31st Ave, Astoria, Queens) 718-626-4440 (Astoria: N to 30th Ave)
www.order.letsorderonline.com/sevaindianrestaurant
Seva has a fairly substantial lunch special for only $7. They serve more or less standard Northern Indian fare, but they do it well, and will forever hold a special place in the hearts of Astorian vegans for being one of the first restaurants in the hood to (correctly!) use the V word on the menu. The original lunch special here came only with

The Melissa Bastian Vegan 100!
This list incorporates many of my favorite vegan foods, meals, and experiences that can be had in the Big Apple—though by no means all of them! – Melissa Bastian

1. Cornbread at Angelica's Kitchen
2. The Zen slice at Viva Herbal
3. Lemongrass seitan on rice vermicelli patties at Lan Cafe
4. Cake batter soft serve ice cream at Lula's Sweet Apothecary
5. Vegan Treats' Peanut Butter Bomb cake
6. The "Penny Lick" at Penny Licks
7. Oyster mushrooms and grilled asparagus at Gobo
8. Dosas from the vegan dosa cart at the southwest corner of Washington Square Park.
9. Coconut tofu soup at Pukk
10. Camarones y coco at Vegetarian Paradise 2
11. Soul Chik'n at Red Bamboo
12. Medu vadi at the several restaurants in the mid 20s on the east side serving southern Indian food
13. Dinner at Hangawi
14. "Wings" at Foodswings in Williamsburg
15. The Ethiopian vegetarian combo at Awash
16. Raw nutmeats from Bonobos
17. Sunflower lentil paté and other vegan tapas at Sacred Chow
18. White chocolate wonderful peanut butter from Peanut Butter & Co.
19. Sweet & Sara marshmallows with toasted coconut where they're made in Long Island City.
20. Ginormous lollipop from Dylan's Candy Bar
21. Seitan scallopini at Blossom
22. Baked veg meat bun at Buddha Bodai
23. Thanksgiving dinner (prix fixe) at a vegan restaurant like Candle Cafe, Angelica Kitchen, Blossom, Gobo, or Curly's Vegetarian Lunch
24. Fresh apple cider at the Union Square Greenmarket in the fall
25. "Turkey" salad by Suneen Foods from a downtown bodega
26. Red sonjas at Mundo in Astoria
27. Sausage roll from Vinnie's on Bedford in Williamsburg
28. A dragon bowl at Bliss on Bedford
29. A Red Bamboo soul chik'n sandwich
30. Ravioli of the day at Caravan of Dreams
31. Spaghetti squash spaghettini at Counter
32. Dessert from the Pure Food and Wine takeout counter
33. Ramen at Souen on 6th
34. Dumplings at Franchia
35. The vegan panini at 'sNice
36. Chocolate hazelnut ice cream at Stogo

37. A falafel pita with way too many crazy toppings at Maoz
38. Black sesame sweet tofu (soft serve) at Kyotofu
39. Black tea with agar cubes at Saint's Alp
40. An Ess-a-Bagel bagel with their tofu cream cheese
41. Brunch at Curly's Vegetarian Lunch
42. Sake pina colada at the V-Spot
43. Peanut butter and banana sandwich at Think Coffee
44. Tofu scramble at Kate's Joint
45. Cupcakes from Babycakes
46. A fig and almond cake from Dean & Deluca
47. Pulled sugar candies from Papabubble
48. Bean curd and broccoli from a Chinese takeout place
49. A plate of goodness from Veggie Castle
50. Beers at the Brooklyn Brewery
51. Seitan satay sticks at Tiengarden
52. Zucchini fries and black bean soup at the Organic Grill
53. Sake lemonade at Goodbye Blue Monday
54. Lasa momos at Tsampa
55. Dinner at the secret 4 Course Vegan supper club
56. A burrito from Benny's
57. A vegan meal at one of Flushing Chinatown's veg restaurants
58. A plate of "soul food" at Cafe Veg
59. Watercress dumplings at Vegetarian Dim Sum House
60. Rice at Rice
61. Omusubi at Oms/b (but not the soup)
62. Pakora at Seva
63. Bread from Balthazar bakery
64. Vegan Drinks on Thursdays at Angels & Kings
65. The ZenHarvest burger at Zen Burger
66. The vegetarian appetizer combo plate at Bread & Olive
67. The midtown-bodega-deli it-should-be-vegan lunch
68. Entenmann's individual apple pie (the kind in a little paper pouch)
69. Fresh fruit or vegetable juice from a juice cart (my favorite is at 48th and 3rd Ave)
70. Knishes at Yonah Schimmel
71. The "Elvis" (peanut butter and banana) at Papa's Empanadas in Jackson Heights
72. A soft pretzel from a cart, with mustard
73. Nuts for nuts! (sugared almonds or cashews)
74. Sorbet from Ciao Bella
75. Cornmeal crusted tofu at Spring Street Natural
76. Mango slices that have been arranged on a stick to look like a flower in bloom.
77. Zeppoli from a street fair
78. Funnel cake in Coney Island that you watched them fry
79. Pommes frites in a paper cone
80. The Mexican chocolate milkshake at Curly's
81. The Bandeja Paisa and empanadas at The V-Spot

82. Falafel from Mamoun's
83. Thai iced tea at Pukk
84. Ice cream cookie sandwich and artisan chocolates at Stogo
85. "Ribs" at Imhotep in Crown, Heights, Brooklyn
86. Pasta with marinara in Little Italy
87. Quinoa pasta at V-Spot
88. A slice of vegan cake while waiting for a band to start playing in the basement of Cake Shop
89. Your bagel on the subway
90. Dosas at Dosa Hut in Queens
91. Dark chocolate bark from The Chocolate Room (Park Slope)
92. Black coffee from a bodega or street cart—or opt for tea instead
93. Soy hot chocolate from Oren's Daily Roast
94. Mango maki at Tanaka
95. Dim sum at Buddha Bodai
96. Pierogi in or from Greenpoint
97. A cheeseless pizza or Siciliana from Rizzo's
98. Marzipan from a bakery in Astoria or Little Italy
99. A soy latte from the Starbucks on Roosevelt Island
100. Hand-cut pasta at Candle 79

THE
PRIME
BURGER
51ST &
FIFTH AVE.

mulligatawny, which for some reason Seva makes with chicken stock. But they've seen the light and now offer it with a delicious butternut squash soup. Their dinner combination isn't a bad deal at $13, and even comes with a vegan dessert offering! When you're done with dinner you can hop right next door to Sweet Afton, one of Astoria's most charming pubs. – Melissa Bastian

BREAKFAST
Morning, sunshine! Most important meal of the day, no matter when you eat it.

MANHATTAN

Chinatown

Good Dumpling House
214-216 Grand St (btwn Mott & Elizabeth) 212-219-9228
(Little Italy: B/D to Grand)
If you're up for adventure at 7am, come here for a "Chinese breakfast," a $1.75 eye opener of steamed sticky rice with pork and green beans. It's not the world's cheeriest spot, but since breakfast is served in the same banana leaf it was cooked in, you'll have no trouble schlepping it to Sara Roosevelt Park, a few blocks away, where you can listen to the Hua Mei birdies sing.

East Village

Sidewalk Bar & Restaurant
94 Ave A (@ 6th St) 212-253-8080
www.sidewalkmusic.net (East Village: F to 2nd Ave)
Breakfast served 21 hours a day (24 on the weekend)! Dig into a diner-ish breakfast, eat it outside on the sidewalk even, but it's going to run you nearly three times the $1.99 price that baffled me when I first moved to NYC. The ghost of bargains past still lingers in the form of coffee and tea, free 'til 2pm. Across the street is 7A, which is pretty much exactly the same story.

Cafe Mogador
101 St. Marks (btwn 1st Ave and Ave A) 212-677-2226
www.cafemogador.com (East Village: 6 to Astor Pl)
Cafe Mogador for breakfast, lunch or dinner! Brunch on the weekends is over-priced and scenester; you'll find yourself waiting for a table, etc. The place is better during the week when you can go in with your book or laptop and chill. The breakfast special is plentiful with organic eggs! – Andria Alefi

Panya
10 Stuyvesant St (btwn 11th St & 12th St) 212-777-1930
(East Village: 6 to Astor Pl)
This Japanese bakery looks like a convenience store with Zen monastery pretensions. It is the place to go to put a green tea/red bean spin on your continental breakfast. The low-priced breakfast specials of Around the Clock, the address's former tenant, have been reincarnated as eggs any style, home fries, salad, and your choice of meat and bread from 7:30am to 11am for a mere $3.75! If you're feeling flush and Tokyurious, try the Japanese breakfast. It's a bit of a splurge at $8.50, but you get a beautifully broiled piece of fish, miso soup, rice, a small serving of the side dish du jour, pickles, an airline-packet of nori and, most authentically of all, natto (fermented soybeans). I usually ask them to hold the natto because I think it smells like semen. If you're feeling more continental, the curry pan is the brilliant offspring of a doughnut and a steamed Chinese bun.

Gramercy Park

Galaxy Global Eatery
15 Irving Pl (btwn 15th & 16th St) 212-777-3631
www.galaxyglobaleatery.com
(Gramercy Park: 4/5/6/L/N/Q/R to Union Sq)
This restaurant is lit almost entirely in pale blues and features a model of the galaxy built in tiny, fiber optic lights implanted in the ceiling. The swirling lights, shimmering blue shadows and smooth black bar feel serene and calming, at least on weekdays. Galaxy is also notable for having tons of things on the menu that are made with hemp products. I suggest the Solar Hemp Waffle with vanilla ice cream and warm berry compote. My wife prefers the Baguette French Toast with bananas and walnuts in warm maple syrup. Both items are best with their sweet-as-candy fresh orange juice and coffee. They have lots of dishes with egg whites, turkey bacon, corn meal tamales, and more. If you're staying within 10 blocks of this place, they'll bring breakfast to your hotel room, and if you know a better way to show the world you're really

Kay Thompson & Hilary Knight • City on Fire

fucking living it up in New York, I'd like to hear about it. – Josh Saitz

Hell's Kitchen

Tulcingo del Valle
665 10th Ave (btwn 46th & 47th St) 212-262-5510
www.tulcingorestaurant.com
(Midtown: C/E to 50th St)
The Desayunos Mexicano are spectacular and huge and oh my god, the beans, so good! The bathroom is around the corner, accessible only from another entrance to the building.

Midtown

Ess-a-Bagel!
831 3rd Ave (btwn 50th & 51st St) 212-980-1010
(Midtown: E/M/6 to Lexington-3rd Ave-51st St)
&
359 1st Ave (near 21st Ave) 212-260-2252
www.ess-a-bagel.com (Murray Hill: L to 1st Ave)
Many people, myself included, consider these to be the best bagels in NYC. I would contend that this would actually make them the best bagels in the world, because, really, where are you going to find a better bagel than New York City? They generally have about five flavors of vegan cream cheese. Order it toasted and add lettuce and tomato and the whole gigantic round still comes out to about $4. – Melissa Bastian

Morningside Heights

La Cabaña Salvadoreña
4384 Broadway (@ 187th St) 212-928-7872
(Washington Hts: A to 190th)
Great breakfast food, and great arepas. They feature very cool artwork on the walls, too; it's almost like a little gallery! – Jerry the Mouse

BROOKLYN

La Guera
4603 5th Ave (btwn 46th St & 47th St, Sunset Park, Bklyn)
718-437-0232
www.sunset-park.com/mall/LAGUERA/index.html
(Sunset Park: R to 45th St)
La Guera started out as a tamale stand on 46th street, but business was so good they moved around the corner and became a full-on restaurant. Get yourself some tamales con queso or mole for $1 each from the cooler next to the front door, and then walk down the street to the actual

Sunset Park, where you can eat them with the stunning panoramic harbor view from one of the highest points in Brooklyn. – Lauren Jade Martin

Cinco de Mayo Restaurant
1202 Cortelyou (@ E 12th St, Ditmas Park, Bklyn)
718-693-1022
(Ditmas Park: Q/B to Newkirk Ave)
I love breakfast at Cinco de Mayo. Both the huevos rancheros and the Desyano Mexicana are really yummy. And the coffee, which has a hint of cinnamon, is delicious. For lunch and dinner, the meals can get a little pricier, so I recommend the huaraches. The veggie one (beans only) isn't listed on the menu, but it's only like $3.50 and it's pretty filling. – Amanda Plumb

BRUNCH

Restaurants that serve brunch aren't necessarily open for breakfast on other days of the week, so those seeking non-weekend waffles are advised to inquire before striking out for any of these locations.

MANHATTAN

The Sunburnt Cow
137 Avenue C (btwn 8th St & 9th St) 212-529-0005
www.thesunburntcow.com (East Village: L to 1st Ave)
&
Bondi Road (the Cow's sister location)
153 Rivington St (@ Suffolk) 212-253-5311
www.bondiroad.com (LES: F/J/M/Z to Delancey-Essex)
These both have a killer brunch deal for around $15 bucks. *Unlimited* Bloody Marys, mimosas, Fosters (they're Aussies), greyhounds, and screwdrivers with your brunch entrée! Guaranteed good times! Attentive, attractive, accented Aussie staff! The Sunburnt Cow is the crazier location, more of a pub vibe, with "football" matches playing all the time, and wall-to-wall young folks from all over the world. Bondi Road is airier and more kick-back (though there's still a wait around 1pm). It has surf videos projected on the back wall, the same menu, the same deal, the same tendency for the bartender to pass out passion fruit shots to the entire restaurant. Amazing! Try the Queen Adelaide (Eggs Florentine with salmon or crabcakes) or The Stack—a hamburger with everything in the world on it: beet, pineapple, bacon, tomato, etc, etc. It's just freaking delicious! – Dear Drunk Girl

Trilogy (Paradise Row, Dreamland, Striver's

Polonia Restaurant
110 1st Ave (btwn 6th St & 7th St) 212-254-9699
(East Village: F/M to 2nd Ave)
If you're looking for quality Polish cooking outside of
Greenpoint, this might be the place to go first. The coffee
is great. Challah French toast—awesome. Babka French
toast—more awesome. Cucumber salad, blintzes with
apple sauce, boiled sauerkraut pirogi with sour cream...
wonderful. – Heath Row

Congee Village
100 Allen St 212-941-1818
www.sunsungroup.com/congeevillage
(LES: F/J/M/Z to Delancy-Essex)
At Congee Village you can get a traditional Cantonese
breakfast of congee (rice porridge) and dim sum fairly
cheaply. The full menu is available from opening time.
Dishes range from the vegan Chinese greens with garlic,
bean curd, and mushrooms (hold the pork) to the more
exotic sour stomach and goose blood. *Not* a good place
to take your meat-and-potatoes eating relatives or hosts
though – Victoria Law (Except if they're open to the idea
of lychee martinis come Bloody Mary time. – AH)

BROOKLYN

Mug's Alehouse
125 Bedford Ave (btwn 10th St & 11th St) 718-486-8232
I'm a big brunchface, like everyone gets to be in NYC, but
I'm also a cheapface. The best cheap brunch I've found is
at Mug's, which gives you an egg dish, coffee/tea, mimo-
sa, bloody or "brunch beer," sausage/bacon and toast—all
for five bucks! It's also a great place for a million types of
beer and their dinner selection is great. – Dear Drunk Girl

Enid's
560 Manhattan Ave (btwn Driggs & Nassau, Williamsburg, Bklyn) 718-349-3859
www.enids.net (Williamsburg: G to Nassau)
Under $10—no special deal but some nice veggie options.
Sometimes a long wait, but great hipster-watching and
serve-yourself coffee. Also a lively late night bar. - Dear
Drunk Girl (It's a bit pricey, but you can't beat the food.
Biscuits and gravy are quite good, as are the rice and
beans. Get a Harrison, the house drink of citrus juices,
triple sec, and tequila. – Eric Nelson).

Relish
225 Wythe Ave (@ N 3rd St, Williamsburg, Bklyn)
718-963-4546
www.relish.com (Williamsburg: L to Bedford)
Relish = HUGE portions and yummy tofu scramble, but

be sure to tell them you're vegan to make sure you get a
butter-free meal. – Dear Drunk Girl

Lodge
318 Grand St (btwn Havemeyer & Marcy, Williamsburg,
Bklyn) 718-486-9400, www.lodgenyc.com
(Williamsburg: G/L to Metropolitan-Lorimer)
If you go for brunch it's 2-4-1 Bloody Marys and mimosas
so that's like a cheap bar! – Megan Garrity

Robin des Bois
195 Smith St (btwn Warren & Baltic, Boerum Hill, Bklyn)
718-596-1609
www.sherwoodcafe.com (Boerum Hill: F/G to Bergen)
If noon finds you somewhat green around the gills, a full-
length fun house mirror and almost life-size sculptures
of penitent saints may sound less than inviting, but you'll
feel better after some coffee and Eggs Benedict in this
pleasantly jumbly antique store-cum-café-bar-restaurant.
The cute slacker-Frenchy staff run on their own time,
though the dining room offers plenty of interesting
memorabilia about which to speculate while you wait for
your food to arrive.

Eclipse
4314 4th Ave (btwn 43rd & 44th, Sunset Park, Bklyn)
718-965-1602
www.eclipsebrooklyn.com (Sunset Park: R to 45th St)
If you want a more bourgie Sunset Park Mexican restaurant experience, Eclipse is great for brunch or burritos,
and also is a good spot for vegetarians craving the real
deal. – Lauren Jade Martin

QUEENS

Jade Asian
136-28 39th Ave (btwn Union & Main, Flushing, Queens)
718-762-8821 (Flushing: 7 to Main St)
Get here early on the weekends if you want to avoid a
long wait. As with most other dim sum places you may
be seated with another group, but you aren't expected
to make conversation with the others. Don't neglect to
order a pot of tea. The food is consistently good and the
ha cheung (shrimp in rice rolls) are a personal favorite. On
weekdays, everything is discounted, but the deal is off if
you take home leftovers. – Sharon Furgason

DINERS, DELIS AND LUNCH COUNTERS
Forget Seinfeld. Diners, delis and lunch counters will
bring you closer to the mostly vanished New York City of
Taxi Driver.

Row) - Kevin Baker • Free Food for Millionaires

Financial District

Pearl Diner
212 Pearl St (btwn Fletcher St & Platt St) 212-344-6620
www.pearlstreetdinernyc.com (Financial District: (A/C/J/M/Z/2/3/4/5 to Fulton St-Broadway-Nassau)
Tucked deep in the belly of the Financial District, this pearl is a utilitarian one, but that's what I like about it. It's a good reminder that not all Wall Street guys are expense account dicks. If you go off-hours, you'll have plenty of solitude.

Lower East Side/East Village

Classic Coffee Shop
56 Hester St (@ Ludlow) 917-685-3306
LES: B/D to Grand St.
Every now and then a bunch of wrongs add up to a right. Like, eat-in customers should really not be served on paper plates, even if there's just a handful of stools and a couple of tables. For that matter, where's the fucking stove? Why close so early? Are you even interested in making a living? But Carmine's been running this joint for more than three decades. He says he's got a fair, community-spirited landlord, essential for any LES dining establishment whose best customers are school kids and crossing guards. It's really sweet to watch him in the morning, greeting students headed to the public elementary across the street. I say we let him continue to do things exactly the way he likes, and honestly if my

labor of love had ventilation issues, I'd probably forgo the bacon, too.

Castillo de Jagua
113 Rivington St (@ Rivington) 212-982-6412
(LES: F/J/M/Z to Delanccy-Essex)
Dirt cheap Dominican breakfast specials. The bacon and plantains are delish, but what really gets me rhapsodizing is the slurpy, soupy oatmeal and the fresh lemonade.

Shopsin's
120 Essex St Stall 16 (in the Essex St Market) 212-924-5160
www.shopsins.com (LES: F/J/M/Z to Delancey-Essex)
The crazy, Macy's Day balloon-sized personality of Kenny Shopsin and his family-run biz made Shopsin's a *cause celebre* long before his *Eat Me* cookbook, the Calvin Trillin piece in the *New Yorker*, and the documentary film *I Like Killing Flies*, the title of which stems from a casual remark Kenny makes on camera. The original location and its Carmine Street successor fell to high rents. This little outpost in the back end of the Essex Street Market may well be your last crack at the hundreds of quirkily-named menu items Kenny and his kids can mix, match, and vegan-ize in umpteendillion different combinations, seasoned with a lifetime's collection of spices. The food's enough to make a regular of anybody, but Kenny's hairpin mood swings scare me out of anything that might smack of overfamiliarity. I keep my head down and obey the rules, which are numerous, and not made in jest. Start yapping into your cell phone if you think it's such a joke.

El Nuevo Amanecer
117 Stanton St (btwn Essex & Ludlow) 212-387-9115
(LES: F/J/M/Z to Delancey-Essex)
I went here after my first ABC No Rio experience. I was undergoing an intense reconnection to my culture during that year and was on an undying quest for amazing Latin food in what seemed to be my future home. Amanecer served up killer rice and beans with plantains. I also had mofongo, but simply getting beans/rice/plantains is fulfilling for the vegetarians. – Cristy Road

Katz's Deli
205 E Houston St (@ Ludlow) (212) 254-2246
www.katzdeli.com (LES: F to 2nd Ave)
Vegan anarchists, consider yourselves warned. Katz's catch phrase is Send a Salami to Your Boy in the Army. But it's also a cultural treasure, a far-from-dead ghost of the Lower East Side's storied Jewish past. The sandwiches are thicker than most human mandibles are high. Every time I'm in there, there's like four different people reen-

acting the scene from *When Harry Met Sally* where Meg Ryan demonstrates how to fake an orgasm. However, it is an interesting, authentic demonstration of the way things used to work in the pre-creamy-dreamy-sour-appletini age: you get a ticket upon entry, you give it to the deli man when you place your order, he scribbles on it, gives it back with your sandwich, and woe to fucking you if you lose it en route to the cashier. – AH (This is kind of a cool place and has survived gentrification, so if you do hot pastrami, go to Katz's. – Fly)

Casa Adela Restaurant
66 Avenue C (btwn 4th and 5th St) 212-473-1882
(East Village: F/J/M/Z to Delancey-Essex)
A true neighborhood place dating to 1976, Casa Adela specializes in authentic Puerto Rican cuisine. It's the real, old-school, Alphabet City deal, as is anything that's been on Avenue C since the Bicentennial. If you eat meat, you can fill your tank for a mere four bucks with a bowl of sancocho, a stew of oxtail, root vegetables and plantains. After the noon news, you'll be able to catch up on your waitress' favorite Spanish language soap. The black and white photos covering the white brick walls provide a great, personal history of Loisaida (that's the Latin Lower East Side), from afros and elevator shoes onward.

Moonstruck
88 2nd Ave (@ E 5th) 212-420-8050
www.MoonstruckEastVillage.com
(East Village: F to 2nd Ave)
Favorite burger and fries in the city. – Andria Alefhi (Oh, now, see, I find Moonstruck overpriced and even when the waiters don't have that many customers, they act like they're in the weeds. – AH)

Veselka
144 2nd Ave (@9th St) 212-228-9682
www.veselka.com (East Village: 6 to Astor Pl)
I must be mellowing. Back when I lived a block away, I would only go to Veselka under duress. Veselka was so clean and lofty, and eating there put me in a bad mood because it left me exposed to those, including myself, who thought it was for posers. But the food is good, and if Ukrainian fare doesn't do it for you it's possible to get a salad, a burger, a turkey burger, even a veggie burger, chili, a tuna melt, a piece of pie. Every time I come here, I think about what an ass I was, acting like it was Johnny Rockets or something. - AH (I find them overpriced and busy. Only good thing is the Borscht. – Andria Alefhi) (Oh my god, does she think I'm a poser? – AH)

Neptune
194 1st Ave (btwn 11th St and 12th St) 212-777-4163
(East Village: L to 1st Ave)
Not so very long ago, this strip of First Avenue was chockablock with excellent Polish diners. We used to get sides of pierogi and blintzes to go with our bacon and eggs. The unironically unnatural blonde (and/or hived) waitresses weren't exactly sunshine in a bottle, but they were game to substitute fries for hash browns. The long wait for their back gardens was always worth it. Neptune is a hearty reminder of those good old days, especially the mashed potatoes, which seem to have several sticks of butter in them. If you've never had pierogi before, get them boiled with applesauce and sour cream on the side.

Greenwich Village

Hector's Place
44 Little West 12th St (@ Washington St) 212-206-7592
(Meatpacking District: A/C/E/L to 14th St-8th Ave)
Hector's doesn't open at 2am because that's when the clubs close. It opens at 2am because it's been opening at 2am since the '40s, to suit the needs of actual meatpackers, the guys who drive the trucks, and a variety of tranny hookers, all of whose ranks have been dwindling as the neighborhood continues to spiral upward. Not surprisingly, the burgers are really good.

Washington Square Diner
150 W 4th St (@ 6th Ave) 212-533-9306
(Greenwich Village: A/B/C/D/E/F to W 4th St)
Great burgers and fountain Coke, which is perfect.
– Heath Row

La Bonbonniere
28 8th Ave (Btwn 12th St & Jane St) 212-741-9266
(Greenwich Village: A/C/E/L to 14th St-8th Ave)
Greasy, and with windows down its entire narrow length, La Bonboniere is a classic hangover spot. Those who don't drink might enjoy loitering on the sidewalk, admiring all the gray faces inside, hovering like queasy moons over the only kind of food they can possibly face.

C H E L S E A

La Taza de Oro
96 Eighth Ave (btwn 14th and 15th) 212-243-9946
(Chelsea: A/C/E/L to 14th St-8th Ave)
It's not often a New York City establishment can stay both open and perfectly preserved, without losing its fangs and succumbing to self-mythology. Especially if it has

Kapralov • Lotus Crew – Stewart Meyer. The

padded vinyl stools. Maybe the secret to this Puerto Rican lunch counter's success is that no one's ever tried to shoot a Hollywood romance here. Mondongo and Mofongo, mmm. You can't go wrong, unless you're a vegetarian. I dig the quilted splash guards behind the grill, and the way the counter guys are really nice to kids.

Flatiron/Gramercy Park

Joe Jr.
167 3rd Ave (btwn 15th and 16th) 212-473-5150
(Gramercy: L to 3rd Ave)
The food's not all *that*, but they've got it down pat. The corner location holds old-timey visual appeal, the waiters are courteous, and they can put a Greek salad together. Some contend that the burgers are the best in New York.

Eisenberg's Sandwich Shop
174 5th Ave (btwn 22nd & 23rd St) 212-675-5096
www.eisenbergsnyc.com (Flatiron: N/R to 23rd St)
No-frills service, deli counter that extends for miles, killer egg cream. – Robyn Jordan (Those smooth cheeked pilgrims lining up at the Shake Shack in nearby Madison Square are off their rockers. The Eisenberg Sandwich Shop—raising NYC's cholesterol since 1929—is where it's at! I love the high ceilings, the worn wooden shelving, the black marble counter, and the three-pronged enamel milkshake mixer that looks like it's been on active duty since the place opened. Sit at the counter for the full experience, and while you wait for your food, see how many of the celebs appearing in photos with the jolly, mullet-ponytailed owner you can identify. This is the place where I learned that 'with boots" is an acceptable synonym for "to go". But for sure, get it to stay. – AH)

Upper West Side

Big Nick's Burger Joint & Pizza Joint
2175 Broadway (@ 77th) 212-362-9238
www.bignicksnyc.com (Upper West Side: 1/9 to 79th St)
I defy even the staunchest anti-breeder to not love, in some part of their grinchy hearts, a restaurant that serves its kid's burger "until midnight *only*." Big Nick's is a masterpiece of accumulation. There's signage everywhere you look. The carryout menu is bigger than most zines. Nothing's ever retired here. If there's a pulled pork sandwich, it's a safe bet that there will soon be a pulled pork pizza and a pulled pork omelette, "served 24 hours a day," even though, technically, the restaurant is only open for 23. Despite his obvious pride in the 1lb, char-broiled, 100% Angus Sumo Burger, Big Nick's got the herbivores cov-

ered too, right down to a mozzarella tofu cheese that can be melted over the vegetarian meat ball hero! Desserts deserve a holler too—all the standard meringue and malted suspects, but also zeppoles and ekmek kataifi, an ambrosial Greek mash-up of walnuts, pistachio, honey, figs, and whipped topping! I hope you get my favorite waitress, a German lady of a certain age who dresses sexy and will call you darling at least 50 times between order and bill.

Upper East Side

Viand Coffee Shop
673 Madison Ave (btwn 61st St & 62nd St) 212-751-6622
(Upper East Side: N/R to 5th Ave-50th St)
&
1011 Madison Ave (btwn 78th St & 79th St) 212-249-8250
(Upper East Side: 6 to 77th St)
&
2130 Broadway (btwn 74th St & 75th St) 212-877-2888
(Upper West Side: 1/2/3 to 72nd St)
www.viandnyc.com
Viand's fries are the best part about the place. Sometimes diner fries suck, but these are good. – Josh Medsker (The lower Madison location saved my heiner on a couple of occasions when hypoglycemia went into overdrive in this fancy neighborhood. – AH)

BROOKLYN

Acapulco
1116 Manhattan Ave (btwn Box St & Clay St, Greenpoint, Bklyn) 718-349-8429
www.acapulcodeliandrestaurant.com

(Greenpoint: G to Greenpoint Ave)
This infamously cheap little Mexican diner in Greenpoint has unbeatable prices, fresh food, and later hours than most restaurants in that neck of the woods. It's a clean atmosphere, with an incredibly extensive menu and guacamole that's off the hook.– Caitlin McGurk

Mike's Coffee Shop
238 DeKalb Ave (@ Hall St, Clinton Hill, Bklyn)
718-857-1462 (Clinton Hill: G to Clinton-Washington)
Mike's is an authentic alternative to the dismal Pratt student cafeteria. I'm invariably there late on a Saturday morning, when the clamor for a seat is so high, you'd have to be pretty dim not to recognize it as an eat-and-get-out situation.

Tom's Restaurant
782 Washington Ave (btwn Sterling Pl & St Johns Pl, Prospect Hts, Bklyn) 718-636-9738
(Prospect Hts: 2/3 to Eastern Pkway)
This cozy Brooklyn diner has been perched on Washington Avenue in the Prospect Heights neighborhood since 1936. It's a beloved neighborhood hangout. During the riots following the death of MLK, locals formed a human chain in front to protect it from the looting that devastated the surrounding community. Inside, there's a buoyant, shrine-like feel...the walls are covered with tributes, tsotchkes, and twinkling festive lights. The grub is grand, and there's a bona fide soda fountain where they serve lime rickeys and egg creams, not because it's the cool retro thing to do, but because they always have. The vibe is friendly from the owners down to the waitstaff. Makes a nice pit-stop during a day at the Brooklyn Museum, several blocks away on Eastern Parkway. – David Goren (Yes, like the Suzanne Vega song. – AH)

QUEENS

Court Square Diner
45-30 23rd St (@ Jackson Ave, Long Island City, Queens)
718-392-1222, www.courtsquaredonerlic.com
(Long Island City: 7 to 45th Rd-Courthouse Sq)
The bracingly diverse clientele is not surprising given their location right below the 7 train, but it still gives me a warm fuzzy, enough to make me overlook the fact that they put carrots in their Greek salad. The milk shakes are full of ice cream and the booths to the left of the entrance come with a complimentary eyeful of Five Pointz. A good place for art lovers to Belgian Waffle up before or after PS1...or really, any time, given that they're open 24 hours.

Neptune Diner
3105 Astoria Blvd (btwn 31st & 32nd St, Astoria, Queens)
718-278-4853 (Astoria: N to Astoria Blvd)
At Neptune Diner the burgers kick-ass. Even though the shakes are a bit expensive, they are huge. – Josh Medsker

DOWNSCALE BYOB
A handful of upscale restaurants think they're cute, touting their lack of liquor license only to ram the bottleneck up your heiner with astronomical corkage fees. Fortunately, not every place that serves food but no alcohol is looking to FYUTA on BYO. These are just a few to get you going. If your destination is a dive, by all means, slip a corkscrew in your pocket as it's quite likely the management is open to customers supplying their own beverages. It's their call, but if they have over 20 seats they're supposed to have a bottle club license or risk being fined for your pleasure.

MANHATTAN

East Village

Snack Dragon Taco Shack
199 E. 3rd St (btwn Ave A & B) 917-733-5126
www.myspace.com/snackdragon (East Village: F to 2nd Ave)
This itsy-bitsy, ephemera-filled indoor/outdoor taco counter will appeal to anyone who ever enjoyed playing Restaurant as a kid. It opens late (like 5pm), stays open later, and its cramped, highly decorated quarters help create a convivial atmosphere in which strangers may easily converse, especially if everyone's coming from the same show at The Wild Room a few doors away. There's a plethora of hot sauce options, and the quickly assembled

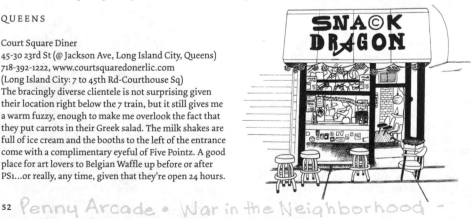

Penny Arcade • War in the Neighborhood

tacos are as tasty as they are cheap. Beer up at any of the neighboring bodegas on Ave B.

The "Indian" restaurants on East 6th St between 1st and 2nd Ave (East Village: F to 2nd Ave)
The legends surrounding this strip include a plausible enough assertion that they're Bangladeshi-run, and have been since the beginning, a whopper about them all sharing one kitchen, and an apocryphal tale in which blood bubbles up from the drains. One thing I know for sure is that most of them will let you bring your own beer or wine. Double-check your pick's liquor license status with the guy posted outside the entrance (act undecided and he may slip you a discount coupon), then trot around the corner to Dual Specialty Store (91 1st Ave) for some high alcohol content Indian beer!

East Village Thai
32 E. 7th St (btwn 2nd and 3rd Ave) 212-673-4610
(East Village: 6 to Astor Pl)
Food's great, there are only three tables, and they've been open for years! How do they do it? Duh, carry out! But I like to eat in because it reminds me of eating in Thailand. New York Thai food, while good, often fails to live up to the hype. This is not the case here. Speaking of authenticity, the Village Farm grocery, a couple of blocks north at 146 2nd Avenue, has Singha beer!

Zaragoza Grocery
215 Ave A (btwn 13th and 14th St) 212-780-9204
(East Village: L to 1st Ave)
The 24-hour party people throw down (as opposed to up) here on Fridays and Saturdays when it's open late to accommodate nightcrawlers, but I find it ever so much more pleasant at lunch, when you're more likely to be sharing your table with a crate of just-delivered cerveza rather than some boozed-up NYU Betty falling off her platform shoes. Homestyle taco components are kept warm in a variety of Crock-Pots behind the counter. Rather than bringing your own beer, you can buy some from the refrigerator case. Tall customers may be recruited to wiggle a packet of corn husks free of a pegboard display rack, as the short cashier stabilizes the folding chair on which you're standing. *Muy simpatico.*

Angelica Kitchen
300 E. 12th St (btwn 1st and 2nd) 212-228-2909
www.angelicakitchen.com (East Village: L to 1st Ave)
Nothing raises your spirits like a hit of your own spirits when your burdock arrives at your communal table a bit blander than you hoped at this famed temple of organic,

vegetarian eating. A great choice for strict vegans whose commitment to health includes a self-administered medicinal tipple. – AH (Plus they have a take-out side. You can go there early in the day & get cheap day-old baked goods. – Fly)

Hell's Kitchen

Wondee Siam Thai Restaurant
792 9th Ave (Between 52nd & 53rd St) 212-582-0355
(Hell's Kitchen: C/E to 50th St)
Start the healing process by drowning your sorrows and cutting your losses after some tepid Broadway fiasco. Forget the pad thai. Bring on something from the "Secret Thai Menu," conveniently located in a plastic sleeve on every table.

Island Burgers & Shakes
766 9th Ave (btwn 51st St & 52nd St) 212-307-7934
www.islandburgersny.com (Hell's Kitchen: C/E to 50th St)
Island Burgers doesn't serve fries, but it makes me think of them because it rivals the Belgian Frites place in the East Village in its commitment to baroque, counter-intuitive, but usually delicious toppings. The best reason to not b-y-o b would be to order a shake. Wait, maybe you could doctor that shake…

Harlem

Amy Ruth's
113 W. 116th St (btwn Lenox Ave & Adam Clayton Powell Blvd) 212-280-8779
www.amyruthsharlem.com (Harlem: 2/3 to 116th St)
Uptown Southern-cooking wise, I'm devoted to Miss Mamie's Spoonbread Too. I feel like I'm two-timing her even mentioning another wholesome, upstanding chicken-and-wafflestablishment, but Amy Ruth is that rare mistress who doesn't mind you bringing your own bottle when you pay her a call.

BROOKLYN

Fast and Fresh Deli
84 Hoyt St (btwn Atlantic Ave and State St, Boerum Hill, Bklyn) 718-802-1661
(Boerum Hill: A/C/G to Hoyt-Schermerhorn)
Don't be fooled by the blandness of the name. This little joint, run by a friendly family from Pueblo, serves the best tacos in downtown Brooklyn and tamales on the weekend. They stock beer at to-go prices and no one will stop you from cracking it open in house, even if you're

a construction worker who'll probably be expected to operate heavy machinery after your lunch break. That's the rowdiest time of day at Fast and Fresh. If the weather's nice, take a seat in the cement-heavy back garden, and raise a brew or two with the hardhat crew.

Stir It Up

514 Atlantic Ave (btwn Nevins & 3rd Ave, Boerum Hill, Bklyn) 718-643-3716
(Boerum Hill: B/D/M/N/R Q /2/3/4/5 to Atlantic Ave-Pacific St)
Good homey Jamaican food where meat-eaters should be forewarned that bones will be contributing to the authentic Island experience.and no amount of brought-beer will wash 'em down. Just one of the reasons why I recommend the roti. Vegetarians get the best-named dishes on the menu, hands down, from the sweet and sour Sweet Source to the poultry-free Ha Ha Chicken Balls.

PIZZA

Grabbing a slice is no prob in this burg. There's a pizza joint on every other corner, and the ones who insist you buy the whole pie tend to plaster their windows with strongly-worded signs to that effect. Pizza by-the-slice is rarely memorable from a culinary standpoint, but it serves its purpose, especially if it's late at night and you've been drinking something stronger than root beer. To eat it like a real New Yorker, fold it in half vertically, allowing the excess oil to gutter off the tip onto the sidewalk or the pizza joint's overflowing garbage can. There are several 99¢ slice places near Port Authority's western edge. Otherwise, an average slice runs around two bucks. If you anticipate that you'll require more than one, you might want to see if there's a recession special whereby two slices qualify you to receive a free soda.

By the Slice

Lower East Side/East Village

Rosario's
173 Orchard St (btwn Houston St & Stanton St) 212)-777-9813
(LES: F to 2nd Ave)
I moved to New York to perform in a long-running late-night show whose motto was "When We Sell Out, We Order Out." The audience dug it when we dragged the phone out so they could see us ordering a pizza (just one) for everybody to share at the end of the performance. When the pizza arrived mid-show, we'd bring the delivery boy onstage and demand that he be given a round of applause. Rosario's was the closest late-night delivery

option. Sal became a semi-auxiliary cast member, sporting a chef's toque and a born showman's grin, asking "Does-a anybody want some pizza?" He's the short Italian guy with the big nose and the baseball cap. If you want to make someone's day, go ask Sal about his stint with the people who did that crazy show on Ludlow Street. Even if you think the pizza's nothing special, I'm telling you, the pizza man sure is.

Two Boots
42 Ave A (@ E 3rd St) 212-254-1919
(East Village: F to 2nd Ave)
&
74 Bleecker St (btwn Broadway and Mercer) 212-777-1033
(NoHo: B/D/F/M to Broadway-Lafayette)
&
201 W 11th St (@7th Ave) 212-633-9096(Greenwich Village:1/2/3/F/L/M to 14th St-7th Ave)
&
384 Grand St (btwn Norfolk & Suffolk) 212-228-8685
(LES: F/J/M/Z to Delancey-Essex)
&
109 E 42nd St (@ Park Ave in Grand Central's Lower Dining Concourse) 212-557-7992
(Midtown: 4/5/6/7/S to Grand Central)
&
625 9th Ave (@ 45th St) 212-557-7992
(Hell's Kitchen: A/C/E/N/Q /R/S/1/2/3/7 to 42nd St-8th Ave)
&
1617 2nd Ave (btwn 83rd St & 84th St) 212-734-0317
(Upper East Side: 4/5/6 to 86th St)
&
514 2nd St (btwn 7th Ave & 8th Ave, Park Slope, Bklyn) 718-499-3253
(Park Slope: F/G to 7th Ave)

Herbert Selby Jr. • How I Became Hettie Jones—

www.twoboots.com

Two Boots makes the best slices in New York. These pies have a lot of personality. So much so that they're named after memorable supporting characters of both big and small screen. Mel Cooley and Mr. Pink aside, I'm pretty partial to the Bayou Beast, a spicy mouthful of barbecue shrimp, andouille sausage and jalapeño. My favorite Two Boots location is the old standby on Avenue A, once notable for having its own movie theater, surely one of the most interestingly programmed screens in town until, like, so many other beautiful, crazy projects in this neighborhood, they were done in by toxic rent increases. The Den of Cin, a super-cute and, for New York, affordable party space in the basement remains. The one in Park Slope is the only one I avoid. – AH (I did a mural on the interior wall of the new-ish place on Grand St, so you should go just to see that!!! – Fly)

Viva Herbal Pizzeria
179 2nd Ave (btwn 11th St & 12th St) 212-420-8801
(East Village: L to 3rd Ave)
Viva Herbal Pizzeria's "slice" is a quarter of a pizza! They have lots of vegan options, as well as pizzas with "real" cheese for those who just can't give up the goat. – Melissa Bastian (Viva Herbal also has kosher options, vegan desserts and yummy teas. I love this place! – Fly)

Artichoke
328 E. 14th St (btwn 2nd Ave & 1st Ave) 212-228-2004
www.artichokepizza.com (East Village: F to 1st Ave)
Not the most revelatory slice I've ever had—in fact, it didn't really taste like pizza. It tasted like this warm, cream cheesy artichoke dip my mother used to serve at cocktail parties and open houses. At $4 a slice, good for those of us who like artichoke dip and the occasional retro thrill.

Pala
198 Allen St (btwn Stanton & Houston) 212-614-7252
www.palapizza.com (LES: F to 2nd Ave)
Wonderful pizza nouveau that's neither too alien-gourmet nor too cute for its own good...just inventive, well-prepared, well-presented, and absolutely delicious. – Heath Row (They've got an entire menu for vegan pizza lovers, too, as well as some gluten-free models. They're on the pricey side. – AH)

Morningside Heights

Koronet
2848 Broadway (110th & 111th) 212-222-1566
(Morningside Hts: 1 to 110th St)
In terms of flavor, Koronet's $3.25 jumbo slice does not merit a special trip, but those with hollow legs may dig the novelty of eating something as long as a 5'7" adult's forearm. This utilitarian university hang provided the setting for the most full-on senior-citizen-on-pigeon action of my life, when an Eastern European grandma in one of those snap-front, sleeveless housecoats made a daring, bare hands rescue of a panicked and sickly-looking specimen who, having blundered in from Broadway, was freaking out behind some stools.

Whole Pie Places

MANHATTAN

Nolita

Lombardi's
32 Spring St (btwn Mott & Mulberry) 212-941-7994
www.firstpizza.com (Nolita: J/M to Bowery)
Lombardi's has that old-timey look which starts getting your hopes up that maybe a bunch of '30s-era gangsters will come barging in, Tommy Guns a-blaze. (And then Marty Scorsese will call, "That's a wrap! You can keep your costume, honey.") Immature people snicker at the mention of Clam Pie, but get it out of your system now because this is a nice place, a family place, and they don't want a buncha hyenas yukking it up over their menu.

Greenwich Village

John's
278 Bleecker St (btwn Jones & Morton) 212-243-1680
(West Village:A/C/E/B/D/F/M to W 4th St)
&
260 W. 44th St (btwn 8th Ave & Shubert Alley)
212-391-7560
(Hell's Kitchen: A/C/E/N/Q /R/S/1/2/3/7 to 8th Ave-42nd St)
&
408 E 64th St (btwn 1st Ave & York) 212-935-2895
Upper East Side: N/R/4/5/6/ to 59th St-Lexington Ave)
www.johnspizzerianyc.com
The abundance of graffiti and knife-related vandalism at the Village John's makes me sad that I never met the Ramones, especially now that CBGBs is but a memory. Did they ever eat here? I don't know, but it seems like they would have. The pizza's really good, and the wording on the "no slice" signs fairly snarls at the tourists coming in off of Bleecker.

Kettie Jones • Please Kill Me – Legs McNeil •

Upper East Side

Slice, the Perfect Food
1413 2nd Ave (btwn 73rd & 74th St) 212-249-4353
(Upper East Side: 6 to 77th St)
&
535 Hudson Street (btwn Perry & Charles) 212-929-2920
(Greenwich Village: A/C/E/B/D/F/M to W 4th St)
www.sliceperfect.com/
Slice is a pizza place on the Upper East Side that will
deliver pizza to you in Central Park, which is amazing.
It's more expensive than most, but everything is organic.
You can get it gluten-free or vegan or any of those hippie
varieties. They even have organic wine and beer, which I
assume they would also deliver. If you can think of a better
way to spend a day than having beer and pizza in the middle of Central Park, let me know. I can drive. – Josh Saitz

BROOKLYN

Nina's Restaurant & Pizzeria
635 Meeker Ave (@ Kingsland, Williamsburg, Bklyn)
718-389-8854, www.ninasbrickovenpizza.com
(Williamsburg: L to Graham)
This place is awesome. At one entrance, it looks like your
run-of-the-mill pizzeria with standard fare. But if you
walk around the corner to the side-entrance, you enter
an old-school Italian family restaurant. The main dining
room is decorated and designed like it used to be part of
a Chinese restaurant, but the Italian menu is solid. It's
a great surprise date location if you're looking to take
someone special to somewhere special but not pretentious, artificial or already known. A must go for long-
time locals. Don't ruin it. – Heath Row

Roberta's
261 Moore St (btwn White & Bogart, Bushwick, Bklyn)
718-417-1118
www.robertaspizza.com (Bushwick: L to Morgan)
Roberta's is a crazy Bushwick Cinderella story, the glass
slipper on the DIY toe of a completely-within-the-demo-
graphic artsy dude who heard about a wood-fired pizza
oven for sale not long after he decided on a whim that
it would be fun to open a pizzeria. Dude! Add artisanal
ingredients, wood tables you could raft down the Mis-
souri on, a semi-bombed-out location and of course it's
only a matter of time before *The New York Times* and Alice
Waters are fawning like Bambi over this scruffy, young
visionary 'n' friends.

Grimaldi's
19 Old Fulton St (@ Elizabeth Pl, DUMBO, Bklyn)
718-858-4300
www.grimaldis.com (DUMBO: A/C to High St)
Yet another frequent winner of the Best Pizza in New York
City stakes, Grimaldi's fresh mozzarellific, crisp crusted
beauties are deserving but, from a dine-in perspective,
only fun if you enjoy waiting in line at Epcot Center.
You know what I do? I give them a call from right about
where you'll be getting off the subway. By the time you've
strolled downhill and fought your way past all those
stressed-out, queued-up suckers, your pie will be at the
counter, all boxed-up and ready to go! No nicer way to
spend a Sunday afternoon than sitting on the Fulton
Ferry Landing, watching the Chinese bridal parties pos-
ing for photos as you eat slice after slice.

Sam's Restaurant
238 Court St
(Btwn Warren & Baltic, Cobble Hill, Bklyn) 718-596-3458
(Cobble Hill: F to Bergen St)
A New York City secret—I hate to even divulge it—is that
the eggplant, ricotta, and fresh garlic pizza at Sam's Restaurant on Court Street is the best in the city. The service
can be slow (they only make one pizza at a time), a roach
might crawl across the table, the servers are crotchety and
may not serve you if they don't feel like it, but it is worth
it... – Amy Burchenal

Totonno's
1524 Neptune Ave (btwn 15th St & 16th St, Coney Island,
Bklyn) 718-372-8606
(Coney Island: D/F/N/Q to Stillwell Ave)
&
1544 2nd Ave (btwn 80th St & 81st St)
(Upper East Side: 4/5/6 to 86th St)
www.totonnos.com/NYC.html
Totonno's serves an entirely different species of pizza
from the flaccid specimens a short constitutional away on
the Coney Island boardwalk. (Note: That walk is not short
enough to attempt it in your bathing suit, while your
hungry friends guard your beach towels.) The homemade
mozzarella and wood-fired crust is justly celebrated,
as is the deeply-ingrained surliness of service. The narrow wood benches are murder on the heiner, but that's
just part of the fun, especially when you're out on the
sidewalk wishing someone would move their ass so your
party can be seated.

CHRON!IC!RIOTS!PA!SM – FIy• The Big Rumpus –

Di Fara Pizzeria
1424 Avenue J (btwn 15th & 16th, Midwood, Bklyn) 718-258-1367
www.difara.com (Midwood: Q to Ave J)
If Tom's Restaurant is a happy shrine, constantly celebrating itself, then Di Fara's Pizzeria is a grim cell, thick with an air of suffering that clings like dough to the adult children who assist their father, Domenico DiMarco, in making truly amazing pizza. It's worth the $5 a slice, so priced because of the ingredients imported daily from Italy, to slow the orders enough to be able to satisfy demand, and, yes, to encourage you to buy a whole pie. Which you should. Go early. Eat outdoors while browsing the shops of heavily Orthodox Jewish Avenue J. – David Goren

BRONX

Louie & Ernie's
1300 Crosby Ave (@ Paine St, Pelham Bay, Bronx)
718-829-6230 (Pelham Bay: 6 to Buhre Ave)
This is the slice I suggest everyone try—the best in the borough, and maybe the whole city. The crust is a perfect melding of dough and salt, baked to a crispness that would have you thinking it's brick oven (it's not.) The sauce contains actual seasoning. Creamy mozzarella is melted to a scalding stretch-happy temperature. A smoky, mouth-watering slice of heaven! Louie & Ernie's is not-so-conveniently located about a mile from the Buhre Avenue stop on the 6 train, but I assure you the trek is worth it. – Genevieve Texeira

CARRYOUT AND STREET CARTS
For when you want your food with boots.

Financial District
Among other choices...

Ruben's Empanadas
64 Fulton St (btwn Cliff & Gold) 212-962-5330
(Financial District: A/C/J/M/Z/2/3/4/5 to Broadway-Nassau)
&
149 Church St (btwn Chambers & Warren) 212-513-1448
(Civic Center: A/C/E/2/3 to Chambers-St-Park Pl)
&
122 1st Ave (btwn 7th & St. Marks) 212-979-0172
(East Village: F to 2nd Ave)
&
77 Pearl Street (btwn Coenties Alley & Hanover Sq)
212-361-6323 (Financial District: R to Whitehall St)
&

76 Nassau Street (btw John & Fulton) 212-513-1486
(Financial District: A/C/J/M/Z/2/3/4/5 to Broadway-Nassau)
&
505 Broome Street (@ Watts St) 212-334-3351
(SoHo: C/E to Spring St)
Hooray for the queerest empanadas in Lower Manhattan! I'm not even close to 100% sure about that, especially when these multiple locations are reputed to have more than one owner (supplied by a single Long Island factory), but what the hell. These Argentinean turnovers come with a wide variety of fillings, the juicier the better as they can run a little dry. I'd say go for the Chili (Veggie or Meat) or the Shrimp in Creole Tomato Sauce over the Chopped Broccoli. You can eat them in, but they're so portable it would be a shame not to take them out. Buy an extra to keep in your pocket as a spare.

Chinatown/Little Italy

Rice Noodle Cart
Rutgers and East Broadway
(Chinatown: F to East Broadway)
What a wonderful world it would be if every street cart traded in their flavorless, stale bagels and suspect *souvlaki* for some of this lady's fat rice noodles, with or without the curried squid. She's always got a big pot of eggs keeping warm in the tea in which they were hard-boiled—three for a buck. My favorite is a very comforting bowl of *congee* (that's rice porridge to you, sonny) with pork and duck eggs for...wait for it... $1.25.

Fried Dumpling (a.k.a Shan Dong Dumpling)
106 Mosco St (btwn Mott & Mulberry) 212-693-1060
(Chinatown: J/M/Z/N/Q /R/6 to Canal St)
They are pork. They are fried. They are cheap (5 for $1). When we are starving on our way to dinner, we stop here for an appetizer. They are not good for you, so I try to just have a bite of someone else's. There is also hot and

sour soup in a sort of glutinous broth. A large soup is two containers of small soup. This is a very straightforward place. It's a true hole in the wall. It's a mess. – Esther Smith (Haul your dumplings a few steps downhill to Columbus Park's playground and burn some postprandial calories on the adult-sized monkey bars. - AH)

Tai Pan Bakery
194 Canal Street (btwn Mott St & Mulberry) 212-732-2222
(Chinatown: J/M/Z/N/Q /R/6 to Canal St)
&
37-25 Main St (@ 37th Ave, Flushing, Queens) 718-888-1111
(Flushing: 7 to Main St)
&
42-05B Main St (@ Maple Ave, Flushing, Queens)
718-460-8787 (Flushing: 7 to Main St)
www.taipan-bakery.com
I was wary of Taipan Bakery at first, since it's right on the "touristy" strip of Chinatown and I figured that the more memorable food would be on a quieter alley, but the place is always mobbed. The bean buns are oftentimes so fresh they're steaming in the little plastic bags they put them in. – Marguerite Dabaie

Deluxe Food Market
79 Elizabeth St (btwn Grand & Hester) 212-925-5766
(Little Italy: B/D to Grand St)
Communicating to the mostly non-English-speaking steam table attendants which three items you'll have over rice at this seething, semi-subterranean grocery-cum-food court can be a harrowing experience, but you should give it a whirl. Yes, there is a chance that the succulent-looking, barbequed item the attendant halting describes as chicken fingers will turn out to be chicken feet, but who cares when you've got two other dishes and the whole Styrofoam clam shell weighed in at $4.95. If the intensity of the grocery-shopping crowd, the brusque staff, and the unfamiliar scene put you in danger of wimping out, fortify yourself with an egg custard and a pork bun or five, then take a deep breath and try again. Really. It's an experience!

Viet-Nam Banh Mi So 1
369 Broome (btwn Mott and Elizabeth), 212-219-8341
(Little Italy: J/M to Bowery)
You can get both meat and vegan sandwiches in this little shop for less than $6 apiece, and their sandwiches are HUGE. – Victoria Law (Fresh squeezed sugar cane juice, be still my beating heart. – AH)

Lower East Side/East Village

Punjabi
114 E 1st St (Btwn Ave A & 1st Ave) 212-533-9048
(East Village: F to 2nd Ave)
Punjabi is the darling of the zine-publishing NYC public. Not everyone who sings its many praises knows its name, but somehow, it's not just the city's 44,000 licensed cab drivers who know about this humble hole where you can get insanely good *samosas* for a buck a piece. Everyone but the cab drivers thinks it's on Houston, but thanks to an unassuming traffic median-type park-strip, it's actually on 1st. I'm sure my fellow patrons at the Sunshine Cinema really appreciate when I smuggle half-a-small-popcorn's worth of those delicious deep-fried babies into the matinee. – AH (I can't eat there without burping it up the rest of the evening – Jessica Max Stein)

Juicy Lucy
85 Avenue A (btwn 5th St & 6th St) 212-777-5829
www.myspace.com/juicylucynyc
(East Village: F to 2nd Ave)
My second fave—after Jefferson Market! – Matana Roberts

Yonah Schimmels Knish Bakery
137 East Houston St (btwn 1st & 2nd Ave) 212-477-2858
www.knishery.com (LES: F/M to 2nd Ave)
These Old World potato dumplings could more than prop

John Joseph • Fuck You Have a Nice Day –

a door, but they must qualify as health food for Yonah to be celebrating his centennial. Some pushy non-traditional flavors have crowded their way onto the menu over the last century. This is one place where it doesn't pay to get too *avant*.

Tompkin Park Gourmet Deli
94 Avenue B (@ E 6th St) 212-677-3131
(East Village: F/J/M/Z to Delancey-Essex)
Giant takeout tuna salads for six bucks, great for eating in the big community garden right across the street, or the other community garden further east on 6th.
– Jessica Max Stein

Baoguette & Baoguette Café
37 St. Mark's Pl (btwn 2nd & 1st Ave) 347-892-2614
(East Village: 6 to Astor Pl)
&
61 Lexington Ave (btwn 25th & 26th St) 212-532-1133
(Flatiron: 6 to Park Ave S)
&
9 Maiden Lane (Broadway & Cortlandt) 212-233-3400
www.baoguette.com (Financial District: A/C/J/M/Z/2/3/4/5 to Fulton-Broadway-Nassau)
The classic *banh mi* sandwich is $5, and big enough for two meals. As for a place to eat it, if you've purchased your Baoguette from the Lexington Avenue location, head two avenues west and you'll find yourself in Madison Square Park. Beware 10lb aggro squirrels. From Saint Marks Place, head two avenues east and you'll find yourself in Tompkins Square Park. Beware 100lb amorous crackheads. There's also a little known office park behind that heinous glass Chase bank building south of Astor Place. – Kate Black

Otafuku
236 E 9th St (btwn 2nd Ave & Stuyvesant) 212-353-8503
www.otafukusauce.com (East Village: 6 to Astor Pl)
Otafuku's opening was cause for major celebration. I had fallen in love with *okinomiyaki* in Japan, but it struck me as a taste sensation unlikely to catch on in the States. It's a jumbo, omlette-y pancake thing, gloopy with brown sauce, studded with scallions and shrimp, and topped with bonito flakes that the heat inside the plastic clamshell container causes to wave around like they're alive. If the tiny bench out front is occupied, or something on the sidewalk is curdling your appetite, take it to Tompkins Square, the little yard by St. Mark's church, or, my favorite, the Grassroots Tavern.

The Mudtruck
4th Ave & 9th St (right by the subway entrance north of the Cube)
www.themudtruck.com (East Village: 6 to Astor Pl.)
It's possible to get your Mud without wheels, most notably at the Mud Spot (307 E 9th St (btwn 1st and 2nd Ave) 212-288-9074), but their full restaurant menu makes me worry that the waitstaff feels a bit irritated at non-to-go "just coffee" orders, even if you play fair by hunching up in the drafty, flyer-strewn window seat. Save everybody the *tsuris* by taking your Mud from the orange and brown truck where it all started? I find it inspirational that the couple-with-a-baby who founded the Mud empire didn't let having a kid and being too broke to rent a storefront stand in their way!

Pommes Frites
123 2nd Ave (btwn St Marks Pl & 7th St) 212-674-1234
www.pommesfrites.ws (East Village: F to 2nd Ave)
Pommes Frites is this amazing french fry place. They have tons of sauces, things like mango chutney and basil rosemary mayo. – grace janove (You know they're extra healthy when they're fried twice! I must admit the paper cone in which they're served gives me an undeniable Belgian hang, as does the doll-sized wooden fork adding some small amount of daintiness to the act of waddling down 2nd Avenue, pile driving fries. I cannot bring myself to eat these with anything other than traditional, straight up mayo. – AH)

A&C Kitchen
136 Avenue C (btwn E. 8th and 9th St) 212-677-8112
(East Village: 8 to E 10th & Ave C)
Fast food Chinese with a lot of vegetarian dishes, including a really awesome hijiki tofu burger dinner. – Victoria Law

SoHo

Lahore Deli
132 Crosby St (btwn Houston & Prince) 212-965-1777
(SoHo: B/D/F/M to Broadway-Lafayette)
Some would say three ripped bar stools plus a wall display of single serving antacid packages = no atmosphere, but I'm not averse to parking it at Lahore, even though I have no cab. The only problem with eating in is the samosas are so good I usually wind up huffing like five times the recommended daily calorie intake for a woman my size. Eat here *after* leaving Housing Works Used Book Café, because you're going to greasy up the pages if you do it the other way around.

Greenwich Village

Jefferson Market
450 Ave of the Americas (btwn 10th & 11th) 212-533-3377
(Greenwich Village: A/B/C/D/E/F/M to W 4th St)
If you are into liquid foods, my fave juice bar is in this
health food store on 6th Ave and 11th St. – Matana Roberts

N.Y. Dosas
50 Washington Sq South (@ Sullivan) 917-710-2092
(Greenwich Village: A/B/C/D/E/F/M to W 4th St)
This Washington Square cart is especially fantastic for
veganistas! 4 bucks for a huge delicious dosa. – Matana
Roberts (If you're merely puckish, you could order a few
vegan drumsticks on a sugarcane stick! This is a weekday,
11-4 sort of treat. – AH)

Garment District

E-Mo Kimbab
2 W 32nd St (btwn 5th Ave and Broadway) 212-594-1466
(Murray Hill: 6 to 33rd St)
The only thing this place sells, besides the drinks to
wash 'em down, are *kimbab*, Korean seaweed rice rolls,
like those California rolls you see hanging around the
salad bars of the corner deli, except made fresh to order
by an extremely nice lady and, in the event of a rush, her
husband. My favorite is Jalapeno, followed by Spicy Tuna,
though someday curiosity or a finicky child may lead me
to investigate the one stuffed with American cheese.

Woorijip
12 W 32nd St (btwn 5th Ave and Broadway) 212-244-1115
(Murray Hill: 6 to 33rd St)
Amidst the corporate wasteland of Midtown Manhattan, the Koreatown neighborhood on East 32nd between
Broadway and 5th Avenue is an oasis. Woorijip, a by-the-
pound ($6.50) food bar squeezed in between karaoke clubs
and shiatsu spas, is the oasis within the oasis. Swanky Korean pop plays in the background as you behold a steam
table with more than twenty choices, from the 'baps
(*bibimbap* & *kimbap*) to kale-studded seafood pancakes
and multifarious variations on *kimchi*. Open 24/7! Makes
a nice pit stop before or after a sojourn at Jim Hanley's
Universe – David Goren (If your train's leaving from Penn
Station, Woorijip can help transform any dirty old Amtrak
seat into your personal dining car. Hopefully your fellow
passengers are open to sharing their airspace with the
aroma of Korean food. If you've no train to catch, you could
carry out to nearby Horace Greely Square where little Parisian tables have been set up for your dining pleasure. – AH)

Midtown

Halal food carts of Midtown
Most of the Halal (i.e., kosher) food carts will provide you
with an awesome (big!) platter of falafel, rice, and mixed
vegetables for about $5. These carts are ALL OVER mid-
town, if you're unfortunate enough to be there. Luckily
there are cute little parks and public spaces all over as
well; check out the one with the waterfall on 51st Street
between 2nd and 3rd Aves. – Melissa Bastian

Grand Central Lower Level Dining Concourse
109 E 42nd St (btwn De Pew Pl & Lexington Ave)
212-557-7992
www.grandcentralterminal.com
(Midtown 4/5/6/7/S to Grand Central)
Though the very idea of a food court in polyglot NYC is
a bit absurd, Grand Central's granite floors and vaulted
ceilings take it far from the standard shopping mall
ethos. Most of the stalls are extensions of name brand
NYC eateries. The famed Brooklyn deli Junior's has an
outpost here, as does kosher Mendy's, the reborn Chirpin'
Chicken and Two Boots, which serves cuisine Italiano y
Louisiana. The two seating areas evoke the choo-choo
experience. The booths are reminiscent of heavy wooden
waiting room benches, and the table tops feature a collage of vintage train ephemera, old schedules, and ad-
vertisements. – David Goren (I feel like it's my lucky day
should one of the hard plastic seats designed to look like

Illustrated History of Television - Tim Mitchell

an overstuffed armchair open up right when I'm looking for a place to sit down. Don't forget to swing by the Whispering Wall. – AH)

Oasis Bar
541 Lexington Ave (btwn 49th and 50th) 212-407-2996
(Midtown: 4/5/6/7/S to Grand Central)
&
161 N 7th St (@ Bedford, Williamsburg, Bklyn) 718-218-7607
(Williamsburg: L to Bedford Ave).
They know what they're doing. Plus, you can get a nice, cool *Ayran* while you're at it! – Marguerite Dabaie (You say *Ayran*, I say *Lassi*, but we both crave a refreshing yogurt based drink to wash down cheap *falafel*. – AH)

Kwik Meal Cart
5th Ave and 45th St
&
6th Ave and 45th St
(Midtown: 7/B/D/F/M to 42nd St)
This cart is famous for good reason. The chef used to work at the Rainbow Room, a famous, swanky NYC restaurant, and now his *falafel* cart. Everything about it is superior to your normal *falafel*—the bread is so soft, the *falafel* balls have a little kick to them, they're not overcooked and the sauce—*the sauce*— it's all about the sauce. Although it's the best *falafel* ever, it's not the cheapest. A sandwich is $4.50 and it's a little bit smaller than typical. If I'm hungry, one doesn't really fill me up but two would be crazy. – Amanda Plumb

The Jamaican Dutchy
51st St & 7th Ave, 646-287-5004
www.thejamaicandutchy.net (Midtown B/D/E to 7th Ave)
I'm no fan of flat screen TVs in restaurants, but I'm kind of fond of the one mounted to the outside of the Jamaican Dutchy truck, despite not having any particular interest in soccer, which is apparently what it's there for. I've got to hand it to the Jamaican Dutchy man for pimping his professional ride with such national pride. Beneath that green and black flag is some of the tastiest food in midtown—everything from rotis, patties, and refreshing sorrel beverage to generous $6 and $7 "mini" meals featuring Island specialties like curry goat and jerk chicken with rice & peas, plantains and steamed veg. I pity the fools at the nearby Sheraton Hotel getting their Starbucks and Danish in their lobby, when a block away other early risers are rocking some *callaloo* & saltfish and plantain or peanut porridge.

Café Duke
140 W 51st St (btwn 6th and 7th Ave) 212-445-0010
(Midtown: N/R to 49th St-7th Ave)
&
1450 Broadway (btwn 40th St & 41st St) 212-354-4595
(Garment District: A/C/E/N/Q /R/S/1/2/3/7 to Times Square-42nd St)
&
545 Broadway (btwn Prince & Spring) 917-237-1575
(SoHo: N/R to Prince St)
www.icafeduke.com
Cafe Duke has an excellent hot bar, but it's best to get there before the lunch crowd, otherwise you end up having to dig for anything good. They have a huge and varied selection, deli counter, sushi bar, pizza, salad bar, hot foot, frozen food, beer and almost any snack you can think of. They also make the most amazing *udon*, which is perfect and filling on a cold winter's day. – Josh Saitz

Upper West Side

H&H Bagels
2239 Broadway (btwn 79th St & 80th St) 212-595-8000
(Upper West Side: 1 to 79th St)
&
1551 2nd Ave (btwn 80th St & 81st St) 212-717-7312
(Upper East Side: 6 to 77th St)
&
639 West 46th St (@ 12th Ave) 212-765-7200
(Hell's Kitchen: A/C/E/N/Q /R/S/1/2/3/7 to 42nd St-8th Ave)
www.hhbagels.com
This is what people mean when they talk about the superiority of New York bagels. If you need confirmation, drive six hours to some seaside locale where well-off New Yorkers vacation, and watch for prominently posted "We have H&H Bagels!" signs. Bring a toothpick if you fancy an Everything, or be horrified hours later when some reflective surface hips you to the state of your toothy grin. – AH (Get some for tomorrow's breakfast, but be sure to ask for freezer bags. They're free and they'll keep your bagels fresh. – Josh Saitz) (These can easily be frozen and shipped off. I once brought two dozen bagels in my suitcase with me when I was visiting my mother. The luggage-checkers nodded knowingly. – Marguerite Dabaie)

Washington Heights

El Sabrosito
(St. Nicholas & 186th St)
This big, shiny new kitchen truck has fresh *nopales*, and they make their own fabulous *gordita* bread!! – Jerry the Mouse

In the Shadow of NoTowers – Art Spiegelman

Endless Summer Taco Truck
(Bedford Ave near N 6th St, Williamsburg, Bklyn)
347-400-8128, www.endlesssummertacos.com
(Williamsburg: L to Bedford Ave)
Giving New Yorkers even less reason to relocate to California is Williamsburg's Endless Summer Taco Truck, where fish tacos are a stand-out, effectively preventing me from ever sampling any other variety. The *frijoles* can be weirdly unseasoned, but that's what hot sauce is for and the *arroz* is delicious. McCarren Park is but a short walk north, though an appealing weekend alternative is to take them on a little field trip to the Brooklyn Brewery.

Turkey's Nest Tavern
94 Bedford Ave (btwn 11th & 12th St) 718-384-9774
(Williamsburg: L to Bedford Ave)
This bar will put their giant frozen Margarita slushies in Styrofoam cups. I know! Bad for the environment, but good for walking out to McCarren Park with! – Dear Drunk Girl

El Loco Burrito
345 Graham Ave (btwn Conselyea St & Metropolitan Ave)
718-388-8215
(Williamsburg: G/L to Metropolitan-Lorimer)
Shrimp tacos! They also have an extensive menu of hippie burrito options, including grilled veggies, tofu, soy cheese, brown rice, whole wheat tortillas, etc. – Dear Drunk Girl (Love love love El Loco Burrito. The woman who works the register is always so so friendly and you can get 3 bean tacos for like $3. – Megan Garrity)

Manna
572 Grand St (@ Lorimer) 718-384-2122
(Williamsburg: G/L to Metropolitan Ave-Lorimer St)
Manna on Grand for late night *falafel* sandwiches 24 hours a day! – Dear Drunk Girl

Yummy Taco
941 Manhattan Ave (btwn Java & Kent, Greenpoint, Bklyn)
718-349-7731
Though it's got that weird Chinese Restaurant turned imitation Mexican feel, Yummy Taco in Greenpoint kiiiiiiiind of knows what's up more than most take-out joints. I'd recommend the tostada salad. It's big enough to come in a cakebox! – Caitlin McGurk

Red Hook Ball Field Food Vendors
Clinton St at Bay St, Red Hook, Bklyn, Weekends only
www.myspace.com/redhookfoodvendors (Red Hook: F to Smith & 9th)
Nothing beats a weekend dip in the Red Hook Pool followed by a plate of *pupusas*, some *horchata*, a plastic cup of *ceviche* and a cheese-and-chili-trimmed ear of corn. The food is amazing, the trashy grounds worn bald, and the lines increasingly long, though it won't be such a trial to wait in them if you remember that they represent a true victory for the little guy. When a big, hairy real estate deal threatened to put the kibosh on this beloved scene, the vendors banded together with the community and a couple of key politicians and reporters. Things were touch and go for awhile, but in the end, the vendors got a lease, agreeing to trade in their makeshift stalls for trucks and certificates from the Board of Health. There's no indoor option here, so don't go if it's raining, or the sun's about to set. Buy some fresh coconut and some trashy plastic toys on the way out!

Halal Paradise Truck
22 4th Ave (btwn Pacific & Atlantic, Boerum Hill, Bklyn)
(Boerum Hill: B/D/M/N/R Q /2/3/4/5 to Atlantic Ave-Pacific St)
A bright green paradise awaits both the post-worship faithful spilling down the stairs of nearby Masjid Al-Farooq and infidels returning from Target or ukulele classes at the Brooklyn Guitar Center. Falafel sandwiches are served on nice, fat bread, and the sauce has a certain tang. If school's not in session and no one's playing soccer, you can eat it in on the Astroturf inside PS38's playground's running track, a block to west.

A+A Bake and Doubles
481 Nostrand Ave (btwn Fulton St & Halsey St, Bedford-Stuyvesant, Bklyn), 718-230-0753
(Bed-Stuy: A/C to Nostrand Ave)
Bed Stuy Indo-Caribbean food. The doubles (curried chickpeas sandwiched in fried dough) are the best—worth traveling for. Closed on Sundays. – Robyn Jordan

Green Pirate Juice Truck
The pirates are mysterious about where they plan to dock! Check the website: www.green-pirate.com
Name me a buccaneer who can resist the liquid squeezings of green apple, celery, cucumber, ginger, and lemon that make up this mobile juice stands signature drink, and I'll show you a scurvy-ridden corpse-in-waiting! They compost their organic waste, run on bio-diesel, and distribute Green Pirate pins as a reward to anyone bringing their own 16-ounce cup. Almost makes me want to choke

down some wheatgrass in solidarity! But first a Cantaloupe Creamsicle and some Hot Pink Limeade...

QUEENS

Flower Drum House
2105 31st St (btwn 21st Ave & Ditmars Blvd, Astoria, Queens) 718-956-3677
(Astoria: N to Ditmars Blvd)
Flower Drum House is your usual Chinese take-out place, but they have a mega-serving of wonton soup for three-fifty, which is a meal in itself. It comes with these fried wonton chips which you are supposed to put in the soup, but I eat them solo. Good for eating in nearby Astoria Park.– Josh Medsker

Sammy's Halal
73rd St @ Broadway (Jackson Hts, Queens)
www.sammyhalalfood.com
Whoo, that long ride to Queens can make a Manhattanite hungry! Despite the hundreds of *halal* carts serving their own borough, the pilgrims have been flocking here ever since Sammy's cart won the *Village Voice's* coveted Vendy Award.

CARNIVOROUS TREATS

MANHATTAN

Papaya King, Papaya Dog, Grey's Papaya, Papaya Overlord... New York City hot dog stands...what's the difference? Grey's splintered off the King sometime in the '70s. The Dog is a copy cat. The Papaya Overlord will reveal himself when you are ready. All have jet sprays filled with exotically named, non-alcoholic beverages that fall disappointingly short of tasting like you're rolling around in the surf with Deborah Kerr and Burt Lancaster. The décor remains a stagy NYC pleasure, lots of fake fruit and boastful signage dangling from the ceiling. I commend Grey's for keeping the Recession Special on the menu no matter what the economy's up to...no meat-eating New Yorker should have to go without an affordable lifetime supply of lips, anuses, and insect parts. It may be an illusion, but these do seem marginally less sleazy than the dirty water dogs you can get from a street cart.

Papaya King
179 E 86th St (btwn 3rd Ave & Lexington) 212-369-0648
www.papayaking.com (Upper East Side: 4/5/6 to 86th St)

Papaya Dog
400 W 42nd St (btwn 9th Ave & Dyer Ave, Hell's Kitchen)
212-629-0632 (A/C/E/1/2/3/S/7/N/Q /R to 8th Ave-42nd St)

Grey's Papaya
402 6th Ave (btwn 8th & 9th St) 212-260-3532
www.grayspapaya.com (A/C/E/B/D/F/M to W 4th St)

Chinatown/Little Italy

Singapore Malaysia Beef Jerky
95A Elizabeth St (Btwn Grand & Hester) 212-965-0796
www.malaysiabeefjerky.com (Little Italy: B/D to Grand)
Oh, hell to the Slim Jim *yeah!* A quarter pound of Spicy

weiler - E·L· Konigsburg

Pork Jerky will set you back a staggering $4.95, but before we start whining about price, consider the enterprising uptown charlatan who is no doubt plating this culinary sensation up with a Pernod-infused crabapple and a shaving of white chocolate, the resulting appetizer-sized portion selling for $30. It's that good. You're supposed to refrigerate it, so best eat it all on the walk to the subway.

East Village

Crif Dogs
113 St. Mark's Pl (btwn 1st Ave and Ave A) 212-614-2728
www.crifdogs.com (East Village: 6 to Astor Pl)
If there's a giant weenie with the words Eat Me over the door, you should open it. That maxim applies particularly here on St. Mark's Place, where basement-level Crif dishes up all manner of tube steaks, including a veggie model that looks a bit too much like panty hose for my taste, but certainly hit the spot back when I was off the meat. My current obsession is the Spicy Redneck, featuring chili, bacon, jalapeños, and Cole Slaw. Cheap beer, late hours, a wall-mounted novelty marital aid dispenser, and plenty of 'tude.

Greenwich Village

Corner Bistro
331 W. 4th St (btwn Jane St and 8th Ave) 212-242-9502
www.cornerbistro.ypguides.net (Greenwich Village: A/C/E/L to 14th St-8th Ave, 1/2/3/F/M/L to 14th St-7th Ave)
Corner Bistro's burgers are especially delicious because it feels no need to toot its goddamn horn. It's been there forever, as the scarred wood tables attest. Would that every "bistro" in New York sold beer in plastic pitchers. – AH (When you order, they don't ask how you want it done. Trust the cook! The fries are a cross between old-school KFC fries and grade school lunch room fries. It's all served on paper plates. If you want a seat and you want to eat, best arrive early. – Heath Row)

Upper West Side

Barney Greengrass
541 Amsterdam Ave (btwn 86th & 87th St) 212-724-4707
www.barneygreengrass.com (Upper West Side: B/C/1 to 86th St)
It may not seem like it from all the Old Navys and Barnes & Nobles, but there are still a lot of people on the Upper West Side who can put a Mel Brooks spin on, "What am I, chopped liver?" If you want to sample this classic New York delicacy, Barney Greengrass (the Sturgeon King) has been at it for over 100 years. (Some would send you down to Sammy's Roumanian on the Lower East Side, but I quail at their practice of setting schmaltz in syrup containers on every table.)

The Smoke Joint
87 S Elliott Place (Btwn Fulton & Lafayette, Fort Greene, Bklyn) 718-797-1011
www.thesmokejoint.com (Fort Greene: 2/3/4/5/M/N/Q/R/B/D to Atlantic Ave-Pacific St)
Don't expect a free shot if you hop on the counter and wiggle out of your bra. This ain't Hogs & Heifers. *That* joint = Meat Packing nightmare. *This* one has awesome pulled pork sandwiches, groaning paper plates heaped with ribs 'n' tips, and ludicrously cheap cans of Pork Slap from the upstate Butternut Brewery. After your meal, drag your carcass over to BAM Rose Cinemas, where you can sit through a rarefied retrospective of some under grossly under-recognized director, annoying the folks in the surrounding rows by smelling like something that crawled out of the 'que pit.

Nathan's Famous Hot Dogs
1310 Surf Ave (@ Stillwell Ave, Coney Island, Bklyn) 718-946-2202
www.nathansfamous.com
(Coney Island: D/F/N/Q to Stillwell Ave)
Hot dogs were invented in Coney Island around 1870 when a German immigrant named Charles Feltman began selling sausages in rolls. So a trip to Coney Island should really include a stop at Nathan's Hot Dogs. Only problem is, they don't have veggie dogs. Never fear, there is a solution: Craig and I prepared our own veggie hot dogs and buns at my place, then brought them with us. At Coney Island, we ordered fries and sauerkraut from Nathan's. The old guy working there laughed when I ordered a side of kraut, and gave it to me for free. Then we sat at their picnic tables and chowed down. I think we had an authentic eating experience. – Amanda Plumb

Cevabdzinica Sarajevo
37-18 34th Ave (btwn 37th & 38th St, Astoria, Queens) 718-752-9528 (Astoria: G/R/M to Steinway)
Cevapci is the Bosnian national dish—a greasy grilled lamb sausage, served with pita and onions. Better pick up some mints for after! A good choice for ravenous meateaters coming from the Museum of the Moving Image.

3 inesters' Favorite Movies About NYC : Pieces

SWEETS

Desserts are usually something of a luxury. But you're on vacation! So there's nothing wrong with having an ice cream cone for lunch. (Same goes if you live here, well, as long as you don't make it an everyday thing…)

Doughnuts

The Doughnut Plant
379 Grand St (@ Norfolk), 212-505-3700
Krispy your Kremes with fresh, non-corporate cakes and glazeds in such flavors du jour as Pistachio, Tres Leches, Meyer Lemon, and Blackout (a nod to the star attraction of the long-gone Ebinger's Bakery). The Doughnut Plant also churns out churros for those too timid to buy the $1 versions from rush hour DIY subway vendors. – AH (I would recommend the glazed doughnut. Why? Because it's a vanilla glazed doughnut, and once you try it, you'll wonder why on earth all glazed doughnuts are not vanilla doughnuts. – Amanda Plumb)

The Doughnut Pub
203 W. 14th St (@7th Ave) 212-929-0126
(Greenwich Village: 1/2/3 to 14th St)
This longtime mom and pop remained stalwart in the shadow of an interloping Dunkin'. They've got a counter with stools, and are open 24 hours for all you Night-hawks at the Diner, but there's no customer bathroom so monitor your coffee intake.

Mochi Doughnuts from Café Zaiya
18 E. 41st St (btwn 5th and Madison) 212-779-0600
(Midtown: B/D/F/M/7 to 42nd St-Bryant Park)

&

69 Cooper Sq (@ E 7th St) (East Village: 6 to Astor Pl)
www.zaiyany.com
There's something vaguely alien about doughnuts made from pounded rice. They've got this stretchy unborn bathmat texture that's counterintuitive in doughnut-land. Even for those of us who aren't vegan or allergic to wheat, they're a fun culinary proposition, particularly the chocolate-dipped version. I'm not too down with Café Zaiya's brightly-lit food court vibe, so when possible, I chopper these babies out to the nearby steps of the New York Public Library to enjoy in the shadow of my lion friends, Patience and Fortitude.

Cider Doughnuts from the Wilklow Orchards stand
Borough Hall Greenmarket (T, Th & Sat)
388 Cadman Plaza W (@ Montague St, Downtown, Bklyn)
212-788-7476
www.cenyc.org (Downtown Bklyn: A/C/F to Jay St)
These wholesome cheapies are available year round, but

are particularly nice on autumnal mornings when one can lounge upon the marble steps of grand, old colonnaded Borough Hall, watching dozens of field-tripping nursery schoolers milling around on pumpkin and apple related fact-finding missions.

Peter Pan Bakery
727 Manhattan Ave (btwn Norman & Meserole, Greenpoint, Bklyn) 718-389-3676
(Greenpoint: G to Nassau Ave)
I thought jelly doughnuts were something to leave in the box for the suckers coming later until I unknowingly got one in a bag of holes on my first visit to this no-frills Greenpoint stalwart. There's a counter where you can sip coffee and admire the spot where the payphone used to be. The customers are a healthy mix of old men and clueless but heartfelt young hipsters.

Cupcakes

Magnolia Bakery
401 Bleecker (@ 11th St) 212-462-2572
(Greenwich Village: A/C/E/L to 14th St-8th Ave)
&
200 Columbus Ave (@ 69th St) 212-724-8101
(Upper West Side: 1 to 66th St)
www.magnoliacupcakes.com
I liked them fine back when all they reminded me of was my grandmother, who also baked with Crisco and favored vintage pastels. Now, thanks to a significant role in Sex and the City, the corner of Bleecker and 11th is jammed with trendy-bag-carrying, cupcake-crazed nim-nims in something the fashion editors refer to as "strappy" sandals. But after Chris Parnell and Andy Samberg immortalized it in their awesome Lazy Sunday rap, I can't not list it. Baker's dozen! Mack on that cupcake, cousin. – AH

Chickalicious
203 E 10th St (btwn 1st Ave & 2nd Ave) 212-995-9511
www.chikalicious.com (East Village: 6 to Astor Pl)
The best cupcake ever is the black and white at Chickalicious. Yes, I am aware of the cupcake opinions of others and cupcake guide books, etc, and I don't give a fuck.
– Andria Alefhi

Ruthy's Bakery and Café
75 9th Ave (@15th St in the Chelsea Market) 212-463-8800
www.ruthys.com (Chelsea: A/C/E/L to 14th St-8th Ave)
Taste may be beside the point here. I was moved to include it after seeing a giant cupcake sculpture of one of the Teenage Mutant Ninja Turtle's heads. Count on

Ruthy for all your over-the-top, baseball-sized Muppet head cupcake needs, too. (If you're seeking a total sugar meltdown, as long as you're in the Chelsea Market, see if Amy's Bread has any chocolate cherry rolls left, and swing by Fat Witch Bakery after 5pm, when all brownies are half off.

The Cupcake Café
545 9th Ave (btwn 40th and 41st), 212-465-1530
(Hell's Kitchen: A/C/E to 42nd St)
&
18 W 18th St (btwn 5th & 6th Ave) 212-255-2415
(Chelsea: N/Q /R to 23rd)
www.cupcakecafe-nyc.com
Also a New York institution. They've got their detractors, but if you want my tongue's two cents, the pretty, flower-

trimmed chocolate buttercreams here are the best cupcakes I have ever eaten outside the ones my mother bakes
using her black bottom recipe. The flagship's interior is
an inviting BoHo cave of mismatched wooden furniture,
high ceilings, and insufficient lighting, a welcome surprise in that shady area behind Port Authority.

Downtown Atlantic
364 Atlantic Ave (@ Hoyt, Boerum Hill, Bklyn) 718-852-9945
www.downtownatlantic.com
(Boerum Hill: A/C/G to Hoyt-Schermerhorn)
As a restaurant, Downtown Atlantic is not my cup of
tea. It's nothing personal. It's just hard for me to get it
up about another bistro-apron, $19 entrée, maybe-take-
your-parents-there-type place unless it's in the middle
of a Midwestern suburb whose only other options are
Panda Express and TGI Fridays. Their gigantic, and quite
possibly copyright-infringing, "Hostess" cupcakes are
another matter entirely. There's a to-go counter up front
for the likes of me.

Little Cupcake Bakeshop
9102 Third Ave (@ 91st, Fort Hamilton, Bklyn) 718-680-4465
www.littlecupcakebakeshop.com
(Fort Hamilton: R to 95th St)
These $2 cupcakes come in a myriad of flavors to tempt
and satisfy any taste. The only downside is it's located in
the ass end of Brooklyn by the Verazanno Bridge, which
you can see looming at you like the mouth of hell, leading
to Staten Island. – Genevieve Texeira

Martha's Country Bakery
36-21 Ditmars Blvd (btwn 36th & 37th St, Astoria, Queens)
718-545-9737(Astoria: N to Astoria St)
&
70-30 Austin St (@ 70th Rd, Forest Hills, Queens) 718-544-0088
(Forest Hills: E/F/G/R to 71st Ave)
&
41-06 Bell Blvd (btwn 41st & 42nd Ave, Bayside, Queens)
718-225-5200 (Bayside: Q13 Bus to Bell Blvd and 41st Ave)
www.marthascountrybakery.com
After the Great Queens Blackout of 2006, all the ice cream
shops in Astoria appeared to have gone out of business.
While on a quest for anything other than a grocery store
pint, I came across Martha's. They don't have ice cream,
but they do have gelato and milkshakes (chocolate milkshake: recommended). They also have a whole display
of cupcakes, in flavors like red velvet and black forest,
though I still prefer regular old butter cream. They've got
indoor and outdoor seating, so you can stay a while. The
best time is the morning, when everything's fresher. –

Shayna Marchese

Cupcakes Take the Cake
www.cupcakestakethecake.blogspot.com
Multiply all the cupcakes in New York by two, and that's
the number of opinions you'll find regarding which one's
the best and which one sucks. Not only that, a new supplier seems to spring up every week. Stay abreast of all
the latest New York City cupcake dish with this blog, the
brainchild of writers Nichelle Stephens and Rachel Kramer Bussel (editor of *The Best Sex Stories of 2009* for those of
you who equate dessert with orgasms).

Hot Chocolate

Max Brenner Chocolate by the Bald Man
841 Broadway (@ E 14th St) 212-388-0030
www.maxbrenner.com
(Union Sq: L/N/Q /R/4/5/6/ to Union Sq)
I'm sure the foodies are right that it's no Jacques Torres,
but my underage companions' criteria runs more toward
"Can I inject myself orally with a chocolate syringe? Are
there brown pipes running along the ceiling filled with
something other than poo?" It's charming in an upscale
chain-y kind of way, and they serve alcohol. Don't be in a
rush to go in, as they've often got an employee handing
out samples close to the entry.

The Chocolate Bar
19 Eighth Ave (btwn Hudson & 12th St) 212-366-1541
www.chocolatebarnyc.com
(Greenwich Village: A/C/E/L to 14th St-8th Ave)
The clean lines of the décor here speak to my inner met-
rosexual, a creature that has yet to make it to the surface
where others can see him. Thus far I have not been refused service for being unkempt, hairy, and invariably
in the company of some seriously jacked-up and about
to become more so kids. In addition to their extremely
worthwhile hot chocolate, their slickly designed, humor-
ously labeled in-house product line could be just the
ticket for your cat-feeding neighbor and/or ass-covering
co-worker.

Jacques Torres
66 Water St (btwn Dock & Main, DUMBO, Bklyn) 718-875-9772
(DUMBO: A/C to High St)
&
350 Hudson (@ King St) 212-414-2462
(SoHo: 1 to Houston St)
&
285 Amsterdam (btwn 73rd & 74th) Upper West Side

212-414-2462 (Upper West Side: 1/2/3 to 72nd St)
www.jacquestorres.com
Sweet chocolate Jesus, here it is. Hot chocolate heaven, like drinking molten pudding. Get the kind with hot peppers in it. (You won't develop the ring of fire, I promise.) The DUMBO shop is tres ooh la la, with antique-y looking cases of petits bon-bons looking and costing like something you'd find in a dowager's jewel box. Having weighed the costs, I do stick by my assertion that the hot chocolate is good for the masses, not every day, but to mark or make a special occasion. I like to take mine out to Empire Park, to sip slowly atop the goose droppings, watching the boats go by the bridges.

Pastry

Nice One Bakery
47 Bayard St (btwn Bowery and Elizabeth) 212-791-9365
(Chinatown: J/M to Canal St)
Every New Yorker thinks their favorite coconut buns are the best coconut buns in New York, but seriously, these ones are. It would be a shame for you to blow your 75 cents in any other Chinatown bakery, unless of course, it's right next to the subway station or something. Yes, it looks like an overgrown hot dog bun, and if your first bite is too shallow, it may taste like one too, but keep going.

Ferrara
195 Grand Street (btwn Mulberry & Mott St) 212-226-6150
www.ferraracafe.com (Little Italy: B/D to Grand)
Pass yourself off as a wedding-cake-shopping-bride-to-be and you just might find yourself enjoying a complementary piece of booze-soaked sponge cake, with your choice of almond, espresso, or vanilla flavored cream between the layers. That's what I did. Of course, I did end up buying a wedding cake, but...

De Robertis Pasticería and Caffe
176 1st Ave (btwn 10th and 11th St) 212-674-7137
www.derobertiscaffe.com (East Village: L to 1st
In addition to the fist-sized chocolate rum balls, the chocolate-dipped cannoli, and the dour-faced marzipan lambs that appear around Lent, the thing I really like here is Grandpa De Robertis' silver dollar, embedded right in the middle of the black and white tile floor, back where the tables are. Seriously old school.

Atlas Cafe
73 2nd Ave (btwn 4th & 5th) 212-539-0966
www.orderatlascafe.com (East Village: F to 2nd Ave)
Atlas Cafe on 2nd Avenue has the best cakes and pies and cupcakes and an amazing extruding tofutti machine that will mix in whatever you want with the frozen yogurt or tofutti. Super-fun. – Megan Garrity

Big Booty Bread Co.
261 W 23rd St (btwn 7th & 8th Ave) 212-414-3056
www.bigbootybreadco.com (Chelsea: C/E to 23rd St)
I like to think this place exists to give those physique-obsessed Chelsea boys a chance to cultivate true body acceptance, beginning with a couple corn pancakes and a guava turnover. It's definitely a case of subversion from within. Nice t-shirts, natch.

Beard Papa
2167 Broadway (@ 76th) 212-799-3770
www.muginohointl.com (Upper West Side: 1 to 79th St)
Beard Papa represents a major technological advance in the annals of cream puffery. After your order is placed, a feminine creampuffologist pulls a handle on a custom-built machine, inseminating Beard Papa's patented pie crust lined with puff pastry shell with the custard filling of your choice. Be prepared, because the second you take a bite, a couple of tablespoons of that custard will come glooping out the other end. Even if you plan on saving the bag for the old man fisherman logo, don't plan on carrying those suckers around all day. Like snowflakes, they're best consumed immediately.

Sweet Things Bake Shop
136 Avenue C (@ E 9th) 212-982-1714 (LES: L to 1st Ave St)
&
La Tiendita (inside the Essex St Market)
120 Essex St (@ Rivington St) 212-388-0449
(LES: F/J/M/Z to Delancey-Essex)
www.girlsclub.org/store
If you're like me, you've got a knee jerk reaction to any cookie that's done up to look like a purse or a high-heeled shoe. It's like, is this a cookie or a post-feminist insult? Well, you can put your knees down, Mother Jones. All proceeds of the Sweet Things Bake Shop go to the Lower East Side Girls' Club, whose youthful members are learning the ins and outs of making dough by baking dough. It must be working, as they've branched out into Fair Trade chocolate and Latin-influenced handicrafts. One step closer to world domination.

Moishe's Homemade Kosher Bake Shop
115 2nd Ave (@ E 7th St) 212-505-8555
(East Village: 6 to Astor Pl)
Picture a chihuahua in a tricorn hat. Now put some jelly on it and take away the chihuahua. That's how's big

Moishe's hamentaschen pastry is. Another of the few remaining hold outs from 2nd Avenue's glory days as the Broadway of Yiddish Theater.

D'Aiuto Pastry Corporation
405 8th Ave (btwn 30th & 31st) 212-564-7136
www.newyorknewyorkcheesecake.com
(Chelsea: A/C/E to 34th St)
Also known as Baby Watson's, thanks to aggressive signage to that effect which I first noticed as a visitor to New York. It still applies. Yes, there really was a Baby Watson. He got a cheesecake named after him, and grew up to take over the family business. His signature product is quite delicious, though vegans may want to give this joint a miss as there's not much there for them beyond coffee and t-shirts depicting Baby Watson's infant self lounging nude on a—problematic, I would assume—fur rug.

The Hungarian Pastry Shop
1030 Amsterdam Ave (btwn 110th & 111th) 212-866-4230
(Morningside Hts: 1 to 110th St)
The stick-up-the-bum formality of Budapest's most celebrated pastry cafe made it difficult for me to savor my pousse-café whilst traveling abroad. I'm far more at ease in the blood red murk of the Hungarian Pastry Shop, surrounded by Columbia students debating Heidegger and flirting whilst I hork down a $3 hazelnut confection that looks like a chocolate dipped...Baby Ruth. A really big one. Oh, speaking of which, go to the bathroom, because the graffiti is wall-to-wall brilliant.

Steve's Key Lime Pie
204 Van Dyke Street
(btwn Conover and Ferris, Red Hook, Bklyn) 718-858-5333
www.stevesauthentic.com (Red Hook: B61 Bus to Van Dyke St)
If Captain Ahab can drag the crew of the Pequod from here to Xmas in pursuit of a great white whale, surely you can get your butt on the B61 bus to Red Hook for some honest-to-god key lime pie. (Though keep your eyes peeled for Steve's vintage delivery vehicle. You may be able to score some at a street fair.) The bad news is it'll ruin you for anyone else's key lime pie. The good news is Red Hook has incredible views of the Statue of Liberty, and free weekend water taxi rides back to Manhattan, courtesy of Ikea. If no one is around when you come in, don't be shy. That bell's not just for show.

LaGuli
2915 Ditmars Blvd (btwn 29th St & 31st St, Astoria, Queens) 718-728-5612
www.laguli.com (Astoria: N to Ditmars Blvd)
LaGuli has amazing canolis, cheesecakes big and little, Italian cookies, almond horns, all sorts of pastries, *and* Italian ices. – Josh Medsker

Ice Cream

Chinatown Ice Cream Factory
65 Bayard St (btwn Mott & Elizabeth) 212-608-4170
www.chinatownicecreamfactory.com

(Chinatown: J/M/Z/N/Q /R/6 to Canal)
If you order the chocolate fucking chip, I swear to god, I'll grab the nearest switchblade and do unto your nose as Roman Polanksi's henchman character did unto Jack Nicholson's. This is Chinatown! Don't be part of the bovine vanilla menace. Get the lychee. Get the red bean!

The Big Gay Ice Cream Truck
www.biggayicecreamtruck.com
Inspired hand-mixed flavor awaits you at the end of this big gay rainbow, which is often to be found brightening the northwestern reaches of Union Square. (Check the website for the daily coordinates) Even though it would mean sacrificing our fix, I'm rooting for the big gay ice cream man to take his truck on a cross country trip to spread tolerance, up the national ice cream ante, and terrorize the bigots.

Lula's Sweet Apothecary
516 E 6th St (btwn Ave A & B)
www.lulassweetapothecary.com (East Village: L to 1st Ave)
Lula's was the first all-vegan ice cream joint to open here in NYC. (Do we have more than one? Yes we do, thanks for asking!) It's olde time soda shoppe meets East Village hip, in the very best of ways. You will always find one of the charming and interesting owners behind the counter, scooping out flavors like Gingersnap, Green Juice, Peanut Butter, or whatever else they've whipped up that day. (Of course everything is made in-house, so flavors change frequently.) If you're not feeling like a scoop, you could go for their phenomenal, soon-to-be-if-not-already famous soft serve. And if you don't want ice cream at all, they also carry a range of delectable vegan sweet treats like Sweet and Sara marshmallows and chocolate bars I've never seen anywhere else. Despite its diminutive size, Lula's just may be the ultimate vegan sugar-coma destination. – Melissa Bastian

Nino's Pizzeria
131 Saint Marks Place (@ Ave A) 212-979-8688
ninospizzany.com (East Village: F/M to 2nd Ave)
Shout out to the soft serve machine that consoled my pregnant heiner after midnight when all my cronies were out tossing back the delicious, healing alcohols. Back in the day, a portion twice the size of Mr. Softee's went for a buck. Now it's the prices that are doubled, but it's still an inexpensive lick to take to Tompkins Square across the street. They also sell pizza by the slice, but save room for dessert by starting with it.

Penny Licks
158 Bedford Ave (@ N 8th St, Williamsburg, Bklyn) 718-384-0158
(Williamsburg: L to Bedford Ave)
The "penny lick" at Penny Licks does not, unfortunately, cost a penny. But it only costs a dollar. What is it? A lil' scoop of ice cream on top of the cutest ice cream cone you ever saw! – Melissa Bastian

Rice Pudding

Rice Pudding from East Village Pizza & Kebabs
145 1st Ave (@ 9th St) 212-529-4545
www.eastvillagepizza.net (East Village: 6 to Astor Pl)
Remember what I just said about saving room for dessert? Two blocks away from Nino's is East Village Pizza & Kebabs. It forms a triangle with yet another by-the-slice place, Stromboli's, on St. Mark's and 1st, which some say has better pizza, but I have no opinion, as my loyalty is pledged to he who has the rice pudding. My late grandmother would have been devastated had she known a New York City pizza-by-the-slice place makes rice pudding better than hers. On the other hand, she'd most definitely approve of the bargain price, the generous serving size, and the reusable aluminum tin in which it is served.

Egg Cream

Ray's Candy Store
113 Ave A (btwn 7th St and St Marks Pl) 212-505-7609
www.myspace.com/rayscandystore
(East Village: F to 2nd Ave)
I've been pulled toward egg creams ever since reading an article about them in *Dynamite* magazine at an impressionable age. There sure is a lot of debate about the proper way to make one given the paucity of ingredients (seltzer, chocolate syrup, milk...no eggs). Actually, I guess the same holds true for martinis. Many contenders vie for the crown, and I've never had a bad one, but a truly atmospheric choice is to get one from Ray's, a magazine stand so unpretentious that it's never bothered to advertise its real name. Maybe it will now that Ray came perilously close to closing his doors in Xmas '09, after 35 years of service. A bunch of neighbors and longtime customers made a concerted effort to keep him afloat.

CAFES

Even if you don't drink coffee, we know you're eager to find a place where you can hole up with your notebook, sketchpad or laptop for a couple of hours.

Planet • El Super • Smoke • Crooklyn • Tootsie •

MANHATTAN

Chinatown

Silk Road Café
30 Mott St (btwn Mosco & Pell) 212-766-8665
(Chinatown: J/M/Z/N/Q /R/6 to Canal St)
They have tables both inside and out. One guy I knew pretty much sat at the outside tables all day. – Victoria Law (Bring your student ID and they'll knock a couple of quarters off your bubble tea. – AH)

Lower East Side/East Village

88 Orchard
88 Orchard St (at Broome) 212-228-8880
www.88orchard.tumblr.com
(LES: F/J/M/Z to Delancey-Essex)
Perennially packed, the ground floor is in "café in sunny corner, everyone can see me" mode, unless it's raining or you've been relegated to the additional basement seating at the bottom of steps so steep you should probably have a game plan for which you'll save if you trip, your coffee or your laptop.

Cake Shop
152 Ludlow St (btwn Stanton and Rivington), 212-253-0036
www.cake-shop.com (LES: F/J/M/Z to Delancey-Essex)
Cake Shop has hosted many an endless night of drawing and school work for me in the past few years, and they're guaranteed to be playing good music all night. Open til 2am, free wifi, and the kind of barista you can happily pass the time staring at to avoid work. – Caitlin McGurk (Cake Shop's ground floor has a vintage rec room feel. I know I'm supposed to be hunched over my computer but the flimsy wood paneling and all those old album covers make me want to slow dance. There's even a raised conversation pit type thing in the back. Hungry? They have a full compliment of sandwiches named for famous musical Micks, including Jones, Ronson, and Fleetwood. – AH) (You can also buy used records there, have a grownup beverage, or see a cool band downstairs. I've sat there on my laptop for hours! – Dear Drunk Girl)

Earth Matters
177 Ludlow St (btwn Houston and Stanton) 212-475-4180
www.earthmatters.com (LES: F to 2nd Ave)
I am partial to the upstairs segment of Earth Matters. The coffee and tea is expensive but you can sit there forever. - Matana Roberts (I tend to think of this more as a health food store with seating and free wifi, but it's true, you can hang out forever! So long that when you start feeling guilty and/or hungry you can order something much more nutritious than a scone. – AH)

Sugar Café
200 Allen St (@ Houston) 212-260-1122
www.sugarcafenyc.com (LES: F/M to 2nd Ave)
This 24-hour restaurant is so narrow, the windows so floor to ceiling, that pretty much anywhere you sit, you're going to get an in-your-face Allen St view to rival the up-close-and-personal, other-side-of-the-glass orangutan action of the Prospect Park Zoo. Particularly good when it's raining, snowing, or sleeting—anything that causes passerby's umbrellas to assume the inside-out position. Speaking of the zoo, there's some anthropological fun to be had out on the sidewalk, peering in at everyone tapping away on their laptops (free wifi, but oh, the glare). For such an exposed establishment, they're pretty lax about appearances, gnarly bar rags and the lit-from-behind artworks' electrical cords left out for all to see, along with a hastily handwritten sign stating that Bathroom is For Customers ONLY. (I guess that one makes sense.) They've got burgers, big salads, and, notably, breakfast-served-in-perpetuity. Price-wise, unless it's pouring and/or the dead of night, I'd rather save a couple bucks by trying my luck else-

where. No foam rubber. Lots of the title ingredient.

Native Bean Coffee and Tea
49 1/2 First Ave (@ 3rd St) 212-533-9948
(East Village: F/M to 2nd Ave)
The guys behind the counter exude warmth, and they try to remember your order by your second visit. I'm a big fan of their vegan tofu, which more or less mimics egg salad and is delish. It's a little pricey at $4.99, but they overstuff it and it fills your belly. My spouse hearts their egg and cheese on a roll. I also appreciate that they know the sweetener goes in the tea before the water, and they do it for you behind the counter. They have free wifi, and the unmatched tables and chairs are comfortable enough. It would be nice if there were more power outlets, but that's my only complaint. - Jenna Freedman (Cushy window seats and lots of sunlight make this cafe ideal for drawing or reading. The surrounding neighborhood is fun to explore, and of course, the people-watching is good. – Becky Hawkins)

Ninth St Espresso
700 E. 9th St (btwn Ave C & Ave D) 212-358-9225
(East Village: L to 1st Ave)
&
341 E. 10th St. (btwn Ave A & Ave B) 212-777-3508
(East Village: L to 1st Ave)
&
Chelsea Market, 75 9th Ave (@ 15th St) 212-228-2930
(Chelsea: A/C/E/L to 14th St-8th Ave)
www.ninthstreetespresso.com

Ninth St Espresso is not cheap at all. Go after you sell a few zines. Worth it! – Andria Alefhi (Ooh, they make fancy designs in the cappuccino foam! And around 5pm, in the Chelsea Market, it's quite the scene. - AH)

Café Pick Me Up
145 Ave A (@ 9th St) 212-673-7231
(East Village: L to 1st Ave)
Café Pick Me Up pulls off a homemade Café Reggio vibe. Many of the habitués exhibit the pallor of those who spend a considerable amount of time in terminally underlit surroundings, taking themselves very seriously. I appreciate that sort of darkness in a café, especially when I've got a lot of time to kill. I'm also a fan of rickety chairs. On gorgeous days, there's a lot of competition for the open-air sidewalk seating along Avenue A, where addled scruffies patrol the other side of the barrier, shouting, sparechanging, and receiving transmissions from their home planets. It's possible to split the difference by sit-

ting just inside the floor to ceiling windows, which open to the elements, European-style.

Ost Café
441 East 12th St (@ Ave A) 212-477-5600
www.ostcafenyc.com (East Village: L to 1st Ave)
Ost turns out to be a very civilized sort of place, and a gracious, large windowed base in which to take in the beauty of an East Village snowstorm. There were others who would have gladly taken my place, of course, which is good for the café, not so much for marathon sitters like me. The waitress will remove your small-ish (but while it still contains liquid, expertly brewed) cup after a couple of hours, but no one will be so rude as to suggest it's time to disconnect from the teat of their free wifi and hit the road.

Ciao for Now
523 E 12th St (btwn Ave A & Ave B) 212-677-2616
www.ciaofornow.net (East Village: L to 1st Ave)
So what if the proprietors aren't the first East Village couple to name their baby Django? They've got fine coffee, delicious pastries and sandwiches and the counter staff knows how to be nice to kids. Go here for the food and the friendlys, not to skulk on your laptop. They make it easy for you by hiding the outlets. The only front-of-the-counter one I can suss services a vintage TV whose programming had been replaced with a working aquarium. (Ciao for Now also runs a pleasant little outpost in the back of Sustainable NYC, the eco-friendly emporium at 139 Avenue A, 212-254-5400)

The B Cup
212 Ave B (@ 13th) 212-228-4808
Outside of its name, do I even like the B Cup? I can't quite get a grip on their tacky looking pay-per-minute-Internet setup when the Tompkins Square branch library is right down the street and the café's wifi is itself free. I'm also no fan of the way the staff comes swooping around the counter, as if I might pocket my cup now that its down to just dregs and foam. That said, I do sort of like The B Cup. I like the orangey lighting, and the little nook back behind the bathroom where you can sort of hide out, provided your back doesn't go into a spasm on the broke ass loveseats they've got crammed in there. They definitely win the prize for the least inviting thrift store furniture. Good salads, though!

Simone Martini Bar
34 1st Ave (@ 6th St) 212-982-6665
www.simonemartinibar.com (East Village: F to 2nd Ave)

& Candle • The Goodbye Girl • Step Right

Forgive me, I have to include this place, because out of the ten East Village cafes I reviewed over ten years ago in East Village Inky #3, it is one of only two who are still with us. (The other is Café Pick Me Up.) That's shocking. How can this be the one to excape the ax? Back in the day, it was called Simone Espresso and Wine Bar, and it seemed very unlikely that it would last a year. Its espresso was fine, but its gilt mirrored, red walled, black laquered Orientalist Bordello in old New Orleans pose seemed like such an unappetizing one. The neighborhood was already supporting Lucky Cheng's, a drag-queen staffed restaurant that's a fave with the bachelorette party crowd (also still kicking). I don't get it. And yet, here it is. I suspect Simone's survival owes to a well-timed name change.

Cha-An Tea House

230 E 9th St, 2nd fl (btwn 2nd & 3rd Ave) 212-228-8030
www.chaanteahouse.com

My friend Amy tried to take me here at least three times, and every time there was a private party or a long wait and we wound up elsewhere. I had written it off, but she kept telling me how much I'd like it. Finally she insisted we try again and we were one of two occupied tables. The prices for small portions can be a bit much, but the tea is well worth it on its own and some of the desserts are great. Inside, the place looks just like a teahouse in Japan, and we hung out for ages without receiving any dirty looks when asking for teapot refills. – Shayna Marchese

The Bowery Poetry Club

308 Bowery (btwn Bleecker and E. 1st St) 212-614-0505
www.bowerypoetry.com

The Bowery Poetry Club has a little café in the front section where you can get fair-trade coffee & Lower East Side Girls Club chocolate bars! – Fly

Saint's Alp Teahouse

39 3rd Ave (btwn 9th and 10th St) 212-598-1890,
(East Village: 6 to Astor Pl)
&
164 Bedford Ave (btwn 7th and 8th St, Williamsburg, Bklyn) 718-486-3888
(Williamsburg: L to Bedford Ave)
www.saintsalp.com.hk

Japanese club kids and Middle Schoolers aren't the only ones hooked on highly sugared tapioca pearl tea. The East Village branch of this Hong Kong chain are early NYC *boba* pioneers, though now, of course, rabbit turds you suck through an oversized straw (fun!) are a common feature of pretty much every Vietnamese sandwich shop and Chinatown bakery. It's a step up to have it here though

You'll feel like you're playing tea party—the portions are so ladylike and everything served just so, in plump little pots and on compact, napkin-topped plates. Indulge in the full golden age of jet travel meets hipsterville experience with dainties like tea eggs, deep fried cuttlefish balls, or toasts topped with butter and condensed milk, or act like you're in a real restaurant by ordering a heartier noodle dish.

NoHo

The Yippie Museum Café

9 Bleecker St (btwn Lafayette and the Bowery) 212-677-5918
www.yippiemuseum.org (NoHo: B/D/F/M/6 to Broadway-Lafayette/Bleecker)

Yes, as in Abbie Hoffman. Go here for $1 cups of coffee or tea and unlimited loitering near the banner that Abbie and friends unfurled over Wall Street. – Kate Black (The Yippie Café is staunchly egalitarian. If you're having trouble booking a venue for your event, be it a reading, a performance, or an act of a musical nature, try snagging an available space on their online calendar, first come first serve. Charge whatever cover you like, but be ready to fork over half the bread, man. – AH)

Greenwich Village

Think Coffee

248 Mercer (btwn 3rd St & 4th Street) 212-228-6226
(Greenwich Village: B/D/F/M to Broadway-Lafayette)
&
1 Bleecker (btwn Bowery & Elizabeth St) 212-533-3366

(NoHo: B/D/F/M to Broadway-Lafayette)
&
123 4th Ave (btwn E 12th & E 13th St) 212-614-6644
(East Village: L/N/Q /R/4/5/6 to Union Sq)
www.thinkcoffeenyc.com
All three locations will let you sit there pretty much forever. The only problem with this is that the NYU students know it, and they camp! This can make it hard to get a seat. But Think is worth it—they source their coffees, milks, and foods responsibly, and give back to the communities in which they do business. And vegans, take note: there's always soymilk right there on the bar. No special requests, no extra charges. The Bowery and Mercer locations also have beer and wine, free live music as well as speakers and art shows. – Melissa Bastian

Oren's Daily Roast
31 Waverly Pl (btwn Greene St & University Pl)
212-338-0014
(Greenwich Village: A/C/E/B/D/F/M to W 4th St)
&
434 3rd Ave (btwn 30th St & 31st St) 212-779-1241
(Murray Hill: 6 to 28th St)
&
830 3rd Ave (btwn E 50th & E 51st St) 212-308-2148
(Midtown: E/M/6 to Lexington-51st St)
&
(and other locations throughout the city)
www.orensdailyroast.com
I am fond of Oren's Daily Roast. They also source their beans responsibly and drinks are usually priced a full dollar cheaper than $tarbucks - which is nice, as in Midtown they are pretty much the only alternative to that ubiquitous megacorp. – Melissa Bastian

Café Reggio
119 MacDougal St (btwn Bleecker & W 3rd St) 212-475-9557
www.cafereggio.com
(Greenwich Village: A/B/C/D/E/F/M to W 4th St)
This ancient, dark café is the real Village McCoy. Its hulking steampunk of an espresso machine reported for duty years before the Beats discovered bongos. It's the perfect place to sit scribbling in your notebook or reading *The Evergreen Review*, except it's so damn dark, you're probably better off just staring moodily into the middle distance. As far as its acting chops, Café Reggio was damn good in *Next Stop Greenwich Village*. Check out the scene where young-but-already-preternaturally-creepy Christopher Walken gets his comeuppance. And make sure you go to the bathroom. I'm not going to spoil the surprise by saying why.

Esperanto
114 MacDougal St (btwn Bleecker & W 3rd St)
212-475-8900
www.esperantocafe.com
(Greenwich Village: A/B/C/D/E/F/M to W 4th St)
Esperanto is a Seattle-style café like all us old hipsters grew up with! They let you sit after your coffee/tea is done and read the paper, or whatever. – Josh Medsker

'sNice
45 8th Ave (@ 4th St) 212-645-0310
(Greenwich Village: A/C/E/L to 14th St-8th Ave)
&
315 5th Ave
(btwn 2nd & 3rd St, Park Slope, Bklyn) 718-788-2121
(Park Slope: M/R to Union St)
'sNice in Park Slope is a really cozy place. Only some of the tables are available for computer use and there's no internet, but they'll leave you alone for a good long while. It's a good energy and space. – Megan Garrity

Grey Dog
90 University Pl (btwn 11th St & 12th St) 212-414-4739
www.thegreydog.com (Greenwich Village: 4/5/6/L/N/Q /R to Union Sq)
Grey Dog is a tiny, packed coffee shop with delicious veggie sandwiches and coffee and worth the (sometimes) wait for a table. – Megan Garrity

Chelsea

Buon Italia
Chelsea Market, 75 9th Ave (@15th, in Chelsea Market) 212-633-9090
www.buonitalia.com (Chelsea: A/C/E/L to 14th St-8th Ave)
This tiny *gelateria* and café fronting the Chelsea Market's Buon Italia grocery has only 5 tables marooned on a brightly lit platform by the olive oil, but it's a good place to get a little free wifi. I've sat here by myself for nearly two hours on occasion. It's in their best interest to let customers sit until long after those guilty feelings have commenced to tug. It might translate to picking up some almond paste, a sprig of just-picked olives, a bottle of imported anchovies, a Kinder-egg, some squid ink pasta and a spray that supposedly mimics the flavor of fresh basil.

Paradise Café
141 8th Ave (btwn 16th & 17th St) 212- 647-0066
(Chelsea: A/C/E/L to 14th St-8th Ave)
The wonderfully funky little Paradise Cafe is relatively narrow, so busy mornings can be quite bustling. There

Quicksilver (obviously shot in San Francisco in

are a couple of chalkboards up by the register outlining the cafe's rules: If you order using Starbucks lingo, they'll charge you Starbucks prices. "Regular" means different things to different people; say exactly what you want. The staff knows they're wonderful; you don't need to tell them. – Heath Row

Café Grumpy
224 W. 20th St (btwn 7th and 8th Ave) 212-255-5511 (Chelsea: 1/9 to 23rd St)
193 Meserole Ave (btwn Diamond & Jewel, Greenpoint, Bkly) 718-349-7623 (Greenpoint: G to Greenpoint Ave) &
383 7th Ave (btwn 11th and 12th St, Park Slope Bkln) 718-499-4404 (Park Slope: F/G to 7th Ave)
www.cafegrumpy.com
The Greenpoint Grump is light and open, with an interesting orange color scheme and about 10 small tables. It's on the top of my short list of comfortable places to work. The wifi is a little slow, but one can't complain about what's free. And their coffee—$1.25 a mug—is great. The proprietors hang out at the big corner table, and are friendly enough. The other two locations aren't as distressed or lived-in as the Meserole St home base, and they don't have wifi. The Chelsea shop's innovation is to weigh out the beans needed for your order and grind them before brewing. – Heath Row. (A mug featuring their disgruntled logo-head could make a nice souvenir for those who find it difficult to parade around with a smiley face anything. – AH)

Central Park

Café in the Central Park Boat House
East 72nd St & 5th Ave, Central Park, 212-517-2233
www.thecentralparkboathouse.com
(Upper East Side: 6 to 68th St)
Have no money for $29 entrees, but want to sit, eat a sandwich, drink hot chocolate, and have a view of the lake by the Boat House, anyway? AND be able to sit as long as you want without a Human Penguin giving you dirty looks? The Café in the Central Park Boat House has seats for the Modern Proletariat. I once sat there, carefree and food-free, for at least two and a half hours chatting with friends, myself getting not even a Poland Spring while they ordered a large chocolate chip cookie and French fries (not more than three to four dollars each.) – Ling Teo

Morningside Heights

Hungarian Pastry Shop
1030 Amsterdam Ave (btwn 111th St & Cathedral Pkwy)
212-866-4230 (Morningside Hts: B/C/1 to Cathedral Pkwy)
You can sit there forever. They would love that! Bring your paper, your homework...I knew a professor who held office hours there! –Jerry the Mouse

Washington Heights

Buenos Días Bakery Cafe
1486 Saint Nicholas Ave (btwn 184th & 185th St)
212-923-0202 www.buenosdiasbakerycafe.com
(Washington Hts: 1 to 181st St)
I do sketching there sometimes—that's how cool they are with your hanging out. –Jerry the Mouse

El Grullon Bakery
1493 St. Nicholas Ave (btwn W 184th & W 185th Sts)
212-923-0098 (Washington Heights: 1 to 181st St)
Fabulous everything, and the best coffee ever. If you ever

want good coffee, you MUST go to a Dominican bakery, because everything else pales in comparison. – Jerry the Mouse

BROOKLYN

Phoebe's Café
323 Graham Ave (Btwn Ainslie & Devoe, Williamsburg, Bklyn) 718-599-3218
www.phoebescafe.com (Williamsburg: L to Graham Ave)
Sit forever, they don't care in the least – Megan Garrity

The Rabbit Hole
352 Bedford Ave (btwn S 4th and S 3rd St, Williamsburg, Bklyn) 718-782-0910, www.rabbitholebakery.com
The Rabbit Hole is a restaurant in the back and a cafe in the front. Since it's a little out of the way, way down Bedford near the Williamsburg bridge), you can sit a long time. It's a nice place. – Dear Drunk Girl (A good place to go when you're in the mood to branch out from the funky and mismatched, though I wouldn't go during boom time brunch or dinner hours, unless you announce plans to tip like you're a four-top with Eggs Benedict and Bloody Marys all around. I like their Farenheit 451, a reanimating tincture of coffee, espresso and mocha. - AH)

Café Orwell
247 Varet St (btwn White St & Bogart St, Bushwick, Bklyn) 347-294-4759 (Bushwick: L to Morgan)
A laptop-using crowd escapes the confines of its respective apartments here during the day. Its nighttime programming is so robust it puts me in mind of the library in an off-season tourist town. Apparently keeping the locals happy and occupied is something Café Orwell takes very seriously. It didn't take them long at all to inaugurate a monthly reading series, Sunday night BYOB film screenings, and Bushfolk, a twice-monthly musical gathering.

Tiny Cup Cafe
279 Nostrand Ave (btwn Clifton Pl & Lafayette Ave, Bedford-Stuyvesant, Bklyn) 718-399-9200
(Bed-Stuy: G to Bedford-Nostrand Aves)
Sit until your ass gets tired / no rules. – Robyn Jordan

Outpost
1014 Fulton St (between Grand & Downing, Bedford-Stuyvesant, Bklyn) 718-636-1260
www.outpostlounge.com
This is a nice coffee shop on the cusp of Fort Greene in Bed-Stuy. It doesn't seem to be propagated as a queer business, but honey, it is queer-run, and very queer-friendly. They offer a vast array of local queer rags (Go,

HX, and more) and it's very important for me to have something like this in my neighborhood. Inside you'll find people of all identities. While hanging here, I often feel a positive connection to the neighborhood, whereas a lot of new businesses in Bed-Stuy feel awkward and removed. Also, there is also a nice back patio, wifi and a full bar! I sit here all day, basically. And they love it even if I just order one chai latte! – Cristy Road

Gorilla Coffee
97 5th Ave (btwn Park Pl & Warren, Park Slope, Bklyn) 718-230-3244, www.gorillacoffee.com
Strong fair trade coffee with loud music and an atmosphere of artsy concentration. Feel free to sit there with your journal or sketchpad for hours, if you can find a seat. The free wi-fi often fills the place up with 20- and 30-somethings on laptops. – Becky Hawkins

Flying Saucer
494 Atlantic Ave (btwn Nevins and 3rd Ave, Boerum Hill, Bklyn) 718-624-0139
(Boerum Hill: B/D/M/N/R Q /2/3/4/5 to Atlantic Ave-Pacific St)
This coffeehouse is my personal favorite for its comfy couches, fun music, colorful decor, laidback vibe, back-garden seating, and cute baristas/clientele. The menu includes coffee, tea, sandwiches and munchies. Best enjoyed in conjunction with a walk to Bergen St. Comics or the Salvation Army. – Becky Hawkins (If you've got a spare alien laying around that you no longer have use for, I'm sure the staff would be happy to stick it on their tip jar. They've got wifi, and such a lax attitude about customers hanging out all damn day that it's usually possible to move to a table near a coveted outlet or extension cord before the battery runs out. – AH)

Muppets Take Manhattan • Hamlet (directed

Tillie's
248 Dekalb Ave (btwn Clermont & Vanderbilt, Fort Greene, Bklyn) 718-783-6140, www.tilliesofbrooklyn.com (Fort Greene: C to Lafayette Ave)
Good music, quirky architecture and proximity to Pratt Institute give this coffeeshop a studious, artsy vibe. The menu includes coffee, food, baked goods and Italian sodas. – Becky Hawkins (Sometimes less studious, but no less artsy, when the mommies of Fort Greene descend with their strollers, and why wouldn't they? The café goes out of its way to provide things kids like to eat. – AH)

QUEENS

Communitea
47-02 Vernon Blvd (@ 47th Ave) Long Island City, Queens) 718-729-7708
www.communitea.net (LIC: 7 to Vernon-Jackson Ave)
Communitea is an awesome coffee place, and they have a whole wall of tea! They also have paninis and salads and the usual coffeehouse stuff. The super high ceilings and big windows are one of the main reasons I go there. That and the coffee! Check out the crazy artwork on the window. Apparently someone tagged it with a glass cutter, so the owner had to go and paint over it to make it look planned. - Josh Medsker (If you're sick of your reading material, Communitea has a swap shelf. I wish they'd reinstate their grand social experiment of letting customers name their own price for paninis, salads, and sandwiches on Wednesday evenings. – AH)

Waltz Astoria
23-14 Ditmars Blvd (Btwn 23rd & 24th St, Astoria, Queens) 718-95-MUSIC
www.waltz-astoria.com (Astoria: N to Ditmars Blvd). Waltz Astoria is great. They have open-mic nights, comedy nights, music, etc... You can sit for long after your drink is finished and read. They also have books for sale when you walk in, and a little outdoor seating. – Josh Medsker

Bookstores Harboring Cafes

Bluestockings Bookstore & Café
172 Allen St (btwn Rivington & Stanton) 212-777-6028
www.bluestockings.com (LES: F/M to 2nd Ave)
The hushed seats that line the window serve as a safe haven from all those noisy, impossible relationship post-mortems going on in other LES cafes as if thespeakers were in their own personal living rooms. (Which they

sort of are.) At Bluestockings, you may overhear the odd tidbit about organizing sex workers or what should be done about an insensitive collective member's revealing breach of gender-un-neutrality, but balls-out yapping is rare. You certainly won't hear any such thing coming out of Foxy, the unbearably cute canine volunteer. The eats are pretty Spartan—vegan multigrainish sprouted Rice Krispy square type things – but the Fair Trade coffee's a non-medicinal virtue, and the tea has obviously been selected by someone who cares about such things.

Housing Works Bookstore Café
126 Crosby St (btwn Houston & Prince) 212-334-3324
www.housingworks.org/bookstore
(SoHo: B/D/F/M to Broadway/Lafayette)
The coffee's affordable. There are a limited but quality range of snacks made by cafe volunteers. Profits go to people living with HIV/AIDS. And there are a lot of used books in close proximity. GOOD used books. – Kate Black (They are great!! You can sit there for a month and they will not bother you. Reasonable prices, restrooms, books—yeah!—I fckn love that place! – Fly) (Factor in free wifi, limited outlets, shared tables and knishes from nearby Yonah Schimmel. – AH)

Books of Wonder
18 W 18th St (btwn 5th Ave & Ave Of The Americas) 212-989-3270
www.booksofwonder.com & www.cupcakecafe-nyc.com (Flatiron: F/M/L to 14th St-6th Ave)
This is a children's book store, and as such their outpost of the Cupcake Café is no place to seek hours of tranquil concentration. But if you are traveling with children, you probably need a triple espresso by now.

Kinokuniya
1073 Avenue of the Americas (btwn 40th & 41st St) 212-869-1700, www.bookweb.kinokuniya.co.jp (Midtown: B/D/F/M/7 to 42nd St-Bryant Park)
Upstairs in this Japanese bookstore is a little café with fish sandwiches, dessert and coffee drinks. Since Coliseum Books closed, the neighborhood was in desperate need for a coffee shop. – Amanda Plumb (It's actually a branch of Café Zaiya, of Mochi Doughnut fame! – AH)

Hue-Man Bookstore & Café
2319 Frederick Douglass Blvd (Between 124th and 125th St) 212-665-7400, www.huemanbookstore.com
(Harlem: A/B/C/D to 125th St)
My system of breaking up working in a café with a little literary reward can kind of backfire when the café is in

a bookstore, and what's on the shelves beckons more interesting than the article I'm in the middle of. Hue-Man shelves some small-press things I'm unlikely to stumble upon elsewhere. – AH (Hue-Man is a great place to hang out when you're waiting to go to the movies at the Magic Johnson Theater. I like the coffee, and the pastries are pretty good. It's kind of upscale-ish, but it's nice. And they let you use the bathroom, which counts for a lot. – Jerry the Mouse)

Every Thing Goes Book Café and Neighborhood Stage
208 Bay St (btwn Victory Blvd and Hannah St, New Brighton, Staten Island)
www.etgstores.com/bookcafe
(walk from Staten Island Ferry or SIR to Tompkinsville)
There is a community of people (okay, it's totally a cult: www.ganas.org) in Staten Island who own three businesses and a whole bunch of houses. Since Staten Island doesn't have that much going on, if you want to go thrifting, or get some coffee at a non-chain, or buy a used futon, you're probably going to end up at one of their establishments. The first area of the shop is a café that serves decent drinks and snacks like bagels and fresh pies from the local farmer's market. The back of the shop and the entire upstairs area is devoted to used books, DVDs and VHS movies, and a small selection of old albums. The place is kind of a trip, but in a good way. – Kelly McClure

Bars

MANHATTAN

Chinatown

169 Bar
169 E Broadway (btwn Essex & Jefferson) 212-473-8866
www.169barnyc.com (Chinatown: F to East Broadway)
Back before it was a *Flight of the Conchords* exterior, 169 was an excellent end-of-the-evening dive in which to get a jump on the next day's hangover remedy with multiple baskets of free, alcohol absorbing popcorn. I hope its hipster street cred doesn't go to its head.

Lower East Side

Mehanata Bulgarian Bar
113 Ludlow St (btwn Rivington & Delancey) 212-625-0981
www.mehanata.com (LES: F/J/M/Z to Delancey-Essex)
My kind of party! Yours too, if you share my predilec-

tion for dancing around to gypsy wedding music, and circused-out Balkan brass! The only thing wrong with this party is it doesn't start hopping 'til late, and I get sleepy. Eugene Hutz from Gogol Bordello DJs here when not on tour.

Fontana's
105 Eldridge St (btwn Broome & Grand) 212-334-6740
www.fontanasnyc.com (LES: B/D to Grand)
This is a great rock and roll bar. It's got horseshoe-shaped booths, a formidable jukebox, acres of room, and a certain amount of pridefulness with regard to its lack of pretension.

Welcome to the Johnson's
123 Rivington Street (btwn Essex St & Norfolk St)
212-420-9911 (LES: F/J/M/Z to Delancey-Essex)
Welcome to the Johnson's looks like my parents' house in the early '80s, if they'd hung out with scuzzy twenty-somethings and had a $2 cocktail happy hour. Good times! – Dear Drunk Girl (…though not on a weekend night when it's too packed and ick. But for non-typical drinking days, yes – Megan Garrity)

Happy Ending
302 Broome St (btwn Eldridge St & Forsyth St)
212-334-9676
www.happyendinglounge.com (LES: B/D to Grand St)
From the outside, Happy Ending is a nondescript little joint. It still bears the awning from its days as a "health club" (massage parlor). They host a number of independent reading and performance series. – Kate Black

Sid and Nancy • Do the Right Thing • Born

Rockwood Music Hall

196 Allen St (btwn Houston & Stanton) 212-477-4155
www.rockwoodmusichall.com (LES: F/M to 2nd Ave)
Similar to Toad in Cambridge, Massachusetts, Rockwood is a comfortable, cozy venue that focuses its attention on the music. About twice the size of Toad, the Rockwood feels more open and airy, but the limited table seating can feel relatively cramped when it's flush against the stage. With no cover charge, the venue makes do with a one-drink minimum and by passing a pail for donations to the bands. It's not a bad method. The beer list is ample, and a bottle of Sierra Nevada will run you $6. The wine list is also surprisingly solid. It's the kind of place you can stop by any night of the week and find something going on. – Heath Row

Local 269

269 E. Houston St (btwn Ave A & Ave B) 212-228-9874
Web (East Village: F/J/M/Z to Delancey-Essex)
Local 269 is owned by two of the nicest Ireland replants I have ever met. – Matana Roberts

East Village

Mars Bar

25 E 1st St (@ 1st Ave), 212-473-9842
www.time2shine.com/mars.html (East Village: F/M to 2nd Ave)
Talk about divey. If truly grimy is what you're after, this is your place. It feels authentic and free from hype. Good for philanderers and folks nostalgic for the "old" East Village. - Robyn Jordan

d.b.a.

41 1st Ave (btwn 2nd & 3rd St) 212-475-5097
www.drinkgoodstuff.com (East Village: F/M to 2nd Ave)
Beer beer beer beer beer beer beer. If you love beer, you should come here—dozens of kinds to make you cheer! (And an outdoor garden and mad crowds, to name just two things that don't rhyme with beer. Swing by on the early end if the goal is to sit and converse like a normal human being.)

KGB Bar

85 E 4th St. (btwn 2nd and 3rd Ave), 212-505-3360
www.kgbbar.com (East Village: F/M to 2nd Ave)
What a history! The building in which it's housed was once the Ukrainian Labor Home, a socialist social club with its own speakeasy. Not to mention, a couple of years back, when I was performing in the theater downstairs, some guy slit his throat in KGB after a female improv comedian performing in the building's other theater gently rebuffed his confession of love! (He survived.) Even on a quiet night it's appealing and somewhat secret feeling, as befits its name. I like the sober party portraits, the high ceilings and the thick drapes. The unisex bathroom stalls are so dark, you risk falling into the toilet. Forget about refreshing your lipstick, unless you want to look like a clown. It's famous for its literary events.

Joe's Bar

520 E 6th St (btwn Ave A & Ave B) 212-473-9093
(East Village: F/J/M/Z to Delancey-Essex)
I won't tell you my favorite bar, for probably obvious reasons, but Joe's on 6th Street between 1st and A is pretty good, too. – Jenna Freedman

McSorley's Old Ale House

15 E 7th St (btwn 2nd and 3rd Ave) 212-473-9148
www.mcsorleysnewyork.com (East Village: 6 to Astor Pl)
This bar has been in operation since 1854, give or take. E.E. Cummings (yeah, yeah, capital letters) wrote a poem about the place. It has so much history, you can touch it. Hint: Don't. Look around at the pictures and magazine and newspaper clippings, the wishbones hanging from the light fixture, and the sign that offers what might be the best barroom rule ever: Be Good or Be Gone. Professor Seagull tippled here at least once, I'm sure. Beer-wise, the choices are simple: Light or dark. They brew their own, and for every beer you order, you get two glasses of the frothy goodness. I suggest you order half and half, one light and one dark. – Heath Row

Angel's Share

8 Stuyvesant St 2nd floor (@ 3rd Ave) 212-777-5415
(East Village: 6 to Astor Pl)
OMG, looks like you'll totally have to have your screeching bachelorette party elsewhere, Brittany! Angel's Share prohibits loud talking of any sort, so as not to distract those meditating on the zen perfection of their heavenly martinis. The name refers to the volume of distilled spirits lost to evaporation during the aging process. I think this means it's a place for those who don't mind behaving like grown-ups.

Grassroots Tavern

20 St. Marks Pl (btwn 2nd and 3rd Ave) 212-475-9443
(East Village: 6 to Astor Pl)
Attention real estate speculators! Forget about transforming this St Mark's Place hole into an American Apparel or an upscale yogurt chain. The scuzz factor is too high, and that's why we love it. Yes, even the bathrooms. Get a pitcher and gouge your name into the sticky wooden

in Flames • Rosemary's Baby • Party Girl •

table. Everyone else has.

Burp Castle
41 E 7th St (btwn 2nd & 3rd Ave) 212-982-4576
www.burpcastlenyc.wordpress.com
(East Village: 6 to Astor Pl)
If you like to explore various beers, especially Belgian
ales, go. They keep the bottles downstairs, and you have
to order a little in advance so the building's super, who
brings up the beer, doesn't have to make too many trips.
– Heath Row (They're chummy with the Pommes Frites
folks, and order some for all the patrons to share every
Sunday, Monday, and Wednesday, around cocktail hour. If
you've got something fermenting in your kitchen, come
to the New York City Home Brewer's Guild meeting here
every third Tuesday, starting around 7:30. – AH) (Nice selection, nice bartenders, and nice murals. Plus, the name.
– Marguerite Dabaie)

7B / Vazacs Horseshoe Bar
108 Avenue B (btwn 6th St & 7th St) 212-473-8840
(East Village: F/M to 2nd Ave)
I like the jukebox at 7B. – Josh Saitz (I like the cheap
breakfasts a block away at 7A. – AH)

Manitoba's
99 Ave B (btwn 6th & 7th St) 212-982-2511
www.manitobas.com
(East Village: F/J/M/Z to Delancey-Essex)
Manitoba's is run by Handsome Dick Manitoba of the legendary Dictators but I just don't hang out in bars. – Fly (I
was pleased to see them open on Thanksgiving Day, serving pumpkin pie during happy hour. – AH)

Decibel Sake Bar
240 E. 9th St (btwn 2nd and 3rd Ave) 212-979-2733
www.sakebardecibel.com (East Village: 6 to Astor Pl)
It's hard to accept that Decibel is really just an East Village basement. After spending time in both East Village
basements and Japanese izakaya, I'm pretty sure Decibel
is in Tokyo. It looks like it, and English is not necessarily
the default tongue, though if you're a sake newbie in need
of guidance, and your waitress doesn't have the fluency
to explain the choices to non-Japanese speakers, she'll
fetch a server who does. From the outside, it looks like
it could be a private club. It took me a long time to work
up the guts to enter, and an even longer-feeling time
for a table to open, but once installed in a booth in this
graffiti and sake label decorated cave, I was like, "Ooh,
I'm gonna come here every day!" If you missed your dinner (because you were waiting in line), it's easy (if a bit

expensive) to cobble together a meal from the Japanese
bar snack menu. Just don't think about how you'd escape
in case of fire.

Sing Sing Karaoke
81 Ave A (btwn 5th & 6th St) 212-674-0700
(East Village: F/M to 2nd Ave)
&
9 St. Mark's Pl (btwn 2nd & 3rd Ave) 212-387-7800
(East Village: 6 to Astor Pl)
www.karaokesingsing.com
So aptly named. There is a definite chance you will start
to feel as if you are in a maximum security prison being
tortured by corrections officers doing off-key renditions
of "Living on a Prayer." This might not seem like the hottest of hot spots in our fair city, but I promise it's well
worth the trip. With countless song binders of Top 40,
show tunes, rock, country *et al*, there really is something
for everyone. They even have Vampire Weekend. Don't expect cheap drinks, or strong ones. The wait to sing is long,
longer if you want a private room. – Genevieve Texeira

Lakeside Lounge
162 Ave B (@ 10th St) 212-529-8463
www.lakesidelounge.com (East Village: L to 1st Ave)
Lakeside Lounge has super-cheap cans of Beast and a
photobooth! – Megan Garrity (A photobooth that my children have been in many times. They also have a no nonsense stage for live music, up close and personal. – AH)

Banjo Jim's
700 E. 9th St (@ Ave C) 212-777-0869
www.banjojims.com (East Village: L to 1st Ave)
There are no hospitable, cheap NYC bars on weekend
nights, but if you're able to go out on a Monday, these
guys've got good live swing until 2am. – Victoria Law
(Melody Allegra Berger of *F-word* zine is a frequent fiddler
here. – AH)

Teneleven Bar
171 Ave C (btwn 10th & 11th St) 212-353-1011
(East Village: L to 1st Ave)
I recommend 10/11 because it has the Star Fucking Hipsters on the jukebox – Fly

HiFi
169 Ave A (btwn 10th and 11th) 212-420-8392
www.thehifibar.com (East Village: L to 1st Ave)
HiFi has a kick-ass jukebox—indie rock, punk, etc, and
the pool tables are usually free. – Josh Medsker (Grandma
here remembers when HiFi was Brownies, a legendary

Times Square • Coming to America • Rhinestone •

live music venue. HiFi's owned by one of the guys who owned Brownies, and his digitized music collection is what powers that jukebox. – AH)

Planet Rose
219 Ave. A (btwn 13th & 14th St.) 212-353-9500
www.planetrosenyc.com (East Village: L to 1st Ave)
Planet Rose would be your average dive bar if it weren't for the zebra print couches, red walls, and, oh yeah, the karaoke. There's no stage at this bar —when it's your turn you just grab a wireless mic and sing from anywhere. It's best on a weeknight when it's easy to take over the place with a group of friends. Songs are $2. On weeknights, the first song is free when you buy a drink. You can bring in food. No cover, but they do card. Warning: Broadway-wannabes frequent Planet Rose, and if you do not load the request board you may be stuck listening to "Suddenly Seymour" all night long. – Amanda Plumb

Otto's Shrunken Head
538 E. 14th St (btwn Ave A & B) 212-228-2240
www.ottosshrunkenhead.com (East Village: L to 1st Ave)
Otto's is one of the few venues left in the East Village where punks, rockabilly kids, goths, and art freaks can

still be found relaxing and performing in their natural habitat. A tiki den extraordinaire with Polynesian décor and stiff, fruity, flaming drinks, this place hosts an impressive array of local bands, comedians, open mics, and general neighborhood weirdness in it's tiny backroom while DJs spin classic tracks up front. – Emily Rems (Potent tiki drinks are about $10. Pang's Punch is the one with the glowstick, but the Zombies taste better. – Kate Black) (I do dream of queerifying Otto's. It's a pretty straight rockabilly tiki-themed dive bar, but the décor is to die for. The crowd is a diverse sub-cultural range fitting to its rockabilly, ska, metal, surf, and punk-themed nights. On soul/ska/reggae/dub night on Thursday, fantastic DJs who spin nothing but classics. The walls are covered in old Polynesian wallpaper, and other random tiki-objects, grass, sea creatures, animal prints, etc. The interior is cluttered to my preference and the blowfish lamps hanging over the bar are the most beautiful fixtures I've ever seen. – Cristy Road)

Crocodile Lounge
325 E 14th St (btwn 1st Ave & 2nd Ave) 212-477-7747
(East Village: L to 1st Ave)
&
Alligator Lounge
600 Metropolitan Ave (btwn Leonard St & Lorimer St, Williamsburg, Bkln) 718-599-4440
www.myspace.com/alligatorlounge
(Williamsburg: G/L to Metropolitan-Lorimer)
Both of these reptilian Lounges give you a free pizza with every pint you buy. The pints are overpriced, of course, and the pizza is shitty, but it's still a cheap way to "wine and dine." – Robyn Jordan (I don't want to discredit myself, but I think the pizza's non-shitty. It's cooked in a wood oven. It's free. They'll put toppings on for a buck. Is that so wrong? – AH)

Beauty Bar
231 E. 14th St (btwn 2nd & 3rd Ave) 212-539-1389
(East Village: L to 3rd Ave)
&
921 Broadway (btwn Melrose & Arion Pl, Bushwick, Bkln)
347-529-0370 (Bushwick: J/M/Z to Myrtle Ave)
www.beautybar.com/ny/home.html
I've enjoyed drinking in bubble-domed hair dryer chairs since the age of four, when my mother used to drag me along for her weekly wash and set, bribing me with an orange Crush from her beautician's *tres glamoreuse* vending machine. The Beauty Bar pushes things into more grown-up territory with its $10 manicure-and-martini happy hour special. It's a gimmick, but a well-implemented one.

9 to 5 • I Like Catching Flies • Miracle on 34th

I prefer the original 14th Street location, in a for-real former beauty salon not unlike the one my mother took me to. Bushwick feels closer to a Farrah Fawcett 'do in spirit.

SoHo/NoHo

Milady's Bar & Restaurant
160 Prince St (Btwn Broadway & Thompson) 212-226-9340
(SoHo: C/E to Spring St)
Cheaper than the Ear. Even if you're not feeling like you're on the brink of insolvency, this is still a good, grounded place for hanging out in SoHo, with pub grub, pay phone, and pool table.

Ear Inn
326 Spring St (btwn Greenwich & Washington)
212-226-9060, www.earinn.com (SoHo:C/E to Spring St)
Crowded and convivial every night despite its where-the-hell-am-I location in that desolate strip by the Holland Tunnel in far western SoHo. It's the kind of solid, homey, warped wood floored, allegedly haunted by the ghost of a dead sailor joint where an unlikely local sex symbol might go when he wants people to treat him like just another unpretentious, barrel-chested, balding guy. When there's live jazz it's very hard to hold a conversation, and very easy to appear rude—a good time to take your pint out to the front sidewalk with the other nature lovers.

Antarctica
287 Hudson St (just below Spring) 212-352-1666
www.antarcticabar.com (SoHo: C/E to Spring St)
They have one of those "name nights" where if it's your name you drink for free, and you can request a name for a future date. It's really spacious and nicely dark, and the bartenders are always friendly without being fake or pretentious. – Megan Garrity (Their motto is "Where the drinks are big, and the memories are short. Also, the drinks are big." – AH)

Botanica
47 E Houston St (btwn Mulberry and Mott) 212-343-7251
www.brooklynbotanica.com
(SoHo: B/D/F/M to Broadway-Lafayette)
It can be loud but it's always fun. The drinks are crazy strong and the back room is excellent for illicit make-out sessions. – Megan Garrity

The front room of the Art Bar is perfectly adequate. But step through the curtain at the back... ...and it's awesome!

Greenwich Village

Peculier Pub
145 Bleecker St (btwn Thompson and W. Broadway)
212-353-1327
www.peculierpub.com
(West Village: A/B/C/D/E/F/M to W 4th St)
On a Saturday evening during the semester it's packed to the gills with raucous NYU party guys and gals whooping it up. Earlier in the evenings, though, the spacious if dim and low-ceilinged bar is perfect for boring folks like me who just want to enjoy the extensive beer list, booth seating, beer-bottle-cap-adorned walls, and table service. Extra bit of fun? There's an entertaining webcomic by Jonathan Rosenberg called *Goats* which, for the first few years of its existence, took place largely in this bar. My favorite character was the fish who lived in beer. If you stop by, try the Brooklyn Brewery Black Chocolate Stout—I've only ever seen it at Peculier, and it is AMAZING. – Melissa Bastian

Fish Restaurant
280 Bleecker St (btwn Commerce St & Jones St)
212-727-2879, www.fishrestaurantnyc.com
(West Village: 1 to Christopher St)

Street • Elf • Crossing Delancey • A Tree

It's not really a bar but they have a deal where you get six oysters or clams and a glass of house wine or Pabst Blue Ribbon for eight bucks. – Robyn Jordan

Fat Cat Jazz Bar

75 Christopher St (@ 7 Ave) 212-675-6056
www.fatcatmusic.org
(Greenwich Village: A/B/C/D/E/F/M to W 4th St)
Where else can you get in for $3 to hear jazz all night 'til dawn, play chess, ping-pong, Scrabble, table-soccer, shoot some pool, play some weird table version of the French game boules, schmooze with friends, talk to strangers, drink beer, have Bleecker Street Pizza delivered to you, watch people, and feel like you're living the lazy hazy days of college again? You don't even need to have any cuing action at the pool table—the atmosphere is that relaxed and forgiving! – Ling Teo

White Horse Tavern

567 Hudson St (@ W 11th Street) 212-243-9260
(Greenwich Village: A/C/E/L to 14th St-8th Ave)
Take a tip from former regular Dylan Thomas, and don't have 18 whiskeys in a row, unless you're keen on expiring permanently later in the evening. Even those who don't love Dylan Thomas should raise a glass in his honor in his favorite pub, which has kept its connection to the great man alive with a room decorated in his honor. I'm not sure if the rowdy parties sharing pitchers at the picnic tables they put on the sidewalk in warmer months are aware of the history.

Art Bar

52 8th Ave (btwn Jane and Horatio) 212-727-0244
www.artbarsc.com
(Greenwich Village: A/C/E/L to 14th St-8th Ave)
This place is stellar. It's not a scene bar. The wait staff is helpful and attentive. The back room, complete with fireplace, feels like someone's basement. The Last Supper painting, featuring Jim Morrison as Jesus, is intriguing. – Heath Row

Flannery's

205 West 14th St (@ 7th Ave) 212-229-2122
www.flannerysny.com
(Greenwich Village: F/M/L 1/2/3 to 14th St-6th Ave)
Flannery's is just an all-around fun place to go if you want to tie a few on with a big group of people. A great cross-section on the jukebox, too. – Josh Medsker (Free darts + big groups of tied-on people = recipe for...? – AH)

Garment District

Mé Bar

17 W. 32nd st (top floor, btwn 5th & Broadway)
212-290-2460
mebarnyc.com (Garment District: B/D/F/M/N/Q /R to 34th St)
The illusion that the Empire State Building is growing out of your head is definitely the best reason to drink a $6 bottle of beer on the roof of a tatty chain hotel. No doubt the Four Seasons begrudges La Quinta Inn this happy accident of location. Don't go if it's inclement and don't get too bent out of shape if there's a table full of squealing Midwestern tourists. I know they made it seem all underground and hip when it served as the final destination in *Nick and Nora's Infinite Playlist.*

Hell's Kitchen/Times Square

Rudy's Bar and Grill

627 9th Ave (btwn 44th St & 45th St) 212-974-9169
rudysbarnyc.com
(Hell's Kitchen: A/C/E/N/Q /R/S1/2/3/7 to 42nd St)
Whatsamatter, hon', did some shitty Broadway musical that started as a Disney movie make you feel dirty in the wrong way? Rudy's will restore you to the Times Square of yore, with free hot dogs, cheap drinks, and an old school funk no amount of warbling mermaids, lion cubs, and candlesticks can wipe clean.

Smith's Bar & Restaurant

701 8th Ave (@ W 44th St) 212-246-3268
www.smithsbar.com
(Theater District: A/C/E/1/2/3/S/7/N/Q /R to 42nd St)
Smith's is a lot like Rudy's, except the crowd seems a bit older and more permanently installed. You can be pretty sure the ancient, half-in-the-bag customer a few stools down is a former chorus girl, or at least a former stripper. Buy the lady a chicken fried steak, why don't you? The food seems as old and done-in as everything else, but complaining about quality in a place like this is an activity best left to troublemaking yuppie tourists with rooms at the Marriott Marquis. Smith's has a beautiful old New York sign. They have live music Wednesdays through Saturdays. I've never been to karaoke Tuesdays but can only imagine.

Grows in Brooklyn • Cloverfield • I Am

BROOKLYN

Brooklyn Brewery
79 N 11th St (btwn Berry St & Wythe Ave, Bklyn) 718-486-7422
www.brooklynbrewery.com (Williamsburg: L to Bedford)
It's like a cafeteria where you drink local beers. You can
order pizza to be delivered to you while you're there.
– Robyn Jordan (But only on weekends, when the experience is enhanced by free educational tours, offered on
the hour. Speaking of education, this is a wholesome bar
setting for taking the kiddies along—so prepare to see
some. – AH)

Brooklyn Bowl
61 Wythe Ave (btwn N 12th St & N 13th St, Williamsburg,
Bklyn) 718-963-3369, www.brooklynbowl.com
(Williamsburg : L to Bedford Ave)
Brooklyn Bowl has great food, great music, bowling,
and often no cover charge. – Amy Burchenal. (If you're
bowling on the weekend, go early, as those lanes fill up
fast! – AH)

Supercore
305 Bedford Ave (btwn S 1st St & S 2nd St, Williamsburg,
Bklyn) 718-302-1629
www.supercore.tv (Williamsburg: L to Bedford)

Supercore is a Japanese coffeehouse/bar/tapas place. I like
going there on weeknights, as they stay open nice and
late. Tuesdays and Wednesdays I think they still offer 1/2
price bottles of wine or sake. – Dear Drunk Girl

Union Pool
484 Union Ave (@ Meeker Ave, Williamsburg, Bklyn)
718-609-0484, www.myspace.com/unionpool
(Williamsburg: G/L to Metropolitan-Lorimer)
When my roommate and I first moved here and were
swingin' single gals, we liked Union Pool for its huge
social backyard with a firepit, and uncommon-in-
NYC dudes > gals ratio. Now it's a bit more packed and
douchey, but we still on occasion enjoy drinking in the
backyard and getting snacks from the snack truck, watching the men troll for ladies at the "sloughing hour" (3am),
or seeing a show and dancing in the huge back room.
It's also still great on a weeknight, where a DJ spins old
country or old soul inside the bar. – Dear Drunk Girl (So
much space, the best bartenders, shows sometimes, perfect backyard for summer, cheap, liberal buy-backs...the
perfect bar – Megan Garrity)

Barcade
388 Union Ave (btwn Ainslie & Powers St, Williamsburg,
Bklyn) 718-302-6464, www.barcadebrooklyn.com

(Williamsburg: G/L to Metropolitan-Lorimer)
It's a bar and an ole skool arcade. I have been there once and I wouldn't go back, but if you want to play pinball or an '80s arcade game you can do it there. It was insanely overcrowded. - Genevieve Texeira

Metropolitan
559 Lorimer St (btwn Devoe St & Metropolitan Ave, Williamsburg, Bklyn) 718-599-4444
www.myspace.com/metropolitan11211
(Williamsburg: G/L to Metropolitan-Lorimer)
This is the local Williamsburg queer dive bar that I've been visiting since I first moved here. It's mind-boggling to see the transition from one year to the next of the communities that exist here. Many people have come and gone, and like any nightlife scene, the energy comes and goes, but it always comes back, especially on ladies night (Wednesday). In the summer, they have a rad free BBQ every Sunday. Every Tuesday is Queer-a-oke. - Cristy Road

The Second Chance Saloon
659 Grand St (btwn Leonard St & Manhattan Ave, Williamsburg, Bklyn) 718-387-4411
www.myspace.com/thesecondchancesaloon
(Williamsburg: L to Graham Ave)
I like Second Chance for its working-man/punkish bar feel and pricing. A lot of bike punks and messenger types hang out there, which makes me feel youthful and dirty, and they're always playing Danzig or some such toughness. Allegedly they have BBQs on occasion in their lil' backyard. - Dear Drunk Girl

Harefield Road
769 Metropolitan Ave (btwn Graham Ave and Humboldt St, Williamsburg, Bklyn) 718-388-6870
(Williamsburg: L to Graham)
Harefield Road is my favorite bar right now. Cheap beer and wine, specials, nice mixed crowd, candlelit, wooden tables, classy cabin feel. - Dear Drunk Girl

Palace Café
206 Nassau Ave (btwn Humboldt & Russell, Greenpoint, Bklyn) 718-383-9848 (Greenpoint: G to Nassau Ave)
The Palace, all the way! This is probably my favorite bar in town. Not only does it look like a Tudor castle on the inside, but there's nothing but old metal on the jukebox and they serve Bud drafts for $1.50! - Caitlin McGurk (The Palace is a neighborhood fixture, a holdover from when the Irish outnumbered the Polish, and still run by family. Best known for its jukebox and cheap beer (with an aggressive buyback schedule), the bar has also branched out

into music shows, occasionally scheduling bands in the back room, which used to be a restaurant, hence the Café part of the name. Every so often, it's rented out as a function hall. - Heath Row)

Lulu's / Alligator Lounge II
113 Franklin St (@ Greenpoint Ave,Greenpoint, Bklyn) 718-383-6000 (Greenpoint: G to Greenpoint)
This Greenpoint bar has seen many faces. It used to be covered in carnivalesque decor, with dim red lighting and a skee-ball game. It felt like home. I loved that vibe, but it's changed over its various episodes of being bought and sold. The fragility of local dive bars in any city is frightening. I've learned to love and accept Lulu's new decor of classier off-white walls and antique iron lamps. One positive change has been the transition from one free hotdog with each drink, to one free pizza pie with each drink. They have punk shows, like, everyday, it seems. - Cristy Road (It's now owned by the people behind the Alligator Lounge and Crocodile Lounge, which would explain the pizzas. Mezzanines on either side give a choir loft feel, nice for observing the proceedings for those not itching be in the thick of them. - AH)

t.b.d.
224 Franklin St (btwn Eagle St & Freeman St, Greenpoint, Bklyn) 718-349-6727
tdbrooklyn.com (Greenpoint: G to Greenpoint)
t.b.d. is awesome, with nice loungy-ness inside as well as a HUGE outdoor space with picnic tables and grill food. If you're lucky, you'll catch Dan Walker doing one of his infamous Robot Monkey battles. - Melissa Bastian

Tip Top Bar & Grill
432 Franklin Ave (btwn Greene and Gates, Bedford-Stuyvesant, Bklyn) 718-857-9744
(Bed-Stuy: C/S to Franklin)
Tip Top is a tiny bar by my house. The times I've gone it's been relatively empty, but I tend to go pretty early. The staff is wonderful and seemed to be very excited to meet new people of the neighborhood. It's been around for eons, and a really beautiful staple of this part of Bed-Stuy. They also have a nice patio. I definitely fell in love here. - Cristy Road

Sonny's
253 Conover St (btwn Beard and Reed, Red Hook, Bklyn) 718-625-8211
www.sunnysredhook.com (B61 Bus to Beard or IKEA water taxi)
Like many longstanding Brooklyn establishments, Sonny's comes with more than one great story. Back

when longshoremen were a fixture of Red Hook, it was a longshoreman's bar belonging to Sonny's family. As a young man, Sonny split on a journey of discovery, handily coinciding with the groovy '70s, coming home when his dad fell ill. His uncle ran the bar as a hobby, and after he died, Sonny took over. It's just a great, great, great, great bar, with a nautical feel to both the decorations and the older patrons. Local author Gabriel Cohen runs a reading series here on Sunday afternoons that seems particularly in synch with its sponsoring venue.

Montero's Bar & Grill
73 Atlantic Ave (@ Hicks, Cobble Hill, Bklyn) 718-624-9799
www.monterosbar.com
(Cobble Hill: M/R/2/3/4/5 to Court St-Borough Hall)
Montero's is a great, old, family-run longshoremen's bar. Friday night has the best laid-back karaoke. Theater geeks mixed with 50-year-old granny singing Sinatra… classic. Cheap beer and buybacks too. –Amy Burchenal (Montero's had a family feud with the Long Island Restaurant, a block away down Atlantic Avenue. The *New York Times* did a story about how a young niece was trying to patch things up, but the old women ruling the respective roosts refused to budge. I can believe it. Those ladies were hardcore. – AH)

Last Exit to Brooklyn
136 Atlantic Ave (btwn Clinton St & Henry St, Cobble Hill, Bklyn) 718-222-9198
www.lastexitbar.com (Cobble Hill: M/R/2/3/4/5 to Court St)
This place is home to many people who have grown up in the area and love to talk about "the olden days" but still welcome newcomers into the fold. The back is always filled with rotating art from local artists. I did a painting once of the front of the place from a photo I took late one night while on my way out. It was bought by a couple who got married in the bar. The feel is what the locals call incestuous. – Adam Suerte

Hank's Saloon
46 3rd Ave (@ Atlantic) 718-625-8003
www.hankssaloon.com (Boerum Hill: B/D/M/N/Q /R/2/3/4/5 to Atlantic Ave-Pacific St)
The neighborhood dive bar. The flames that are painted on the side have been there forever. It is rumored that they are only closed four hours a day (from 4am to 8am). Regular honky tonk and free BBQ are staples here all week 'round. – Adam Suerte (My neighbor, Joe, still refers to Hank's as the Indian bar, because he remembers it as the hang out of the Navajo steelworkers whose uncles and dads built the Empire State Building and many other NYC landmarks. There's a great essay about them and their connection to the neighborhood in Joseph Mitchell's *Up in the Old Hotel*. Nowadays, put your hands together for Live Band Kuntry Karaoke pretty much every Monday night. – AH)

The Bell House
149 7th St (btwn 2nd and 3rd Ave, Gowanus, Bklyn) 718-643-6510
www.thebellhouseny.com
(Gowanus, Bklyn: F to Smith & 9th St)
The folks behind the Bell House excel at whipping up non-stop live fun. The space is a giant, converted warehouse on a lonely street near the Gowaus canal. Their stage has hosted all sorts of great live music, some of it pretty dang high profile, rarely costing more than $10, but what really warms my cockles are inspired participatory events like the Brooklyn Chili Takedown, the World's Biggest Connect Four Championships, amateur ping pong tournaments, meetings of the Secret Science Club, and the high point of every Tri-State alternative librarian's social calendar, the Desk Set's Biblioball Dance Party!

Great Lakes
285 5th Ave (btwn 1st St & 2nd St, Park Slope, Bklyn) 718-499-3710
(Park Slope: M/R to Union)
The jukebox is made up of bartender mixes and is super-indie-rock. – Megan Garrity

Bar Reis
375 5th Ave (btwn 5th & 6th St, Park Slope, Bklyn) 718-832-5716 (Park Slope: F/M/R to 9th St-4th Ave)
When I lived in Park Slope this was my Cheers. Reis and staff are the best at making everyone in the bar feel like they are family. You'll likely find someone willing to play you and your friends without any attitude at the downstairs pool table. Not having beer on tap is no problem once you've had a perfectly mixed drink (a whiskey sour—they make it a special way) followed by a beer and taco special. The garden outside is perfect for a group of your hoodlum friends or just you and a special someone, possibly someone who wants to smoke. Big Ups, Bar Reis!! – Heath Row (This well-kept, candlelit bar inspires me to drink like an adult, and not just because I've got a kid across the street, taking a free workshop at the Brooklyn Superhero Supply. – AH)

Barbès
376 9th St (corner of 6th Ave & Park Slope, Bklyn) 718-965-9177
www.barbesbrooklyn.com (Park Slope: F/G to 7th Ave)

Mutual Appreciation• West Side Story •

If I lived a little closer I would seriously consider making Barbès my own personal better-than-Cheers. Barbès' tiny flea circus of a back room has exactly the kind of programming I crave, from traveling cinema to live vintage Hawaiian swing to the sweaty pits frenzy that is the weekly Slavic Soul Party, starring the band of the same name. The front bar is so dark that I am guilty of tying up the much more brightly-lit single seater bathroom, too impatient to leave the calendar of upcoming events for homeward-bound subway reading.

The Freak Bar
1208 Surf Ave (@ W 12th, Coney Island, Bklyn)
718-372-5159 (Coney Island: D/F/N/Q to Stillwell Ave)
No better place to drink a Coney Island Lager while admiring your bartender's full sleeve tattoos. Born of recent renovations in the building housing Sideshows by the Sea and the Coney Island Museum, it's also a great place to fortify yourself for, decompress from, or relive the glory of a guy tripping a rat trap with his tongue or hammering a railroad spike up his nasal passages. Rest assured he drinks there too. It's available for rentals. I tell you this in hopes that you'll get married there, and invite me.

Cha-Cha's
Coney Island Boardwalk (@Stillwell, Coney Island, Bklyn)
718-946-1305, www.chachasofconeyisland.com
(Coney Island: D/F/N/Q to Stillwell Ave)
Like many establishments on the Coney Island boardwalk, it's open for the season only when leathery, sand-

paper-voiced regulars start making an evening of it quite early in the afternoon. (In their defense, it gets dark here by 4pm in the winter.) An excellent vantage point from which to watch drunken young ladies falling off their platform shoes as they stroll along the uneven boards, sipping *piña coladas* from fluorescent plastic souvenir glasses reminiscent of bongs.

QUEENS

Sweet Afton
30-09 34th St (btwn 30th Ave and 31st Ave, Long Island City, Queens) 718-777-2570
www.sweetaftonbar.com (Long Island City: N to 30th Ave)
A relative newcomer to the Astoria bar scene, this English-style pub is a refreshing change from the more clubby, pseudo-Mediterranean joints that line 30th Avenue. Slipped discreetly onto 34th Street just a few doors south of 30th Ave and just three blocks from the train, Sweet Afton focuses on "local." It makes a point of sourcing its meats, cheeses, vegetables, and fruits from small purveyors in the NYC area. They'll even tell you about the shop that cured the cucumbers for your fried pickles (it's in Brooklyn.) Specialty cocktails are all delightful and pack a punch, including a Dirty Pickle Martini, a French 75, a Spicy Cherry Margarita, and numerous others.
– Melissa Bastian

Bohemian Hall & Beer Garden
2919 24th Ave (btwn 29th and 31st St, Astoria, Queens)
718-274-4925
www.bohemianhall.com (Astoria: N to Astoria Blvd)
Until quite recently, the Bohemian Hall & Beer Garden was *the* beer garden. This was the one place that could draw frat boys, office drones, and hipsters alike all the way to Queens for a night out. Upon entering the front door, you'd think, "Okay, I'm in a mid-sized, Germanic-themed bar with a few tables. Whatev." But then you'd go out the back door, and like stumbling through the back of a wardrobe, suddenly you had emerged in BeerNarnia! And then you understand that maybe, just maybe, Queens isn't such a bad place after all. – Melissa Bastian

Studio Square
35-33 36th St (btwn 35th Ave and 36th Ave, Astoria, Queens) 718-383-1001
www.studiosquarenyc.com (Astoria: G/M/R to 36th St)
Astoria's second beer garden is a place well-worth visiting—very polished with great attention to detail in the decor, lots of beers on tap, and accommodating indoor

and outdoor spaces. It's a fantastic place for a large group, which can't be said for many NYC locations. Just be on the lookout when you're headed there; while the inside is impressive, out front it's so unassuming that it's not hard to walk right past it. – Melissa Bastian

McCann's Pub and Grill
36-15 Ditmars Blvd (@ 36th St, Astoria, Queens) 718-278-2621
www.mccannspubnyc.com (Astoria: N to Ditmars)
McCann's is a pretty typical but still cool dive-y neighborhood bar. They have cheap drinks and a pool table. The juke is nothing special—Steve Miller-Led Zep-usual bar stuff. – Josh Medsker

Crescent and Vine
25-01 Ditmars Blvd (@ 25th St, Astoria, Queens)
718-204-4774 (Astoria: N to Ditmars Blvd)
Crescent and Vine is a great wine bar. They have free olives at the table and a great cheese plate. – Josh Medsker

GROCERIES AND FOOD SHOPPING
Eating every meal in a restaurant can start wearing you down after a while, so why not pull together a picnic, or treat your hosts to a homecooked meal?

MANHATTAN

Chinatown/Little Italy

New York Supermarket
75 East Broadway (under the Manhattan Bridge, btwn East Broadway & Henry St) 212-374-4088
(Chinatown: B/D to Grand)
The New York Supermarket is my Manhattan Chinatown go-to. One of the things I like the most, next to the mountains of cheap greens and the barrel of live frogs (um, they're *pets*, right?) is the fact that you practically have to be an international spy to find it. They are hidden behind (inside?) a more-than-building-sized pillar of the Manhattan Bridge. Start by circling around that southern leg, where the vendors are hawking Saran-wrapped something or others (get that sesame pancake sandwich Calvin Trillen loves so much, the 75 cent-er stuffed with greasy, tangy greens.) You can also reach it by going through the little mall-type thing. Eventually, you'll hit this shady, covered, alley-type place where there are bins of produce and guys waiting to weigh it. Go through the sliding doors and bingo, you're in a supermarket filled with all manner of roast meats (almost as many mock as not), herbal remedies, snacks, joss paper, noodles, the list goes

on and on and on. There's also a back entrance that lets you out onto Henry Street, but where's the fun in that?

Kam Man Food Products
200 Canal St (btwn Mott St & Mulberry St) 212-571-0330
(Chinatown: J/M/Z/N/Q /6 to Canal)
This Chinatown supermarket has every possible Chinese or Japanese item you want. Downstairs they have an amazing array of beautiful ceramics of all kinds, decorative chopsticks, and all sorts of nifty things. You can buy gorgeous ceramic bowls there for $2-3 or even less. And they also have lanterns & paper screens, and musical instruments—everything! – Jerry the Mouse

Bangkok Center Grocery
104 Mosco St (btwn Mott and Mulberry), 212-732-8916
www.thai-grocery.com
(Chinatown: J/N/Q /R/W/Z/6 to Canal)
Bangkok Center Grocery is your place for one-stop shopping whenever Thai is on the menu. It's okay if you don't feel up to cracking your own coconut; they've got some killer refrigerated curry pastes that'll last even the laziest cook for nearly a year provided you can get 'em through airport security. The friendly owners make for impressive cultural ambassadors, eagerly steering their *farang* customers toward the tastiest snacks and the best brand of fish sauce (Golden Boy, if you must know). This is also a good place to pick up kefir lime leaves, which can live outside the freezer until you make it back home.

Ten Ren Tea and Ginseng Parlor
75 Mott St (btwn Canal & Bayard St) 212-349-2286
(Chinatown: J/Z/N/Q /R/6 to Canal)
&
79 Mott St (btwn Canal & Bayard St) 212-732-7178
(Chinatown: J/Z/N/Q /R/6 to Canal)
&
138 Lafayette St (btwn Canal St & Grand St) 212-343-8098
(Chinatown: J/Z/N/Q /R/6 to Canal)
&
5817 8th Ave (btwn 58th St & 59th St, Park Slope, Bklyn)
718-853-0660
(Borough Park: N to 8th Ave)
&
135-18 Roosevelt Ave (btwn Prince & Main St, Flushing, Queens) 718-461-9305 (Downtown Flushing: 7 to Main St)
&
83-28 Broadway (btwn Dongan & St. James Ave) Elmhurst, Queens) 718-205-0861 (Elmhurst: G/R to Elmhurst)
www.tenren.com
I hate the idea of spending $4 on 20 bags of tea. I do like

• Midnight Cowboy • Frankie & Johnny •

the idea of tea connoisseurs coming to Chinatown for their fix, though, and one day it would be nice to slow down long enough to take a class, so that I, too, might learn to savor something so elegant and ancient. The staff at 75 Mott behave as if they're working in a jewelry store, but they're quite accustomed to dealing with tour bus groups, and know how to remain professional in the face of gross ignorance. They will pour samples for any bumbling Yankee, even George Bush Sr. (as evidenced by a yellowing news clipping). All the other locations serve bubble tea, a substance which may as well have come from another planet, its temperament is so different.

May Wah Healthy Vegetarian Food

213 Hester St (btwn Baxter & Centre) 212-334-4428 www.vegieworld.com (Chinatown: J/Z/N/Q /R/6 to Canal) Where do you think that fake meat on Chinatown's vegetarian restaurants' menus comes from? Tofurkey Town? No, here! (It's also widely available in Chinatown's large Asian supermarkets, but I like this place because the staff is so jolly, and I can relate to the fanzine-like fervor that leads them to hit one culinary note, over and over.) Hope there's an ice chest in your backpack, because a lot of the stock's in a freezer case.

Kong Kee Food

240 Grand St (@ Bowery) 212-966-1350 www.kongkeefood.com (Little Italy: B/D to Grand St) What? A store full of tofu? Yup. There is heaven on earth. They've got all sorts of tofu (silken, firm, skins, puffed...). They also have fresh, thick, rice noodles. I fried up some tofu in agave nectar, sautéed some veggies and served them with the rice noodles. Yum! The store has a surprisingly good website with photos, including a slideshow of how they make tofu. – Amanda Plumb

Lower East Side/East Village

Guss Pickles

87 Orchard St (@ Broome) 212- 334-3616 www.gusspickle.com (LES: F/J/M/Z to Delancey-Essex) Brilliant old-school New York for foodies. Fresh pickles, pickled peppers, and other pickled items for sale from barrels on the sidewalk. You can get a single half-sour pickle for 50 cents or a larger container for about $6. Fresh, fun, and a bit of history worth maintaining! – Heath Row

The Essex Street Market

120 Essex St (btwn Rivington and Delancey) 212-388-0449 www.essexstreetmarket.com (LES: F/J/M/Z to Delancey-Essex)

Shopping for produce on Flatbush

Lots of interesting little shops that demonstrate the variety of the LES. If you don't mind all the dead animals for sale, Jeffrey's Meat Market stall has rotating exhibits of art by local artists and school kids. – Victoria Law (Put some Blisters on your Sisters at Shopsin's, after which you can do the right thing by swinging by the Lower East Side Girls Club's La Tiendita stall. – AH) (This place is amazing! You can get all your groceries, fruits and veggies very cheap. You can even get a curse lifted! The only thing is that they close very early, I think around 5pm. – Fly)

Russ and Daughters

179 E. Houston (btwn Allen & Orchard) 212-475-4880 www.russanddaughters.com (LES: F/M to 2nd Ave) My sister-in-law's maternal grandmother is one of the three Daughters, which makes me, a Hoosier Protestant, mishpachah by marriage! Hot damn! I wonder if I'll ever get up the nerve to flout my familial connection in hopes of qualifying for discounts on caviar, lox, and creamed herring. Don't leave without tasting the pistachio halvah and admiring the forethought that kept my kinsmen and women from ripping out the gorgeous vintage fixtures when other New York institutions were succumbing to '70s and '80s remodeling urges.

Whole Foods Beer Room

95 E. Houston St (btwn Chrystie and Bowery) 212-420-1320 www.wholefoodsmarket.com/stores/bowery (LES: F/M to 2nd Ave) The Whole Foods on Houston Street is fantastic and overpriced. This one also has a little annex where they only sell a ridiculous variety of beers from around the world. You can get a Sapporo Special Reserve that was flown

The Seven Year Itch • The Sweet Smell of Success

in from Japan, an organic hemp beer from Northern California or a fuckin' Pabst Blue Ribbon in a can. – Josh Saitz (You can buy a brown glass growler, and then haul it with you to refill from one of their five or six taps of local microbrews whenever you're in the neighborhood. Good local choices that you can't find in any old corner bodega are Coney Island and Butternut Brewery – AH)

Bowery & Vine

269 Bowery (btwn Houston & Prince) 212-941-7943
www.boweryandvine.com (LES: F/M to 2nd Ave-Houston)
It's been around forever, but on the surface it would seem that Bowery & Vine is complicit in the gentrification of this neighborhood. So I consider it very decent of them to keep some drinkable cheap stuff prominently displayed by the door.

Sunrise Mart

29 3rd Avenue, 2nd floor (at 9th St) 212-598-3040
(East Village: 6 to Astor Pl)
Unless they're totally swamped, the cashiers at this Japanese supermarket over St. Mark's Bookstore will shout out a hello the moment the elevator doors open. Rice balls and an Asahi tallboy would make a pretty good picnic, don't you think? So would a big old squeeze bottle of Kewpie mayonnaise. They also have a small but intriguing selection of Japanese cosmetics, housewares, and cleaning products.

East Village Cheese Shop

40 3rd Ave (btwn 9th and 10th St) 212-477-2601
(East Village: 6 to Astor Pl)
When I want to indulge in some nice cheese and still stay on a budget, I head to the East Village Cheese Shop. You'll know you're in the right place by the sign-covered windows. The two front cases often have triangles of brie for $1 and logs of chevre for under $2. Some of the cheeses are a little past their prime (aka the expiration date), but I've never had a problem with any of the ones I purchased. They also sell breads, coffee, crackers, and spreads.
– Amanda Plumb

M2M

55 3rd Ave (@ 11th St) 212-353-2698
(East Village: 6 to Astor Pl)
&
2935 Broadway (@ 116th St) 212-280-4600
(Morningside Hts: 1 to 116th St-Columbia University)
Ignore the rowdy party of NYU coeds and the imperious homeless dowager giving them the stink-eye, and the East Village location of this "convenient mart" feels like a sit-down version of something you'd find in a Tokyo Metro station. I buy my Japanese groceries at Sunrise Mart, but come here for below-restaurant-price udon and low-quality sushi. Sometimes I pick up the components for making bubble tea at home, but I always end up giving them to someone in need of a present. The Morningside Heights location feels cheerier.

Trader Joe's

142 E 14th St (btwn 2nd and 3rd Ave) 212-529-4612
(East Village: L to 3rd Ave)
&
130 Court St (@ Atlantic Ave, Boerum Hill, Bkln)
718-246-8460 (Boerum Hill: F/G to Bergen)
www.traderjoes.com
In addition to being the cheapest source of quality, regular groceries around, TJ's is great for movie treats - buy snacks and cans of Simpler Times —3.99/six pack!—and sneak 'em into the theater. – Robyn Jordan (You can also get very cheap great ready-made meals here. Don't let the line fool you! It might seem long but it goes really, really fast!!! – Fly)

Astor Wines

399 Lafayette St (btwn 4th St & Astor Pl) 212-674-7500
www.astorwines.com (East Village: 6 to Astor Pl)
There's wine out the bahootie in this well-lit landmark, not to mention frequent tastings and a staff that can suggest something drinkable at rot gut prices.

Union Square

Union Square Greenmarket – Monday, Wednesday, Friday, Saturday
1 Union Square W (btwn 14th & 17th) 212-788-7476
www.cenyc.org/greenmarket
(Union Square: L/N/Q /R/4/5/6 to Union Square)
The Union Square Farmer's Market is well-known and completely worth a walk-around. Not only is there a large selection of wonderful foodstuffs for sale but there's so many people to watch! – Marguerite Dabaie (Get there before 8am to see chefs in checked pants and rubber clogs absconding with wheelbarrows heaped with wild leeks, pea shoots, edible pansies, and the like. They'll be on the menu tonight and I bet they'll taste great. Look for the chevre vendor who displays portraits of her goats, Bags for the People people at the Hawthorne Valley Stand, and the Cat Grass is Wheat Grass sign. – AH)

• Fame • Requiem for a Dream • Cruising •

SoHo

Dean and Deluca
560 Broadway (@ Prince) 212-226-6800
www.deandeluca.com (SoHo: R to Prince)
This SoHo institution offers us just-browsers a chance to
rubberneck at the pampered Airedales who shop here as
if it's a regular grocery store. It's kind of stomach churn-
ing, but so is looking at a facelift, and you'll see plenty of
them here, along with extremely tight jeans tucked into
extremely high heeled boots. Don't plan to buy anything
here unless you're flush, but there are free samples to be
hovered over.

Greenwich Village

Porto Rico Importing Co
201 Bleecker St (btwn 6th Ave and Macdougal) 212 477
5421 (Greenwich Village: A/C/E/B/D/F/M to W 4th St)
&
40 1/2 St. Marks (btwn 1st and 2nd Ave) 212-533-1982
(East Village: 6 to Astor Pl)
&
107 Thompson St (btwn Prince and Spring) 212-966-5758
(SoHo: C/E to Spring)
&
120 Essex St (in the Essex Street Market @ Delancey)
212-677-1210 (LES: F/J/M/Z to Delancey-Essex)
&
636 Grand St (btwn Manhattan Ave & Leonard, Williamsburg, Bklyn) 718-782-1200
(Williamsburg: G/L to Metropolitan-Lorimer)
www.portorico.com
Porto Rico Importing Co. know their shit. They have
about 40 different varieties of coffee and about 20 different kinds of tea from all over the world. They aren't the
most friendly, so you can't stand there and have a convo
with them about Kenyan AA vs. Tanzanian Peaberry, but
the coffee is the shhhiiitttt. They can also trick you out
with coffee-makers, espresso machines, and accoutre-
ments. – Josh Medsker

Lifethyme
410 Ave of the Americas (btwn 8th & 9th St) 212-420-9099
www.lifethymemarket.com
(Greenwich Village: A/B/C/D/E/F/M to W 4th St)
If you want "live" vegan take-out then go to Lifethyme.
They are a bit pricey but live food is a specialty and it is
pretty good. They have a place to eat upstairs and a bathroom. – Fly

Integral Yoga Natural Foods
229 W 13th St (between 7th Ave & Greenwich Ave)
212-243-2642, www.integralyoganaturalfoods.com
(Greenwich Village: 1/2/3 to 14th St)
IYNF is a good-sized, all-vegetarian grocery that stocks
everything you could possibly want for your LOHAS
(Lifestyles of Health and Sustainability) lifestyle. Most exciting is the salad bar. In addition to the basic salad makings, there's also hot food. It's like homemade without
actually having to cook. – Heath Row

Myers of Keswick
634 Hudson St (btwn Horatio and Jane) 212-691-4194
www.myersofkeswick.com
(Greenwich Village: A/C/E/L to 14th St-8th Ave)
Anglophiles and UK expats jonesing for Uncle Joe's Mint
Balls can satisfy that and any number of other packaged
food cravings here, but the real attraction is a deli case
filled with individual-sized savory pies, none of them
costing more than $4. Interest you in a Jammy Dodgie,
luv? No? What about a Scotch egg, washed down with a
postcard of the Queen?

Chelsea

The Chelsea Market
75 9th Ave (btwn 15th and 16th st) 212-243-6005
www.chelseamarket.com (Chelsea: A/C/E/L to 14th St-8th Ave)
Well worth a visit, provided your loins are girded for field
trip groups of New York City schoolchildren and legions
of Food Network fans praying that their gods will descend
from the closed-to-the-public upper floors where most of
the shows are filmed. Nowadays it's all about over-the-top
cupcakes, fancy kitchenwares, imported ingredients, and
the occasional fashion shoot or sample sale. There are
several bonafide markets within the market. The Manhattan Fruit Exchange does a brisk trade in exotica from the
produce world, offered alongside more standard fare...

fiddlehead ferns, starfruit, Hen-of-the-Woods, and all manner of itsy bitsy, teeny tiny "baby" versions. Buon Italia corners the market on olive oil, sun-dried tomatoes, and ancient Parmesan. The market recently leased space to Posman Books, and set up a feeding station on the High Line. It hosts trivia nights, grown-up spelling bees, Rooftop Films' off-season programming, and unusually compelling art and photo exhibits.

Garment District

Hanh ah Rheum
25 W 32nd St (btwn Broadway & 5th Ave) 212-695-3283
www.hmart.com
(Garment District: B/D/F/M/N/Q/R to 34th St)
This Korean supermarket has a higher mark-up on the same products you'd find in Chinatown, but it's still pretty cheap, and if it's giant jars of kimchi you're after, you have come to the right place! A reliable supplier of the delicious and improbably named Angelo Pietri brand sesame-miso salad dressing. When a time-crunch rules out the made-to-order preparation of E-Mo's Kimbabs up the street, I can't say no to the prepackaged ones near the register. As with any Asian market, the candy aisle is something special, and while we're ruining our health, you may as well pick up some single serving packs of the sesame oil-soaked roaster laver seaweed that my son Milo loves even better than Angelo Pietri dressing. It's high in magnesium, and the smaller sheets cut down on the mess, if not my personal consumption.

Hell's Kitchen

Giovanni Eposito & Sons
500 9th Ave (btwn 37th St & 38th St) 212-279-3298
(Hell's Kitchen: A/C/E to 34th St-8th Ave)
&
357 Court St (btwn Union & President, Carroll Gardens, Bklyn) 718-875-6863
(Carroll Gardens: F/G to Carroll St)
Italian-Americans (to make a sweeping generalization) make everyone else look like rank amateurs when it comes to decorating the walls of their NYC businesses with autographed photos of celebrity fans. The ones opposite the cases of this 3rd generation "meat store" are particularly poignant, given the proximity to Broadway. My hunch is that for many of the actors hanging alongside bonafide celebs like Cher and Brenda Vaccaro, the star treatment never got much further than signing a possibly-unasked-for headshot for their butcher. But to turn to happier subjects, that homemade sopressato will

last for a couple of days without refrigeration. The Carroll Garden's location, properly referred to as the G. Esposito Pork Store, is too tough to pay much attention to thespians. The biggest ham there is the erect fiberglass pig, dressed as a chef, out on the sidewalk.

International Grocery
543 9th Ave (btwn 40th & 41st) 212-279-1000
(Hell's Kitchen: A/C/E/N/Q/R/S/1/2/3/7 to 42nd St-8th Ave)
Old world charm, with olives, cheese, condiments, and spice from Italy, Spain, and Greece, it's one-stop Mediterranean shopping.

Stiles Farmers Market
569 9th Ave (btwn 39th and 40th) 212-695-6215
(Hell's Kitchen: A/C/E/N/Q/R/S/1/2/3/7 to 42nd St-8th Ave)
The Stiles Farmers Market provides a perverse, but democratizing counterpoint to all that locally-grown, artisanal, slow food chocolate and cheese-ism, that can, in its media depiction, begin to seem exclusive and a bit untethered from the real world. What it lacks in terms of sunshine and preciousness, it makes up for in proximity to Port Authority and laminated prayer cards taped to the registers.

West African Grocery
524 9th Ave (btwn 39th and 40th) 212-695-6215
(Hell's Kitchen: A/C/E/N/Q/R/S/1/2/3/7 to 42nd St-8th Ave)
I need a tour guide to talk me through this no-frills purveyor's staple ingredients. Senna Pods? Yam fufu? Big knobby roots? I'm particularly fascinated by the gallon milk jugs filled with bright orange and red palm oil, though at $25 a pop, you'll want to have some recipes lined up before making the investment.

Murray Hill

Kalustyan's
123 Lexington Ave (btwn 28th St & 29th St) 212-685-3451
www.kalustyans.com (Murray Hill: 6 to 28th St)
When there's no trip to Queens' Patel Brothers on the horizon, I'll duck in here for some frozen paneer, bulk Indian spices, or a cup of rose-flavored ice cream served with an old-fashioned wooden spoon. It's a bit "As Featured in *Gourmet Magazine*," but the packages aren't gummy like in some other establishments and the mango powder appears to have been packed in this century. Always quick to identify a business opportunity, Kalyustan's has lately jumped on the café-within-a-grocery bandwagon, carving out some space upstairs, a nice respite from the tension-filled squeezing-past-the-stockboys going on in the aisles

downstairs. One thing I really like picking up here is a bag of breath-freshening fennel seeds with some bright gerbil turd-sized candies mixed in.

Midtown

The Bridgemarket Food Emporium
401 E 59th St (@ 1st Ave) 212-752-5836
www.thefoodemporium.com
(Sutton Place: N/R/4/5/6 to 59th St-Lexington)
Food Emporium is a NYC supermarket chain. The one under the 59th Street Bridge and is actually *built into the bridge*. It is stunningly gorgeous, with vaulted ceilings, floor-to-ceiling windows, a mirrored wall, and tiled columns that match the bridge's architectural details. The history of the bridge is quite interesting. For many years it provided the only access to Roosevelt Island, formerly known by many names, one of which was Welfare Island. This is where New York City effectively stored the people it didn't know how to handle, including the terminally ill, the criminal, and the insane. A trolley ran across the bridge to Long Island City, Queens and stopped at an elevator midway which allowed access down to the the island, but only with special identification. Now this upscale, foodie sort of grocery store has taken up residence—not to mention the pricey condos that now populate the island. The grocery has the most amazing selection of flowers and plants, a gorgeous bread counter, and a divine selection of handmade chocolates, as well as some nice salad and hot food bars. I like to put myself together a little lunch and then sit in the comfy seating area upstairs (where there is also a tea bar) and ponder the situation. – Melissa Bastian.

Upper West Side

Fairway
2127 Broadway (btwn 74th St & 75th St) 212-595-1888
(Upper West Side: 1/2/3/9 to 72nd St)
&
2328 12th Ave (btwn 132nd St & 133rd St) 212-234-3883
(Harlem: 1 to 125th St)
&
450-500 Van Brunt St, (@ Reed St, Red Hook, Bklyn)
718-694-6868 (Red Hook: B61 bus to Beard St)
www.fairwaymarket.com
The Broadway flagship is classic NYC food shopping—tight aisles, all sorts of seductive condiments you hadn't even realized you craved, and octogenarian Upper West Siders ramming their baskets into your kidneys as you try to double back for something you forgot. They have

Sahadi's Bulk Bins

excellent fresh bread. If you like waterfront dining, get a Spring Joy salad at the Brooklyn outpost, where outdoor seating has been installed to capitalize on the zillion dollar view of the Statue of Liberty, also viewable from the parking lot. – AH (I like to help myself to free samples from the olive bar and then wander around looking for other samples to munch on. – Amanda Plumb)

Upper East Side

Eli's Vinegar Factory
431 East 91st St (btwn 1st and 2nd Ave) 212-987-0885
www.elizabar.com (Upper East Side: 4/5/6 to 96th St)
If you want to be sickened but amazed, go to Eli's Vinegar Factory, on the Upper East Side. Everything is insanely overpriced, but delicious and well-presented. – Josh Saitz

BROOKLYN

The Bushwick Farmers Market
Corner of Linden & Gates – every Wednesday
(Bushwick: J to Gates)
The Bushwick Farmers Market is run by a really great group of people who push their goods every Wednesday on the corner of Broadway and Linden and also host free seasonal fairs with workshops and concerts. Not all of the produce is as cheap as one might like, but it's the best quality by far in this area. – Caitlin McGurk

Red Hook Community Farm
590 Columbia St (btwn Sigourney and Halleck, Red Hook, Brooklyn) 718-855-5531
www.added-value.org (Red Hook: B61 Bus to Beard St or the IKEA water taxi)

If you fetishize pumpkins fertilized with elephant and rhino dung, head to this Red Hook Saturday farmers' market and get a child farmer from the nearby housing project to give you the full scoop on one of New York City's most heart-warming urban agricultural successes. You're welcome to help weed and water, too.

Sahadi's
187 Atlantic Ave (btwn Court and Clinton, Boerum Hill, Bklyn) 718-624-4550 www.sahadis.com
(Boerum Hill: 2/3/4/5/M/R to Court St-Borough Hall)
Our most venerable Middle Eastern grocery can generate some crazy lines, particularly around Christmas, Easter, New Year's Eve, or 5pm. So if you're just dashing in for some yogurt soap or a pack of pita bread, try the Damascus Bakery further up the block, or the Oriental grocery across the street. If it's hummus you're after, take a number, because nobody does it better. They've got a deli (offering a bargain lunch combo), bulk bins galore, marzipan, homemade halvah, teas out the wazoo, belly dancing videos, an olive bar, fruit leathers in every color of the rainbow, and Greek Easter egg dye in season. – AH (Spices, couscous, preserves, cheeses, olives, dolma, anchovies, capers, honey...their gourmet foods cost less than the factory-farmed, big agribusiness fare from more traditional markets. – Kate Black)

Park Slope Food Coop
782 Union St (btwn 6th and 7th Ave, Park Slope, Bklyn) 718-622-0560
www.foodcoop.com (Park Slope: M/R to Union St)
You can't actually shop here if you're not a member, but it's totally worth coming in for a tour of one of the largest and oldest member-owned food cooperatives in the country. – Lauren Jade Martin (Most events are free and open to the public. In addition to screenings of documentaries about sustainable agriculture, the horrors of factory faming, and *Who Really Killed Robert Kennedy*, look for musical performances and lectures on topics like Meditation and Acupuncture & the Treatment of Digestive Disorders. Try to snoop around the community bulletin boards—a trove of sublets and bikes for sale! – AH) (Anarchist heaven or Stalinist hell? You decide. – Jessica Max Stein) (There is another tiny food coop at 58 E. 4th St in the East Village that is open to all. – Melissa Bastian)

Susie Farm Grocery
752 Flatbush (@ Clarkson, Flatbush, Bklyn) 718-826-9429
(Flatbush: Q to Parkside Ave)
Given my attraction to unfamiliar food and accents more melodic than my own plains stater, Susie's, an airy open-

front West Indian grocery spilling onto Brooklyn's most tropical street, is total catnip. Get yourself to Susie's, and you'll be well-situated to explore all sorts of Caribbean produce markets, groceries, bakeries, and restaurants.

The hotspot for Russian groceries is in Brighton Beach, Brooklyn. Alight from the B/Q train at the Brighton Beach Stop. Explore Brighton Beach Avenue. There are two main shopping strips, one under the elevated train tracks and one across Coney Island Avenue. – David Goren

QUEENS

Sai Organics
3607 30th Ave (@ 36th St, Astoria, Queens) 718-956-1793
(Astoria: N to 30th Ave)
&
3021 30th Av (@ 31st St, Astoria, Queens) 718-278-1726
(Astoria: N to 30th Ave)
Sai's two locations are both on 30th Avenue, one right next to the subway station on the northwest corner, and the larger, original location further east near 36th Street. They're run by people with a strong dedication to providing healthy food to their customers. They live in the neighborhood and form relationships with their customers. They only carry vegetarian products and make a real effort to support small, ethically-run food producers and organic farmers. As Queens does not have a co-op, this is definitely the next best thing. – Melissa Bastian

Parrot Coffee Market and Mediterranean Grocery
31-12 Ditmars Blvd (@ 31st St, Astoria, Queens)
718-545-7920 (Astoria: N to Ditmars)
&
58-22 Myrtle Ave (@ Forest Ave, Ridgewood, Queens)
718-821-2785
www.parrotcoffee.com (Ridgewood: M to Forest Av)
Parrot Market is a wonder. It is actually not much for coffee, but it has more olives than I have ever seen in my life, about eight different kinds of feta cheese, a wide selection of Balkan and Middle Eastern delicacies, *and* European candy. So bad ass. – Josh Medsker

Patel Brothers
42-92 Main Street (btwn 37th Ave & Roosevelt Ave, Jackson Heights, Queens) 718-661-1112
www.patelbrothersusa.com
Go here for all your Indian cooking needs. If you like cumin or cardamom or pistachios, get them here, because there is no place cheaper. You can also get henna kits with excellent designs, lentils for dal, and good incense. – Jerry

the Mouse (Not to mention some seriously out-there snacks and sweeties. You'll need a bigger sari stat once you start dipping into that shit. – AH)

Pacific Market
75-01 Broadway (@ 75th St, Elmhurst, Queens) 718-507-8181
(Elmhurst: E/F/G/R/M/7 to 74th St-Roosevelt Ave)
The employees are kind of rude if you don't look local, but this West Asian supermarket has the best selection of seaweeds and etc. for cheap. – Matana Roberts

FREE EATS

Grub
At Rubulad
338 Flushing (btwn Classon & Taaffe Pl, Bedford-Stuyve-sant, Bklyn) 718- 782-8523
www.myspace.com/anewworldinourhearts
(Bed-Stuy: G to Flushing Ave)
Grub is the free community dinner sponsored by the In Our Hearts Anarchist Collective, who dumpster most of the ingredients for this delicious, home-cooked meal on the 1st and 3rd Sunday of every month. Dinner's served at 7pm, but if you want to get to know your hosts before pulling up at their table, arrive at 3:30pm to help cook. (You could also toss them a small donation to keep 'em in dishwashing liquid.) It goes without saying that vegan options abound.

Food Not Bombs
Get a crash course in cooking for a vegetarian crowd, then dig in to make sure you're not poisoning the people. See? Mama was right about things tasting better when you cook them yourself. Details in the Volunteer section.

The Church of the Holy Apostles
The volunteer meal served after this soup kitchen has closed its doors to the public is a chance to break bread— or more likely a filling casserole of some sort—with folks who may be outside your usual demographic. That's never a bad thing, especially when you're all working toward a common goal. Want to brainstorm ways to get a higher level of activist commitment? Chat up the parishioners who have been pulling regular volunteer shifts here every other day for years! Details in the Volunteer section.

Wisteria
What, you thought only fairy princesses were allowed to eat pretty purple flowers? Not so, if you're here when the arbors of our public parks wrap themselves in their an-nual mantle of wisteria blooms (late April or early May).

They taste peppery, like nasturtiums. There's an outside chance an old lady will go apeshit on you, not from any concern for your health, mind you. *Those plantings were put there for everybody to enjoy, young (wo)man!* Some particularly fertile grounds to seek this seasonal treat are

Central Park's Conservatory Garden and the arbor-shaped walkway close to the left of the W. 72nd entry, on that path that leads to the lake, as well as in Christopher Park, the West Village tiny plot at the intersection of Christopher, Grove, and W. 4th, that is also home to George Segal's Stonewall-commemorating *Gay Liberation* sculpture.

Gingko Nuts
I've heard the fruit of these trees compared to vomit, dia-pers, wet dogs, feet, and rotten goat cheese. Mmm! Bring on the recipes! If you're up for a lot of sound and fury, resulting in lots of fun and a very small amount of some-thing people in other parts of the world consider a deli-cacy, grab your gloves and join the harvest. Or do what I do and just wash your hands! The stink comes off! Unlike apples, the good, ripe ones are on the ground. Pinch the fruit until a little nut squirts out. Put the nut in a bag— and here I will go on record as saying that this is one case where you *don't* want to use your reusable, up-cycled cloth bag—go for a disposable plastic one. Leave the pulp under the tree. Take the nuts inside, hose them off, and blot them dry. Crack them with a nutcracker or your two front teeth. Remove the softer interior nut, and submerge it in boiling water for 20 seconds. This will make it easy to remove the amber-colored film—just rub it off with your fingers. You will be left with a handful of soft, white nuts. Don't eat them yet, though— they're still toxic! Put a little olive oil in a pan, and stir-fry the nuts until they turn

bright emerald tree boa green. Sprinkle with salt, add to an Asian dish, or make a big to-do about gathering your non-squeamish friends to help you eat them in a highly ceremonial fashion. The trees grow all over the place. Their leaves are fan-shaped and only the females bear fruit. If you want a pastoral experience, look for them in Central Park. Or take the F train to Bergen Street, and wander the streets of Boerum Hill, Brooklyn.

Happy Hours and other alcohol-related enticements
Even if you don't drink, you should pay attention when you peruse those ZG2NYC bar listings! Time it right, and you can snag pizza, hot dogs, Belgian frites, and Italian Appertivo! Don't say we never gave you nothing.

FOOD FESTIVALS AND COOKING COMPETITIONS
Used to be every time I turned around, someone was opening a French bistro on the premises of a recently vacated Puerto Rican men's social club. Now cook-offs appear to be all the rage. They're multiplying like yeast! A good source for finding out about the latest clambakes of this sort is the blog Not Eating Out in NYC—the same people who bring you the Five Obstructions (www. noteatingoutinny.com/category/events/).

The Brooklyn Chili Takedown – multiple times throughout the year
www.chili-takedown.com
Tell your stomach to watch the fuck out, because once a year is not enough and the competitors are unfettered by any official rules save a mandate to bring enough to feed the crowd! Who knows what they'll put in that pot in their pursuit of chili excellence! For about 10 bucks, you can sample 20 or so. Get in "free" by registering to compete—though be forewarned, it'll cost you a lot of beef, beans, stress, and heartache. Wisely, this mother of all hipster cook-offs is always scheduled at a venue where alcohol is sold, a practice that extends to its many spawn, including, but not limited to, tofu, cookie, fondue and bacon takedowns.

Ninth Avenue International Food Festival – May, the weekend after Mother's Day
9th Ave from approximately 42nd St St to 50th St
www.hellskitchen.bz/info/ninthavenuefoodfestival.shtml
Don't listen to the Eeyores who do nothing but complain about how great this festival used to be. I mean, they're probably right, but we can't all turn back the clock. There's still plenty of good, diverse eating to be done if you blind yourself to the mercenary Italian sausage stands spreading their botulism from street fair to street

fair with no regard for personality or history. Resolve to support only the vendors who are in some way tied to the restaurants and groceries of Hell's Kitchen.

Brooklyn Kitchen Cupcake Cook-Off – May
www.thebrooklynkitchen.com/cupcake.html
Brace yourself if you're planning on competing, and pace yourself if you're merely there to eat. These cupcake fetishists know how to put the sugar on top, and will spend hours of prep work getting it right. Even the pros go into this one with trembling knees.

The Brooklyn Beer Experiment – June or July
www.thefoodexperiments.com
Yay, beer! Fun to drink and fun to cook! Who will win? The scientific home-brewer or the inspired punk home chef whose secret ingredient is a six-pack of whatever's in the dumpster? How about both! Enter if you dare—it won't cost you anything but the price of your ingredients. Even if your timing prevents you from attending, it's worth a gander at their website as they've been known to stage other competitions, notably a Chocolate Experiment that resulted in the creation of a dish named "Chocolate Black Beans with Cauliflower and Pork Belly #9."

The Great Hot Dog Cook Off - July
www.thegreathotdogcookoff.com
Vegetarians! At long last, your competitive weenies will be accorded the respect they deserve as sought after competitors in the Great Hot Dog Cook Off. Is it going too far to say that one of their number could take Best In Show? They supply the charcoal and grill, you bring enough of everything for eight lead-bellied judges to eat a whole one and another 150 dog lovers to try a bite. It's recommended that you recruit a couple of friends to be in your pit crew. As for spectators, a $15 admission may seem a little steep compared to all the papaya places' Recession Specials, but it all goes to City Harvest, a major player in feeding NYC's genuinely hungry.

Craft Beer Week – September
www.nycbeerweek.com
Bring your knee-pads. Most of this festival's hoopla strikes me as something I could patch together on my own for way cheaper, but there are always a couple of lower budget, not-your-average-bear type events that hold appeal, like the Brooklyn Scary Dive Bar pub crawl or a free samples tour of local home-brewers' small apartment set-ups. The Gotham Cask Festival-within-the-festival is also a good deal as the only thing you're paying for there is the rarefied stuff you end up pouring down your gullet.

Harry Met Sally. The Cruise. Somewhere in

Chili Pepper Fiesta – usually the first Saturday in October

The Brooklyn Botanic Garden
1000 Washington Ave (btwn Flatbrush Ave, Washington Ave, & Eastern Pkwy, Prospect Hts, Bklyn) 718-623-7200 www.bbg.org (Prospect Hts: 2/3 to Eastern Pkwy or B/Q to Prospect Park)
You have to pay to get into the garden, and any dish that may result in the ring of fire is a la carte, and, but jalapeño-shaped temporary tattoos are free, as is hobnobbing with live in-person chefs, cookbook authors, and food bloggers, and ear-warming live music from such chili-rich locales as Mexico, India, and Louisiana.

International Pickle Day – October
Orchard St & Grand St, 212-966-0191
www.nyfoodmuseum.org/_phome.htm (LES: J/M/Z to Essex)
What a surprise to find all this garlicky, fermented fun going on on two closed-to-traffic blocks of the Lower East Side. It just seems so much better suited to the Palm Court at the Plaza. Expect lots of green face paint and a guy in a gherkin suit.

The New York City Dumpling Festival - October
www.dumplingfestival.com
LES
Dumplings of the world, unite! Good, now that we have them all in one place, let us fall upon them and eat them! Better, perhaps, to leave the eating contest to the big boys (and girls), though you can share in their bellyaches by methodically stuffing yours several inches beyond its recommended capacity, going stand to stand for pirogi, potstickers, gnocchi, and other such filling-filled dough pockets.

Casserole Crazy – October
www.casserolecrazy.com/the-casserole-party
Greenpoint or Bushwick, Bklyn
Grandma always claimed to have invented that cream-of-mushroom-soup, crushed-potato-chip, chicken-and-noodle dish you love so well, but if the casserole historian behind this annual event recognizes it for a previously-published chestnut from the pages of *Family Circle* or *Women's Day*, you've blown your shot. Original recipes only! If you've got one, and can bring it in hot and ready to rumble, by all means enter the fray via the online registration. Otherwise, buy a ticket and dig in.

Enid's Annual Apple Pie Bake-Off - October
560 Manhattan Ave (@ Driggs, Williamsburg, Bklyn) 718-349-3859
www.enids.net (Williamsburg: G to Nassau)
Attention, rest of the country! We're tired of you thinking you're so great just because you've got good, wholesome family values and a local 4-H kid who raised a prize-winning hog. Our hipster bar apple pie contest is gonna kick your State Fair's ass.

Brooklyn Underground Chili Extravaganza (BRUCE) - October
Barcade
388 Union Ave ((@ Powers St, Williamsburg, Bklyn) 718-302-6464 www.barcadebrooklyn.com (Williamsburg: G/L to Metropolitan-Lorimer)
www.myspace.com/brucechili
BRUCE's rule is that every chili must have at least three exotic ingredients and a name, thus ensuring that some will taste better than they sound, and vice versa. I'm not sure anyone will ever be able to top the Handsome Barnyard (No Furry) which has duck, lime juice, and coconut milk that won a couple of years back. If you're coming in from out of town, it could be tough to compete. Rather than registering first come-first serve online, you fill out a form and stick it in a ballot box that magically appears in Barcade around this time of year.

The Chocolate Show – late October/early November
Metropolitan Pavilion
125 W.18th St (btwn 6th & 7th Ave) 866-CHOC-NYC
www.chocolateshow.com (Chelsea: 1/9 to 18th St)
Twenty-five bucks is way too dear for me to spend on getting in to what feels like a trade show, even if it does come
with unlimited free samples of fancy chocolate. (I think,
technically, they're supposed to be limited, but it's not
like you'll be ejected after you complete your first lap of
the Metropolitan Pavilion.) However they do let two kids
in free with every paying adult, and I have two kids who
would quite rightly judge me the nicest mother in the
world were I to treat them to such an event.

The Brooklyn Pie Bake-Off
www.brooklynpiebake.tumblr.com
All right! A pie annual! This event combines crust (no
ready-mades allowed) and community (at least one ingredient must be grown within a 200-mile range) consciousness while simultaneously raising money for a worthy
cause. Can you bake a pie? Good, neither can I, but I gave
it my best shot anyway. I think I spent more on the Mast
Brothers chocolate that was my local ingredient than if I'd
paid $10 to just eat, and later, one of the judges blogged that
it isn't really a baking chocolate. Well hell, next time I'll go
to the farmer's market for some apples like everybody else!
I'm no sore loser, though—those individual duck tarts that
placed first in the Savory category were DEE-lish.

Food Obstructions – Several times throughout the year
www.noteatingoutinny.com
Food Obstructions numbers as one of the best things
about having to live on the same planet as my least favorite filmmaker, Lars Van Trier, whose film *The Five Obstructions* inspired this cook-off event. Each year, there's a new
set of impositions that contestants must work around.
Last year's entries had to contain an ingredient beginning
with the letter "K", rosemary, something that was grown
or produced in Brooklyn, something with seeds, and no
butter. There's a cookbook in there somewhere, folks.
Tickets to feed are really cheap—five dollars will get you a
bite of everything.

ENTERTAINMENT

MUSEUMS
Museums in NYC can be outrageously expensive. I have a
friend who used to work for a museum in Texas, and while
in NYC he would just demand to be let in for free...*and it*

worked. I am a little too passive for that. – Cecile Dyer

All the museums that charge admission have a few hours
every day (or month) when rabble like us can come in for
free, though be forewarned, you will invariably wind up
cheek to gill with everyone else who can't or won't pay. On
the plus side, the lack of financial investment frees you
up to blow that cultural popcorn stand whenever you've
had enough—no need to worry that you're bailing before
you've gotten your money's worth.

A few of the biggies have a suggested admission charge,
but it's in no way obligatory. We all have our own interpretations. The main thing is to hold your head up as you
offer up your pittance.

Actually, most museums are actively seeking to cultivate
the younger crowd. I don't know how to put this politely,
but they're banking on one of you growing into the sort of
wealthy, childless specimen whose death yields a healthy
financial return. So what if you don't like art, culture or science? They've got live bands, DJs, stand-up comedians, cash
bars, late-night movie screenings, boogie oogie oogie and party arty arty! Surely that alone is worth a sizable endowment.

Art Museums

The Museum of Comic and Cartoon Art (MOCCA)
594 Broadway, Suite 401 (btwn Prince St & Houston St)
212-254-3511, www.moccany.org
(SoHo: B/D/F/M to Broadway-Lafayette St)
Admission: $5
I pray that one day MOCCA will be the size of MOMA. For
now, it's just a couple of rooms, so don't go expecting the
Louvre. If you're a comics fan, do try to make it to one of
their artist-in-person openings.

The New Museum for Contemporary Art
235 Bowery (@ Prince) 212-219-1222
www.newmuseum.org (LES: N/R to Prince St)
Admission: $12, Seniors: $10, Students: $8, Under 18 years
old: Free
Free Thursday 7pm-9pm
This is one museum where I would never ever go when
it's not free. They've got a lot of floor space, but they don't
always fill it up. I had a good time there with a friend who
knows even less about art than I do. After scratching our
heads for several floors, I was able to wring some pleasure
from his enthusiasm for a very slow, pretty video that was
fortunately screening in a room with many comfortable
bean bag chairs. We liked how the Museum supplement-

Century. The Godfather, Parts 1, 2, & 3 • Super

ed a sort of compelling Iraq war exhibit with a schedule of guests who might have an interesting point-of-view—authors, scholars, returned soldiers, and Iraqi citizens—but, instead of public lectures, they booked them to sit in the gallery to engage visitors in conversation. To end things on a positive note, the gift shop is hot, if mostly out of our price range.

Rubin Museum of Art

150 W. 17th St (btwn 6th & 7th Ave) 212-620-5000
www.rmanyc.org (Chelsea: 1/2/3 to 14th St)
Admission $10, Seniors/Student: $2
Free Friday 7 PM - 10 PM
Specializing in Himalayan art, the Rubin is one of my favorite museums in the city, even if the guards do get a trifle stern when the atmosphere of cultivated serenity causes the feral young to bust out in a fit of giggling. It has tons to offer, including a beautiful children's room with a great big fuzzy yak and thoughtfully supplied magnifying glasses for peering at the fingernail-sized demons and heroes populating the Tibetan thanka paintings, but for some reason, it's not high on the tourist and school group agenda. Which means there's never more than one or two people ahead of you for a rice bowl in the beautiful, open plan café. Hanging out here is what passes for spiritual pursuit with me. There's a Himalayan Happy Hour every Wednesday evening, a live music series, and movies relevant to the current exhibition on Friday nights, free as long as you ante up for seven bucks worth of refreshments.

International Center for Photography

1133 Ave of the Americas (@ 43rd St) 212-768-4682
www.icp.org
(Theater District: B/D/F/M/7 to 42nd St-Bryant Park)
Admission: $12, Seniors/Students: $8, Children under 12: free
This medium always brings things to life so vividly... which is why I like it in the first place. I don't come here as often as I'd like because some of the things brought so vividly to life are not so child-friendly.

The Museum of Modern Art (MOMA)

11 W 53rd St (btwn 5th and 6th Ave) 212-708-9400
www.moma.org (Midtown: E/M to 5th Ave-53rd St)
Adults: $20, Seniors: $16, Students: $12, Under 16 years old: Free
Free (and PACKED) every Friday from 4pm–8pm.
Dang, they're not playing with that $20 admission, and even on non-Friday afternoons you may find yourself in a line stretching halfway down the block for the privilege of forking over all that dough. Famous Picassos,

Matisses, Van Goghs, and Andy Warhols that blew the establishment's mind in the olden days are still here. And it continues to be a magnet for weird, interesting work from people who we hope have a lot of work left in them. And the people watching is sublime. I know you're going to want to spend all day tromping from floor to floor, justifying that whopping admission fee, but there are opportunities for relaxation that go beyond a black padded bench. The mezzanine level bookstore has long tables where you can sit for hours, flipping through the merch. The garden is a glamorous haven on a long, sunny morning. With all that fabulousness on the walls, take a few minutes to gaze out the window. Guided tour headsets are free, as is the worthwhile coat check, which generally has a long line. Avoid the inviting but pricey 2nd floor café and duck out to Menchanko-Tei instead.

American Folk Art Museum

45 W 53rd St (btwn 5th and 6th Ave) 212-265-1040
www.folkartmuseum.org (Midtown: E/M to 5th Ave-53rd St)
Admission: $9, Seniors/Students: $7, Children under 12: Free
Free Friday, 5:30–7:30 pm (includes live music!)
The phrase "folk art" makes me think of wooden ducks wearing calico bows and potpourri-trimmed straw hats, but this museum is really a hotbed of Outsider Art (which

makes for a mad-good gift shop). There's even a study center devoted to Henry Darger, a Chicago custodian whose secret life's work was writing, illustrating, and quite possibly believing a sprawling history of The Vivian Girls, the leaders of an army of female and hermaphrodite children, fighting men in Civil War uniforms, frequently to the point of disembowelment and beheading. The restraint the Museum shows in not putting any of that on their totebags should be considered a shining example for others in its line of work. – AH (Compared with the high art in the Met and MOMA, folk art tends to be more accessible. Much of it is practical—furniture, quilts, and signs; and it's often made out of everyday items. While the MOMA will be crazy-packed, free Fridays are a great time to check out the American Folk Art Museum. Despite its many floors, it's pretty small and doable in one visit. – Amanda Plumb)

MOMA's Annual Artists Pass
If your artwork has ever been exhibited in NYC (not on a lamppost), or your illustrations have been published in something that might conceivably be described as a "real" magazine, or you're one of those smoothies who could sell sex toys to a nun, gather up your supporting evidence and try your luck at the Visitors Services desk near the coat check. (I went armed with a copy of my zine and a few issues of BUST, in which I have a column that I also illustrate by the hair of my chinny-chin-chin.) If the attendant finds your claims credible, you can purchase a $25 Artist's Pass that allows you to come and go as you please for a year and gets you into their film screenings for free as well. Even if you don't plan on visiting New York again in the year, the friends upon whose couch you're staying may be willing to hold onto those photo-free credentials for you, especially if your first name corresponds to one of their genders.

The Museum of Art and Design (MAD)
2 Columbus Circle (@ 59th St) 212-299-7727
www.madmuseum.org (Midtown: A/C/B/D/1 to 59th St-Columbus Circle)
Admission: $15, Students/Seniors: $12, Under 12 years old: Free
Pay-What-You-Wish every Thursday 6pm - 9pm
MAD's exhibits tend to showcase the gnarly, crafty things dear to my heart—a giant tapestry of a sweatshop worker composed entirely of garment labels, a five dollar bill embellished with enough French knots to give Honest Abe an awesome 'fro, a resident artist who loads his fresh-off-the-pottery wheel creations into a briefcase, totes them around the New York City subways, and then displays the resultant mass as sculpture—among many others. Like so many other NYC cultural institutions, MAD has recently upgraded to a fancy new building, but Studio Sunday, their 2pm all-ages workshop, is still a good dealio for people without children, in that the $10 all-inclusive, per-person workshop + museum entry works out to $5 less than the standard adult admission. If your cell phone plan includes unlimited weekend calling, check out their bang-up free audio tour for cell phones. Every December, they throw a DIY Salon, a beer-and-DJ-enhanced craft party, where you can hop from station to station, making (or learning how to make) things like throwies, merit badges, magic lanterns, and paper jewelry.

The Whitney
945 Madison Ave (btwn 74th & 75th) 212-570-7721
www.whitney.org (Upper East Side: 6 to 77th St)
$18, Seniors/Students/, 19–25 years old: $12: $12/ Under 18 years old: free
Pay What You Wish Friday, 6–9 pm
My Whitney drill goes something like this: Friends with their fingers on the art world's pulse fly in from Chicago or London, specifically to catch some show at the Whitney by a famous artist I've never heard of. They take me with. I enjoy myself. I resolve to enrich myself with every-other-monthly visits, but don't purchase the membership that would make such a resolution financially sensible. Then before I know it, the phone rings, and the friends from London and Chicago are flying in again. I did manage to hear about and subsequently go see a very galvanizing Kara Walker retrospective there. If you want to come off fashionably blasé, bust on the famous Whitney Biennial—all the critics do.

Metropolitan Museum of Art
1000 5th Ave (@ E 82nd St) 212-535-7710
www.metmuseum.org (Upper East Side: 4/5/6 to 86th St)
Suggested Admission: $20
This enormous museum has one of the best collections of art in the world. You could spend a day just in one section. It might take you a week to do the whole museum. Like the Natural History Museum, the Met also has a good African art collection. – Andy Singer (And no one should pay more than a dollar to enter! There are plenty of philanthropists who keep that place going; they don't need your 20 bucks. Go sit and absorb the sights and sounds of the Temple of Dendur; think about the history of the people who created that structure, and then about the events that led to it sitting in a big room on 5th Avenue instead of in Egypt. Apparently this object, unlike some others, actually was a gift from that country, so don't feel

SYRIAN
IRANIAN
TURKISH
ARMORS
15.00 AD

guilty about enjoying it. But respect it. While you're in that section, check out the statues of Hatshepsut, Egypt's female pharaoh. And of course the blue hippo, which the museum has named William and adopted as its unofficial mascot. – Melissa Bastian) (Additionally, I'll be blocking the exits until you've seen the hunky Hanuman sculpture in the South Asia Galleries, the Chinese Garden Court, the Japanese armor (check out the helmet with the bunny on it!) and the bed where the kids sleep in *From the Mixed-Up Files of Mrs. Basil E. Frankweiler*. If it's nice outside, get your ass up to the roof. Also, while my purse and often taste buds recoil from most museum cafés, the Met offers two lovely options that aren't too expensive. The first is a sandwich on the Great Hall's balcony, and the other is a self-serve breakfast by the big window in the Petrie Court Café and Wine Bar before it morphs into a fancy restaurant for lunch.

The Guggenheim
1071 Fifth Ave (btwn 88th St & 89th St) 212-423-3500
www.guggenheim.org (Upper East Side: 4/5/6 to 86th St)
Admission: $18, Seniors/Students: $15, Under 12 years old: Free
Pay What You Wish Saturday 5:45 pm - 7:15 pm (museum closes at 7:45)
Being inside the Guggy is like being in a larger than life conch shell. Have you ever been to the top floor and looked down? Vertigo! I have seen some good exhibits there, but it is the famed building by Frank Lloyd Wright itself that is the real work of art. – Ling Teo (It is most definitely worth a visit. Admission is a bit steep, which is part of what makes pay-what-you-wish Saturdays so great. They'd be great anyway though: People from all over the world fill the museum with unbridled excite-

ment and a sense of expectant awe, which makes it feel like being at the most important art opening ever. Start all the way at the top floor, and slowly spiral downward, stopping at each exterior gallery. The museum's collection is no less stunning than its changing exhibits. You'll see original works the images of which you've known all your life. To me, such things never cease to be breathtaking. – Melissa Bastian) (The Guggenheim acts far younger than its 50 years on the first Friday of the month, when it throws an Art After Dark bash for young members, though non-members can get in for a steep $25 (drinks not included). They're prone to party tricks like letting the first hundred people wearing red in for free, so do a little research before hitting the ATM. – AH)

El Museo de Barrio
1230 Fifth Ave (btwn E 104th & E 105th St) 212-931-7272
www.elmuseo.org (Upper East Side: 6 to 103rd St)
Adults: $6, Seniors/Students: $4, Children under 12: Free
Free the third Saturday of every month. Seniors free on Wednesdays.
Now that its building's all spiffed up and ready to party, the tourist hordes may stop petering out before they hit El Museo de Barrio. The Day of the Dead is a biggie here, as is Three King's Day (January 6) when the Museo sponsors a procession complete with camels.

The Studio Museum in Harlem
144 W 125th St (@ MLK Blvd) 212-864-4500
www.studiomuseum.org (Harlem: 2/3 to 125th St)
Admission: $7, Seniors / Students: $3, Under the age of 12: Free
Free Sundays 12pm – 6pm
Would that all "studios" in NYC were this size, with new plumbing, hardwood floors, and some really great art on

Zinester's Favorite Songs About New York: New York

the walls. The exhibition materials which they give away free make the big bananas seem like cheapskates. They have great family workshops and free movie screenings. If you are an emerging artist or filmmaker of African descent, promise me you will go for one of the three giant brass rings the Museum offers annually: a $20,000 fellowship, a free, non-live-in (sorry) studio, and $1,000...which ain't exactly a year's rent but would for sure make a dent in the clay budget.

The Cloisters
99 Margaret Corbin Dr (@ Ft Tryon Pl, Fort Tryon Park)
212-923-3700, www.metmuseum.org/cloisters
(Inwood: A to Dyckman St-200th St)
Suggested Admission: $20
It appears that the Cloisters are well-known only to German tourists, so you will really get to see everything up close. Check out the book room, where illuminated manuscripts are displayed that will blow your mind. – Jerry the Mouse (The Cloisters contains the bulk of the Met's medieval collection, and are housed in a gorgeous monastic structure cobbled together from bits and pieces of 12th to 15th century architecture. Late spring is a particularly great time to visit, as the courtyard gardens will have busted out with flowering herbs, pretty flowers, and a discreetly positioned cappuccino machine that makes for some of the most pastoral sipping this side of Verona. –AH)

The Brooklyn Museum of Art
200 Eastern Parkway (btwn Grand Army Plaza & Washington Ave, Prospect Hts, Brooklyn) 718-638-5000
www.brooklynmuseum.org
(Prospect Hts: 2/3 to Eastern Parkway)
You may remember some considerable flap about Chris Ofili's *The Holy Virgin Mary*, who was depicted as a black woman (not a problem), partially rendered in such non-traditional materials as cut-outs from porno mags and elephant dung (big problem). It all went down in *this museum!* Before that dust-up, the Brooklyn Museum was this world-class museum that could never get the respect it deserved because it wasn't in Manhattan. Even though it was the one that started this whole party trend with its First Saturdays, not as an excuse to sink its vampire fangs into comely youth, but more to celebrate its excellent exhibits with the community, with dancing preceded by dance lessons, film screenings, live music, interactive art projects, and free admission. Much as I love a party, there's a certain beauty to first Sundays too. You could fire a cannonball through the joint and not hit anybody.

MOMA PS 1
22-25 Jackson Ave (@ 46th Ave, Long Island City, Queens)
718-784-2084
www. ps1.org (LIC: E/M/G to LIC-Court Sq)
Admission: $5, Senior/Student: $2 – Free with MOMA ticket stub used within 30 days (not valid for events)
PS1 is one of my personal favorite museums in New York City. It's out of the way and thus less crowded than the places on Manhattan's Museum Mile all along 5th Avenue from 82nd to 104th Street. It's housed in an old public school in the Long Island City section of Queens (thus the title) and hosts weekly $10 dance parties (admission included) on summer Saturdays, with out-of-town DJs spinning, so after you're done viewing the exhibits, you can come outside and dance or lounge in the gravel area. It's a great place to meet people, even though the parties themselves get super crowded. – Eric Nelson (The art's fun too! There's always something there to make me laugh, often on video. Go see James Terrell's *Meeting* an hour before sunset, the only time you *can* see it, provided of course it's not raining. And that's all I'm going to say about that. – AH)

Isamu Touching Garden Museum
9-01 33rd Rd, (@ Vernon Blvd, Long Island City, Queens)
718-204-7088, www.noguchi.org (LIC: N to Broadway)
Admission: $10, Seniors/Students: $5, Children under 12: Free
Pay what you wish: 1st Friday every month
Leave your monkey mind in Manhattan and pick a beautiful day to enjoy the tranquil indoor/outdoor flow that carries you around Japanese sculptor Isamu Noguchi's simple shapes. It's a long walk from the subway, but once you get there, the Socrates Sculpture Park is in spittin' distance. The museum's website gives detailed instructions for following the artist's personal route, which involved taking the Roosevelt Island tram from Manhattan, then hoofing it across a bridge to Queens. Fun!

Fisher Landau Center for Art
3827 30th St (btwn 38th & 39th Ave, Astoria, Queens)
718-937-0727
www.flcart.org (Astoria: N / W to the 39th Ave)
Admission: Free
Always free and usually very sparse in visitors, this is a fantastic place to see modern art. I saw my first Yoshitomo Nara in person here. – Melissa Bastian

The Queens Museum
NYC Building (in Corona Park, Flushing, Queens) 718-592-9700
www.queensmuseum.org
(Flushing: 7 to Willets Point/Shea Stadium)

City ~ Cub and They Might Be Giants • New York

Suggested Admission: $5
The Queens Museum inhabits one of the old fair buildings out by Shea Stadium, in Flushing Meadow Park, the
site of the World's Fair in 1939/40 and again in 1964/65.
It sometimes has really good art shows by excellent,
lesser-known contemporary artists. The ride there on the
#7 from 42nd Street in midtown Manhattan is the best,
because, after leaving Manhattan and going a couple of
stops into Queens, it comes above ground and runs on elevated tracks all the way. There are great views of Queens.
– Andy Singer (One of the Queens Museum's most notable
features is a comprehensive model railroad sized version
of NYC. Find your friend's building! Find your favorite
restaurant! There's even a tiny jet taking off from mini-
JFK! The former fairground site has a neglected ghost
town feel which can make for some fun running around.
Check out the Unisphere. – AH)

Cultural, Science, and History Museums

The Ellis Island Immigration Museum
Starts at Castle Clinton, 26 Wall St, 1-877-LADY-TIX
www.nps.gov/ellis/index.htm
(Battery Park: 1 to South Ferry)
Admission: $12, Seniors: $10, 4 to 12 years old $5, Under 3
Years old: Free
There's a lot of site-specific oomph to this exhibit on immigrant experience, and the curators don't put too much
of an apple pie spin on the hardships many endured. (The
taped audio tour is, by contrast, kind of sanitized.) Anyway, don't let the foam rubber Statue of Liberty crowns
for sale at the ferry's embarkation point fool you into
thinking that this is some sort of cheesy give-it-a-miss
tourist attraction. The arrangement of bundles, trunks,
and carpet bags running the length of the lobby never
fails to give me a lump, as does imagining that Great
Hall jammed with confused, exhausted families, some of
whose jackets would be chalked with rejection marks that
would dash their chances for entry. There's an interactive
database where you can search for the names of relatives
who came through here on their way from the old country. The trip out (you're technically paying for the ferry,
the museum itself is free once you get there) is expensive,
but worth it. Save a little dough by opting out of the
Statue of Liberty stop—you'll pass by close enough to get
a good look at the old girl's pores. Do you really need to
join the teeming masses swarming around the base? If
the answer is yes, it's free to get out and stroll around.

The Museum of Jewish Heritage: A Living Memorial to
the Holocaust
Edmond J. Safra Plaza, 36 Battery Pl (Btwn 1st Pl & West
St) 212-968-1800
www.mjhnyc.org (Battery Park: 4/5 to Bowling Green)
Admission: $12, Seniors: $10 Students: $7, Under 12 years old: Free
Free Wednesday 4pm – 8pm
The subject matter is heavy, yes, but inarguably compelling. The implications and experiences are examined
through so many lights, there's always new information.
The Museum has some tips for planning a visit with kids,
and areas where the focus shifts to more peaceful periods
of Jewish life. Nighttime events run a serious gamut, as
titles ranging from *The End of the Jews* to *Is Diss A System?
A Milt Gross Comic Reader* attest.

National Museum of the American Indian
1 Bowling Green (intersection of Broadway & Battery Pl)
212-514-3700
www.nmai.si.edu (Financial District: 4/5 to Bowling Green)
Free

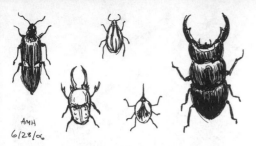

AMH
6/28/06

This is a gem of a museum—and underrated! I can't believe its building, a beautiful Beaux Arts customs house, sat vacant for years before the museum moved in. I saw a great exhibit of Fritz Scholder paintings here, as well as an exhibit on dressmaking with dresses dating back to 1850, a healthy multimedia aspect that shared the faces and names of the dressmakers, and an oral history of the craft. Strong women with important stories represented here. Thank you, Smithsonian! The small gift shop on the main floor has a wide-ranging selection of books on Native Americans, and is well worth perusing on its own. – Heath Row

The South Street Seaport Museum
12 Fulton St (Btwn South St & Front St) 212-748-8786
www.southstreetseaportmuseum.org (Financial District:
A/C/J/M/Z/2/3/4/5 to Fulton St-Broadway-Nassau)
Admission: $12, Seniors/Students: $10, Children 5-12: $8
I love me a good scrimshaw, but what I'd head to first and foremost is *The Peking*, a tall ship you can board to learn about the scurvy conditions endured by your average seaman not a hundred years back. Lots of rotten potatoes and more than a few musical evenings involving mops on the head and coconut shell bras, to go by the charmingly abused, bawdy-but-innocent-seeming photographic enlargements posted below decks. If you do take the extremely tall escalator back to the museum after your time aboard, try to see if they're showing a video of the vintage film shot by a guy riding the top of *The Peking*'s mast during some seriously squally swells!

Bodies Exhibit
11 Fulton St (btwn Front and Beekman St) 1-888-9BODIES
www.bodiesny.com (Financial District:
A/C/J/Z/2/3/4/5 to Fulton St-Broadway-Nassau)
Admission: $26.50, Senior: $22.50, Children age 4-12:
$20.50. $1 more expensive on weekends/holidays. Call
about student discount.
I'll yammer on to anyone who'll listen about the cadaver dissection I participated in as part of my massage school training, and how once I'm done with my body, you're welcome to pass it around and eat it if that's how it would be of the most service, but I suspect my ghost would be royally pissed if my preserved remains wound up spending eternity displayed in some uncharacteristically athletic pose. Surely my flayed corpse would prefer to be exhibited hunched over a long-armed stapler, or maybe checking its email when it's supposed to be starting dinner. At any rate, the education department of this now-permanent NYC attraction is working hard to make sure their charges' dance cards stay filled, with the most intriguing event being artists' Sketch Nights several times a month. And while that admission fee is enough to make your optic nerve pull a Big Daddy Roth, Theatermania. com and all the other online brokers offering discount theater tickets usually have some cut-rate deals to Bodies going too. Which I guess clears up the question as whether or not this freak show is truly intended as science.

Museum of Chinese in America
215 Centre St (btwn Howard St & Grand St) 212-619-4785
www.mocanyc.org (Chinatown: J/N/Q /R/Z/6 to Canal)
$7. Seniors/Students: $4. Under age 12: Free
Free Thursday 11 am - 9 pm
Their new building, designed by Maya Lin, makes for one of the most beautiful museums in the city. Video portraits of Chinatown hometown heroes anchor an incredible ephemera collection demonstrating the overt racism that greeted the first Chinese immigrants, and persisted to the recent past. There's a full-scale recreation of an herbalist's shop with lots of explanations as to what everything is. Check their website if you want in on one of their frequent eating tours of Chinatown. Ditto if you've got some video to upload about your town's Chinatown, or are a Chinese-American who'd like to contribute to their Story Map. – AH (They have an amazingly interactive permanent exhibit on Chinese immigration. – Victoria Law)

Side – The Magnetic Fields ● Walk on the Wild Side

Museum of Sex
233 5th Avenue (@ 27th St) 212-689-6337
www.museumofsex.com (Gramercy Park: N/R to 28th St)
Admission: $14.50, Seniors/Students: $13.50
There's a case to be made for the curatorial expertise that drags all this stuff into the light to exhibit in one tastefully designed location. Someone's definitely got a sense of humor about the subject, as evidenced by a recent survey of the animal kingdom's balls-out mating rituals. If you're in the mood, you can probably rustle up a discount coupon from an ad in *The Onion* or off the museum's own website. Or at least swing by the gift shop to see the love doll for dogs, the penis-shaped stemware, and the hot pink banana vibe. (Love imagining what the carry on baggage inspectors would make of that one.)

Japan Society
333 E 47th St (Btwn 1st Ave & 2nd Ave) 212-832-1155
www.japansociety.org
(Midtown: 6/M to Lexington Ave-53rd St)
$10. Seniors/Students: $8. Under 16-years-old: Free
Free every Friday 6-9PM
A restful exhibit space and cultural center near the UN, the sedate-seeming Japan Society is more than capable of busting the sort of indecorous move I crave, showing Yoko Ono's *Fly* and *Film No. 4 (Bottoms)*, and salting the cute Hello Kittyishness of an anime exhibit with some seriously perverted examples of the form. Evenings are the time for film screenings, performances, and food forums.

American Museum of Natural History
Central Park West (btwn 79th and 81st St) 212-769-5200
www.amnh.org (Upper West Side, B/C to 81st St)
Suggested Admission: $16
Their "suggested" admission will make your eyes bleed, so pay what you will, with the understanding that only those who throw down the full amount will be getting into the non-negotiable special exhibit. The museum has incredible collections of stuffed animals, plants, fish, dinosaur bones, and African, Central American, South American, and Asian art. It is a paradise for people who like to sketch. It's also a good place for anyone interested in natural history, the biological sciences or non-European art and artifacts. It's a *huge* museum so you could spend a day just in one section. – Andy Singer (I recently discovered the Margaret Mead Hall. It's wonderful and overlooked by most visitors. – Victoria Law) (Fucking real dinosaur bones, all put together. A blue fucking whale hanging from the ceiling. Unbelievable dioramas of Native American culture. They even have a dodo bird. I went once for a hothouse exhibit of rare butterflies inside a

tent. Some of them landed on me. People dream of getting their science shit into this museum. It only has the best exhibits and the best people working there. – Josh Saitz) (Like Seymour Cassel, Ruth Gordon, Lou Jacobi, and Walter Matthau, the Museum is one of New York's great character actors. *The Squid and the Whale, Manhattan, Election, Gertie the Dinosaur,* and the totally botched *Night At the Museum* number among its many on-screen appearances. It too has a sideline as a party promoter, throwing a DJ-enhanced shindig called "One Step Beyond" on the first Friday of every month in the attached Rose Center for Earth and Space. And because it's accustomed to dealing with kids, it hosts the Valhalla of all kids parties—a slumber party, limited to kids 8–12 and their deep-pocketed parents. – AH)

Hayden Planetarium Space Show at the American Museum of Natural History
My spouse and I paid $24 apiece to get into the museum and see a half-hour long space show in the Planetarium. Although AMNH is pay-what-you-wish, you have to pay at least $20 to see special exhibits, IMAX films, and the space show, so giving them the extra $4 they recommended seemed reasonable. I am sorry to tell you it wasn't. Both of us had fond memories of the Planetarium from our childhood visits. The whole Rose Center for Earth and Space was majorly overhauled recently, so we were psyched to see what it was like now. I'm not sure if it's the kind of thing that's just more fun for kids (not to mention stoners) or if the new design just isn't as happening. A lot of the interactive elements were already out of commission. The Hayden Planetarium Theater was just as cool as ever, but I was disappointed in the show. Speaking of

kids, the place is crawling with loud school groups.
– Jenna Freedman

The New York Historical Society
170 Central Park West (btw W 76th & W 77th St) 212-873-3400
www.nyhistory.org (Upper West Side: B/C to 72nd St)
Admission: $12. Senior: $9. Student: $7. Under 12: Free
Pay what you can: Friday 6-8PM
Coming here just makes me think of how much less I
would dig any New York that doesn't have a Chinatown.
I do kind of enjoy going on the Fourth of July when they
give you free popcorn and let you in free if you're wearing
red, white, and blue, and costumed reenactors get real
serious about patrolling the sidewalk in front of the entrance with their muskets, as double-decker busloads of
tank-topped tourists roll hooting past.

The Jewish Museum
1109 5th Ave (@ 92nd St) 212-423-3200
www.thejewishmuseum.org (Upper East Side: 6 to 96th St)
$12. Seniors: $10. Students: $ 7.50. Under 12: Free
Free on Saturdays
I find it New York-y in the best way that the Jewish Museum closes for Martin Luther Day but is open on the Sab-
bath. It's housed in a beautiful old building, and has more
than enough art and culture to make its mother proud.
Moving on to the museum café, this is one place where
you need not worry about breaking any kosher laws. The
permanent and very interactive Archeology Zone kids
exhibit is one of the best of its kind, with seriously fun
dress-up, role-playing activities.

The Museum of the City of New York
1220 5th Ave (@ 103rd St) 212-534-1672
www.mcny.org (Upper East Side: 6 to 103rd St)
Suggested Admission: $10
An overlooked museum right there on Museum Row, but
up a little north-ish. They do phenomenal and detailed
exhibits on New York history, art, and the history of the
"built environment," not just architecture proper—they
have an exhibit now on Eero Saarinen—but also things
like the parks and the development of the park system
of the city. They are family friendly, and have held a children's holiday party for the past 40 years. Children 12 and
under and members get in free, as does *anyone* who lives
or works in East Harlem above 103rd Street. Just say "I'm
a neighbor" if you live or work in the neighborhood, and
you get in free. – Jerry the Mouse (Know your address,
neighbor, or the ticket desk person is going to think
you're a total *putz* for not just flipping them a quarter and
saying, "Here's your suggested admission!" – AH)

The New York City Transit Museum
Boerum Place and Schermerhorn Street - underground
(Downtown Bklyn) 718-243-3060
www.mta.info/mta/museum (Downtown Bklyn:
M/R/2/3/4/5 to Court St-Borough Hall)
Here's your chance to drive the bus, though prepare to
wait if a three-year-old beats you to the steering wheel.
I prefer to pretend that I'm a passenger on the many
vintage subway cars on the lower level's disused tracks.
Those rattan seats take me back to a pre-air-conditioned
time, when a girl could wear white gloves and dream of
being Miss Subways. (Viva the 21st century, when the City
Reliquary resurrected the tradition with a Miss G Train
pageant—first runner-up was a violin-playing man in
drag!) Every now and then, there's an opportunity to ride
one of these babies for real, when the Museum rolls it out
in service of a special event. There's lots of chilling information for claustrophobes regarding the sandhogs who
built the subways, and a kick-ass gift shop where you can
pledge allegiance to your favorite train line with a t-shirt
or a Xmas ornament featuring a circle bearing its letter
and color. True buffs might enjoy the frequent tours of
maintenance shops and Old City Hall station, or just chat-
ting up the very talkative retired volunteers, all of whom
share your passion.

The Museum of the Moving Image
3601 35th Ave (@ 36th St, Astoria Queens) 718-784-0077
www.movingimage.us (Astoria: N to 36th Ave)
This highly participatory monument to movie and tele-
vision-making has been undergoing major renovations
and is due to reopen on January 15, 2011. Count on a pricey
admission that will deliver as long as you go with kids, or
similarly uninhibited adults. My friend and I had a stone
blast on a weekday visit, deliberately scheduled for a time
when my children would be in school. The paper print-
out of our video flip book is priceless. Other visits have
allowed me to get up close and personal with Gumby and
Alien's Alien Queen. A ham like me can never get enough
of capering in front of that green screen. Naturally, this is
also a prime place to catch screenings of both classic and
rarely shown films.

Littler Museums

Federal Hall
26 Wall St (btwn Broad St & Nassau St) 212-509-1595
www.nps.gov/feha (Financial District: J/Z to Broad St)
Free
If you are like me, a bit of a history dork and a fan of im-

Harry • New York City Don't Mean Nothing – Savage

pressive architecture, Federal Hall is a great (free) stop. In its original form the building served as the first capitol of the US, and the bill of rights was passed there. (T.I.G.H.T.) They usually have some sort of historical exhibition going on, and it's amazing to walk around the rotunda. – Cecile Dyer

The Lower East Side Tenement Museum
108 Orchard St (btwn Broome St & Delancey St)
212-431-0233
www.tenement.org (LES: F/J/M/Z to Delancey-Essex)
Admission: $20, Senior/Student: $15
The Lower East Side Tenement Museum gives a great history of the Lower East Side housing, labor, and immigrant scene, and also does walking tours of the neighborhood. And they have a gift shop. – Jerry the Mouse (The actual exhibition space is in a couple of tenements across the street, where apartments have been done up as period-accurate representations of what life would have been like for the families who lived there at various times over the last century and a half. It helps put these pioneers' unbelievably sweet rents in perspective to imagine what a blast it would be to stand over the sink, hand-laundering your nine children's soiled linen after a 12-hour shift at the Triangle Shirtwaist Factory. They also host interesting guest speakers. – AH) (The museum folks learned that the father of a Jewish family who lived in one of the units died of TB, so the apartment has medical tools from the treatment and signs that the family was sitting Shiva. The Baldizzi family's apartment has a cool story. Josephine Baldizzi was walking down Orchard Street one day and noticed a sign on the tenement building where she had grown up, explaining that a museum based on the real lives of immigrants who lived in the building was in progress. She went in and started talking with the curators who then worked with her to design an apartment based on the one she grew up in. There is even a little audio of her talking about the apartment. Because the building is not up to code, there is a limit to the number of people who can be on each floor at any given time, so tours are small, kind of pricey and each tour only shows you a portion of the building. – Amanda Plumb) (Expect some of the grimmer realities of life on the LES to be a bit soft-pedaled if you take a tour geared for all-ages. – AH)

Reverend Jen's Lower East Side Troll Museum
122-24 Orchard Street #19 (btwn Delancey and Rivington)
212-777-2875
www.societyofcontrol.com/coal/rev_troll.htm
(LES: F/J/M/Z to Delancey-Essex)
Pay what you wish – By appointment only

While the focus of this museum is admittedly narrow in scope, you're unlikely to find a larger collection of troll dolls in a semi-open to the public setting. Your tour will be conducted by the museum director. (She's partial to Budweiser if you'd like to bring a hostess present.)

Merchant's House
29 E 4th St (btwn Bowery & Lafayette) 212-777-1089
www.merchantshouse.org
(NoHo: B/D/F/M to Broadway-Lafayette)
$8. Seniors/Students: $5. Under 12: Free
This little-known museum is a great example of what a single-family home was like in the early- and mid-19th century. It used to be an informal museum run by a family member who wasn't trained in museum design or preservation, and some alterations were made that aren't truly in line with what a professional would have done. I'd go back just to talk to the gardener, who is friendly, well-informed about the property, and given the amount of time he's been working there, truly and deeply cares about the place. – Heath Row (This hidden-in-plain-sight historical site has got its own one-shot zine, detailing all the spooky, ghostly encounters visitors and staff have had in the Merchant's House. Note to self: Do not apply for a job here. – AH)

The Center for Book Arts
28 W 27th St 3rd Floor (btwn 5th and 6th Ave) 212-481-0295
www.centerforbookarts.org Flatiron: N/R to 28th St)
Free
In front of the work area where students and Center members position type and ink it up on four vintage Vandercook presses is a small gallery that's a source of constant interest to those with a soft spot for getting the word out DIY-style. My favorite show here included a ton of one-shot zines from the Chicago-based collective, Temporary Services, dangling from the ceiling on strings that allowed visitors to paw through them to their hearts' content. They have great artist talks that tie into the exhibits and a monthly Friday night Book Arts Lounge, where for a $10 suggested admission, you can learn all sorts of nifty tricks, like making pop-up books or continuous flexagons. Enter your poems in their annual chapbook competition, and you may find yourself with a reading, a thousand bucks, and a limited-edition, letterpress run of your work, printed and bound by artists at the Center. If you're more hands-on, you may elect to nominate yourself for a full scholarship to their four-day spring Letterpress Printing & Fine Press Publishing Seminar For Emerging Writers.

The Museum at FIT
Seventh Ave at 27th St, 212-217-5558
www.fitnyc.edu/museum (Chelsea: 1/2 to 28th St)
Free
I don't give half a fraying shoelace for sample sales and the latest fashion trends, but I have a costume designer's interest in both outrageous get-ups on order of Bjork's swan dress, and beautifully constructed vintage garments that make me wonder how our foremothers dealt with such fleshy realities as menstruation, shitting babies, 90° days and waistlines commensurate with sustaining life. The Fashion Institute of Technology is serious about preserving these artifacts, in a peaceful, temperature controlled, low-lit atmosphere, perfect for restoring one's tranquility when the honk and screech starts to overwhelm.

James A Farley PO Postal Museum
421 8th Ave (@ 31st St) 212-330-3291
(Garment District: A/C/E to 34th St)
Free
To see the whole collection, some of which is upstairs, you have to make an appointment with "Mr. Paul". Even if you don't connect with this mystery man, if you have a zine or any other project that travels by the mail, you owe it to yourself to pop into the post office's grand old lobby.

There are several interesting displays of postal memorabilia at either end, including a really cool old delivery bike that I dream of wheeling around town.

The Asia Society Museum
725 Park Avenue (btwn 70th St & 71st St) 212-288-6400
www.asiasociety.org (Upper East Side: 6 to 68th St)
$10. Senior: $7. Student: $5. Under 16: Free
Free every Friday 6-9pm
Go for the frequently changing array of exhibits and the exciting, "young" feel. This is the coolest place to check out new art from Asia, and I mean all of Asia—not just the Far East, but also India, Nepal, the Philippines, and all points of the diaspora. And they're inexpensive for a museum. They even hold hands-on art-making workshops if you want to meet some contemporary artists and have them show you how they do what they do. – Jerry the Mouse

Hispanic Society of America
613 W 155th St (btwn Broadway & Riverside) 212-926-2234
www.hispanicsociety.org (Washington Hts: C to 155th St)
Free
An amazing free museum focusing on Spain, Portugal, and Latin America, as well as a historic library with lots of beautiful illuminated manuscripts, Renaissance pieces, and a large and varied collection put together in the early days of the New World. It's one of NYC's hidden uptown treasures. You can actually go and just browse old books on subjects like Jewish and Islamic art in Spain and Latin America, imagery in particular artists' works, and more.

You But You're Bringing Me Down - LCD Sound

The knowledgeable curator and archivist speaks Spanish and English (and probably a lot of other languages), and is extremely helpful and enthusiastic. There are free 45 minute tours of the building and collections given by museum curators or the Education Department at 2pm on Saturdays. – Jerry the Mouse

Morris-Jumel Mansion
65 Jumel Terrace (@ Sylvan Terrace, 1 blk E of St. Nicholas Ave) 212-923-8008
www.morrisjumel.org (Morningside Hts: C to 163rd St)
$4. Seniors/Students: $3. Children under 12: Free
This is the oldest house in Manhattan; a must for any local antiquarian. H.P. Lovecraft wrote of his visit in the early '20s. Barbara, the caretaker, is a dear. Spend some time walking the grounds, sit on a bench along the edge of the property, and be sure to check out the row of clapboard houses nearby. And ask Barb about the ghosts that people see from the Triple Nickel next door—especially the man in the white feather coat. – Heath Row

City Reliquary
370 Metropolitan Ave (@ Havemeyer St, Williamsburg, Bklyn) 718-782-4842
www.cityreliquary.org (Williamsburg: G/L to Metropolitan-Lorimer)
Pay what you wish
The City Reliquary *rules*. Its contents include collections of everyday objects on loan from everyday people—like jars of found street sweeper bristles, Statue of Liberty postcards with different tints and vantage points, seltzer bottles, and bits of salvaged brickwork from buildings. It also includes amazing core samples, old tools, and the rubbish and rubble of a city chock full of people. It's usually staffed by one volunteer in a cramped, dusty, and very well-organized little space. Imagine taking the best parts of a salvage yard, a book about New York history, and a crazy old lady's tchotchke shelf. - Cecile Dyer (If you have a collection, you can share and show it at their occasional collection nights. And if you're into newfangled bikes—high riders and the like—people involved in the project also dabble in that. – Heath Row) (This is one museum to which I heartily advocate making a non-dinky donation. I love the dimestore passion in evidence here. For instance, there's a piece of a really old shovel, found in the New Croton Aqueduct, earnestly labeled "Really Old Shovel." Those with an interest in burlesque will appreciate the corner devoted to Little Egypt—complete with a mirror that will morph you into a creepy mannequin in belly dancer costume with a push of a button. I'm partial to the attempt to recreate Petrella's newsstand, a Chinatown

landmark that passed away with Mr. Petrella, an amateur artist specializing in Bruce Lee portraits. Given its location and underground vibe, the Reliquary doesn't need to do too many backflips to attract young museum-goers, but it's still sinking its teeth into the museum party pie with Third Thursdays. Live bands and refreshments compliments of the Brooklyn Brewery make the proceedings feel like a house show, complete with back yard to escape to when the display cases start to fog up. If the Reliquary's not open when you're in the 'hood—or even if it is—go around the corner to Grand and Havermeyer, where the Museum's original location, a window in a ground floor apartment, is still operating, and a painted-on signpost supplies distances to other Williamsburg landmarks. – AH)

The Waterfront Museum & Showboat Barge
290 Conover St, Pier 44 (@ Reed St, Red Hook, Bklyn) 718-624-4719
www.waterfrontmuseum.org
(Red Hook: B61 bus to Beard St or IKEA water taxi)
Pay what you wish
This museum is entirely contained within an old barge, which a Brooklyn family found filled with over two tons of mud and purchased for the fixer upper price of $1. They restored it themselves and live below decks, maintaining the upper level as a museum devoted to the history of showboats, and the performers who appeared on them (as well as their own rescue of this particular craft, a subject the father, David, is always up for discussing with visitors. He'll also set the kinetic Rube Goldberg device he built at one end into motion for you.) Summer brings Circus Sundays, when the museum hosts a variety of matinée performances for around $15 a ticket.

Center for Thanatology
391 Atlantic Ave (@ Bond St, Boerum Hill, Bklyn) 718-858-3026
www.thanatology.org
(Boerum Hill: A/C/G to Hoyt-Schermerhorn Sts)
Free
A labor of love from a Brooklyn woman who's really interested in the study of death rituals! Call to make an appointment!

The Wyckoff Farmhouse Museum
5816 Clarendon Rd (btwn 59th and Ralph, East Flatbush, Bklyn) 718-629-5400
www.wyckoffassociation.org
(East Flatbush: F to 18th Ave then B8 to Rockaway Ave)
$5. Seniors/Students: $3. Under 10 years old: Free
Is your last name Wyckoff ? If so, congratulations, you're descended from the original owners of this cozy, his-

toric home. The head curator would like to roll out the metaphorical red carpet for you in a significant, pleased-to-meet-you way. Time has marched on since the first settlers plunked down roots in Brooklyn, marooning the brave little farmhouse amidst many fast food joints and auto parts stores, but there's always a good time to be had in a churn-your-own-butter, wow-*how*-many-kids-did-that-family-pack-in-here kind of way. The staff's remark-ably flexible. I once saw a couple of public school kids talk them into building a fire in the front yard in order to pop some corn to go with that just-churned butter.

Weeksville Heritage Center Hunterfly Road Houses
1698 Bergen St (btwn Buffalo & Rochester, Crown Heights, Bklyn) 718-756-5250
www.weeksvillesociety.org (Crown Hts: A/C to Utica Ave)
$4. Under 12: Free
Weeksville, which has been absorbed by Crown Heights, was settled in the 1830s by African-Americans seeking to establish an economic, political, cultural, and social base that would put a little space between them and some trouble-making Manhattan yahoos. The three surviving houses, one inhabited as recently as 1968, have been deco-rated to reflect a range of historic periods, and stand in stark contrast to the surrounding projects. You can take a guided tour Tuesday through Friday afternoons (call if you've got a hankering to come earlier) and Saturdays from 11am to 2pm.

The Coney Island Museum
1208 Surf Avenue, 2nd floor (@ W 12th St) 718-372-5159
www.coneyisland.com/museum.shtml
99¢
A delightfully creaky budget museum filled with the kind of memorabilia you'd step on a baby's finger to run across in an out-of-the-way flea market. A dilapidated wicker rolling chair! (Tour the boardwalk in style!) Postcards featuring the long-ago-burned-down Elephant Hotel! Creepy, fringe-trimmed circus punks! (The kind a sailor hurls baseballs at to win a kewpie for his favorite doll!) On nights when movies are scheduled, they drag a screen out and show it here. There's also a bathroom that far surpasses the ones the Parks Department maintains for beach-goers, well worth the admission price. It's open weekends year-round, and more frequently in summer.

We Know the Secret of the Colors
Beginning from Spring St and Avenue of the Americas (SoHo: C to Spring St)
www.theabsurdists.com/weknowthesecret.html
Okay, art freak, I hope you've got a lot of memory there on your downloader, because these files are gargantuan, but totally free. You can load them onto your MP3 player before leaving home, but don't give in to the temptation to hit play until you're standing on the corner of Spring Street and Avenue of the Americas with two hours to kill before sunset.

Central Park Conservancy tours of Central Park
Wednesdays, Thursdays and Fridays from mid June to mid August
Phone: 311
www.nyc.gov/parks/rangers
Even those who don't want some damn park ranger tell-ing them what to do may benefit from having him or her tell them about Frederick Law Olmstead and Calvert Vaux. Such information could come in useful when you're de-signing your own massive city park.

Wildman Steve Brill's tours of Central Park
Bimonthly in seasons conducive to foraging
914-835-2153
www.wildmanstevebrill.com
If you enjoy eating wisteria off the arbors of the Conserva-tory Garden, Wildman Brill can show you how to take it up a notch without accidentally poisoning yourself in the deeper wilds of Central Park. For instance, that bottlecap? Not food. Cigarette butt? Also not food. Goldfish crackers under a bench in the Diana Ross Playground? You can do better. The guy's a total pith helmet-wearing, dandelion-eating ham. He'd better be if he has a suggested dona-tion of $15 (with a no-change policy should you hand him a twenty). Perhaps an experienced dumpster diver like yourself can look him in the eye, as you hand him your zine and a monetary donation that fits within your budget.

Lower East Side History Project Walking Tour
Every day
Headquartered in the Bowery Poetry Club
308 Bowery (btwn Houston & Bleecker) 347-465-7767
www.leshp.org (East Village: F to 2nd Ave)
$15
Those who worry that walking tours are geared toward retirees sporting fanny packs without shame should

Springsteen • Harlem Shuffle - Bob & Earl •

be reassured that the history project organizing these rambles is based in the Bowery Poetry Club. (Less reassuring is how many Bowery Poetry Club regulars of my acquaintance don't look like they could survive two hours of walking, especially in broad daylight.) The topics mulch a lot of good underground dirt up to the surface, with themes running the gamut from Beat Writers & Poets to Historic Women. These used to be pay-what-you-can but have now settled into a hard and fast $15. (The Gangsters: Birth of Organized Crime tour is ten bucks more.) The first Tuesday of every month is a free Sacred Spaces tour, departing from the Church of the Most Holy Redeemer on 3rd Street between Avenues A and B. The guides are deeply invested in their subjects and a great many of them are neighborhood residents of long standing, including Thom Corn, a founding member of Bullet Space squat on 3rd Street between C and D, who leads Sunday's tour on the African-American Experience. Make sure that you know where to meet for your tour, as they all start in different locations.

Hey, I'm Walkin' Here!
www.burnsomedust.com
The main guy who leads these free expeditions is taking a break to walk across America. Not sure when, if ever, he'll be back, but in the meantime others are filling his shoes and maps of all previous walks are archived on his website. Print them out and beat a lonesome path. Each one has a theme or goal, such as noticing how people get around eastern Queens once the subway tracks run out. Shoes are even more important here than in the Atlantic Subway tunnel, as the hoofing can go on for 12 or 15 miles.

New York City Food Crawl
nycfoodcrawl.blogspot.com
Plenty of commercial tour operators stand at the ready to squire visitors in and out of Katz's, Joe's Shanghai, Crif Dogs, and other such real New York City deals, but given that you're reading this book, I doubt *you* need a paid escort holding your hand to get you across unfamiliar thresholds. It is nice to make friends though, and the free monthly NYC Food Crawl sets strangers up with one hell of a deft ice breaker by concentrating on one dish only. Dumplings? Samosas? Hot chocolate? Surely you have an opinion on the subject. You'll be provided with a scorecard, a map, and organized into teams so that no one stop on the itinerary gets slammed to the point where it's no fun anymore. All you'll pay for is what you eat.

Sketchcrawl
www.sketchcrawl.com/forum
Sketchcrawl is a global drawing marathon started by Pixar artist Enrico Casarosa. Whether you go solo or in groups, take a day to journal and draw your surroundings. You can find out more about meeting with the New York City group on the website. We tend to meet at museums, parks, and cafés. Last time, it was the Chelsea Market and the High Line. – Alisa Harris

Forgotten NY Tours
www.forgotten ny.com/tours.html
A few times a year, Forgotten NY brings their expertise off of the internet and out into the real world, with walking tours designed to help you notice such richness as vintage lampposts, fading ads for long-closed businesses still painted high up on side walls, and grand pre-war ornamentation decorating buildings downgraded to parking lots and the like. You have to keep checking the website. The tours are only announced about two weeks before they're due to take place. They're not free, but they're worth it, and you can bet your sweet bippy that the tour guide will be a fanatic about how great all this stuff is! Past tours are lovingly documented on the website with lots of photos and commentary.

The Surveillance Camera Players' Walking Tours of New York
www.notbored.org/the-scp.html
A pox on the Surveillance Camera Players for moving to Cincinnati of all places! I wish them well, but it's put a serious crimp in the number of Free Surveillance Camera Walking Tours of New York, which is currently hovering around zero. The SCP may be making their mischief somewhere east of us these days, but they very thoughtfully left their hand-drawn maps of camera locations in various New York neighborhoods, as well as instructions for how you can learn to spot these things for your own cartographic activities. Just go to their website and click on Walking Tours, which will eventually lead you to the maps.

Marching Bands of Manhattan – Death Cab for

Lower East Side Jewish Conservancy Tours
www.nycjewishtours.org/events_calendar.htm
As expected, a lot of this non-profit's tours take place on
the Lower East Side, but there are also ones designed to
hip you to the Jewish community of Revolutionary New
Amsterdam and Harlem's Jewish history. Say what now?
They'll run you $18, but if you factor in that each tour is
at least three hours, you're paying well below minimum
wage. Two dollars off if you're a student, and another $2
bucks off if you register in advance.

Free Sunday morning tours of the Flatiron District
11am, SW corner of Madison Sq, 23rd & Broadway,
212-741-2323
www.flatironbid.org/tour.php (Flatiron: R to 23rd St)
The Flatiron/23rd Street Partnership leads free walking
tours of the area every Sunday at 11am. This is an opportunity to rub shoulders with more mainstream tourists,
and tour guides, and is probably nothing you couldn't
do on your own. However, maybe you're traveling with
a nervous grandma, and doing something that she will
enjoy will make her feel like it's okay for you to leave her
at the hotel later in order to catch a Bed-Stuy house show
that won't end 'til 4 in the morning. You've got to give a
little sometimes, you know? Ask your tour guide about
"23 skidoo."

Free Saturday afternoon tours of Union Square
2pm, Abraham Lincoln statue, midpark @ 16th St
www.unionsquarenyc.org/walk.html
If the Flatiron's not your bag, you can learn about the
social and political history of Union Square (there's a lot
of it) for free every Saturday at 2pm. One thing I learned is
that that hideous "Metronome" sculpture installed on the
south end is really a clock.

Brooklyn Brewery Tours
Every Saturday and Sunday
79 N 11th St (btwn Berry St & Wythe Ave, Williamsburg,
Bkyn) 718-486-7422, www.brooklynbrewery.com
Free
Damnit! No more free samples! It's still a worthwhile 20
minutes just to get the deets on how the hard work of
others ultimately causes your midriff to pooch out like
you've got a dang joey in there. And after, you can buy
some to drink in their extremely makeshift (all part of the
fun) tap room, and maybe pick up a deeply price-chopped
post-seasonal case.

Brooklyn Historic Railway Association Atlantic Avenue
Tunnel Tours
Down a melonfarming MANHOLE at the intersection of
Atlantic Avenue & Court St, Boerum Hill, Brooklyn
718-941-3160, www.brooklynrail.net/proj_aatunnel.html
(Boerum Hill: M/R/2/3/4/5 to Court St-Borough Hall)
$15
Folks seem to love this! I'm sure I would too, if I didn't
equate descending into the unknown, one-at-a-time, via
metal rungs sunk into a narrow subterranean cylinder
with being buried alive! The tours are led by Bob Diamond, who spelunked this, the world's oldest subway
tunnel, back into existence in 1980. There's one every
month, usually on a Sunday, and if you're down, you need
to make reservations. Leave your high heels at home.
Bring a flashlight. If you really have no fear, maybe you
should attempt to schedule an art or performance event
down here. (Email your proposal to Brian Kassel, bkas-
sel@brooklynrail.net)

Don't forget that the museums—particularly ones devoted to preserving the traditions and history of a particular
immigrant group—lead awesome walking tours (for a
price). Check out the ones departing from the Museum of
Chinese in America, El Museo del Barrio, and the Lower
East Side Tenement Museum.

HISTORIC BUILDINGS

Eldridge Street Synagogue
12 Eldridge St (btwn Canal & Division) 212-219-0888
www.eldridgestreet.org (LES: B/D to Grand)
$10. Senior/Student: $8. Ages 5-18: $6
Eldridge Street Synagogue is a wonderful restored synagogue, and the first (I believe) in New York City; it has
some really amazing stenciling and painting, carefully
restored by a non-profit and documented well. Its gift
shop is good for souvenirs, including puzzles and coloring books for kids, and good picture and history books.
– Jerry the Mouse

The Flatiron Building
175 Fifth Ave (Btwn 22nd & 23rd)
(Flatiron: R to 23rd St-Broadway)
The Flatiron Building comes almost to a point and gets
wider as it goes south and it really is a marvel. – Josh Saitz
(It's one of the oldest skyscrapers in the world and Spiderman works here! A strange little etymology yarn goes
that guys used to hang out at the north end (23rd Street),
hoping the wind would funnel past the building and
blow women's skirts up. The beat cops would tell them

Cutie • Parade – Kimya Dawson • The Stoop –

to scram, or who knows, maybe even to skidoo, and thus, the phrase "23 skidoo" was born. I guess that's kind of a dumb story, and possibly not even true since a competing anecdote says a jockey invented the phrase to illustrate the hardships of being the 23rd horse in line, but it does illustrate something New Yorkers used to do for fun before the invention of TV.

The Empire State Building
350 5th Ave (@ 34th St) 212-736-3100
www.esbnyc.com/index2.cfm
(Murray Hill: B/D/F/M/N/Q /R to 34th St)
Admission to get to the top: $20, Senior/Students: $18
&
The Chrysler Building
405 Lexington Ave (@ 42nd Street)
(Midtown East: 4/5/6/7/S to Grand Central)
Both are amazing examples of Art Deco and have beautiful lobbies and design. The Empire State has an observation deck that's open every day. With the World Trade Centers gone, these two are the highest buildings in New York. – Andy Singer (You can gander at the Empire State Building's Art Deco lobby for free, if you don't want to pay the freight to go to the top. – David Goren) (You'll enjoy the Empire State Building more at night because there are no school groups and fewer old people. It's open until midnight for your touristy viewing needs. It takes a while to get to the top, but the view is spectacular, especially at night. It's usually not crowded in winter, but good weather attracts tourists. Don't buy postcards there; just walk right across Fifth Avenue where you can get them at 90% off retail prices. And please don't buy the cheesy shit. Don't be a dork. Be yourself. Enjoy. Soak it in. Don't feel like you have to keep moving because unless you relax, you won't have any fun. Don't bother trying to take pictures at night, because unless you know what you're doing, they won't come out. Just get postcards from across the street and keep them. – Josh Saitz)

The Brooklyn Bridge
Park Row & Center St in Manhattan to your choice of Cadman Plaza East or Johnson & Adams St in Brooklyn
(Financial District: 4/5/6 to Brooklyn Bridge-City Hall) or
(Downtown Bklyn: M/R/2/3/4/5 to Court St-Borough Hall)
Whenever I walk across it, I hug an arch the same way other people hug trees. Not to get too sentimental and weepy, but I'm so glad this iconic, borough-connecting beauty hasn't been blown up by terrorists. Except when it's hailing liquid Slurpees and -20° with the wind chill, there is no nicer thing than a leisurely hike across the Brooklyn Bridge. Depending on what time of year it is,

you may encounter multiple school groups doing the exact same thing. There are informative plaques at the midpoint, a gentle incline, benches, and many tourist couples who would probably love you if you offered to take their camera to snap a photo of the two of them together.

Louis Armstrong House
34-56 107th St (btwn 84th & 86th St, Corona, Queens)
718-997-3670
www.satchmo.net (Corona: 7 to 103rd St-Corona Plaza)
$8. Seniors/Students/Children over 4: $6. Under 4: Free
I'm of the opinion that there's always something to be gleaned from visiting the natural habitats of those we admire (like Eleanor Roosevelt's nun-like sleeping quarters, sandwiched between her husband's bedroom and that of his overbearing mother, or the many homemade frog beanbags Edward Gorey didn't quite manage to give away to all his friends). I wish the great man were still alive to see all the little kids trick or treating as Louis Armstrong here on Halloween.

The Elephant Hotel
Elephant Hotel (aka The Elephantine Colossus, formerly located on Surf Avenue, Coney Island)
The Elephant Hotel is no more, but you can see photos and learn more about it in the Coney Island Museum. It was quite the thing when it opened in 1882, but quickly became hot in another way, so many prostitutes plying their trade that "seeing the elephant" became a Victorian euphemism for having sex. – AH (I am fascinated by the elephant-shaped hotel. There were stairs in the trunk and two floors of guest rooms. Like most everything else in vintage Coney Island, the hotel was made out of wood

and burned down - Amanda Plumb).

Extra Place
1st St btwn Bowery & Second Ave
(East Village: F to 2nd Ave)
Perhaps you would like to go throw some beer, a used condom, some dirty needles and a rose in the alley behind CBGBs where umpteen bands, the Ramones to name but one, posed for iconic photos and presumably got up to some other stuff too. Ever since the Department of Transportation blacktopped it in honor of the luxury housing that was erected across the way, it's been a vastly cleaner affair in every sense of the word.

PUBLIC ART

Life Underground by Tom Otterness (2000)
14th St & 8th Ave, in the A/C/E/L subway station
www.tomotternessstudio.com/exhibitions_subway.html
A permanent installation of Tom Otterness' humorous, rolypoly bronze figures running amok in the passageways (as well as on platforms, girders, and a bench.) Despite commissions from private collectors with serious means, Tom's sympathies are firmly with the proletariat, a POV that plays

well with those of us who rely on public transportation to get around. My favorite is the babushka taking a reading break atop a top-hatted swell. If you like what you see here, keep your eyes peeled for more Otterness-y goodness outside the Times Square Hilton, and in Battery Park, Brooklyn's Metrotech Center, the Bronx's New York Botanic Garden, and the waters off Roosevelt Island.

De La Vega
102 St. Marks Pl (btwn 1st Ave and Ave A) 212-876-8649
www.delavegamuseum.blogspot.com
(East Village: 6 to Astor Pl)
De La Vega's most iconic image is a fish jumping out of the bowl with the slogan "Become Your Dream." He draws this on discarded desks, broken TVs, abandoned futons, even garbage bags. I respect that he just has to create art and he's not just hustling to make a buck. I see his work all the time and a local liquor store paid him to draw posters for them. – Josh Saitz (James De La Vega has the makings of a million dollar motivational speaker. The man knows how to push a message. He maintains a tiny East Village "museum" from whence he peddles tiny paint-

Display Your Own On Street Poles!
One morning I came out of my building to find that someone had screwed a small, square painting to the street sign where I lock my bike. (This was particularly nice as the nocturnal activities surrounding that pole usually result in stolen wheels or bikes that go missing altogether.) In the month or so it lived on our block, I grew very attached to that painting, and was much concerned for its welfare. Then one morning I bumped into my downstairs neighbor, Alvaro, who asked me if I had noticed that our painting had disappeared. Apparently, someone had gone ahead and done what I was many times tempted to do, but as a good citizen did not!

To make your own street pole art, use a board that's not going to stick out so far that someone whaps their head on it. Avoid watercolors. Subject-wise, keep in mind that parents with little kids and community-spirited old ladies will be among the multitudes, and words or images they deem unsuitable for viewers of all ages will come down a lot faster than otherwise. Drill holes in the board; fill your pockets with appropriate-sized bolts and wing nuts; come to NYC and install. Drop us a line so we can attend your exhibit before someone steals it!

← calling all wingnuts! Use this life-size NYC street sign pole template to drill holes in your artwork prior to free outdoor display.

be so fortunate as to be able to support themselves selling their work, even if the price tag for one of his digest-size zines almost made coffee come out of my nose (and I hadn't had any coffee since like 6 o'clock that morning.) His fish stuff wears a little thin with me, but I will never weary of his drawings of his mother. For a provocative photo op on a non-rainy day, sit in one of the beat up chairs on the sidewalk outside the museum, each labeled as reserved for a distinct racial group. –AH)

The Mosaics of the East Village
(East Village: 6 to Astor Pl)
Jim Power is the Mosaic Man. Look for him as he works on them on St Mark's Place with his dog, Jesse Jane. (You

can see his mosaics all along St Mark's.) If you do see him try to give him a donation; he gets no funding and is often homeless. – Fly (Several businesses on Avenue A and side streets leading to Tompkins Square feature Jim's mosaics, too. They're lucky to have them. – AH)

Alamo by Tony Rosenthal (1967)
Astor Place, Lafayette @ 8th St
www.tonyrosenthal.com/Alamo.htm
Very few New Yorkers know that the Astor Place Cube can spin, and even fewer know its real name, so they may look at you like you're nuts when you shout, "Remember the Alamo!" and set it in motion with a well-placed shove. But you know what? They're the ones who are ignorant.

Sticker Mural in the Ace Hotel lobby
20 W 29th St (@ Broadway), 212-679-2222
www.acehotel.com/newyork (Murray Hill: R to 28th St)
You're not staying here, are you? Didn't think so, but provided everything about you isn't screaming, "Kick me out!" a non-guest can check out this mural, culled from the street graffiti sticker collection of Michael Anderson.

Library Way
E 45th St btwn 5th Ave & Park Ave
(Midtown: S/4/5/6/7 to Grand Central))
Exercise your mind and body as you stare at the sidewalk, where the Grand Central Partnership commissioned sculptor Gregg LeFevre to install 96 plaques worth of rousing literary quotes. The words are definitely inspiring, though the graphic flourishes can get a little New Age poster-ish. I do enjoy standing there, contemplating the meaning of it all as office workers rush around me. Goes good with a mochi doughnut from Café Zaiya.

The Grand Central Whispering Wall
Grand Central Station, 42nd St @ Park Ave
(S/4/5/6/7 to Grand Central)
More a naturally-occurring architectural phenomenon than a deliberate work of public art, you and a friend could definitely turn it into a performance. It's outside the Oyster Bar, where there's a large arched intersection into which three passages filter. Stand in one corner, face to the wall, and get your friend to do the same in the corner diagonally opposite. Whisper into the wall and your friend will hear your message plain as day! Fun! People who aren't in on the acoustic secret will assume you are stoned. – AH (Check out the Holiday Laser Light show on the astrologically designed ceiling of the main terminal's Vanderbilt Hall, every half-hour throughout December. – David Goren)

Peace Fountain by Greg Wyatt, 1985
Cathedral of St John the Divine's Great Lawn
Amsterdam Ave @ 112th St
www.stjohndivine.org
(Morningside Hts: 1 to 110th St, Cathedral Pkwy)
All hail hippie *Godspell* Jesus when the Second Coming is at hand, but 'til such time as then, I'll cast my lot with this outlandish vision of good and evil. The *Peace Fountain* is totally off-its-rocker, depicting St Michael the Archangel beheading the devil atop a giant crab while nine tiny giraffes frolic nearby. Dominating the lurid scene is a happy moon face who looks like he may have the same baby daddy as the one singing, "Welcome To Our World of Toys" down at FAO Schwartz. The fountain is ringed

HOW **DARE** YOU CRITICIZE NEW YORK!?!
NEW YORK IS **THE GREATEST CITY ON EARTH** !!!

with bronzes cast from New York City schoolchildren's animal sculptures. Did I mention there are live peacocks? And that one of them's albino?

Graffiti Hall of Fame
106th & Park Ave
(East Harlem: 6 to 103rd St)
Lots of NYC public school playgrounds sport murals on their low walls. Keep your eyes open and you'll see plenty of anti-drug, anti-drop-out, pro-literacy messages starring Dora the Explorer, Curious George, Clifford the Big Red Dog, and other unlicensed household names. If you're a connoisseur, or in the mood for something a little more mature, the Graffiti Hall of Fame ringing the basketball courts of Central Park East Secondary School (HS 555) may merit a special trip. It was founded by famous graffiti writers and does not stick to the usual Board of Ed approved script.

Cereal Killers
Wythe Avenue & N 13th St
(Williamsburg: L to Bedford Ave)
There's awesome graffiti on the border of Williamsburg and Greenpoint. The *Cereal Killers* mural shows icons of popular children's breakfast cereals drawn up to be gangsters. It takes up the entire side of a building and should really be checked out. After, you can walk a few blocks to the East River State Park on Kent and 13th and get a gorgeous view of Manhattan. The area is deserted so it's best to go during the day or (my preferred time) sunset. – Eric Nelson

Ellis G
www.ellisgallagher.com
Ellis G is a graffiti artist who traded his spray cans for chalk, outlining shadows cast by such things as hydrants, street signs, and chained-up bikes. His work pops up in Brooklyn's Cobble and Boerum Hills a lot, particularly near the entrances to the F/G stop on Bergen and Smith.

5 Pointz
Jackson Ave (@ Davis St, Long Island City, Queens)
www.5ptz.com
Even before former mayor Rudy Guiliani's totalitarian Quality of Life campaign took a Brillo pad to NYC, the subways' complimentary crash course in hip-hop art appreciation had pretty much disappeared, though you can still ride the MTA to the 5 Pointz Institute of Higher Burnin'. It's a 200,000-square-foot factory building turned graffiti grail. On the weekend, aerosol artists from all around the world can be seen piecing and wildstyling the exterior walls, without having to worry about getting snuffed by a train. In fact, you, too, can paint on Saturdays and Sundays between noon and 7pm and weekdays by appointment. Obtain a permit by emailing the manager, Meres, at meresone@aol.com.

Murals and Memorial Walls
Take a picture, because for sure it will last longer. It always makes me sad when some young person's memorial wall gets covered over. They're particularly thick in the eastern portions of the East Village and Lower East Side, Spanish Harlem, and Harlem, though they can spring up anywhere. There are also many vibrant community murals, promoting ethnic pride and reminding kids to stay in school because crack is wack. Of course, all it takes is one little regime change or real estate developer to clear the slates. (There's a great mural tale with a bitter ending in John Mejias' *Paping* zine compilation, *The Teacher's Edition*.) Many independently-owned businesses, particularly in lower income communities, hire artists to create promotional murals on the security grates and sidewalls of their stores. If you don't want to leave things to chance, check the websites of the following organizations to make sure the community wall art you dream of seeing still exists:
City Arts www.cityarts.org
Groundswell www.groundswellmural.org/
Muralistas www.elpuente.us/arts/murals.htm
Tats Cru www.tatscru.com/
Brooklyn Street Art: www.brooklynstreetart.com

New York • Coney Island Baby – Tom Waits •

Guerrilla Knitting

Speaking of street poles, they get very cold in the winter, which is just one of many reasons why you should never lick them. Instead, why not knit colorful cozies to keep them nice and snug, simultaneously bringing joy to the peoples of New York? Don't use your round needles, though. It's not like these poor inanimate creatures can lift their legs out of the cement to slip on a custom made legwarmer. Instead, knit your works square and bring some extra yarn and a plastic needle so you can stitch them on. Magda Sayeg, founder of the original yarn-bombing graffiti crew Knitta Please, has a book coming out soon, that will no doubt give you more (k)nitty gritty instructions (www.magdasayeg.com).

LIBRARIES

Zine Libraries!

ABC No Rio Zine Library
156 Rivington St, 2nd floor (btwn Clinton & Suffolk)
212.254.3697 ext. 21
(LES: F/J/M/Z to Delancey-Essex)
Hours vary, usually Wednesday evenings & Sunday afternoons
ABC No Rio Zine Library is the shit. They have more zines than you can shake a stick at and copies of old stuff too (*Factsheet Five, Rollerderby*, etc).You have to read them at the library, however. Bummer. They also have zine workshops – Josh Medsker. (ABC No Rio recently spent a whole penny to buy the building they've occupied for nearly 30 years, but there's no way owning real estate can force this crew to settle down. It's volunteer-run, so there may be times when you push open that heavy, disreputable-looking door, only to feel like...*helloooooooo?...Is anybody home?* Trust me, there's always a lot going on...print shop, dark room, Food Not Bombs, all-ages hardcore matinée, poetry reading, art show, computer center, some righteous benefit or another...and a handful of people sitting around reading zines! The Zine Library is a humble room with milk-crates and filing cabinets assisting the shelves that hold the 12,000 strong collection. The librarians are a volunteer workforce, so hours may get jimmied to accommodate their schedules. It doesn't hurt to call, especially if you've decided to lug your entire zine collection with you in order to donate it in person.

Barnard Library Zine Collection in Lehman Hall
z3009 Broadway 2nd floor (enter campus @ 117th St, look for the mod white building that looks like it's up on stilts)
212-854-4615, www.barnard.edu/library/zines
(Morningside Hts: 1 to 116th St/Columbia University)
The Barnard zine collection specializes in zines made by women (as in gender self-defined), with topics running the gamut from feminism, activism, anarchism, body image, gender, parenting, queer community, riot grrrl, sexual assault, etc, etc, etc! It's accessible during the library's regular stacks hours (daily until 11pm, except in summer and January intersession when it's M-F, 9-5). While technically open only to Barnard and Columbia University affiliates, one has only to tap Zine Librarian Jenna Freedman for permission to enter, either by phone or by emailing zines@barnard.edu. That, or just tell the desk attendant you're there to see Jenna, and she'll let you up. If you're a zine-making woman, or a zine collecting-woman who's looking to thin out her female-created holdings, you can show the guard the package you're bringing to increase your good friend Jenna's workload. Unlike many academic and public collections, the zines are housed in open stacks, meaning you're free to browse. No need to select off a menu, then have the librarian fetch your choices for you. There are comfy chairs. You can

photograph or photocopy any zine that you find in the stacks. There's also an archives collection. All of the zines are cataloged online at www.icanhaz.com/zinecatalog.

Public Libraries

Of *course* zinesters love libraries! Like half of us are librarians. (The other half works at Kinko's.) For some reason, Brooklyn and Queens each have their own system, while Manhattan shares with Staten Island and the Bronx. They all have free Wi-Fi, and computers which you can use for a half an hour, if you can rally a sympathetic librarian to let you on.

The New York Public Library
Stephen A. Schwarzman Building
5th Avenue @ 42nd Street, 917-275-6975
www.nypl.org/locations/schwarzman
(Midtown: B/D/F/S/M/7 to 42nd St-Bryant Park)
The Library. It's just too beautiful. The Rose Reading Room alone is a work of art. There are often break dancers out front when the weather is good, and the library has great exhibits, such as the one last year of vintage comic books! Have you seen an actual copy of the Gutenberg Bible? I have, at the library—one of only 45 copies printed on vellum. It's worth a visit just to say hello to the lions out front, Patience and Fortitude. – Melissa Bastian (They have everything, including back issues of *Negative Capability*. At least they say they do; I am too lazy to go see for myself. – Josh Saitz) (Apparently you can roam the stacks. I've never done it. I've only ever gone to the amazing exhibits they have there—*and* it's pay what you want. It's a great time. – Josh Medsker)

Mid-Manhattan Library
455 5th Ave (btwn 39th St & 40th St) 212-340-0863
www.nypl.org/branch/central/mml
(Midtown: B/D/F/S/M/7 to 42nd St-Bryant Park)
Mid-Manhattan Library is one of my favorite places in town. If only they had coffee! I found out about this book from William Burroughs from 1968 called *The Electronic Revolution*, that basically predicted the internet. I searched and tried to buy it everywhere, and couldn't find it. That's the kind of essential material they have here. – Josh Medsker (It's not as romanticized as the Schwarzman library, but the hours are longer and the circulation policies are more generous. – Kate Black) (If you want to be completely blown away (but not check out books), go to the Manhattan Research Library. You can temporarily borrow books for research, but not physically leave the building with them. Sometimes I like to go and get research done there, even though I could probably take the same books home from another library. The place is just too amazing. – Marguerite Dabaie) (They also house the famous "picture archives" that used to be way, way more important to me before the internet really kicked in. – Fly)

Chatham Square Branch
33 East Broadway (btwn Catherine St & Market St) 212-964-6598
www.nypl.org/locations/chatham-square
&
Seward Park Branch
192 East Broadway (@ Jefferson St) 212-477-6770
www.nypl.org/locations/seward-park
(LES: F to East Broadway)
The branch libraries in Chinatown often have free Chinese opera performances or music recitals. – Victoria Law (Well, damn, I guess I've never gone at the right time! But given how I rely on these locations as my super secret Chinatown bathroom spots, I feel confident that one day my visit will coincide with the arrival of some Chinese opera singers, who will hopefully be there for reasons that have nothing to do with heeding nature's call. – AH)

Hamilton Fish
415 E Houston (btwn Ave C & Ave D) 212-673-2290
www.nypl.org/locations/hamilton-fish-park
(LES: F to 2nd Ave)
They have a lounge-type area in their children's section where you can sit and read your books with or without kids! They also have a good selection of novels by authors of color, both famous and lesser known. If you are looking for research assistance from a librarian, however, you'd be better off going to a different branch. – Victoria Law

The Ottendorfer Branch
135 2nd Ave (btwn 9th and St. Marks Pl)
www.nypl.org/locations/ottendorfer
(East Village: 6 to Astor Pl)
The Ottendorfer has a less comfortable kids' reading area than Hamilton Fish, and the adult area is usually full, but they have a great selection of books. – Victoria Law (They also have a gorgeous terra cotta Queen Anne façade, as befits New York's first free public library. – AH)

The Jefferson Market Branch
425 Ave of the Americas (@ 10th St) 212-243-4334
www.nypl.org/locations/jefferson-market
(Greenwich Village: B/D/F/M to W 4th St)
If you want to be surrounded by beauty while you study for your chem class, there's the Jefferson Market Library. The building used to be a courthouse and has stained glass windows and lovely details throughout. – Margue-

Yoko Ono • Boy from New York City - The

rite Dabaie (The winding stone staircase makes me want to delve back into some Shakespeare, then break in after hours to act it out. – AH)

Library for the Performing Arts, Dorothy and Lewis B. Cullman Center
40 Lincoln Center Plaza (on W 62nd St btwn Amsterdam & Columbus Ave) 212-870-1630
www.nypl.org/locations/lpa (Upper West Side: 1 to 66h St)
This branch has nifty exhibits, and depending on the hour, you may convince the attendant in the Billy Rose Theater collection to let you view the archival footage of your choice. Fittingly, this one has a lot of live musical events. One thing I always enjoy about coming here is seeing all the little bun-head Julliard students walking around with their toes turned out.

Schomburg Center for Research in Black Culture
515 Malcolm X Boulevard (@ W 136th St) 212-491-2200
www.nypl.org/locations/schomburg
(Harlem: 2/3 to 135th St)
This one's a biggie. They've been collecting, which of course also means preserving books, films, recordings, photographs, art, and other materials documenting pretty much every aspect of black life, not just in this country, but all over the world! It's a great place to bone up on the Harlem Renaissance. Reward your ears with a trip up to the Recorded Sound Division, where they can have their pick of music, radio broadcasts, the voices of Marcus Garvey and Booker T. Washington and/or over 5000 hours of oral history. Like the Schwartzman Building (the one

with the lions), they have a gift shop to be reckoned with.

Brooklyn Central Library
10 Grand Army Plaza (@ Flatbush Ave, Prospect Heights, Bkln) 718-230-2100
www.brooklynpubliclibrary.org/central
(Prospect Hts: 2/3/4 to Grand Army Plaza)
Brooklyn's main library is a) huge and b) the front steps are a great place to soak up sun and people-watch. – Becky Hawkins (It's got a gorgeous façade, and it isn't nearly as crowded as the Mid-Manhattan Library. – Marguerite Dabaie) (Find sustenance in a ground floor café, and another one out on the newly refurbished plaza, where you can ponder the bookish quotes, and literary friezes above the library's entrance. On Saturdays, the NYC Greenmarket convenes right across the street from the library at the entrance of Prospect Park. – David Goren) (This library often plays host to interesting exhibits, films, and lectures. – AH)

Queens Central Library
89-11 Merrick Blvd (@ 89th Ave, Jamaica, Queens) 718-990-0700
www.queenslibrary.org (Jamaica: F to 169th St)
Funding has been cut, I hear, but when I first went there, they had an amazing exhibit of ancient Chinese printing and early books. What really impressed me was that it looked more like a bookstore, a major commercial bookstore, than a library, full of gorgeous piles of new best sellers, the kind of books you'd need to order and wait months for from Manhattan's public library. I was so jealous of Queens. Apparently anyone in New York City

can get a Queens library card. They collect artist books and limited editions—now it's been limited to Brooklyn, Queens, and Long Island publications. All Queens branches are supposed to be just as good as the Central Library. A real palace for the people. – Esther Smith

Tremont Branch
1866 Washington Ave (@ E. 176th St, Tremont, Bronx)
718-299-5177, www.nypl.org/locations/tremont
(Tremont: Harlem to Tremont)
&
Morrisania Branch
610 East 169th St (@ Franklin Ave, Morrisania, Bronx)
718-589-9268, www.nypl.org/locations/morrisania
(Morrisania: 2/5 to 149th St, then BX55 bus to E 169th)
They're both surprisingly quiet, well-equipped, and have nice light, good books and computer access. – Jerry the Mouse

Francis Martin Branch
2150 Dr. Martin Luther King Jr Blvd
(@ 181st St, University Heights, The Bronx) 718-295-5287
www.nypl.org/locations/francis-martin
(University Heights: 4 to Burnside Ave)
Francis Martin has good children's programming. – Jerry the Mouse

Spuyten Duvil Branch
650 W 235th St (@ Independence Ave, Spuyten Duyvil, Bronx) 718-796-1202
www.nypl.org/locations/spuyten-duyvil
(Spuyten Duyvil: 1 to 231st St, then BX10 bus to 232nd St & Henry Hudson Pkwy)
I really have to give a shout-out to the Spuyten Duvil branch in the Bronx where I did a comix-making workshop a few years ago. I was wondering why they sent me all the way out to the Bronx until the kids there told me that the name of the branch translates to "Spade of the Devil" and then I was like, "ohhhhh...ok...I get it." – Fly

Academic Libraries

Cooper Union Library
7 E 7th St (btwn 3rd & 4th Ave) 212-353-4186
www.cooper.edu/facilities/library/library.html
(East Village: 6 to Astor Pl)
The country's only totally tuition-free university will grant you admission to their stacks if you tell the guard that you're a citizen who needs to examine some public documents. The guard may look at you funny. (You'd think I was the only person ever to take advantage of this fab offer, or maybe he's sussed out that my "research" has yet to steer me toward matters of public record. I'm more the freaky art book type, and they have lots of those.) Don't go expecting the mahogany-scented, ivy-covered golden halls of academia. It's got more of a worn-out conference room vibe, though the windows give you a good ground floor view of Astor Place.

Columbia University Library
Many libraries- go to www.columbia.edu/cu/lweb/indiv/libraries.html for locations or call 212-854-7309
www.columbia.edu/cu/lweb
(Morningside Hts: 1 to 116th St-Columbia Univ)
If you can get access, Columbia University Library has lots of wonderful books, a phenomenal rare books room, and a café too. – Jerry the Mouse

Pratt Institute Library
200 Willoughby Ave (@ Hall, Clinton Hill, Bklyn)
718-636-3684
www.library.pratt.edu (Clinton Hill: G to Clinton-Washington)
The Pratt library is open to the public, so stride through the turnstile with confidence. They have a small collection of art zines, a thrillingly huge collection of the type of current periodicals to which you might subscribe, if you had the money, and gorgeous fixtures, including a glass and iron floor that clears up any doubt about the interior having been designed by the Tiffany Glass & Decorating Company. Plenty of comfy seating in which to read those magazines.

Other Libraries

The Hispanic Society of America
613 W 155th St (btwn Broadway & Riverside Dr) 212-926-2234
www.hispanicsociety.org
(Washington Hts: 1 to 157th St)
The Hispanic Society has a great library and a really friendly and knowledgeable head librarian. It's also a free museum. – Jerry the Mouse

Will Oldham Horror • Jeffrey Lewis • Piss

The Jewish Theological Seminary Library
3080 Broadway (@ W 123rd St) 212-678-8000
www.jtsa.edu (Morningside Heights: 1 to 125th St)
The Jewish Theological Seminary Library is amazingly
light—a beautiful place in which to be. – Jerry the Mouse

The Morbid Anatomy Library
543 Union St (@ Nevins, Gowanus, Bklyn)
e-mail morbidanatomy@gmail.com for appointment
www.morbidanatomy.blogspot.com
The Morbid Anatomy Library is housed in a studio in the
same building as Proteus Gowanus, one of my favorite
galleries. It is a labor of love, born of an interest in the
arcane, and exists to give artists, researchers, and anyone
with an interest in such things access to books and images related to medical museums, anatomy, memorial
practices, mortality studies, and the like. I particularly
like how they value works that other libraries may have
dumped because the information in them is out of date.
These books may not have the best advice on how to
remove a tumor, but many have beautiful—in the Mut-
tar Museum sense of the word—illustrations. No artist
would toss those babies out with the bathwater. If this
were my museum, I would have a hard time not going to
The Vortex and The Thing every other day, wheelbarrow
in hand.

READINGS
Most of the bookstores in this guide, including indie
favorites McNally-Jackson, Bookcourt, and Word and big
used gorillas like Housing Works and The Strand, host
readings and author appearances. Sometimes, though,
it's nice to shut your eyes and let someone read out loud
to you in a venue with a liquor license. Some taverns of
deserved literary repute are:

Lolita Bar
266 Broome St (btwn Allen St & Orchard St) 212-966-7223
www.lolitabar.net (LES: F/J/M/Z to Delancey-Essex)
A bit lounge-y for my taste, until you hit the basement,
home of the awesome, travel-themed Restless Legs Reading series, hosted by my pal David Farley, who wrote
a whole entire book about his quest for Jesus' historic
foreskin. (I'm not going to tell you if he found it. Read *An
Irreverent Curiosity* and find out!)

Happy Ending
302 Broome (btwn Forsyth and Eldridge) 212-334-9676
www.happyendinglounge.com
(LES: F/J/M/Z to Delancey-Essex)
Once *that* kind of massage parlor, now a big literary draw.

What a Cinderella story! Wednesday night reading series.
Sex Worker Literati takes place the first Thursday of every
month. Past and present sex workers read, monologue,
and share their stories. Another fun one is the "How I
learned… " series, a homework assignment of sorts for
the invited authors, who complete the sentence and
then some, according to that week's theme, the fourth
Wednesday of every month. The Animal Farm Series
(2nd Thursday of every month) promotes the idea that all
writers are equal. If the first Wednesday's Pleasure Salon
arouses an itch you're eager to continue scratching, the In
The Flesh series taps a deep vein of smut with Host Rachel
Kramer Bussel on the third Thursday.

KGB Bar
85 E 4th St (btwn 2nd & 3rd Ave) 212-505-3360
www.kgbbar.com (East Village: F/M to 2nd Ave)
The dimly-lit East Village former National Socialist Party
HQ is also a temple of orally-delivered fiction, non-fic-
tion, and poetry. I'm going to lose my scat, though, if they
don't replace the junky, little desklamp that has us non-
20/20 readers hunching over the lectern like someone's
blind granny. You could save both a visually-impaired
author and the day by producing a flashlight from your
bag at just the right moment!

Smalls Jazz Club
183 West 10th St (btwn 4th St and 7th Ave) 212-252-5091
www.smallsjazzclub.com
(Greenwich Village: 1 to Christopher Street)
Smalls is an old-school jazz bar that features poetry readings every other Saturday. It is consistently voted the best
jazz in the city by the folks whose name starts with Z, but
we don't care about that, do we? – Josh Medsker

Pete's Candy Store
709 Lorimer St (btwn Frost St & Richardson St, Williamsburg, Bklyn) 718-302-3770, www.petescandystore.com
(Williamsburg: G/L to Metropolitan-Lorimer)
Pete's gets points for holding readings in a room that
looks like a Punch and Judy theater, and also for paying
readers with drink tickets (though next time I think I'll
save mine until after I've read).

Bushwick Book Club
Goodbye Blue Monday
1087 Broadway (btwn Dodworth St & Lawton St, Bushwick, Bklyn) 718-453-6343
www.bushwickbookclub.com (Bushwick: J to Kosciusko St)
This is one of the most beautiful ideas ever to come out
of Brooklyn, or really the world. Each month, a book is

selected (recent selections include Kurt Vonnegut, Milan Kundera, and Miranda July). Read, or re-read the book so it's nice and fresh in your mind when you show up on the first Tuesday of the month to hear a host of local songwriters singing original compositions inspired by the book in question. They even serve book-related refreshments! They've got a CD, and some of their greatest hits are archived online for your free aural pleasure at www.reverbnation.com/thebushwickbookclub.You ought to be hooked by the first chorus of Jeff Lewis's song for Raymond Carver ("What Do We Sing About When We Sing About What We Talk About When We Talk About Love.")

Art Galleries

There are so many galleries in New York that it's impossible to get to even 1/100th of them, let alone list them in anything resembling a coherent fashion. Better you should get yourself to a neighborhood where a lot of them are, and take it from there. SoHo allegedly died when a lot of galleries jumped ship to Chelsea. And Chelsea is now rumored to be ready for organ harvest, though given the number of galleries clustered around 9th Avenue, I don't think the family's ready to let go just yet. In Brooklyn, DUMBO, Williamsburg, and Bushwick have a lot of galleries, which sprang up around the artists who live there, just like their SoHo predecessors did back in the day. Bushwick's probably the last place of these three where a young artist can afford to live (with three roommates). To find out what's opening, closing and showing in any given week, take a look at www.artcards.cc.com.

These are a few galleries dear to us. They're not snobby by nature. Some of them are known for throwing fun events and/or encouraging visitors to interact with the work. Several feel as if they might be open to considering your work for a group show or something. If you see something you like, ask the person working there to direct you to some galleries they like, because chances are, unlike us, they'll know exactly what's showing right now.

Charming Wall
191 W 4th St (btwn 6th and 7th Ave) 212-206-8235
www.charmingwall.com (Greenwich Village: 1 to Christopher St)
If you're looking to plaster your walls with quirky, accessible prints—think the kind of illustrations that turn up in the pages of *Bust* or *Giant Robot*—this tiny Village storefront will toot your poster tube, for sure. Pricing's a straight up $20 per print. Ain't that democratic? Everyone who works here is really nice, too. If the art you make fits into the general birds on branches, skateboarding bunnies, eerie Red Riding Hoods aesthetic, you should think

about sending some low-res samples or relevant website links to gallerymanager@charmingwall.com.

Cinders
103 Havermeyer (btwn Hope and Grand, Williamsburg, Bklyn) 718-388-2311, www.cindersgallery.com
(Williamsburg: L/G to Lorimer/Metropolitan)
Before Havermeyer became the hip extension of Bedford Avenue that it is now, it was just a handful of bars, a bike shop, some clothing stores, and Cinders. To see this unique art/commerce space still thriving is a testament to the well-curated gallery and store. At the front is the gallery, featuring a new exhibit every month from photos to paintings to collage to textiles. The display is always interesting and it welcomes you into the store, which takes up the back half of the gallery. The art is for sale, as are goods from zines and magazines to t-shirts and postcards. The owners and staff are always so friendly that whether you leave with a piece of art, a zine, or nothing at all, you'll be glad you got a chance to stop in and explore.
– Megan Gerrity

Central Booking
111 Front St, Suite 214 (@ Wall St) 347-731-6559
www.centralbookingnyc.com (DUMBO: A/C to High St)
If you like zines, this one has your name all over it. It's dedicated to the art of the book, and the curators make it plain that the definition is broad enough to include "a pamphlet done inexpensively on a copy machine." Finally, some respect!

Art House Co-op's Brooklyn Art Library
201 Richards St #16
(btwn Coffey & Van Dyke, Red Hook, Bklyn)
www.arthousecoop.com (Red Hook: B61 bus to Coffey St)
Be an artist, even if you're not! Art House, late of Atlanta and a very welcome recent addition to Red Hook, has any number of nifty projects posted on their website and available for your participation—a self-portrait project, a project devoted to creating patterns, a fill-up-and-return sketchbook project. Create a profile, pay a nominal participation fee, and agree to abide by a few parameters (for instance, the self-portraits all had to be a uniform, 2-D size). Then book a trip to NYC to attend your gallery opening, art star! Get in touch before hopping the bus to Red Hook, though, as their hours are irregular.

Proteus Gowanus
543 Union St (@ Nevins, Gowanus, Bklyn) 718-243-1572
www.proteusgowanus.com (Gowanus: R/M to Union)
Proteus Gowanus is my favorite gallery in New York. Its

N•J•) • Rockaway Beach – The Ramones • New

Japanese Young Artists' Book Fair
February: Chelsea & Williamsburg, Bklyn
www.peppers-project.com
How nice. A hundred young artists, several really cool bookstores and an alternative art festival all coming together to make me feel like my zine looks like it was made by a monkey. That's okay, though. Admiring these cunningly folded and bound objects has enriched my life, and helped me realize I have nowhere near the patience to attempt something on this order myself.

Pulse NY
March
330 West St (@ Houston) 212-255-2327
www.pulse-art.com (SoHo: 1/9 to Houston)
$20 Seniors/Students: $15. Under 12: Free
It ain't as cheap as gallery hopping, but you won't have to deal with the irritation that comes from having to fight your way to the free wine, only to realize that it's all gone. If you want to see who the establishment has selected as the rising stars of the Contemporary Art scene, take a look. There's usually some performative aspect or at least a video lounge where you can watch videos that you could probably catch right now on YouTube. Hmm, maybe you should just go to MOMA...

Bushwick Open Studios and Arts Festival
June: Bushwick, Bklyn
www.artsinbushwick.org
This is more of my speed, a throwback to what the DUMBO Arts Festival used to be, without the distractions of those beautiful bridges and the cooling breezes of the East River. The artists open their studios, but the dance, street installations, and hopefully gorgeous early June weather make it feel like more of a big outdoor party. Count on the party to eventually make its way to 3rd Ward, in order to rage all night long. (www.3rdward.com) My god, those people know how to have a good time.

Atlantic Avenue Art Walk
June: Boerum Hill, Bklyn
www.atlanticavenueartwalk.com
Everyone jumps on this bandwagon! The Atlantic Avenue merchants' association has been trained well by the Atlantic Antic, the ginormous annual street fair that goes down every September. Expect the holistic veterinarians to roll out some kittens, the café where the moms and toddlers hang out to display children's art, and everyone from the yoga supply store to the Transit Museum to

spirit is closer to a community center, the kind of place that motivates you to get involved rather than just tip-toe around, looking. Every year unfolds under a theme. The first one was "Play," followed by "Mend" and "Transport." It's a short walk from the attractions of both Park Slope's 5th Avenue and the Carroll Gardens end of Smith Street. It's small, so I would try to visit on a day when something's on. Fortunately, there's almost always an event of one kind or another—a craft workshop, a meeting of the Fixer's Collective, or an opportunity to practice constrained writing with the Writhing Society, who are always on the lookout for new playmates to mess around with the mathematical methods invented by the French group, Oulipo. (They'll loosen you up with "free wine for $2 a glass.") If you're in NYC for an extended period and looking for a cheap, quiet, daytime location in which to write or research, Wi-Fi, bread, and coffee included, you can partake of their communal Study Hall for $50 a month.

offer seductive discounts aimed at skimming a little off the Art Walk's top. It's almost laughably respectable compared to Bushwick, but the organizers are still faithful to the spirit of pre-gentrification with block parties, live music, and walking tours of the public murals on some of the rougher-looking streets. In 2009, they even organized the painting of a new mural, which you can see on the corner of Atlantic and Boerum Place.

Art Under the Bridge Festival
September: DUMBO
www.dumboartfestival.org
This weekend extravaganza gets a lot of mileage out of its milieu. You'll find bands, performance artists and site specific installations tucked away in the various loading docks and crannies of DUMBO's ancient waterfront buildings at every hour. My all-time favorite was the formally attired quintet seated on floats in the river, who prepared complimentary cups of tea to order, based on the signals you sent them via semaphore flags. When it was time for the tea to be delivered, the server would pull himself back in along a rope. Just before I left, one of them was swamped by the wake of a passing barge, tumbling into the drink clad in a tuxedo on a chilly autumn day. He got a lot of applause, but from the way his teeth were chattering, I think he may have also gotten hypothermia.

AGAST – Annual Gowanus Artists' Studio Tour
October: Gowanus, Bklyn
www.agastbrooklyn.com
Ooh, this could be the bait to drag you out to Proteus Gowanus. The waters of the Gowanus Canal were so septic

and gross for so long, that the artists who've been here the longest are obviously hearty, determined specimens. They're here for the duration. In addition to their expertise in ironworking, welding, potting, and large-scale painting, they know a hell of a lot about ventilating old warehouses and factories, removing asbestos, and putting in toilets where none exist. That's the sort of stuff you should really be asking them about...you'll get a good history of the neighborhood along with a practical education in how artists operate.

Free Lower East Side Art Walk
The last Sunday of every month at 1pm
Lower East Side Visitor Center
70 Orchard St (btwn Broome St & Grand St) 212-226-9010
www.lowereastsideny.com (LES: F to 2nd Ave)
These community boosters will squire you to some Lower East Side galleries. Hopefully, your guide will be a little more mellow than the chipper voice who narrates their free podcast tours. If you think maybe a self-guided art crawl is more your speed, you can grab a free map from the tiny visitor's center. Your chances of bailing on the galleries in favor of a Lower East Side Dumpling and Beer walk are much less if you join forces with some European tourists on the actual tour.

For all you artist folks coming to the city who want to sell your work, you can do that here in NYC much more easily than elsewhere in the US because there is an actual Supreme Court decision that ARTIST president Robert Lederman (once billed as former mayor Rudy Giuliani's "worst nightmare"!) won against the City a long time ago, in which all art sales were classified as Free Speech. This basically means the City CANNOT force you to pay money or move you off the streets or out of the park if you are selling your artwork in a space no larger than 4x8x5 feet. Robert Lederman has important info about all this in an article called "Selling Art on the Street: The Basics," (www.knol.google.com/k/selling-art-on-the-street-the-basics). He also gives links to all the documents you need to carry with you, in case you run into ignorant Parks officials or police officers who think they need to move you. There are videos, advice, documents, media clippings, and more, all archived in the links provided. You can also join the ARTIST yahoo group. (www.groups.yahoo.com/group/nycstreetartists) ARTIST stands for "Artists' Response To Illegal State Tactics." – Jerry the Mouse

a Graveyard – Mouldy Peaches • 10 Crack

For nearly 20 years, a volunteer collective has been putting on weekly shows featuring independent punk and hardcore bands from around the world. ABC No Rio is much more than a music venue – it's an activist and community resource center, with art exhibits, readings and an honest-to-goodness Zine Library. The folks at ABC are committed to creating a diverse and inclusive scene where all can feel welcome, and never book racist, sexist or queer-bashing bands. Admission is $7. – redguard. (There's great people watching at the popular all-ages Saturday afternoon punk / hardcore matinees. No alcohol at the show. – Victoria Law) (The punk matinee!! Every Saturday at 3pm! I was actually there for the first one in early, early 1990. They came & took drunken photos of us which later appeared in 17 magazines to illustrate the straight-edge movement at CBGB. – Fly) (Perhaps they could use your volunteer services at the door, not that I don't enjoy seeing the petite Ms. Law informing rowdy headbangers nearly twice her size that they can't bring their 40s back inside. – AH)

Bowery Ballroom
"6 Delancey (btwn Bowery & Chrystie) 212-533-2111
www.boweryballroom.com (LES: J/M to Bowery)
One of my favorite music venues in New York. The upstairs performance area reminds me of a lot of the midsized clubs I used to frequent in Chicago and Boston. Bigger than the Lounge Ax or TT the Bear's, smaller than the Middle East Downstairs, it feels like a proper "adult-person" venue. – Heath Row

LIVE MUSIC

MANHATTAN

Financial District

Alwan for the Arts
16 Beaver Street, 4th Floor (btwn Broad & Broadway)
646-732-3261, alwanforthearts.org
(Financial District: 4/5 to Bowling Green)
Alwan for the Arts has amazing cultural mix performances in a downtown space near Wall Street. Dance, music, theater... they even offer Arabic classes now! Tickets are $15 per performance, but they'll let you in for less if you're totally strapped. – Jerry the Mouse

Lower East Side

ABC No Rio Matinee Saturdays
156 Rivington (btwn Clinton St & Suffolk St) 212-254-3697
www.abcnorio.org/events/punk.html
(LES: F/J/M/Z to Delancey)

Cake Shop
152 Ludlow St (btwn Rivington & Stanton)
212-253-0036
www.cake-shop.com (LES: F/J/M/Z to Delancey-Essex)
Cake Shop may be the coolest music venue ever. – Melissa Bastian (Cake Shop has lots of great shows. – Fly) (I spent $7 to see four bands for five hours. Not bad at all. – Josh Saitz)

Arlene's Grocery
95 Stanton Street (btwn Ludlow & Orchard)
212-995-1652, www.arlenesgrocery.net (LES: F to 2nd Ave)
Grandma here remembers when Arlene's really *was* a grocery. Arlene's retained its distinctive red and yellow awning. It's a fine place to hear live music, or inflict some on the masses yourself by signing up to perform Rock N Roll karaoke to a live band, but if it's a popsicle, or a dusty bottle of hydrogen peroxide you're after, you're going to have to hit that bodega around the corner by Bluestockings.

National Underground
159 E Houston Street (btwn Chrystie & Allen)
212-475-0611
www.thenationalunderground.com (LES: F to 2nd Ave)
I was going most every Wednesday, even going by myself,
because the free Dixieland jazz was super authentic. I
could sit in the back on Victorian couches, drink a beer
and eat the best burger, 10 bucks, but what I liked about it
is they dress it up for you, serve it with ketchup and mustard right on it, pickles and everything. – Andria Alefhi

The Mercury Lounge
217 E Houston St (btwn Ludlow and Essex) 212-260-4700
www.mercuryloungenyc.com (LES: F to 2nd Ave)
The appeal of the Mercury is twofold: 1) great shows and
2) small club. In other places, this is a recipe for disas-
ter as you'll be crushed against walls and into people's
armpits as you desperately try to catch a glimpse of your
favorite band, but at the Mercury the complex math of
favorite band + breathing room works. They're great at
booking bands on the upswing of their popularity, right
before they start to sell out places like Webster Hall or
Bowery Ballroom (Mercury and Bowery are part of the
same family of clubs under the "The Bowery Presents"
umbrella). Which means you get to see music you love in
a relatively intimate setting with other fans, and still have
room to lift your beer or move your feet. – Megan Garrity

East Village

Bowery Poetry Club
308 Bowery (btwn 1st St & Bleecker St) 212-614-0505
www.bowerypoetry.com (East Village: F to 2nd Ave)
Bowery Poetry Club does some really great shows although they are a bit more pricey (than the free ABC No
Rio punk matinee) and you can't really hangout after the
show – Fly

The Lower Eastside Girls Club Free Saturday Performance Series
56 East 1st St (btwn 1st Ave & 2nd Ave) 212-982-1633
(East Village: F to 2nd Ave)
The Lower Eastside Girls Club Saturday Performance
Series is a weekly free all ages performance series, featuring line-ups of musicians, singer-songwriters, MCs and
poets. This project embodies the Girls Club's mission of
offering free and innovative cultural programming to
members, connecting the Girls Club to the greater community, and supporting women in the arts. If you're fearless enough to play a room packed with opininated, NYC
teenage girls, email the organizers and lobby to be put on
the bill. Every Saturday at 3pm.

Lit Lounge
93 2nd Ave (btwn 5th and 6th St) 212-777-7987
www.litloungenyc.com (East Village: F/M to 2nd Ave)
Lit Lounge's bar is dark, relatively roomy and comfortable, if it's not overly crowded with people waiting to get
into a show. There's an art gallery in back. The show space
is downstairs. The stairs are really steep, and the quarters
below can get quite tight. But almost everywhere you
stand, you can get a sight line. – Heath Row

Drom
85 Avenue A (btwn 5th & 6th St) 212-777-1157
www.dromnyc.com (East Village: F to 2nd Ave)
Drom attracts acts from Turkey, Spain, Eastern Europe,
Italy, even India and Brazil – anywhere the Gypsy presence has asserted itself musically. Some of the players
are big names in their countries of origin and yet, tickets
are rarely more than $10. They serve food, which makes it
easier for people of all ages to see the show, but if you're
eating, the minimum table tab is $20 per person so get a
slice of pizza on your way. Who sits down for Gypsy music anyway? I know I can't.

Blue Raincoat – Leonard Cohen • Fairy Tale of

The Stone

16 Avenue C (@ 2nd St)
www.thestonenyc.com
(East Village: F/J/M/Z to Delancey-Essex)
With regular Lower East Side *avant* music haunts closing down on the regular (the last being Tonic), the Stone is the soldier still managing to stand and stand up for all that's artsy. Volunteer run with so much love and hope for sound art. – Matana Roberts

Banjo Jims

700 E 9th Street (@ Ave C) 212-777-0869
www.banjojims.com (East Village: L to 1st Ave)
A great place to hear music any night, but especially on Monday nights when the Cargelosi Cards play live swing until 2am. They pass the hat around a couple of times during the performance, but there's no hard and fast door charge. – Victoria Law

C Squat

155 Avenue C (btwn 9th St & 10th St)
www.myspace.com/seesquat155
(East Village: F/J/M/Z to Delancey-Essex)
See Skwat has always been my favorite place for shows. Me & my band, Zero Content, have played lots of shows there over the past two decades. Do not expect those to be advertised anywhere. You have to search that shit out. It takes effort, but it is definitely worth it! – Fly

Otto's Shrunken Head

538 E 14th St (btwn Ave A & B) 212-228-2240
www.ottosshrunkenhead.com (East Village: L to 1st Ave)
You don't have to be a screaming psychobilly to down a flaming tropical beverage from a coconut carved to look like a monkey, and the music here will put you in a great mood, no matter what. Otto's divey back room is a great place to take on some vintage ukulele, rockabilly, swing, or good old rock n roll on the cheapy cheap. The bathrooms have copious adhesive-backed evidence of all who have played here, as well as adult novelty dispensers.

SoHo/NoHo

The Roulette

20 Greene Street (btwn Canal & Grand) 212-925-2050
www.roulette.org (SoHo: J/Z/N/Q /R/6 to Canal St)
This is one of the oldest joints for experimental, adventurous music. It was here way before the Stone or Issue Project Room. In ways, it inspired some of these other spaces and has been able to stay afloat through some incredibly tough times. It's literally on the edge of SoHo and the beginnings of Chinatown. You could see a great show of thought provoking music, then run around the corner to Pearl River! – Matana Roberts

Ace of Clubs

9 Great Jones St (btwn Broadway and Lafayette) 212-677-6963
www.aceofclubsnyc.com
(NoHo: B/D/F/M to Broadway-Lafayette)
This little basement space tucked beneath Acme (one of the city's most scrumptious purveyors of New Orleans-style grub) ain't much to look at. But what it lacks in decor it makes up for in pure volume as one of the only small clubs on the island of Manhattan that books metal bands. The night I played there it was an all-female lineup with more of a hard rock vibe, but on other occasions, I've seen great local metal acts like Hung and IKillYa whose headbanging fans always show up in full all-black regalia to keep the scene alive. – Emily Rems

Joe's Pub

425 Lafayette St (Btwn 4th St & Astor Pl) 212-539-8770
www.joespub.com (East Village: 6 to Astor Pl)
I love Joe's Pub. I hate Joe's Pub. Their booking is high quality and consistent. Every show has been excellent, despite the fact that it was held at Joe's Pub, not because. I've not gone to a more uncomfortable, stand-offish, and expensive place for music in New York City. Tickets cost $25. If you don't have a table or dinner reservation, you're directed back to the bar area, which gets crowded pretty quickly. You're obliged to order a couple of drinks. A ginger ale costs $5. A 7&7 costs $11. Joe's Pub isn't a music venue. It's a dinner theater that hosts music performances. – Heath Row (Amen, Brother! That 2-drink minimum gets me right in the old bread basket. May as well order a grown up drink like a top shelf Scotch on the rocks, so they don't fuck things up as they go about fucking you. Don't get a mixed drink or it'll be all mixer! Under no circumstances should you order dinner here, even though that's the only way to secure a table. The food is appalling. So why buy a ticket to Joe's Pub if it's such a terrible place (and it is)? Sometimes legends come through, and the intimacy of the space get them in its thrall—they drop all diva antics and aloofness, let down their hair, seem to even enjoy themselves. It can make all the difference. – AH)

Greenwich Village

Fat Cat Jazz Bar

75 Christopher St (@ S 7 Ave) 212-675-6056
www.fatcatmusic.org
(Greenwich Village: A/C/E/B/D/F/M to W 4th St)

It's just 5 bucks cover if you go on the early side, and you can bring in take-out. Totally worth it, usually. I think there's live music every single night. It's a huge place. You can pay a small charge to rent Scrabble tiles and a board for a whole night of entertainment. – Robyn Jordan

Bar Next Door
129 MacDougal St (btwn W 3rd and W 4th St) 212-529-5945
www.lalanternacaffe.com
(Greenwich Village: A/B/C/D/E/F/M to W 4th St)
Next Door is a good place to go listen to jazz. On Thursdays you can go listen, get a glass—or four—of wine, some food, and dig the tunes for ten dollars. – Josh Medsker

Gramercy Park

Workshop for Music Performance Concert Hall
31-33 E 28th St (btwn Park & Madison) 212-582-7536
www.wmpconcerthall.com (Gramercy Park: R to 23rd St)
If your ears were nearly fried off at ABC No Rio's punk and hardcore matinee, perhaps your next musical afternoon should be of a more soothing nature. The WMP is a fancy room (19th century chandeliers, gilt mirrors) hosting classical music of the sort that can be fit onto a very small stage. Every Monday at 12:30, they have "Strad for Lunch", a 45-minute long chamber music concert where the musicians get to play on a genuine Antonio Stradivari-made Stradivarius violin. Depending on how you interpret the $10 suggested donation, the experience could prove cheaper and more effective than a bottle of aspirin.

Midtown

The Jazz Church: St. Peter's Church
619 Lexington Ave (@ 54th Street) 212-935-2200
(Midtown: B/D/F/M to 42nd St-5th Ave-6th Ave)
Back in the late 50's, the legendary Reverend John Garcia Gensel established a ministry among the Jazz musicians of New York City. Responding to the claim that jazz was the devil's concern, he wondered why Old Scratch should get the best music. Gensel hung out in the clubs, and became the man that musicians like bassist/composer Charles Mingus could call on day and night to bail them out of jail and soothe their emotional wounds. After Gensel became Pastor of St. Peter's Church at 53rd and Lex, he established it as the spiritual home of New York City's jazz community. He passed on in 1998, but the church continues it's jazz ministry. There's a free concert every Wednesday at noon, jazz vespers on Sunday's at 5:00, and when a jazz musician dies they are sent off with a proper jazz funeral at St. Peters. Every October they hold the "All Nite Soul" fundraiser, where the music goes until dawn. – David Goren

Carnegie Hall Family Concerts
881 7th St, 212-247-7800, www.carnegiehall.org
(Theater District: N/Q /R to 57th St-7th Ave)
Practice, practice, practice and if that doesn't work, hit one of Carnegie Hall's Family Concerts, when you can swan into this world-famous venue for the low, low price of $9. Don't get your nose out of joint if there are a lot of kids there – these afternoons are devised to hook the next generation of music lovers by their tender young ears. You should thank them for giving your old ass the opportunity to soak up the acoustics and vibes, the complimentary cough drops, and the framed photos of all the legends who've performed here.

Upper West Side

The Metropolitan Opera
70 Lincoln Center Plaza (@ 66th & Broadway) 212-362-6000
www.metoperafamily.org (Upper West Side: 1 to 66th St)
The Met is awesome. Tickets can cost as little as $20, and they also have standing room only in the very back. The nose-bleed seats are worth securing, although you might wish for some opera glasses. The translations are on displays at the seat level versus above the stage. The building is just as awe-inspiring. – Heath Row (Those low cost tickets Heath mentions are the 150 rush tickets that are set aside for every (non-super-deluxey-opening-night-type) Monday through Thursday night show, purchasable two hours before showtime. If you're a senior citizen, you can purchase these babies online starting at noon. – AH)

Washington Heights/Harlem

Abyssinian Baptist Church
Tourist Entrance: W 138th St & Adam Clayton Powell, 212-862-7474
www.abyssinian.org (Harlem: B/C/2/3 to 135th St)
Go to listen to the Choir and the 11am sermon at Abyssinian Baptist Church in Harlem on Sunday. – Jerry the Mouse (Wear your Sunday best – no tank tops, flip flops, or the stinky raggedy clothes you've been sleeping in since Cincinnati. Also, don't you even *think* about vacating that pew until the service is over! First come, first served, with days that tend to swell the ranks of any congregation, like Christmas and Easter, reserved for church members only. – AH)

Velvet Underground • Chelsea Hotel No. 2 –

Our Savior's Atonement
178 Bennett Ave (@ 189th St) 212-923-5757
mosaconcerts.weebly.com
(Washington Hts: A to 190th St)
Our Savior's Atonement, the uptown Lutheran Church &
Community Center (OSA), runs a free series of concerts
that are the highest quality around—classical, baroque,
ancient, as well as jazz and modern stuff. – Jerry the
Mouse

Marjorie Eliot's Parlor Jazz
555 Edgecombe Ave, Apt 3F (@160th St) 212-781-6595
(Harlem: A/C/B/D to 145th St ...the neighborhood's really
more Washington Hts, but if Ms. Eliot chooses to call it
the northern tip of Harlem, then so shall we)
The coolest NY experience ever. She opens up the living
room of her Harlem home to amazing musicians. They
pass the bucket, so pay what you can. All are welcome.
– Amy Burchenal (All are welcome, but Ms. Eliot's place
can only accommodate 50 folding chairs, so call ahead to
reserve. – AH)

BROOKLYN

Zebulon
258 Wythe Ave (btwn N 1st St & N 3rd St, Williamsburg,
Bklyn) 718-218-6934, www.zebuloncafeconcert.com
(Williamsburg: L to Bedford Ave)
I love the atmosphere. Great acoustics! Kind of reminds
me of the old Berbati's Pan venue in Portland. It is free
most if not all nights. It is a classy joint, a real musician's
place to hear and see music. – Andria Alefhi

Death By Audio
49 S 2nd St (btwn Kent and Wythe, Williamsburg Bklyn)
www.myspace.com/deathbyaudioshows
(Williamsburg: L to Bedford Ave)
A DIY show place in a warehouse-looking building. Do
people live here? They also sell musical gizmos. – Dear
Drunk Girl (I don't know about living but for sure they
build and sell all sorts of things to make you sound louder
and fuzzier than you already do, viewable at www.death-
byaudio.net - AH)

The Glasslands
289 Kent Ave (btwn S 1st St and S 2nd St, Williamsburg,
Bklyn) 718-599-1450
(Williamsburg: L to Bedford Ave)
The Glasslands is one to beat when it comes to combining
music and art. In your ears, on the walls, installed, pro-
jected...there's even a magnet wall you can noodle around

with upstairs. They run a free afterschool program where
kids explore art and music making, and also, this being
South Williamsburg, learn to DJ. If you and your band are
hitting the road with the four trunk loads of costumes
and video equipment you use in your two hour set, you
should definitely see about getting yourselves booked in
here. It's in the same building as Death By Audio. Given
the address and the number of Glasslands events that
show up on the Nonsense New York list, it seems like ev
ery event would be all-ages, but their liquor license means
mostly not. Damn, an elementary school kid can get in,
but your 19-year-old ass can't? Oh, well, at least they keep
it cheap with lots of $5 shows. If you're really broke, the
bar takes credit cards. An excellent place to partake of Mr.
Jonathan Toubin's Soul Clap and Dance-Offs.

Dead Herring
141 S. 5th St, 1E
(btwn Bedford and Driggs, Williamsburg, Bklyn)
www.myspace.com/deadherringhouse
(Williamsburg: L to Bedford Ave)
DIY loft show place in cool kids' living room. Great house
party feel, and lovely, iconic imagery out the windows,
brought to you by the J/M/Z (the Z is mythical now) and
the Williamsburg Bridge. – Dear Drunk Girl

The Trash Bar
256 Grand St (btwn Driggs and Roebling, Williamsburg,
Bklyn) 718-599-1000
www.thetrashbar.com (Williamsburg: L to Bedford Ave)
Trash Bar is a great venue for catching the most awesome
of the awesome on NYC's indie front. There's an open bar
before 9pm. Meet new and interesting bands and enjoy
the best tater tots in town. – Lola Batling

Leonard Cohen • Chicago, New York - The

Pete's Candy Store
709 Lorimer St (btwn Frost & Richardson, Williamsburg, Bklyn) 718-302-3770, www.petescandystore.com
(Williamsburg: G/L to Metropolitan-Lorimer)
The listening chamber looks like the inside of a gypsy caravan juxtaposed with 1950's American school desks. Free every night for music plus other fun, like trivia night and spelling bees. Sucks going alone. Also cool drinks with elderflower and shit like that. – Andria Alefhi

The Knitting Factory
361 Metropolitan Ave (@ Havermeyer, Williamsburg, Bklyn) 347-529-6696
www.bk.knittingfactory.com
(Williamsburg: G/L to Metropolitan-Lorimer)
Many considered it the final indignity to the disappearing downtown NYC rock scene when the legendary Knitting Factory vacated its original Tribeca digs to take over the former Luna Lounge space in Brooklyn. But you know what? My band just played the new Knit and the place is pretty swell! Conveniently located a stone's throw from Manhattan, the club's main room is intimate enough that you can see no matter where you stand, and the Knitting Factory name still attracts the same caliber of indie super-stars that they've always been known for, only now fans can see their faves up-close. – Emily Rems

Lulu's
113 Franklin St (@ Greenpoint Ave, Greenpoint, Bklyn) 718-383-6000 (Greenpoint: G to Greenpoint Ave)
Lulu's has punk shows, like, every day (it seems) – Cristy Road (Lulu keeps changing her name, from Lulu's, to Lost & Found, then a brief stint as the Alligator Lounge II, and has now back to Lulu's, which I hope will stick, because in my opinion, she looks like a Lulu. Got a tight little dance floor and acres of unclaimed airspace overhead. – AH)

Goodbye Blue Monday
1087 Broadway (btwn Dodworth St & Lawton St, Bushwick, Bklyn) 718-453-6343
www.goodbye-blue-monday.com
(Bushwick: J to Kusciuszco)
Colorful, unpredictable entertainment in a teensy, unlikely-looking venue under an elevated subway. I showed up because one of my friends was playing, and I got to see a fusion band, a burlesque act, a singer-songwriter and a punk duo in one evening! I had a dee-licious cream soda, and they also offer coffee, beer and wine. – Becky Hawkins (It is a rad space with very strict safe-space policies. A sign at the front door says NO SEXISM NO HOMOPHOBIA NO RACISM NO BULLSHIT. – Cristy Road) (Refreshments

are only slightly cheaper than the usual Brooklyn bar prices, but they've got free shows every night of the week. They also have yoga classes, book readings, wifi, computers, comedy nights, and anything that anybody from the community feels like putting on. This place is a serious staple of Bushwick and deserves a lot more attention than it gets. – Caitlin McGurk)

Brooklyn House Shows:
The Boneyard in Crown Heights
1410 Lincoln Pl (btwn Utica Ave & Rochester Ave, Crown Heights, Bklyn)
(Crown Heights: 3/4 Train to Crown Heights/Utica Ave)
&
538 Johnson (@ Bridge St, Bushwick, Bklyn)
www.myspace.com/538johnson (Bushwick: L to Grand)
&
House of Yes
342 Maujer St (Btwn Morgan St & Olice St, Bushwick, Bklyn)
www.houseofyes.org (Bushwick: L to Grand)
&
Surreal Estate
13 and 15 Thames St
(Btwn Bogart St & Morgan St, Bushwick, Bklyn)
www.myspace.com/surrealestatenyc
(Bushwick: L to Morgan)
There is a deep underbelly of independent music in NYC happening at houses. Coming from Florida, where each city I lived in had its staple punk house that held shows, I was amazed at the number of homes creating all-ages venues here. I couldn't believe so many DIY spaces existed at once. All these spaces are rad. I didn't feel too alienated as a newcomer, which is totally possible in small punk scenes, especially when one is a queer girl who can't deal with much bullshit.– Cristy Road (They all host skill shares, workshops, performances and dance parties, too. Surreal Estate's kitchen is where the cooking goes down for Brooklyn's Food Not Bombs (10am every Thursday), and the House of Yes has a crazy, trapeze-equipped sky-box where you can learn to fly. – AH)

Rubulad
338 Flushing Ave (btwn Classon and Taaffee, Bedford-Stuyvesant, Bklyn) 718-RUB-ULAD
(Bedford-Stuy: G to Classon)
Rubulad in Brooklyn does some amazing shows off the radar – Fly (If you show up looking like you're on your way to Burning Man, you may get discounted admission to this big old freaky-deaky warehouse party. (No need to spend hours on your costume. Body paint and a penis gourd will suffice.) People smoke all sorts of things here,

Aisler's Set● Harlem Holiday – Cab Calloway &

so check the exits because these guys are prone to decorating with paper and lots of it. Believe it or not, they also try to host a Kids Rubulad one afternoon a month. The best way to find out what's on the Rubulad horizon is by subscribing to the Nonsense New York list. – AH)

Jalopy Theater and School of Music
315 Columbia St (btwn Woodhull and Rapeleye, Carroll Gardens, Bklyn) 718-395-3214
www.jalopy.biz (Carroll Gardens: F/G to Carroll St.)
Jalopy is a gem tucked away between Carroll Gardens and Red Hook, one of the best places to see free/cheap music, get cheap drinks and go on a date. I adore the place. The owners are an adorable married couple who love roots music and the people who love roots music. The place has a warm, red interior with church pews and bizarre instruments hung like hunting trophies. It really feels like your imaginary coolest-aunt-and-uncle's secret venue in the Catskills, or somewhere just outside New Orleans, off the tourist route. You can see world-class jazz, country, blues, folk, and bluegrass acts for as little as $10, and every Wednesday the free "Roots and Ruckus" features a mash up of great local performers. Tecates are $2.50! You can also take an 8 week class to learn a cool old-timey instrument. Rent an instrument for $25 a month, buy a new one, or get your own fixed up. – Dear Drunk Girl

BAMcafe
30 Lafayette Ave (btwn Ashland Pl & St Felix St) 718-636-4100
www.myspace.com/bamcafelive (Fort Greene: C to Lafayette)
If an esoteric, foreign film at BAM Rose Cinemas leaves you yearning to rub shoulders and possibly more with brainy, arty beauties of both genders, the location could not be more convenient. A drink here fetches some cover-free live rock, jazz or R&B every Friday and Saturday night. Pretty much everyone who plays here is into spicing the standard arrangements with a liberal infusion of world music, or tuba, or some creatively applied classical music training. If you're accustomed to hearing music in beer-pissy back rooms, this historic opera house's soaring, high windowed drinking space will seem like something out of a fairy tale.

Issue Project Room
232 3rd St, 3rd Floor (@ 3rd Ave, Gowanus, Bklyn) 718-330-0313
www.issueprojectroom.org (Gowanus: F/G to Carroll)
This place is close to my heart. With a board of directors that's a who's who of NYC arts awesomeness you can't go wrong here, any night of the week. – Matana Roberts (I hope the board cracked some champagne when they

learned the city had awarded Issue Project Room a new, 5000-sq. foot, landmarked home (110 Livingston – they move in 2011.) 'Til then, if a converted can factory is good enough for board member Steve Buscemi, it's good enough for you! But please keep in mind that he's there for his musician son, not you, ya yutz! Bring your laptop, film clips, digital tuning fork, and connector cables to the Sunday night audio / video jam. A hot spot for experimental, avant-garde, and/or free-form musical composition – AH)

Southpaw
125 Fifth Ave (between Butler and Douglass, Park Slope, Bklyn) 718-230-0236
www.spsounds.com (Park Slope: B/D/M/N/Q /R/2/3/4/5 to Atlantic Ave-Pacific St)
Park Slope's Southpaw is a sprawling, generous, party palace for music lovers that maintains a small club vibe even when hosting big rock acts like Joan Jett, soul bands like Sharon Jones and the Dap Kings, or hip hop legends like Slick Rick. The biggest crowd my pop-punk band ever played to (around 500 people) was at this venue, and man, did that crowd get loose! Excellent interior design offers multiple levels to view the stage from, ample seating for the weary, and plenty of room to bust a move, which is really what you need to enjoy an epic show. – Emily Rems

Barbès
376 9th St (btwn 6th & 7th Ave, Park Slope, Bklyn)
718-965-9177
www.barbesbrooklyn.com (Park Slope: F to 7th Ave)
Barbès does the oft-overlooked Tuesday night a solid
with the Slavic Soul Party, a wild Balkan hootenanny
starring the band of the same name, and like-minded
musical guests. One date was traumatized by the sight of
a middle-aged horn player emptying his spit valve onto
the floor, another by the sweaty pitted, arms-in-the-air
jubilation on the dance floor, but I can't get enough.

QUEENS

Silent Barn
915 Wyckoff Ave (btwn Hancock and Wierfield, Ridgewood, Queens)
www.myspace.com/thesilentbarn
(Ridgewood: L to Halsey St)
Head out to the Bushwick/Ridgewood border and see a
show on almost any night of the week at the Silent Barn.
It's a very chill, low-key DIY venue that serves cheap beer
and just opened a zine library of their own! – Eric Nelson

BRONX

The Bronx Underground
The First Lutheran Church
3075 Baisley Avenue (@ Bruckner Blvd,Schuylerville,
Bronx) 718-829-0650
www.myspace.com/bronxunderground
(Schuylerville: 6 to Hunts Point)
These all ages DIY shows have been popping kids' ear-
drums in the Bronx since 2001 and have amassed a huge
following, drawing up to crowds of over 300. You can
see 4 or 5 bands from different sub-genres of rock for $9.
Local and even nationwide bands are begging for shows
here. There's sometimes as much as a 6-month wait to
play. – Genevieve Texiera

Revolution
Bruckner Bar & Gallery
1 Bruckner Blvd (@ 3rd Ave, South Bronx) 718-665-2001
www.myspace.com/revolutionny (Bronx: 6 to 138th St)
The Bronx Underground also throws these monthly Revolution dance parties at Bruckner Bar. It's $5 if you RSVP on
www.going.com. Live music! Come early or late for drink
specials! Great for all the original scenesters who were at
the first show back in 2000, and are starting to feel a little
too old among 16-year-olds. – Genevieve Texiera

MUSIC FESTIVALS

Carnegie Hall Neighborhood Concerts and Community Sings
www.carnegiehall.org/neighborhoodconcerts
Carnegie Hall's Weill Music Institute sponsors a free
neighborhood concert series from October to June. Artists of all world music stripes, including American gospel
raise the roof beams in venues ranging from libraries,
churches and shelters to The Brooklyn Museum and
Harlem's Apollo Theater. For Free. There are even a few
opportunities for the audience to croak along at the Community Sings.

Zlatne Uste Festival - January
www.zlatneuste.org
Friday $20. Saturday $45. Under 12: Free. Knock $5 - $10 off
with a student ID.
Zlatne Uste is a 2-day Balkan extravaganza where all-age
masses dance in ever-accelerating circles. Those in the
know come prepared with water bottles, which they
safeguard in out of the way locations, labeled with their
names. Our American folk traditions have many things to
recommend them, but when it comes to old ladies dancing with teenaged boys, our Balkan friends have us beat!
There's a ton of live bands and the Saturdays rage 'til the
wee hours, meaning there are plenty of opportunities to
get in free as a volunteer without being doomed to miss
out on all the fun because you're pulling a four hour shift
in the dishroom.

Bang On A Can Marathon - June
The World Financial Center Winter Garden
220 Vesey St (@ West St) 212-945-0505
www.bangonacan.org
(Battery Park: A/C/E/2/3 to World Trade Ctr-Park Pl)
Bang On A Can seeks to further contemporary music, particularly *challenging* new music, by not only commission-
ing, recording, and promoting it, but also by sneaking it
into the ears of the masses. The plan is carried out with
particular gusto at the annual Marathon in the World
Financial Center's Winter Garden, which I have to say,
does make for excellent people watching opportunities.
In addition to the rapt devotees who've had this free event
on their calendar for months, there are plenty of people
who've just blundered in from the waterfront in search of
a bathroom and seize any vacant spot they can find only
to move on a couple of minutes later, shaking their heads
as if to say, "Well, *that* Emperor forgot to put on clothes."
The whole thing runs like clockwork for over 24 hours.
If you've got 500 cds of your contemporary *avant-garde*
compositions in a drawer somewhere, send one in for

NYC is Dead - Lower East Side Stitches •

consideration for the next Marathon.

Siren Music Festival - July
Coney Island, Brooklyn
www.villagevoice.com/siren, 212-475-3333
Since 2001, it's free, it's all ages, there's a ton of bands I won't have heard of, which is always fun. (Note: I have heard of Death Cab for Cutie, New York Dolls, TV on the Radio, Blonde Redhead, Mission of Burma...okay, the list goes on, but they don't all play the same year!) If it tanks, well, it was free and the Cyclone's right there. I love things like this, being out in the hot sun, drinking a beer, getting something for nothing.

JellyNYC Pool Parties - July
East River State Park
90 Kent Ave (btwn 13th St & 14th St, Williamsburg, Bklyn)
www.thepoolparties.com (Williamsburg: L to Bedford Ave)
Free
The free music has left the pool. Hear me, hipsters? The folks who produce these Sunday afternoon parties have moved them to the East River State Park, which, while small, is an actual state park, with rangers who don't really want you drinking, even if you're over 21, which is when they'll grudgingly admit you to a little, cordoned-off alcohol zone. But everyone can play basketball and dodgeball, listen to music, and generally behave as if they're attending some parallel universe MTV Beach Party.

Charlie Park Jazz Festival - September
Tompkins Square
St Mark's Pl (btwn Ave A & Ave B)
(East Village: 6 to Astor Pl)
&
Marcus Garvey Park
124th St & Mt. Morris Park
(Harlem: 4/5/6 to 125th St)
www.cityparksfoundation.org
Free
At the first Charlie Park Jazz Festival I attended in the early 90s, they christened the stretch of Avenue B where he once lived Charlie Parker Place. If you're a jazz fan, or if you listen to WKCR, you know that Phil Schaap, who emcees the event, talks too much. Some people are into that. I'm not one of them. The music is whatever. I like Bird and all, but I prefer musicians playing their own stuff, you know? But don't take my word for it; I wasn't paying close enough attention to say for sure that it was all covers. – Jenna Freedman

New York Gypsy Festival - September
Multiple venues
www.nygypsyfest.com
If I were the sole author of these music listings, you would probably be left with the overwhelming impression that New York City's live music scene is but a larger, starrier version of Sibiu, Romania's, give or take a couple of freaked out marching band costumes. What can I say? I knows what I likes! There's a lot of variety beneath this umbrella, but what I like best are the big, brass filled bands that play the sort of raucous, celebratory dance music you hear at weddings, circuses, and during the first scene of Emir Kusturica's *Underground*, when a horse cart carrying two drunken friends careens through the streets of Belgrade, one of them shooting at the musicians he has hired to run after them. Ooh, yeah, I bet you're in the mood now! I know I am!

CMJ Music Marathon and Film Festival - October
Multiple Venues
www.cmj.com
It's a bit unseemly, New York trying to pass itself off as Austin, Texas, but people do all sorts of things on the

outside chance of being discovered by an industry professional. Bazillions of small labels book their next big things into dozens of venues and then run themselves ragged trying to generate some positive buzz. Can you feel the anxiety and pulsating potential for disappointment? The only sure thing, from my point of view, is the annual Bloodshot Records Barbeque, an afternoon hootenanny where you can kick back in a thrift store cowboy shirt (extra points for full-sleeve tattoos) and wash down a free garden or non-garden burger with some cheap beer and extremely-alt-country music.

BONK Festival - October
Multiple Brooklyn venues
www.bonknyc.info
Admission, but some events are free
Every fall I'd get these messages that the Hungry March Band and the Rude Mechanical Orchestra were off to HONK, the festival of activist street bands in Somerville, Massachusetts, and I'd be like, "Damn! Next year I am definitely figuring out a way that I can go too!" Before that could happen, the festival came to me! I'm counting on BONK to become a regular thing. Hopefully this year it won't rain on the potluck or the parade across the Brooklyn Bridge. (One had to be cancelled, the other relocated.)

SUBWAY SERENADE
My favorite place to hear live music is the subway. Timing is everything, though. In warm weather, Washington Square Park is a good bet, too, and I've met some of my favorite buskers there. At evening rush hour, there's a woman who sings opera in the marble corridors of the Graybar Passage on the east side of Grand Central Terminal. Whether or not you catch an aria, check out the awning outside. The Graybar building facade has a nautical theme, and the lower exterior was made to look like a ship's mooring, complete with concrete rats climbing up the ropes. – Kate Black

There's a lot of great music in the subway. One of my favorites is Mr. Winston Spencer who can most often be found in the Atlantic Avenue terminal on the platform of the B/Q train during the evening rush. With his sweet falsetto, Caribbean lilt, and the reggae rhythm setting on his cheap, electric keyboard, Mr. Spencer can outcroon Aaron Neville. He's usually singing, "The Wayward Wind," and his rueful mid-song chuckle as the song's character contemplates his restless ways will floor you. – David Goren

There is a lady who plays the saw in the Union Square sta-

tion who makes no bones about prominently displaying her website (www.sawlady.com, natch). It's only a matter of time before you investigate her presence in cyberspace, joining the ranks of such fans as Zubin Mehta. – AH

Elizabeth Genco had a great zine called, PLATFORM, detailing her experiences playing her fiddle in the subways. She's moved on to other projects, but maybe you can rustle up a copy in the Barnard Zine Library or at ABC No Rio. –AH

THEATER AND LIVE PERFORMANCE
First off, thank you for entertaining the notion that Theater is not dead. Keeping it on life support sure gets expensive though. For my money, the best stuff is usually Off-Off Broadway, where even the occasional lemon won't run you more than $15 or $20, and the producers are likely to be sweeping the stage as soon as they can get out of their costumes. You better believe those guys are grateful for any full-price ticket purchase that comes their way. Some companies whose work I've enjoyed, none of whom have a permanent home, include Piehole, The Debate Society, and Clancy Productions—seek 'em out!

For the fullest menu of what's playing at any given time, check for reviews and listings in *Time Out New York*. The *Village Voice* also remains willing to chuck thespi-yorkers a bone by listing what's going on.

Here are some good places to see live theater, performance art, puppetry, and sometimes dance, comedy, music and/or movie stars.

Dixon Place
161 Chrystie St (btwn Rivington & Delancey) 212-219-0736
www.dixonplace.org (LES: J/M to Bowery)
After years of talking the fundraising talk, and watching as flophouse neighbors give way to fashionable boutique hotels, Dixon Place grabbed the brass ring. They got their swell new digs, but they're still the same old art freaks at heart. A great place to see performance art, the Five Lesbian brothers, interminable experimental musical exploration, new work by old stalwarts, and for five weeks every summer, the Hot Festival, the world's oldest continuously running celebration of queer performance. And ain't it grand when even the cutting edge has room for volunteer ushers? Sign up by filling out a form on their website. – AH (The new space is spectacular, but I do miss the feeling of being in founding director Ellie Covan's living room. But hey, Dixon Place is always offering exciting, balls-out performances, and now it's in a space

Summer in the City – Regina Spektor, New York

worthy of its influence on the NYC dance scene. It's not only dance, so check out what they got going...it'll move ya'. – Lynn Brown)

The Slipper Room

167 Orchard St (@ Delancey) 212-253-7246
www.slipperroom.com (LES: F/J/M/Z to Delancey-Essex)
The Slipper Room is the center of a modern cabaret scene, a dramatic backdrop to the burlesque shows featuring a rotating cast of characters. – Kate Black (But in true vaudevillian style, the proprietors here book bands and DJs as well as pretty peelers to mix things up. The night my band played, I remember their sparkly red house drum kit was missing some pieces so we had to scramble behind the velvet curtains to find something to prop the floor tom on before the stripping hula hooper Miss Saturn had finished her routine. Ahh, showbiz! – Emily Rems) (The Slipper Room put its pasties on ice when its building scheduled a date with the wrecking ball, but it swears it'll reopen on the 2nd floor of the new structure being built atop the one where La Rems scrounged an ersatz tom shim. 'Til then, check the website to see which nearby venues are hosting the Slipper Room event of your choice. - AH)

Blue Man Group at Astor Pl. Theatre

434 Lafayette (btwn 4th St & Astor Pl, NoHo) 212-254-4370
www.blueman.com (East Village: 6 to Astor Pl)
So what if it's been running for years and has, through frequent television appearances and commercial endorsements, come to be thought of as a "tourist" show? It's still a full-court blast, unless perhaps you're Jello-phobic, or fearful that some firebug might whip out a lighter while the entire theatre is swathed in toilet paper. With ticket prices that rival Broadway's, you may want to hold off on this one until you're traveling with an older relative who's willing to spring for something special for the whole family. Ask for the armband that signals your willingness to participate to the fullest degree.

The Public Theatre

425 Lafayette Ave (btwn 4th St & Astor Pl)
212-239-6200
www.publictheater.org (East Village: 6 to Astor Pl)
Unlike *Saturday Night Live*, The Public never really lost its street cred. Rather than rest on its laurels as the guys who launched Shakespeare in the Park, A

Chorus Line, and a bazillion downtown theater careers, it continues to put on great shows by the likes of Suzan Lori Parks, Lisa Kron, and Mike Daisey. If someone like Liev Schreiber or Peter Dinklage start hankering to be taken even more seriously than they already are, guess where they'll be appearing as MacBeth or Richard III. Its Under the Radar festival brings new theater from around the globe to NYC every New Year. Budding playwrights should consider applying to be one of their Emerging Writers. If accepted, the only downside is they may expect you to start hanging out in their in-house bar and cabaret space Joe's Pub.

LaMama Etc.

74 E 4th St (btwn Bowery & 2nd Ave) 212-254-6468
www.lamama.org (East Village: F to 2nd Ave)
Okay, these guys are really much more way out and experimental than the following anecdote is going to suggest, but my favorite memory of going to LaMama is seeing an extremely foul-mouthed Amy Sedaris in a puffy 1970s bikini, Scotch tape snubbing her nose and a craft fur treasure trail disappearing into her bottoms, holding a vibrating pillowcase that she claimed contained a monkey she was going to sell for parts. This was closely followed by *Faust Gastronome*, which featured a lot of onstage food, a memorable shoe forcing the actress playing the devil to stand with her foot permanently cocked in cloven hoof position, and a bare-assed Faust crouched at the end of a very long table, shitting Adolf Hitler out along with copious amounts of sausage. Um, also, they have a dance festival.

The New York NeoFuturists: *Too Much Light Makes the Baby Go Blind*

When rents collide: the alternative demographic APARTMENT-DWELLING-DOG-OWNER cast going head to head with alternative demographic tiny old Eastern European lady cast.

- Cat Power• Sunday in New York - Bobby

at the Kraine Theater
85 E 4th St (btwn 2nd & 3rd Ave) 212-777-6088
www.nyneofuturists.org (East Village: F to 2nd Ave)
I was a Neo-Futurist, performing *Too Much Light* in both
Chicago and New York for nearly ten years of my life. As
such, my perspective on the whole thing is unreliable, but
fortunately, I can still recite the ol' spiel, word for word:
"Too Much Light Makes the Baby Go Blind is 30 original plays
performed in 60 minutes in random order. Each week, a
roll of the dice determines how many old plays will be cut
the following week, and new plays are written to fill the
holes in the menu...and when we sell out, we order out!"
That said, I was shocked to learn that the audience now
has the option to buy tickets online. Used to be you had to
stand out in the elements, waiting forever for your turn
to roll the die that would determine your admission price.
It started as $1 x the roll. Now it's up to $10 + the roll...
should you choose to exercise that advance purchase option, congratulations, you just rolled a six. (Sucker!)

Performance Space 122
150 1stAve (@ 9th St) 212-477-5288
www.ps122.oorg (East Village: L to 1st Ave)
This old public elementary school building long ago
cast off the shackles of the New York Board of Ed for the
jollier bondage of frequently funny, almost always over-
the-edge performance and dance at extremely reasonable
prices. Eric Bogosian, Spalding Gray, John Leguizamo,
Karen Finley, and a buncha other big bonobos honed their
milk teeth on PS122's stage. Some of them still put in an
appearance here on for old time's sake. Tickets are pretty
much always $20, with $5 knocked off for students and
seniors.

Theater for the New City
155 1st Ave (@ 10th St) 212-254-1109
www.theaterforthenewcity.net (East Village: L to 1st Ave)
Ask a downtown theater person about the long-time left-
ies who founded and still run this place, and you'll get an
earful about some seriously cranky management style.
(Civilians may get a taste of this, depending on who's
working the box office.) From summertime's children's
street theater heavy with political message to a post-
parade Halloween Ball, they've got a long history of giving
back to the community. My favorite annual events are the
Thunderbird American Indian Dancers' Dance Concert
and Pow Wow in February and Bread and Puppet Theater's
Children's Circus matinées on December weekends. – AH
(There's sometimes a used book sale in the lobby– Jerry
the Mouse)

HERE Arts Center
145 Ave of the Americas (btwn Spring and Broome)
212-647-0202
www.here.org (SoHo: C to Spring)
HERE exists in a realm of edges: the entrance to the Holland Tunnel, commercial parking lots, and nighttime
streets that don't see much pedestrian traffic. It presents
wonderful examples of new performance art, theater, and
multimedia work. Their attention to set, lighting, and
sound design is obvious. And the seats seem to be old
lecture hall or theater seats. Each seat sports a small desk
surface that flips up and over, as well as what might be old
ashtrays set into the seat backs. At HERE, I feel like I'm
helping artists bring important work to life. – Heath Row

The New Victory Theater
209 W 42nd St (Btwn 7th Ave & 8th Ave) 212-239-6200
www.newvictory.org (Theater District: A/C/E/N/Q/
R/S/1/2/3/ 7 to 42nd St-Times Sq)
The folks responsible for cleaning up the Times Square
of *Taxi Driver* and *The Robin Byrd Show* have a lot to answer
for, but I acknowledge that someone did the right thing
by restoring this derelict Broadway palace as a New York
home for family fare innovators from all over the world.
You don't have to have a kid to appreciate punk action
acts, *Jason and the Argonauts* brought to life by toy action
figures, or a dreadlocked Rapunzel whose witch is played
by a Cornish actor whose bio lists "organic farmer" as his
day job. You can get balcony seats for as little as $12.50

St. Ann's Warehouse
38 Water St (@ Dock, DUMBO Bklyn) 718-858-2424
www.stannswarehouse.org (DUMBO: F to York St)
I used to wish American theaters could be more like
their engaging Scottish counterparts, with bars and
nice snacks and exposed brick walls that make you feel
all arty-like. Now I don't have to wish anymore. There's
always something intriguing going on here. Annual one-
night stands by The Tiger Lillies...Al Pacino corralling his
famous pals for a reading of *Salome*...Frances McDormand
playing badminton with the Wooster Group...the Toy
Theater Festival...a Mabou Mines production of Ibsen's
A Doll's House in which the tall female cast members tow-
ered over their male counterparts whose heights ranged
from 40 to 53 inches... What's that? You want me to shut
up so you can go volunteer usher? Don't tell me. Talk to
the House Manager at 718-254-9601.

Coney Island Circus Sideshow
1208 Surf Ave (@ 12th St, Coney Island, Bklyn) 718-372-5159
www.coneyisland.com/sideshow.shtml

Darin • This Mess We're In – PJ Harvey & Thom

(Coney Island: D/F/N/Q to Stillwell Ave)
Freak out at the last 10-in-1 sideshow in America! If once
is not enough when it comes to sword-swallowing, fire-
eating, and mousetrap-on-the-tongue antics, you can
sit and watch the performers cycle through their acts all
day long for the cost of a single admission. Although the
acts are suitable for all ages, I get the sense that the majority of the cast engages in some extremely interesting
extracurricular activities. – AH (The sideshow seems to
be a bunch of hipsters/art-stars who have decided to put
themselves on display. There are a couple of times when
they hit you up for more money (but personally, I think
that seeing how Madame Twisto is positioned in a box
avoiding swords is *not* worth $1). When the sideshow is
not in session, the space is home to a Friday night burlesque show, the Coney Island film festival, and B movies
on summer Saturdays. – Amanda Plumb)

Chinese Theater Works
www.chinesetheaterworks.org
Chinese Theater Works does free Chinese performance,
notably excerpts of popular Chinese opera like *The Monkey King* and *Legend of Lady White Snake*. I see that they're
also doing Taiwanese hand-puppet theater as well. They
do both indoor and outdoor events. – Victoria Law

Circus Amok
www.circusamok.org
Acrobats, biting political commentary and parody, and a
bearded lady! They play in public parks throughout the
city in September. You can see them without paying a
dime, but you really *should* throw some green into their
donation bucket. – Victoria Law (One thing I really like

about Circus Amok is the built-in diversity of the audience. It's one thing to see a tattooed, gay, Caucasian slack
rope aerialist preaching to the anti-real-estate-develop-
ment choir, but things become far more interesting when
the audience pool opens itself to church-going Latino
and African-American families from the nearby housing projects, who just happened to be strolling through
the park when the great Circus Amok band kicked up its
squonk. – AH)

NY International Fringe Festival
www.fringenyc.org
Once upon a time, two friends wrote a musical with the
horrible title of *Urinetown*, and rather than putting it in a
drawer when every theater they got in touch with rejected
it out of hand, they put it up as part of the NY International Fringe Festival. The Fringe is a haven for people
who've been incorrectly informed that their work sucks,
as well as presenters too fledgling, solo or just plain
out-there to get a foothold elsewhere. It's certainly had
a positive impact on my family's life. Tickets are cheap,
and with so many shows competing for audience, you can
rest assured that parking your butt in a seat for an hour or
two will mean a great deal to those onstage. If you prefer
the view from their side of the footlights, applications
are accepted from December through February for the
upcoming August.

Brave New World
www.bravenewworldrep.org
I'm a sucker for site-specific performance and theater in
non-traditional venues, making this Brooklyn company
right up my alley, if I had one. They've staged *To Kill A
Mockingbird* on the director's Ditmas Park porch, *On The
Waterfront* on a Red Hook pier, and *The Tempest* on Coney
Island's boardwalk, featuring a Shakespearean Mermaid
Parade. I can't say where they'll pop up next, but let's
meet there, okay?

Shake It Up, Baby!
I've had a sweet spot for it ever since Woody Allen invoked
Shakespeare in the Park as a reason why Tony Roberts
should stay in New York and Tony Roberts tells him,
"They stole my tights." Seeing the official, Public Theater-
produced Central Park version is great if you like to get
up at dawn and have a whole day to kill in line, but it's not
the only game in town:

Lower East Side:
Shakespeare in the Parking Lot
www.shakespeareintheparkinglot.com

Inwood:
Inwood Shakespeare Festival
www.moosehallisf.org

Brooklyn:
Piper Theater Company
pipertheatre.org

Queens:
Hip to Hip Theater Company
www.hiptohip.org

Roving through the Boroughs:
Theater Smarts
www.theatersmarts.com

Theatrical Discount Strategies
But let us say you've heard great things about some
Broadway or Off-Broadway show. (What makes some-
thing a Broadway show, as opposed to an Off or Off-Off
Broadway show, is the number of seats in the house, not
the location, the presence of under-rehearsed puppets
performing sexual acts, and/or the words "zombie" or
"The Musical!" in the title.)

There are several ways to get 'er done:

TKTS Booths (aka the half-price, day-of ticket booths)
226 W 47th St (@ Broadway) 212-221-0013
(Theater District: A/C/E N/Q /R/S/1/2/3/ 7 to Times Square-
42nd St)
&
199 Water St (btwn John St & Fulton St) 212-912-9770
(South Street Seaport: A/C/J/Z/2/3/4/5 to Fulton St-Broadway-Nassau)
&
1 MetroTech Center (@ Jay St & Myrtle Ave Promenade,
Downtown Bklyn) 212-912-9770
(Downtown Bklyn: A/C/F to Jay St)

If you fancy the traditional, wait-in-line forever, chat-
with-theater-students-and-nice-people-from-Ohio, Give
My Regards to Broadway, more stressful experience,
you'll want the original Times Square booth. Downtown
Brooklyn and the Seaport are much saner and sell the
exact same tickets. You'll be choosing from whatever's
available for today. (Though it's possible to buy tickets

to tomorrow's matinées at the Seaport and Brooklyn
locations.) The choices are posted on an electronic board
similar in spirit to the ones listing arrivals and departures
in the airport. Bring cash because that's all they take, and
make sure there's a little fat in the budget, because half
price comes with a surcharge. Once your non-refundable
transaction is completed, put your ticket away in a place
where you'll be able to find it later. Broadway box office
people are tough cookies.

High 5
www.highfivetix.org
If you're a teenager, or are traveling with a card-carrying
one, you can snag $5 tickets to a bunch of really great shit
(including dance, music, spoken word, and BAM's Next
Wave festival) by buying advance via High 5's website. Be
sure to bring that teenage documentation with you to the
box office: anything listing a birth date putting you between 13 and 18, or a current middle school or high school
ID from anywhere in the world. High 5 allows teens to
take an adult escort at that same discount price. You can
also use High 5 to get $5 museum passes—each of which
will get two people in. Check the website's calendar to see
what's available.

Student Rush
If you're a card-carrying student (perhaps through the
miracle of Photoshop), one or two unsold seats can be
yours for $20 a pop. Just show up at the box office a
couple of hours before showtime. A few minutes before
showtime may suffice if this turkey's having trouble attracting an audience. The sad truth is that straight plays
are a much tougher sell than feel-good musical foof
conjured from the corpses of old movies, so even if it won
the Pulitzer prize, you can probably rush a seat to a weeknight performance...unless of course it stars someone
truly famous.

Ushering
Willing to look and possibly feel like a dork for an evening
in exchange for some free Off-Broadway theater? Oh sure,
it sounds like a good deal now, but what about when some
confused senior citizen with a voice like a seagull is giving you hell for not knowing where the bathroom is? I
know I don't feel particularly on my game when it looks
like I'm on my way to a catering gig. (Probably because
I don't own black pants and white shirts, and thus am
always settling for whatever ugly things Goodwill can
cough up at the zero hour...) If you still think you want to
do this, best make haste. Get in touch with the volunteer
coordinators as much as a month in advance:

Empire State of Mind – Jay-Z featuring Alicia

Biltmore Theatre, 212-399-3000, volunteer@mtc-nyc.org

MTC Stage I and Stage II mtchousemanager@nycitycenter.org.

Second Stage Theatre - JSchleifer@2ST.com

Playwrights Horizons 212-564-1235, usher@playwrightshorizons.org

Cherry Lane Theatre, company@cherrylanetheatre.org, 212-989-2020 ext. 23

Lucille Lortel Theater ushers@lortel.org.

Signature Theatre 212-244-7529 housemanager@signaturetheatre.org

Women's Project 212-757-3900, info@womensproject.org

New York Theater Workshop, 212-780-9037

Second Acting It

Please join me in thanking the writers of *The Office* for ruining this time-honored practice for the rest of us. Used to be, if you insinuated yourself with the crowd under the marquee when a show broke for intermission, you could follow them back in and slip into an empty seat for the second act. It wasn't so much seeing a play as getting away with something. But ever since these *Office* characters Second Acted It, ushers have been gunning for bums to throw out. They'd probably let it slide if they were one-night-only volunteers, but with the exception of the

Roundabout, Broadway ushers are union members.

DANCE

Whenever I deliberately set out to see some dance in NYC, I wind up enjoying myself immensely, but it happens so seldom, I can still remember every piece I've seen and count them on the fingers of one hand.

FreeFALL

www.freefallnyc.org

FreeFALL is a low-tech, high-concept dance-theater company run by Lynn Brown and Lynn Marie Ruse. Their stuff is sexy and often site specific. I was recently invited via Facebook to a guerrilla performance of *lie, lay, laid* to be performed every 30 minutes in a room at the Hilton, from check-in time to lights-out at 11:30. If your moves could use some help, check out the Move of the Day videos archived on their blog. And look, I got Lynn B to divulge some of his hot NYC dance tips below!

Movement Research at Judson Church
Judson Memorial Church
55 Washington Square S (btwn Thompson & Sullivan)
212-598-0551, www.movementresearch.org
(Greenwich Village: R to 8thSt-NYU)
Monday, 8pm, Free

This is where I go to see the hippest, grooviest, forwardest thinking dance in NYC. It's a smart, fun, and supportive crowd of movers and shakers, gathering as a tribe to see new experimental work. And might I say dancing there is a dream, crashing and slipping through space that has been shared by all the greats of PoMo dancinghood. Feel the ghosts, and do it for Free. Also look for their Fall and Spring Festivals: more production value at dirt cheap prices. – Lynn Brown

Fall for Dance Festival
New York City Center
131 W 55th St (btwn 6th& 7thAve) 212-581-1212
www.nycitycenter.org/content/stage/ffd.aspx
(Theater District: N/Q /R to 57th St)
September, $10

Independent downtown artists, major ballet companies, and international artists meet on the same stage at City Center, at the Fall for Dance Festival. Ten days every September, five programs, 20 artists, and a wild ride through enough different aesthetics in one night to make your head spin. With joy. At just $10, it can't be beat but everybody knows it, so find out when tickets go on sale, and get in line early if you can. If you go on the 'net, be patient, and start in June. – Lynn Brown

The Love Show
www.theloveshownyc.com 917-363-7065
If you're like me, you think modern dance is sexy. Obviously, the folks behind The Love Show agree with us. They also find ballet and burlesque sexy, thank god, and put together regular shows that celebrate the human form, both male and female, and what it can do. They move around, so keep up with all current news on their doings on their website. - Lynn Brown (Their holiday contribution was an R-Rated *Nutcracker* at Theater for the New City. - AH)

Dance Theater Workshop Studio Series
219 W. 19th St (btwn 7th Ave & 8th Ave) 212-924-0077
www.dancetheaterworkshop.org (Chelsea: 1/9 to 18th St)
$5
My first NYC dance job was sweeping floors at DTW. I know no one confers artist status on you but you, but I confess that I didn't feel totally legit as a choreographer until DTW produced my work. Every New York choreographer you have heard of, and many others who you should hear of, have been presented here. The Studio Series runs approximately monthly, and tickets are $5. Their mainstage productions are more expensive, but you can count on the quality. - Lynn Brown

DanceNow Festival
www.dancenownyc.org
September
The folks at DanceNow had a little idea back when...a festival to open the downtown dance season. It's now a big idea, presenting over 60 artists every year, in an assortment of venues. My all-time favorite memory as a performer was at DanceNow, doing a dance in a life raft off of Chelsea Piers, ending with a dive into the Hudson. Someone called the police, and soon we had a rescue boat and helicopter over the site. Thrilling! I can't promise a police raid, but the dancing will suffice. - Lynn Brown

S.L.A.M. (Streb Laboratory for Action Mechanics)
51 N 1st St (btwn Wythe & Kent, Williamsburg, Bkln)
718-384-6491
www.streb.org (Williamsburg: L to Bedford Ave)
Streb rocks. Fight Club attitude, modern dance aesthetics, and an all-around kick-ass good time. Confront gravity, space, and limits in an environment conducive to defeat them all through technique and smarts. Ongoing $15 drop-in classes and special workshops year-round. And if they are performing in New York, make sure to catch 'em. - Lynn Brown

COMEDY
I invited my friends Ed Herbstman and Melanie Hoopes, who run the Magnet Theater, to do a little improv with me. In this scenario I am a visitor to NYC, who wants to see some comedy on the cheap. And they are the experts who publish zines, except since they don't really, they keep pronouncing it so that it rhymes with the second syllable of vagina! Anyway, enjoy Melanie and Ed's recommendations.

The Upright Citizen's Brigade
307 W 26th St (btwn 8th Ave & 9th Ave) 212-366-9176
www.newyork.ucbtheatre.com (Chelsea: C/E/F/1/9 to 23rd St)
About ten years ago some Chicago Improv people set up shop in Manhattan and completely transformed the comedy world in NYC. They and many of the alumni from their improv classes have gone off to become stars, but many return regularly for a Sunday night show called Asssscat 3000. There are two shows, the 7:30 is ten bucks and the 9:30 is free but you have to wait in line. While most of the top talent has gone off to their new LA location, the revolving cast usually contains a small handful of incredible performers and medium-to-big names. It's become a more buttoned-down operation over the years, but the theater still has that underground feel—it's in the basement of a Gristede's supermarket. - Ed Herbstman & Melanie Hoopes (If you're drunk and/or brave, perhaps you and your friends will sign up to perform a midnight sketch of your own devising in Friday's Liquid Courage. Turn your script in to the box office between 10:30 and 11:30, and then steel yourself because every sketch that's submitted gets picked, and these days, when people hear Upright Citizen's Brigade, expectations are high. - AH)

Made Up Musical
Magnet Theater
254 W 29th St (btwn 7th Ave & 8th Ave) 212-244-8824
www.magnettheater.com (1 to 28th St)
Fridays at 10pm, $7
Bad improv is the worst type of bad comedy. Second worst is bad musical theater. So I must be crazy to recommend that you go to see *Made Up Musical*. Except that lo and behold, I'm one of the guys who founded the Magnet Theater. Maybe I'm biased, but it's brilliant. It's deep, silly, technically superior, and really funny. It manages to be moving, too. And it's a completely improvised musical. - Ed Herbstman & Melanie Hoopes

Thursday Night Out
Magnet Theater
254 W 29th St (btwn 7th Ave & 8th Ave) 212-244-8824

Ono • New York City - Ladysmith Black

www.magnettheater.com (1 to 28th St)
Thursdays, shows at 8pm, 9pm & 10pm, $5
You not only get a night filled with excellent groups of
Magnet graduates for just five bucks, but you can hop
into the 7pm Magnet Mixer, where Magnet students past
and present join improvisers from all the world over and
non-improvisers who just want to play, forming rare and
wonderful one-night-only combinations. Sign-up starts
at 6:30. Plus, there are $1 PBRs. This is the cheapest date in
the tri-state region. – Ed Herbstman & Melanie Hoopes

Story Pirates After Dark
www.storypirates.org, 347-878-6798
Location and price varies, but it's usually less than $20
Of all the comedy shows written entirely by children,
The Striking Viking Story Pirates After Dark has to be the
best. The concept is brilliant and simple—teach children
storytelling skills by taking stories written by kids and
performing them with fully fleshed-out song, dance, costume, and puppets. This freshly post-pubescent group of
Northwestern grads have performed for tens of thousands
of grade schoolers. Each month they do an After Dark
show for the over 18 crowd. Everything is still written by
kids, which makes the darkness darker, the dirt dirtier,
and the show awkwardly fun and twisted. – Ed Herbstman & Melanie Hoopes (These are the guys who've made a
play out of *Found Magazine*'s found notes. – AH)

Don't Quit Your Night Job
Julia Miles Theater
424 W 55th St (@ 9th Ave) 212-757-3900
www.dontquitnyc.com
(Hell's Kitchen: A/B/C/D/1 to 59th St-Columbus Circle)
Monthly
Don't Quit Your Night Job is a monthly late-night comedy
happening, a mish-mosh of improv, music, and sketch
with a revolving cast from Broadway and beyond. Tickets
are $20 and proceeds go to benefit the TDF/Open Doors
program, an arts mentoring program for high schoolers.
Usually I'm skeptical when proceeds go to benefit some
sort of do-gooder cause—methinks it's a way to squeeze
$20 out of me for a $10 show. But previous guests include
Huey Lewis, Hank Azaria, Julianna Margulies, Michael
McKean, Anthony Rapp, Sara Ramirez, George Wendt,
Bebe Neuwirth, David Hyde Pierce, Martha Plimpton, An-
drea Martin, and Mo Rocca. So there! (I know, I had you at
Huey Lewis.) – Ed Herbstman & Melanie Hoopes

LECTURES
Think how intellectual you'll sound when you're able to
preface your remarks with a breezy "I saw her give a lecture in New York and..."

The New York Public Library
www.nypl.org/events/public-programs
Oh how I love those hearty, self-reliant, and above all
opinionated senior citizens trundling through all sorts of
wind and weather to attend free programs at the NYPL.
They think nothing of interrupting an honored speaker
with a request to *speak UP!* They have no hesitation about
rustling plastic bags packed with newspapers fished from
the trash. They subsist on canned tuna fish and righteous
indignation, and damned if they aren't doing their bit to
keep the arts alive! They'll go to anything, but a particularly good place to check them out is the Performing Arts
branch in the Lincoln Center complex, because those renegade oldies loooove them some opera and ballet, and the
programming will be really cool for you too.

Center for Book Arts
28 W 27th St, 3rd floor (btwn 6th Ave and Broadway)
212-481-0295
www.centerforbookarts.org (Chelsea: N/R to 28th St)
Anyone who's capable of running off 30 copies of a messy
cut-and-paste punk zine at work should be capable of sitting through an artist's talk or an interesting discussion
on the history of printmaking, book-binding and self-
publishing, no?

BAMcinématek
BAM Rose Cinemas
30 Lafayette Ave (btwn Ashland Pl & St Felix St, Fort Greene, Bklyn) 718-623-2770
www.bam.org (Fort Greene: C to Lafayette)
You know it's going to be arty if they spell it like THAT! $15 will usually suffice to get you a movie followed by a panel discussion, lecture, or opportunity to gape at a real live blue jean-wearing movie star. The films can be pretty much anything: acknowledged classics, little-seen awesomeness finally getting its due, work by local artists, festival favorites, and most intriguing, (*fill in the blank*) *Selects*, the program where iconic actors and directors get to present a line up of their favorite films.

Nerd Nite
www.nerdnite.com
New York City has long served as a paradise for nerds. Henry Ward Beecher. Emma Goldman. Do you think if they had it to do over again, they'd be like, "Outa my way, I'm snorting some club drugs and hitting Barney's sample sale!" No way! They'd be counting the days until the next Nerd Nite, when proudly curious smarties get together to drink, listen to guest speakers hold forth on such topics as Jewish gangsters, unusual New York City census data, and/or zombies, and occasionally speed date. Tickets hover around $10.

Open City Dialogue at Pete's Candy Store
709 Lorimer St (btwn Frost & Richardson, Williamsburg, Bklyn) 718-302-3770
www.petescandystore.com
Reducing this bi-monthly bar lecture series' name to its initials will get you pretty close to the spirit of the thing. OCD's guest lecturers keep it brief, but they know how to pack a passionate wallop into those 45 minutes. Recent topics have included Greenpoint's rooftop farms, a slide-show of the Domino Sugar factory and other abandoned New York sites, and David Byrne explaining the relationship between creativity and context. And while we're at it, Virginia, how about some non-denominational proof of Santa Claus' existence, culled from a combination of historical fact, ontological argument, and inductive reasoning?

Secret Science Club
Monthly meetings at The Bell House
149 7th St (btwn 2nd Ave & 3rd Ave, Gowanus, Bklyn) 718-643-6510
secretscienceclub.blogspot.com (Gowanus: D/N/R to 9th St-4th Ave)
When I was in 7th grade, my science teacher sweetened

a year-end C- with a little aside to my parents that she thought my interest in theater would probably serve me better than the lessons she'd been trying to get through my thoroughly disinterested skull. I'm not sure I deserve a second chance, but the pointy heads behind Brooklyn's Secret Science Club are granting me one anyway, and damned if the medicine doesn't go down easier with several spoonfuls of alcohol! Astronomers, physicists, marine biologists, neurobiologists, zoologists, mathematicians and all manner of smarties whose college degrees actually led to meaningful employment within their chosen fields show up to disseminate, take Q's, offer A's, and make things explode.

LANGUAGE AND CULTURE
There's also no shortage of cultural recruiting by countries other than our own, some of it in the very tongues these foreign devils speak in their native lands! This is just the Eurocentric tip of the iceberg, mind you...

La Maison Française
16 Washington Mews (btwn 5th Ave & University Pl)
212-998-8750, www.nyu.edu/maisonfrancaise (Greenwich Village: N/R to 8th St-NYU)
Most of the lecturers have a connection with NYU, and when you divide the cost of tuition by attendance at a single class, it's like you're totally scamming the system, even if you have to lay down a ten-spot or so. Other people have to get work study jobs and learn to speak French to learn about Le Corbusier, or participate in round tables like "Translating as a Profession."

Deutsches Haus
42 Washington Mews (btwn 5th Ave & University Pl)
212-998-8660, www.nyu.edu/deutscheshaus (Greenwich Village: N/R to 8th St-NYU)
Also an NYU institution.

Glucksman Ireland House
Washington Mews (btwn 5th Ave & University Pl)
www.irelandhouse.as.nyu.edu (Greenwich Village: N/R to 8th St-NYU)
I'm all like, "Yeah! They speak English!" But they also speak this: *Fáilte romhat go h-Áras Glucksman na hÉireann...* um, I think it's something about fostering excellence. Next thing I know, someone's going to tell me that Glucksman's an Irish name.

Horton Heat • Jamaican in New York – Shinehead •

Goethe-Institut
1014 5th Ave (btwn E 82nd & E 83rd St) 212-439-8700
www.goethe.de (Upper East Side: 4/5/6 to 86th St)
Starting to get a complex about my lack of German...

Instituto Cervantes New York
211 E 49th St (btwn 2nd Ave & 3rd Ave) 212-308-7720
www.nuevayork.cervantes.es
(Midtown: 4/6 to 51st St- Lexington Ave)
Why, oh why, did I take French instead of Spanish, a
language that would have served me much better in my
adopted home? It may not be too late, except the website
with all the info about classes and events is also in Spanish.

If you have an interest in a particular culture or are pre-
paring to travel in a foreign land, try typing that country's name into a search engine, like so: "Jamaican Cultural Center Events NYC". Oh, cooool, look what turns up:

Caribbean Cultural Center African Diaspora Institute
(CCCADI)
408 W 58th St (btwn 9th Ave & 10th Ave) 212-307-7420
www.cccadi.org
(Midtown: A/B/C/D/1 to 59th St-Columbus Circle)
There's so much to learn and do here in NYC, I hope I
don't forget to go to Jamaica (let alone the Francophone
Caribbean island of Guadaloupe).

SPECTATOR SPORTS

Brooklyn Cyclones
Keyspan Stadium
1902 Surf Ave (btwn 19th & 20th, Coney Island, Bklyn)
718-449-8497
www.brooklyncyclones.com
(Coney Island: D/F/N/Q to Stillwell Ave)
There are Met fans and Yankee fans, and then there are
Cyclones fans. The Coney Island Cyclones are one of the
farm teams for the NY Mets, and they play in a little stadi-

um right by the water. I've never seen a game at Yankee or
Shea Stadium, but I can bet you that games are better at
Coney Island. Tickets start at $7 and the stadium is small
enough that any seat is a good seat. Between innings they
have cute little contests. And it's at Coney Island, which
means you can combine the game with a ride on the Wonder Wheel and a bag of cotton candy. – Amanda Plumb

The New York Liberty
Madison Square Garden
2 Penn Plaza (33rd St btwn 7th & 8th Ave) 212-564-9622
www.wnba.com/liberty (Garment District: 1/2/3 to 34th St)
The Liberty plays at the Garden. It ain't cheap, but discounts and ticket giveaways can be scratched up with
a little internet digging. If you're traveling with a rabid
sports fan, a Liberty Game is an opportunity to give 'em a
special treat, feminism getting some highly visible center
court respect! Then you can rightly claim you're all spent
out when they start petitioning to see a Broadway show.

Gotham Girls Roller Derby
Various academic facilities around the city, though they
dream of having their own pro rink someday...
www.gothamgirlsrollerderby.com
Going into my first roller derby I had no idea what to
expect but even though I'm fairly sports impaired, I had
a fabulous time. The basic rules of the game were easy to
follow (and thankfully, outlined in the program) so even
though the game commentary was about as easy to decipher as your typical subway announcement, the cheers
of the crowd made every point won exciting. The players'
costumes and often hysterical nicknames were, of course,
a large part of the appeal and the half-time show (sword-
swallowing!) definitely added to the ambience. – Sharon
Furgason (If you're moving here and dream of joining a
team, the Gotham Girls hold try outs for Fresh Meat (their
term) during the November through February off-season,
and are sometimes looking for Jeerleaders and refs too.
– AH)

The New York City Marathon
All five Boroughs, starting at the Verrazano-Narrows
Bridge and ending in Central Park, First Sunday in November
www.nycmarathon.org 212-423-2249
I love the Marathon, probably because I don't see how
people can force themselves to do it. There's no shortage of Olympics-fit competitors, but nearly as many are
ordinary Janes and Joes (their names often scrawled on
their t-shirts) whose physical condition seems to mirror
my own. You can run it, too, but you have to enter the lot-

tery way in advance, and be prepared to cough up around two hundred bucks in fees, if accepted. You're guaranteed entry if you agree to raise money for one of the charities on the Marathon's website. For those of us who are sane enough to prefer watching this lunacy, don't worry about missing the runners. The front of the pack whizzes by in seconds but it takes the rest of those yo-yos forever to thunder past any given spot.

SUMMER FREEBIES

Yes, summer in NYC can be brutally hot, but we promise to make it up to you with a plethora of fun, festive, Free events.
River to River Festival
www.rivertorivernyc.com, 212-360-1399
Lower Manhattan, including Battery Park, Wagner Park, the World Financial Center and the South Street Seaport
This massive smörgåsbord of summertime fun attracts marquee names like Conor Oberst, Jenny Lewis, and Merce Cunningham, simultaneous with more modest (and often much more gratifying) attractions, like choreographed works by local dance companies and drop in workshops where kids learn to make toy sailboats. The Big Draw goes on under River to River's giant umbrella, as does the Bang on a Can Marathon.

Hudson River Park Take Me To The River Festival
West Street from Houston to W. 55th
www.hudsonriverpark.org, 212-627-2020
I love this park. The bathrooms have toilet paper. The grass is in such short supply, people are inclined to treat it nicely. (Sorry, Rover, no dogs allowed.) As if the view of New Jersey wasn't entertainment enough, they pour on the free programming every July and August, alternating movies with live bands and Sunday night dancing. (The programmers keep things holy by taking Saturdays off.) The one-night-only showboat is the Rumble on the River, where amateur boxers go at it on a ring set up near the *Intrepid*. (www.fridaynightfightsnyc.com)

City Parks Foundation Concerts and Theater Performances
www.cityparksfoundation.org
Tuesdays, Wednesdays, and Thursdays
All five boroughs July and August
If you think doing Shakespeare next to a packed playground and a schizophrenic junkie wondering where his bag went is easy, think again, motherfucker! They do a great job of remembering that not everyone who craves free outdoor entertainment is a college educated Park Slope homeowner with one child in Montessori School

and another on the way. I'm not dissing that demographic, but certainly there are plenty of New Yorkers who, on the whole, would do more than just sit still for some free theater and dance, even if, on average they don't seek it out as frequently as this demographic does.

Summerstage
Rumsey Playfield in Central Park (Midpark around 70th St) 212-360-2777
www.summerstage.org (B/C to 72nd St)
Summerstage concerts run from spoken word and dance to well-selected double-bills of rock, soul, Brazilian, Asian, African, and other world musiques. Most are free with several Big Name fund-raiser concerts sprinkled in. – David Goren (It gets pretty dusty and cramped inside the actual arena. I don't mind partial view if it comes with shade and comfort. Best advice, bring a sarong to spread out under the trees. – AH)

Celebrate Brooklyn
9th St Bandshell
95 Prospect Park W (@ 9th St) 718-855-7882
www.prospectpark.org (Park Slope: F to 7th Ave)
Another free summer concert series that has in recent years leapt in front of Summerstage in terms of the coolest acts, occasionally giving nod to Brooklyn-originated grooves from They Might Be Giants to Antibalas. An annual not-to-miss show is Hall Willner's multi-star

tributes to a single artist. Feted in the past have been Doc Pomus, Leonard Cohen, and Bill Withers. CB also screens silent movies with live soundtracks provided by local bands. – David Goren

Lincoln Center Out of Doors & Lincoln Center's Midsummer Night Swing
70 Lincoln Center Plaza
(Columbus Ave btwn 62nd & 65th) 212-875-5030
www.lincolncenter.org (Upper West Side: 1 to 66th St)
Most of the plentiful free summer music ends by mid-August, but Lincoln Center Out of Doors lives it up all the way to the end of the month. Midsummer Night Swing swings from experimental to jazz to the closing American Roots fest, featuring the likes of Sleepy LaBoeuf, the Knitters, and Patty Smith. – David Goren (The highly audience-participatory programming runs Tuesday through Saturday for three weeks in July. If big band swing dancing leaves you cold, come back the next night when they'll be twistin' the night away. There's mandatory valet parking for bags and purses of any kind, so leave 'em at home, or pay $3 to have 'em babysat while you dance your heart out. – AH)

Quisqueya en el Hudson
173rd St & Audubon Ave, 646-345-3656
(Washington Hts: C to 163rd)
Quisqueya on the Hudson is a new festival for Dominican arts, music, and dance organized by Dominicans in Washington Heights. Last year's festival took place in Highbridge Park on a Sunday in late June. – Jerry the Mouse (If you can't make it to the party, there's a hot and widely available cd of the same name showcasing past participants. – AH)

MOVIE THEATERS
It's a bittersweet experience to see a wonderful movie here, knowing it will never be widely released. On the other hand, knowing that you're seeing something huge before the folks in Denver, Pittsburgh, and San Diego get a chance to is the most delicious kind of *Schadenfreude*.

MANHATTAN

LOWER EAST SIDE/EAST VILLAGE

Sunshine Cinema
143 E Houston Street (btwn 1st Ave and 2nd Ave)
212-777-FILM #687
www.landmarktheatres.com/market/NewYork/Sunshine-Cinema.htm (East Village: F to 2nd Ave)

According to buffs whose standards are far more stringent than mine, this lovely-to-look-at space gets straight As for focus, seat comfort, and popcorn. I would further commend them for showing at least three films I'm interested in seeing at any given time. – AH (They show a new midnight movie every Friday and Saturday. It's an opportunity to get to see an old favorite of yours on the big screen. – Genevieve Texiera)

Anthology Film Archives
32 2nd Ave (@ 2nd St) 212-505-5181
www.anthologyfilmarchives.org
(East Village: F to 2nd Ave)
Blink and you'll miss it—the thing about the Anthology is you kind of have to make the effort to see what's playing. Their films invariably fall into the "Revivals, Special Screenings, and Other" category, so it's not like BAM or Film Forum where you go to see a new release playing a standard engagement, and find out about more esoteric, short-term offerings from postcards scattered throughout the lobby. And—explaining why so many recent NYU film school grads are on the menu—they rent their two theaters out. Go ahead, shoot your feature film and show it here!

Village East Cinema
181-189 2nd Ave (@ 12th St) 212-529-6799
www.villageeastcinema.com (East Village: L to 3rd Ave)
Village East didn't start out showing films; it opened
in 1926 as the Yiddish Art Theater. Since then it's gone
through many name and venue changes, from theater to
film to burlesque to music and back to film. In the early
'90s it was converted into a seven-screen multiplex and
the main auditorium was restored—so if you can see a
movie in there, it's a treat. If not, there's still plenty of
old-theater-goodness in the lobby area. They play typical
art house fare but it's usually (somewhat) less crowded
than the Angelika. – Shayna Marchese

Tribeca/SoHo/NoHo

92YTribeca
200 Hudson St (@ Canal) 212-601-1000
www.92y.org/92yTribeca/ (Tribeca: A/C/E to Canal)
The 92nd Street Y's Tribeca location is a multi-functional
venue, but it has the cutest little theater that shows some
out-there stuff. I saw Road House there! How cool is that?
– Marguerite Dabaie (On Christmas Day, the great bus-
man's holiday of NYC Jews, the Y's downtown outpost
celebrates with Chinese food and a double feature, such
as the back-to-back Mel Brooks classics Blazing Saddles
and Spaceballs. – AH)

Angelika
18 W Houston St (btwn Broadway & Crosby St) 212-995-2000
www.angelikafilmcenter.com
(NoHo: B/D/F/M to Broadway-Lafayette)
There are certain seats where you can feel the theater
shaking as the subway rumbles underneath, but that's
kind of why I like it. The ticket holders' lines do get a
bit psychotic on the weekend, so even if you purchased
tickets in advance, come early and do your yoga breathing. – AH (You'll never forget you're in NYC. This amuses
me. – Kate Black) (It's a beautiful old theater and some of
the screens are a little small, but they show the best indie
films and love what they do. – Josh Saitz)

Film Forum
209 W Houston St (btwn Ave of the Americas and Varick)
212-727-8110, www.filmforum.org (SoHo: 1 to Houston)
Could it get any more rarefied? I'm not saying that everyone who goes here is a film snob. But I nearly had a
nervous breakdown in the middle of To the West, an interminable Chantal Ackerman documentary that is nothing
but silent Russian commuters in big fur hats, stoically
waiting for their trains to arrive. The closest I've come

to Film Forum-osity was my first New Year's Eve in NYC,
when I saw three Satjayit Ray films in a row. One of the
few cash-only box offices remaining, so go with a wad,
or factor in a $1.75 ATM surcharge at the delis around the
corner on Varick.

Greenwich Village

The IFC Center
323 Ave of the Americas (@ W 3rd St) 212-924-7771
www.ifccenter.com
(Greenwich Village: A/B/C/D/E/F/M to West 4th St)
They recently teamed up with the New York International
Children's Film Festival (www.gkids.com), and it seems
like there's always a "best of the fest" feature or shorts
program screening Saturday at 11am, and I would swear
Sita Sings the Blues is on permanent rotation, as well it
should be! I would tend to classify these choices not as
kiddie flicks so much as independent films that audience
members of all ages can enjoy, unlike, say Alvin and the
Chipmunks III or Lars Van Trier's Antichrist, one of which
played there. Guess which. – AH (Be sure to check out the
gallery of vintage movie posters. – Lola Batling)

The Quad
34 W 13th St (btwn 5th Ave & Ave Of The Americas)
212-255-8800, www.quadcinema.com
(Greenwich Village: F/M/L to 14th St-6th Ave)
Small 'n' arty, just the way my teenage Woody Allen-lov-
ing self once imagined all NYC cinemas would be.

Midtown

Big Cinemas
239 E. 59th st (btwn 2nd & 3rd Ave) 212-371-6682
www.bigcinemas.com
(Midtown: N/R/4/5/6 to 59th St-Lexington Ave)
This theater shows films from India that you might not
get a chance to see elsewhere. Even when the film I want
to see is playing at a more convenient location, it feels
good to make the trek here and do my bit to keep 'em in
business. The facility itself is just your average single-
screen neighborhood cinema, but they have samosas for
sale along with the popcorn and Junior Mints. You should
be able to score a copy of Plot, a complimentary fan rag
bursting with photos and breathless interviews. If you
want to supplement your refreshments, Katagiri Japanese
Grocery is on the same block at number 226.

Sony Wonder Technology Lab
550 Madison Ave (btwn 55 th St & 56th St) 212-833-8100
www.wondertechlab.sony.com
(Midtown: E/M to 5th Ave-53rd St)
They hold free screenings every Saturday, and all you
need to do is call ahead to RSVP. You don't get the whole
interactive exhibit experience, however—you just go into
the theater, watch, and leave. That's okay. The theater is
bigger than many screening rooms in New York City, and
the high-definition projection setup is pretty keen. The
sound in the room is amazing. – Heath Row

Upper West Side

Silent Clowns Film Series
Bruno Walter Auditorium at the NY Public Library for the
Performing Arts
70 Lincoln Center (Amsterdam @ 65th St) 212-712-SCFS
www.silentclowns.com (UWS: 1 to 66th St)
When I was a kid, it seemed like every pizza parlor in
town had a Laurel and Hardy flickering on a screen in the
corner, which did nothing but foster resentment. Like,
what's so funny about these guys, they don't even talk,
and why is our pizza taking so long? It took sitting in a
theater with a bunch of reverent, appreciative, adult fans
to really get why these things are so special. My favorite
is Harold Lloyd, and this series puts him on the bill every
season. The screenings take place on alternating Sunday
afternoons from September through April and feature live
musical accompaniment and Q&A with film historians.

Lincoln Plaza Cinemas
1886 Broadway (btwn 62nd St & 63rd St) 212-757-2280
www.lincolnplazacinemas.com (UWS: 1 to 66th St)

A fine uptown option for catching the same films down-
towners are seeing at the Angelika, Sunshine, IFC and
Village East.

Harlem

Maysles Cinema
343 Lenox Ave /Malcolm X Blvd (btwn 127th and 128th)
212-582-6050
www.mayslesinstitute.org/cinema/index.html
(Harlem: 2/3 to 125th St)
How inspiring that after a long and much-heralded documentary career, Albert Maysles (*Grey Gardens, Gimme Shelter*) up and opened himself a movie theater! This beautiful, 60 seat jewel way uptown shows only documentaries
and there's only one showing a night, with a suggested
$10 donation.

BROOKLYN

Union Docs
322 Union Ave
(btwn Ten Eyck & Maujer, Williamsburg, Bkln)
718-395-7902, www.uniondocs.org
(Williamsburg: G/L to Metropolitan-Lorimer)
I feel pretty goddamn blessed to live in a city with not one
but two cinemas devoted to documentaries, even if this
one's also a one-show-per-night type of dealio. It's also
a suggested donation situation! Hooray! Though here, I
suggest paying the actual suggested amount (or more),
which allows this non-profit to give visiting artists an
honorarium.

Cobble Hill Cinema
265 Court St (btwn Butler and Baltic, Cobble Hill, Bklyn)
718-596-9113, www.cobblehilltheatre.com
(Cobble Hill: F/M to Bergen St)
Ghastly paintings of Judy Garland, Vivian Leigh, Laurel and Hardy, John Wayne, and other bygone stars adorn the front of this neighborhood quad, one of the few theaters in NYC to offer bargain matinées before 6pm on weekdays, and first show on Saturday and Sunday. Even better are Tuesdays and Thursdays when all shows are the matinée price.

BAM Rose Cinemas & BAMcinématek
30 Lafayette Ave (btwn Ashland Pl & St Felix St, Fort Greene, Bklyn) 718-636-4100
www.bam.org (Fort Greene: C to Lafayette)
BAM Rose Cinemas screens great films—a minimum of three current releases and frequent revivals or festival offerings. There's nothing quite like pulling open those heavy doors and traversing the Brooklyn Academy of Music's grand old lobby en route to the box office. The red velvet seats are some of the cushiest in NYC. –AH (Sure, there are plenty of places to catch a flick in New York, but not too many theaters regularly show classics on the big screen. Enter *BAMcinématek*, Brooklyn's only daily, year-round repertory film program. It presents new and rarely seen contemporary films, classics from cinema history,

work by local artists, and festivals of films from around the world, often with special appearances by directors, actors, and other guests—all for the price you'd pay to see the latest Hollywood schlock-buster. – redguard)

Summer Screenings

I love seeing movies outdoors, even if I invariably become unseasonably cold, lay on my side to get my feet and knees up under my sweatshirt, and then...zzz, sqwwnnck whuh, is it over? These are by no means all the outdoor movies series in NYC, so check *The Onion*, *The Voice*, or *Time Out*, or subscribe to Free NYC and check your email daily to see what's on when you're hankering for some film *al fresco*.

River to River Festival Monday Movie Nights on the Elevated Acre
55 Water St (btwn William St and Coenties Slip)
www.rivertorivernyc.com
Holy Cow, I have never made it to this one, but given the location, I'll see you there next summer. I wonder if this is the one all the actors go to...Monday's their night off.

Harbour – The New Pornographers • Brooklyn

Hudson River Flicks
July through Mid August, 212-627-2121
www.hudsonriverpark.org
(Greenwich Village: A/C/E/L to 14th St-8th Ave)
Wednesday nights are for people who are old enough to
see R rated movies; Friday nights, for people who wish
they were. There's a very slim chance I could make it
through *Sex and the City: The Movie* if it was free and I
could take frequent breaks to look across the river toward
New Jersey. Free popcorn!

Central Park Summerstage Films
Central Park's Rumsey Playfield
Mid-park around 70th St, 212-360-2777
(Central Park: B/C to 72nd St)
Free
www.centralpark.com/pages/activities/movies.html
Summer Stage films in Central Park are pretty amazing.
They search you for drinks, and get pretty pissed about
people who try to sneak stuff in. Here are my suggestions
(as of yet untried): put a bottle of wine in a Baby Bjorn
wrapped in a blanket, a flask in your pants, or think up
some other ridiculous scheme. – Cecile Dyer

Rooftop Films
718-417-7362, www.rooftopfilms.com
Every summer they show films on rooftops in Brooklyn,
Manhattan, and Queens. Shorts, super-indies...hell, I bet
they would show your home movies if they thought it was
good. It's a worthy cause, so check it out and donate your
time, energy, and movies. – Josh Saitz (It's true what Josh
says. You can submit your movies, if you reverse the usual
formula of Christmas in July. If they don't accept your
film, teach them a lesson by renting equipment from
them and showing it on your friend's rooftop! – AH)

Brooklyn Bridge Park Conservancy Movies with a View
Empire-Fulton Ferry State Park
(Water St btwn Dock & Main, DUMBO, Bklyn)
www.brooklynbridgepark.org/go/programs-/-events/
movieswithaview (DUMBO: F to York St)
The picnic blanket crowds are friendly, unlike the real
estate hogs of Bryant Park's free outdoor film series. Even
better is the location—the screen's set up in front of the
Brooklyn Bridge. When they showed *Moonstruck*, there
was a romantic shot of the full moon hovering over that
very bridge, and I swear the camera operator must've
been positioned right where I was sitting. The crowd went
apeshit. Transportation Alternatives provides valet bike-
parking for this event, and the popcorn is free.

Sneaky!

UA Court
106 Court St (btwn Schermerhorn St & State, Brooklyn
Hts, Bklyn) 718-246-7459
(Brooklyn Hts: M/R/2/3/4/5 to Court St- Borough Hall)
A couple of bad little birds (Lynn Edwards & Brian Bell)
would like you to know they only check tickets here when
you enter, "so do a double feature! The second one is
free!" My goodness, that takes me back! And it's true that
the higher you go, the less staff presence there is, unless
it's some alien-apocalypse-blow-up-the-Statue-of-Liberty
flick that every rowdy unchaperoned teen above the age of
nine is going to try to sneak into. So when you buy your
ticket, make sure that's the film you paid for. Then sneak
into the latest adaptation of Jane Austen. Also, the seats
here rock (as in intentionally, back and forth). And they
show like half an hour of previews before the actual previews, which go for at least 10 minutes.

Robyn Jordan recommends stopping in the screening
room in the back of the Lower East Side Tenement Museum's Shop. It's intended for people waiting to go on tours,
but anyone can sit and enjoy the documentary screenings
about immigration at no cost.

Let us not forget that there are movies aplenty in pretty
much all of the libraries, museums, and cultural centers
mentioned in this book, many of them free with admission! Or, in the case of the libraries, just plain free.
Bluestockings Bookstore has been known to rock (as in
provide) a screening, as has ABC No Rio. Café Orwell in
Bushwick has a little film club that convenes every now
and then and Habana Outpost in Fort Greene also wants
to watch movies with you. If there's some obscure film
that you can't find anywhere, run it through a search
engine with "showtimes NYC" and you may discover
it's showing while you're here, or more likely that it was
showing for a week, but the run ended the day before you
arrived. It's okay. You'll find something else.

Movie Rentals
I know, it's counterintuitive, you're in New York fuckin'
City, you should be out painting everything in sight
screaming FDNY red, but I've had friends come dragging
through, two weeks into a four week tour, and what they
really want to do is rest. Call in some carryout and lie
down on the couch!

Two Boots Video Rental
42 Ave A (btwn 3rd St & 4th St) 212-254-1919
www.twoboots.com (East Village: F to 2nd Ave)
Two Boots used to have a fantastic movie theater, the
Pioneer. It was a sad day when that rent got raised. Fortunately, their video business survives, the highly selec-
tive selection of rental titles is as good as the pizza, and
the idea of combining the two is a stroke of no-brainer
genius.

Kim's
124 First Ave (btwn 7th St & St. Mark's Pl) 212-533-7390
www.mondokims.com (East Village: F to 2nd Ave)
The Kim's legend started in a corner of the owner's dry-
cleaning business and eventually ballooned to 55,000
titles, multiple locations...it was nuts. Unfortunately,
the rental end of the Kim's empire couldn't keep afloat in
the age of streaming video. Now you might not be able
to rent Kim's obscure selections, but you can buy them!
There are many, many titles, from the classic to the cult
to the sub-cult-bizarre on shelves arranged into fringe-y,
highly descriptive categories, or grouped by director,
with a disturbing-as-ever back room. The used titles go
for cheap, and stickers on the case let you know if the film
you're thinking of acquiring is out-of-print.

Film Noir
10 Bedford Ave (btwn Lorimer & Manhattan Ave, Greenpoint Bklyn) 718-389-5773
(Greenpoint: G to Nassau Ave)
Film Noir is the smartest, most focused video rental store
I've ever encountered. Ever. It concentrates on film noir
as well as science fiction, horror, anime, and so on. One
quality many video store employees lack is the owner
Will's knowledge of and enthusiasm for the genres he
carries. This is an awesome rental resource in a neighborhood dominated by Polish video stores. All you need to
do to qualify for an overnight rental is register your credit
card. – Heath Row

FILM FESTIVALS
Count on New York City to have a festival celebrating
the films of every film-producing nation and region in
the world. Bosnia-Herzegovina, Israel, India, the African
diaspora...get busy with the search engine and you'll find
what you want. Don't cry if your beloved country seems
underrepresented. I'll bet it's got a short in the New York
International Children's Film Festival, at the very least.

But why just sit in the audience? All these festivals take

submissions—yes even the Tribeca Film Festival. Win
that one and you get to be Harvey Keitel's next girlfriend.
Some are just too good to pass up. The NY Surf Film Festival? The Bicycle Film Festival? If there is a Second Annual
CHAT D'OEUVRES: The Cat Art Film Fest (there'd better
be!) promise me you will dig up a submission form and a
video camera.

February
New York International Children's Film Festival
www.gkids.com

New York Short Film Festival
www.nycshorts.com

March
New Directors New Films
www.newdirectors.org

April
Gen Art Film Festival
www.genart.org/filmfestival/newyork

Migrating Forms Festival
www.migratingforms.org

Tribeca Film Festival
www.tribecafilm.com/festival
Tribeca Film Festival is supposed to be the shit, but I always seem to miss it. – Josh Medsker

June
Sprout Film Festival: Making the Invisible Visible
www.gosprout.org/film

New York City Food Film Festival
www.nycfoodfilmfestival.com

NewFest: The New York LGBT Film Festival
www.newfest.org

Human Rights Watch International Film Festival
www.hrw.org/iff

Brooklyn International Film Festival
www.brooklynfilmfestival.org

July
African Film Festival
www.africanfilmny.org

New York Used To Be – The Kills • NY's Alright

August

Asian American International Film Festival
www.africanfilmny.org
The venues in which the films are shown aren't anything
to write home about, but the films themselves...wow! –
Victoria Law

Acefest
www.acefest.com

September

New York Surf Film Festival
www.nysurffilm.com

Coney Island Film Festival
www.coneyislandfilmfestival.com
Scary-sounding splatterfests are a favored genre here,
as is anything to do with mermaids or roller derby, but
I have a hunch your ticket to guaranteed acceptance
is a Coney Island location. The old whore just can't get
enough of herself on the silver screen! – AH

Loisaida Cortos Latino Film Festival
www.loisaidacortos.com

New York Film Festival
www.filmlinc.com/nyff

October

Imagine Science Film Festival
www.imaginesciencefilms.com

CMJ Music Marathon and Film Festival
www.cmj.com/marathon

The Royal Flush Festival
www.royalflushfestival.com
Art and film and rock and roll!" – AH

New York City Horror Film Festival
www.nychorrorfest.com/

CHAT D'OEUVRES: The Cat Art Film Fest
This festival's online presence is veiled in mystery, and
yes, it is a film festival entirely devoted to cats. Try seeing
if the Anthology Archives publicist Stephanie Gray can
direct you to the person (code name: Petit Loup) responsible publicity@anthologyfilmarchives.org. – AH

November

Margaret Mead Film and Video Festival

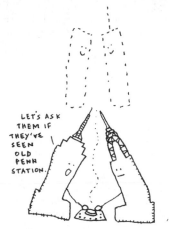

THE EMPIRE STATE AND THE CHRYSLER CONTACT THE TWINS WITH A OUIJA BOARD.

www.amnh.org/mead

December

Bicycle Film Festival
www.bicyclefilmfestival.com
Totally awesome indie and amateur films about all-things
bike, often featuring footage of Black Label and other
such underground scenes. – Melissa Bastian

Zero Film Festival
www.zerofilmfest.com

Monthly

Get Ahead Festival
www.getaheadfest.wordpress.com

If You Like Saxophones – Fear. New York

MAKE! DO!

As gratifying as it can be to kick back and be entertained, there are even greater rewards awaiting those willing to ruin their hairdos by diving in as full fledged participants. Don't worry that you'll have no one to talk to. You will.

TOP HITS
Some of our favorites.

Story Corps Booth
Foley Square (@ Centre St btwn Duane & Worth, across from the courthouse) 646-723-7027
www.storycorps.org/record-your-story/locations/new-york-ny
Be a part of oral history! Back in the day, NPR reporter David Isay had the brilliant idea to create a place where "ordinary" Americans could interview each other about their lives, with the results going into a permanent archive. The original booth was in Grand Central and unsurprisingly, the ordinary turned out to be pretty fucking extraordinary. Book your free appointment well in advance (you'll need a credit card, but it will only be charged if you bag out with less than 24 hours notice, in which case, you just donated $25 to a worthy cause). You've surely got a good story, so let a Story Corps worker draw it out of you. At the end of your 20 minute session you'll be given a CD of your recording.

World Record Appreciation Society
Monthly live events
Various bars in Manhattan & Brooklyn
www.urdb.org
Like most kids, I was fascinated by the *Guinness Book of World Records*, but never dared dream that one day I too could compete. I may not have the stamina (or schedule) to outlast a determined rope skipper or flagpole sitter, but I can for sure show up at a bar, ready to be documented wearing 17 pairs of underpants on my head (provided the world record continues to stand at 16). You may prefer to forge a brand new, never-before-held record. The only requirements are that it be quantifiable, legal, and breakable. There's nothing to stop you from going for the gusto at home, with your video camera as the only live witness, but it's way more of a party to get her done before a supportive crowd of fellow record breakers.

NYC Mix Tape Exchange
First Saturday of every month
Various bars on the Lower East Side
www.myspace.com/nycmixtapeexchange
A chance to simultaneously beef up and show off your music collection. Every month has a theme. If you've got a soft spot for a particular subject or sound, they're open to suggestions. Past mixes have centered on covers, body parts, people's names, and...my favorite...New York City! Whatever this month's theme is, it'll be posted well in advance on the group's myspace page. A great excuse to spend an afternoon or two pawing through your stacks! Make your mix and burn it onto a CD, or push the record button on that old cassette player. The more copies you bring, the more you can take home. The organizers reserve the right to jimmy the date if a really good concert conflicts, so when you're going online to check the theme and the address of this month's bar, double-check that you've got your dates right.

CLASSES

MANHATTAN

Lower East Side

Worm Composting Classes and more!
The Lower East Side Ecology Center
East River Park Fireboat House, 212-477-4022
lesecologycenter.org (LES: B/D to Grand St)
As if roaches and mice aren't enough, the Lower East Side Ecology Center wants us to set up worm bins in our NYC apartments. Possibly figuring that this one could be a tough sell, the Center arranges to conduct these workshops in a variety of locations, for a price that's right (free, though sometimes you'll be asked to kick in a $5 "materials fee.") It's not all worms, thank god. They'll also teach you how to make green roofs, reclaim discarded furniture, and revamp the workplace into a non-toxic office environment.

Times Up! Free Bicycle Repair classes
156 Rivington St, basement (btwn Suffolk & Clinton)
212-802-8222 (LES: F/J/M/Z to Delancey-Essex)
&
99 S 6th St (btwn Berry & Bedford, under the Williamsburg Bridge, Bklyn)
www.times-up.org/calendar/calendar.php
(Williamsburg: J/M/Z to Marcy Ave)
The volunteer staff at Times Up! educate people about the greenhouse effect and non-polluting transportation. Their website has links to tons of bicycle-related events and group rides. Get on their mailing list and they'll keep you in the loop, whether the news be happy or sad, a victory for bike lane legislation, or another felled cyclist to

be commemorated with a ghost bike. Because knowledge is power, they have free bike repair classes where you can learn the basics, and/or work on your own ride. Monday is reserved for women and trans people. Become a member for $25 ($20 for students) and you'll qualify for the free welding class.

Dr. Sketchy's Anti-Art School
www.drsketchy.com
Every other Saturday 4-7pm
For about $10-15, sit in on a burlesque cabaret life-drawing studio and feast your eyes (and pencils) on the loveliest of performance artists. There are also frequently free cupcakes from sponsors. – Kate Black (So what if you already went to art school? Did it have its own coloring book, a cash bar, silly contests and models of all body types preening like peacocks in their own eye-popping costumes? Founder Molly Crabapple is as community-spirited as she is sexy, industrious, talented, and increasingly famous! – AH)

The New York School of Burlesque
212-561-1456 (email is best: contact@schoolofburlesque.com) www.schoolofburlesque.com
2 hour long workshops, $30
Just so we're clear, this is not some dumb-ass lesson in how to Strip For Your Man. This is an opportunity to pick up classic old-time moves from the days when everyone expected exotic dancers to be schooled in more than just polishing poles with their pussycats. Even if you never do so in public, you will feel pride knowing that you are capable of twirling your nipple tassels both bi and uni-laterally. No need to rush off to Frederick's of Hollywood for any specialty items just yet. The school's got more than enough loaner boas, opera gloves, and twirligigs. Just wear whatever you'd wear to aerobics class, except for the sports bra—bring the kind that hooks in the back. If you do take a notion to turn the world on with your smile, the class will also touch on practical matters like costuming and getting gigs, as well as history and plenty of dish.

Sex Toys 101
Babeland
94 Rivington (btwn Essex & Orchard) 212-375-1701 (LES: F/J/M/Z to Delancey-Essex)
&
43 Mercer St (btwn Broome & Grand) 212-966-2120 (SoHo: J/Z/N/Q/R/6 to Canal)
&
462 Bergen St (btwn 5th Ave & Flatbush Ave, Park Slope, Bklyn) 718-638-3820 (Park Slope: 2/3 to Bergen St)
www.babeland.com/events
The teachers are experienced, laid-back, and funny in a way that should put everybody at ease right from the get go. They may call for volunteers, but it's not like they're going to force you to put yourself in that position if you're feeling shy. On the other hand, if the whole point of this $10 exercise is to try something new, why not stick your hand up?

East Village

RePlayground
at Sustainable NYC
139 Ave A (btwn St. Mark's & 9th St) 212-254-5400
www.sustainable-nyc.com & www.replayground.com
(East Village: 6 to Astor Pl)
Second Wednesday of the month, 6-7:30 pm
Upcycle your garbage at these free monthlies. Learn to make ornaments from Metro Cards, picture frames and Valentines from maps, and jewelry from bottle caps, gum wrappers, and magazines. These classes fill up fast, so

even though they're free, you have to register in advance. If you're lacking the required garbage, you can either ask the teacher to give you some or rifle through the recycling bins of east 9th Street on your way to class.

Greenwich Village

Moon Dances in Hudson River Park
Pier 54 (btwn Horatio and W 14th on the Hudson River)
www.pier54.com/moondance
Sunday nights at 6:30 from mid-July to mid-August
You get exactly half an hour to pick up a few rudimentary moves after which you'll be expected to tango, salsa or swing in front of the thousands of New Jersey residents who surely spend their Sunday evenings out on their terraces, high powered binoculars and video cameras in hand. No pressure.

Juggling
Theaterlab Studio
137 W 14th St, 2nd floor (btwn 6th Ave & 7th Ave)
646-785-9494, www.jugglingclasses.com
(Flatiron: F/L/M to 6th Ave - 14th St)

Monday 4:30-5:30 & 5:30-6:30
I figure I'll always be able to work my way around the world as a waitress/massage therapist, but it wouldn't hurt to pad out the resume with a little juggling. If a Flying Karamazov Brother can't teach me how to keep my balls in the air, maybe he can show me how to get a laugh when an Indian club bonks me on the head. Twenty bucks seems reasonable enough for a drop-in group lesson, but as an investment in my global busking tour? Priceless!

Gramercy Park

Society of Scribes
School of Visual Arts (SVA) Annex
214 E 21st St (btwn 2nd & 3rd Ave) 212-452-0139
www.societyofscribes.org (Gramercy Park: 6 to 23rd St)
The Society of Scribes sometimes offers one-day calligraphy classes that aren't too expensive. – Jerry the Mouse

Garment District

Intro to Improv
Magnet Theater
254 W 29th St (btwn 7th Ave & 8th Ave) 212-244-8824
www.magnettheater.com (Garment District: 1 to 28th St)
2 hour workshop, Free
If you're interested in how the mysteries of being creative and spontaneously funny are... un-mystery-fied, take the Magnet Theater's 2-hour free intro class. That's right, I said Free. The secret behind this small but fast-growing improv school is simple: everyone can improvise. And they'll prove it to you. Their master instructors offer this excellent class twice a month in their theater, on their stage. That's how they hook you, the bastards. – Ed Herbstman

Midtown

Museum of Art and Design
2 Columbus Circle (@ 8th Ave) 212-299-7777
www.madmuseum.org
(Columbus Circle: A/B/C/D/1 to 59th St-Columbus Circle)
Sunday, 2pm
Sunday afternoon, intergenerational workshops cost $10 per person and you don't need to be affiliated with a kid. The materials are first-rate, the instructors unflappable, and your fee covers your museum admission as well. That can be a really good deal, when you consider that the mandatory adult admission is normally $15. This event goes down at 2pm but it shouldn't be a problem to get in to the museum earlier. It's aimed at families, but that

110th Street - Bobby Womack • Broadway - The

doesn't mean gluing cotton balls on paper plates to make Easter bunnies. A couple of projects I really dug were embroidering merit badges of my own design and sculpting goblets out of clay.

BROOKLYN

Spacecraft
355 Bedford Ave (@ S 4th St, Williamsburg, Bklyn)
718-599-2718
www.spacecraftbrooklyn.com
(Williamsburg: J/M/Z to Marcy Ave)
Drop-in
Spacecraft is a great place to go pick a craft, pay a reasonable price, and learn how to do it. All the materials are there for you. You don't have to dirty your apartment anymore! – Dear Drunk Girl (Some of their walk-in projects are geared more toward the six-year-old birthday party demographic—presumably you already know how to paint a box and glue things to it. They also have a modest selection of craft kits, supplies, and books. The owners have little kids, who they keep out of their hair with picture books, toys, and a Lego table. If you're traveling with some ankle biters of your own, they're welcome to mess around with that stuff, too, which might just free you up to get crafty for an hour or so. – AH)

Drink and Draw
3rd Ward
195 Morgan Ave (Btwn Stagg & Meadow, Bushwick, Bklyn)
718-715-4961, www.3rdward.com/drink-n-draw
(Bushwick: L to Morgan)
Wednesday, 8-10:30 pm
3rd Ward in Bushwick has some great classes, not always cheap, but every Wednesday night you can take a "life drawing class" called Drink and Draw. It's $15 ($10 if you bring a pal) and you can draw a naked person and drink free PBR 'til you fall over. – Dear Drunk Girl

Etsy Labs
55 Washington St, Suite 512
(btwn Water and Front St, DUMBO, Bklyn) 718-855-7955
www.etsy.com/storque/events
(DUMBO: A/C to High St-Brooklyn Bridge)
Monday, 5pm – 8pm
On Monday evenings, Etsy welcomes ordinary citizens into its inner sanctum. Everything's free...supplies, tools, the expertise of the visiting instructor. ZG2NYC contributor Esther Smith led one Monday night workshop where folks learned how to make rolling ball books and ornaments. Felting, t shirt surgery, homemade plushies, and pincushions...some of this stuff I sort of know how to do, but this is an opportunity to learn from the masters!

The Fixers Collective
Proteus Gowanus
543 Union St (@ Nevins, Gowanus, Bklyn) 718 243-1572
www.fixerscollective.org (Gowanus: N/R to Union St)
Thursday 6-9pm
Bring your broken object in for collective consideration at this weekly workshop in the super cool gallery that fomented this group. The core members are seriously patient, inventive, persistent people, who will help you figure out how to nurse your ailing waffle iron back to health. You're also welcome to lend a hand with fixing others' fritzed-out stuff, regardless of whether or not you have a clue as to what you're doing.

QUEENS

Materials For The Arts
33-00 Northern Blvd, 3rd Floor (@ Honeywell St, Long Island City, Queens) 718-729-3001
www.mfta.org/education_workshop_schedule.html
(LIC: R/M to 36th St)
Materials for the Arts gets it that you'd do just about anything to scam your way into their warehouse, but trust me, they're hardcore about making sure that you're one of the approved representatives of an approved charitable organization. They must feel kind of bad about it though, because every now and then they lower the drawbridge so the general public can freely attend craft workshops. There's pretty much one a week, lurching from stitched books to no-sew costumes to wind chimes and mobiles and beyond.

AROUND TOWN

Gotham Writer's Workshop
Various Venues in Manhattan and Brooklyn
www.writingclasses.com/CommunityEvents/index.php
This is one of the more aggressively marketed writer's workshops in the city. They won't bestow a degree on you, but they have about as many courses per semester as your average college. They're famous for their spendy eight-week boot camps, designed to whip you into such writerly shape you'll graduate with a full-length novel or memoir (and very slack abs). They also offer one-day, six-hour workshops for those with an interest in such specialties as TV, food, and travel writing. Sadly, those six hours are three times as expensive as they would've been had you spent them at Spa Castle. A better financial bet

is to hit one of their free one-hour drop-in workshops. There are a couple of them every month at bookstores around Manhattan and Brooklyn. Obviously, they're a way for the instructor to reel in new students, but who knows, maybe you'll come out of it with a poem or a very short story. If you're here in September, keep an eye peeled for their Open House, when they really bump up the number of free samples.

OPEN MIC

You don't have to jump out of an airplane or sign up for one of those reality shows where contestants are submerged in a tank filled with live eels in order to confront your deepest fears. We have plenty of open mics around town for your convenience. You can find comprehensive, though perhaps not entirely accurate listings here:
www.openmikes.org/calendar/NY

The friend who's coming along to lend moral support will thank you should you choose to try your luck at one of the following. Even if you go down in flames, the folks in the audience will have plenty of opportunities to salvage *their* experience, given these mics' track records of attracting both inspired performers and/or unhinged characters.

The Moth StorySLAM
1st Monday of the month at 7:30 pm
South Paw
125 Fifth Ave (btwn Baltic & Butler, Park Slope, Bklyn) 718-230-0236 (Park Slope: 2/3 to Bergen)
&
2nd Tuesday of the month at 7pm
The Nuyorican Poets Café
236 E 3rd St (btwn Ave B & Ave C) 212-780-9386
(East Village: F/J/M/Z to Delancey-Essex)
&
3rd Thursday of the month at 7pm
Housing Works Bookstore Cafe
126 Crosby St (btwn Houston & Prince) 212-334-3324
(SoHo: B/D/F/M to Broadway-Lafayette)
&
last Monday of the month at 7pm
The Bitter End
147 Bleecker Street (btwn Thompson & LaGuardia)
212-673-7030
(Greenwich Village: A/C/E/B/D/F/M to W 4th St)
www.themoth.org/storyslams_nyc, $7
The MOTH has felt anointed from the get-go, lousy with celebs and *New Yorker* contributors alike, but there's still a chance for rabble like you and me to be discovered sipping our metaphorical sodas on a StorySLAM stool pro-vided we're brave enough to show up half an hour before showtime and toss our names in the aspirant story-teller hat. Ten participants will be selected at random to tell five-minute extemporaneous tales, riffing on that week's theme. (They tend to be of the one word, open-ended variety like "Gifts," "Denial," or "Cars" and are posted well in advance on the website.) Not-so-far-out-on-a-limb participants may prefer to sit in judgment, in which case seek out a Moth staffer and let him or her know you're available to score the evening's proceedings. Or, you could just watch in a supportive, admiring way. Once a year, they host the glamorous, glitzy, open-to-the-public Moth Ball.

Nuyorican Poets Café
236 E 3rd St (btwn Ave B & C) 212-780-9386
www.nuyorican.org
(East Village: F/J/M/Z to Delancey-Essex)
Nuyorican Poets Café is a friggin' downtown in-sti-tution! What can I say about it that hasn't already been said? They have spoken word poetry and hip-hop-type music all week long. – Josh Medsker (Used to feel like going to the ends of the earth. Now feels like a UNESCO site for East Coast slam poets, both aspirant and anointed. There are any number of opportunities if you want to compete, though choose your selection carefully. It's not an Emily Dickinson-loving crowd. – AH)

Sidewalk Cafe
94 Avenue A (@ 6th St) 212-473-7373
www.sidewalkmusic.net (East Village: F to 2nd Ave)
Lach's famed Anti-Hoot has been laid to rest, but the Monday night anti-folk madness soldiers on. This is the scene that spawned, or at least sustained, Kimya Dawson, Jeffrey Lewis, Nellie McKay, Regina Spektor, and the Trachtenberg Family Slideshow Players. Sign-up starts at 7:30, with early birds going first and on down the line until things finally wind down at whatever-in-the-morning, when everyone whose name went on the list has had his or her chance to shine. If you want to get a fan's eye view of the proceedings, there's a Sidewalk regular who faithfully reports his impressions at www.sidewalkatsidewalk. blogspot.com. If you want to see and hear what things were like back in the day, there's a lot of archival footage and a complimentary MP3 player at www.antifolk.net.

Banjo Jim's
700 E 9th St. (@ Ave C) 212-777-0869
www.banjojims.com/gigs.htm (East Village: L to 1st Ave)
Saturdays at 2:30
Every kind of music (mostly guitar-driven folk and rock).

York (Ya Out There) - Rakim • Queensbridge (the

Bowery Poetry Club
308 Bowery (@ Bleecker) 212-614-0505
www.bowerypoetry.com
(East Village: B/D/F/M to Broadway-Lafayette)
Second Saturday of the month, 6pm
If your poetry lacks a certain *je ne sais quoi*, perhaps what it's missing is backing instrumentation, courtesy of a house jazz band. (Reading *a capella* is also an option.) Selected performances will be featured on the Buffalo Quickie video podcast!
&
Fourth Wednesday of the month 10pm
If the idea of getting up at an open mic turns your bowels to fast melting Freezer Pops, Reverend Jen, the Patron Saint of the Uncool would agree that your fear is not without precedent. Her Anti-Slam (www.revjen.com/antislam) was founded in rejection of the traditional slam system whereby those not judged winners not only feel like losers, they have the low score to prove it. (Prior to thinking up the Anti-Slam, she expressed her disapproval by signing up for a slot at the Nuyorican, dressed entirely in head-to-toe, rubber-dog-doo-topped brown, the perfect costume for delivering three minutes of farting noises into the mic.) You have six minutes to do your thing, whatever that may be, and everyone gets a 10. Male frontal nudity is not only acceptable, it's encouraged by the hostess, who feels there's "not enough of it in Western Art." The only uncool thing here would be to snicker at a brave soul who elsewhere might seem out of his or her depth.

Paddy Reilly's Songwriters Open Mics
519 2nd Ave (@29th St), 212-686-1210
www.myspace.com/paddysopenmic
(Murray Hill: 6 to 28th St)
Wednesday at 7pm and Saturday at 5pm
This bar was famous for having nothing but Guinness on tap. They tossed some Bud on there a while back, possibly as a way of ensuring the crowds would continue to drink nothing but Guinness. NYC has so many bars that resemble this one, but Paddy O'Reilly's is indeed something special, open mic wise. On Wednesdays, each participant gets to play three songs. There's a keyboard available if you accidentally left your piano at home.

The Tank Theater
354 W 45th St (btwn 8th and 9th Ave) 212-563-6269
www.thetanknyc.org (A/C/E to 42nd St)
The Tank has small local productions and on Sundays has SLAM Theater. It supports local art, theatre, writing, and so on. Support our local artists! – Josh Medsker (SLAM theater, unlike slam poetry, is performed by someone other than the writer. If you're a strong-bellied playwright keen to hear what a bunch of unrehearsed actors might do to your favorite scene, bring your script, some butter to not melt in your mouth, and a game face mask in the event you start crying on the inside. – AH)

Bar Matchless
557 Manhattan Ave (@ Driggs Ave, Williamsburg Bklyn) 718-383-5333
www.barmatchless.com (Williamsburg: G to Nassau)
Sunday at 8:30pm
Working in bars has done a number on my hearing, but my musician pals tell me this one has a super duper sound system. Turn it up to eleven every Sunday at 8:30pm.

Pete's Candy Store
709 Lorimer St (btwn Frost & Richardson, Williamsburg, Bklyn) 718-302-3770
www.petescandystore.com
(Williamsburg: G/L to Metropolitan-Lorimer)
Sunday at 5pm
The musical open mic packs 'em into the cute little theater every Sunday at 5pm. The bar's in another room, so you won't be playing to people who will talk through the act, just people who may stand up and stagger off for a refill, accidentally kicking over a glass someone else set on the floor.

The Perch Cafe
365 5th Ave (@ 6th St, Park Slope, Bklyn) 718-788-2830
www.theperchcafe.com (Park Slope: F/G to 4thAve)
Sunday at 7pm
Music, comedy, and spoken word in a super-supportive atmosphere. Of course, all the changing tables, toys, and child-friendly food means they're equally supportive of kids and babies. My advice to you is to act like the squalling and shrieking doesn't bug you at all, though keep an

album) - Nas • No Sleep Till Brooklyn - The Beastie

eye peeled for overly permissive or inattentive parents.

Waltz Astoria
2314 Ditmars Blvd (@ 23rd St, Astoria, Queens) 718-956-8742
www.waltz-astoria.com (Astoria: N to Ditmars Blvd)
Waltz open-mic is a couple bucks. It has grown to be a big thing in recent years—and a good time. – Josh Medsker

Guest Bartending
No, no, no, you silly goose, it doesn't matter if you don't really know how to tend bar. Just make it stiff and throw a couple of umbrellas in there. Anyway, no one's giving the regular staff the night off. Play Grasshopper to their Ancient Master and you may pick up some recipes, or at least the proper way to wield a cocktail shaker. In return for this opportunity and tips—which you should most definitely share with your behind-the-bar mentor—most of the establishments below will expect you to bring in at least 20 thirsty friends. The hard part is informing them that they won't be drinking for free. The participating bars aren't particularly distinguished, but I did winnow out the gnarlier midtown joints. This is a plan-ahead type of activity, as most managers will want to make sure you're not an unwashed crackhead or a tap-guzzling Barney Gumble-type before reserving your spot. Fair enough, I guess.

The Dog House Saloon
152 Orchard St (btwn Rivington & Stanton)
646-429-8780 (LES: F to 2nd Ave)
www.doghousesaloonnyc.com/guest-bartend.html
Shouldn't be too hard to get a pack of pre/post-vegan followers to trail you to the Lower East Side when you can bait the hook with an offer of free hot dogs.

Stay
244 E Houston St (btwn Essex & Norfolk) 212-982-3532
http://www.stay-nyc.com/welcome.htm
(LES: J/M/Z to Delancey-Essex)
Hey, Slinky, you could be in with the in crowd (a hefty 25 of whom you're responsible for bringing in) as one of four Thursday night guest bartenders at this Lower East Side lounge. Rule the night by gangpressing another friend to serve as guest DJ!

Village Pourhouse
64 3rd Ave (@ 11th St) 212-979-BEER
www.pourhousenyc.com/book_a_party.php
(East Village: L to 3rd Ave)
They have over a hundred kinds of beers, which is a lot,

and they'll let you jump behind the bar once a mere ten friends have crowded in. Shoot, just invite everyone you inadvertently make physical contact with on the L out from Williamsburg, and you'll have a quorum! With a friend guest-pouring at Bar None the same night as your one-night-only appearance here, you've got yourself a pub crawl.

Bar None
98 3rd Ave (btwn 12th & 13th) 212-777-NONE
www.barnonenyc.com/guestbartending.html
(East Village: L to 3rd Ave)
No need to get gussied up for this dive. You don't want to be overdressed when your patrons are drinking out of fishbowls. If I were to guest bartend, and I'm gonna in honor of this rag's publication, Bar None would be my first choice.

Fiddlesticks Pub
56 Greenwich Ave (btwn 6th & 7th Ave) 212-463-0516
www.fiddlesticksnyc.com/guestbartender.html
(Greenwich Village: 1/2/3 to 14th St)
Pull a wee bit of the Guinness for all your Lepra-Con pals. Malcolm or Nathaniel will tell ye which night o' the week t'will be.

Fat Annie's Truck Stop
131 W 33rd St (btwn 6th & 7th Ave) 212-695-1122
fatanniestruckstop.com
(Garment District: B/D/F/M/N/Q/R to 34th St)
Reward yourself with tater tots if you're still standing after uncapping several hundred beers on a Monday night. Call Roy to set it up. Yankees games bring in a lot of aspirant Bleacher Creatures—if the Yanks hit a home run, these animals will be clamoring for the free shot they know they've got coming.

Bar 12
206 E 34th St (@ 3rd Ave) 212-545-9912
www.Bar12.com (Murray Hill: 6 to 33rd St)
Say what? You want to do your tending in a midtown sports bar? Really? Well, okay...why not? Set it up with Adam, the guy in charge. Bring a bunch of friends, and keep 'em coming as the worlds collide.

Mercury Bar West
493 3rd Ave (btwn 33rd & 34th St) 212-683-2645
mercurybareast.com/events/events.html
(Murray Hill: 6 to 33rd St)
The Mercury is quite handy to NYU Medical Center, should your inexpertly mixed well drinks cause trouble

Boys • Christmas Time in Hollis Queens – Run-DMC

for one of your 30 (that sounds like a lot) guests. We know you want the host establishment to make a lot of money off your popularity, but a real bartender would have cut that guy off. Especially since both Wednesday and Thursday are school nights.

Overlook
225 E 44th St (btwn 2nd & 3rd Ave) 212-682-7266
www.OverlookNYC.com
(Midtown East: 4/5/6/7/S to Grand Central)
They're pretty prideful of the Yankees and the fact they have a room with cartoon walls. Whereas if I had a bar in that neighborhood, I'd be prideful of a room with cartoon walls and my proximity to the Japan Society. Maybe they're proud of that too. Ask Mark or Neil when you call to set it up.

Butterfield 8
5 E 38th St (btwn 5th Ave & Madison Ave) 212-679-0646
www.butterfield8nyc.com/employment.php
(Midtown: S/4/5/6/7 to 42nd St-Grand Central)
If you clean up nice, have the sort of posse who can refrain from smashing the crystal chandeliers (and possibly breast implants), contact Melissa about putting in a Friday appearance (or fill out the online form).

The Banshee Pub
1373 1st Ave (btwn 73rd St & 74th St) 212-717-8177
www.bansheepubnyc.com/guestbartending.html
(Upper East Side: 6 to 77th St)
&
Trinity Pub
229 E 84th St (btwn 2nd Ave & 3rd Ave) 212-327-4450
www.trinitypubnyc.com/guest.html
(Upper East Side: 4/5/6 to 86th St)
&
The Gael Pub
1465 3rd Ave (btwn 82nd St & 83rd St) 212-517-4141
www.thegaelpubnyc.com/guest.html
(Upper East Side: 4/5/6 to 86th St)
These three are kin to each other. Their o'phone numbers be different, but they're all Irish, guest bartending goes down on Thursday, and the ones who'll decide if you fit the bill are Gene or Billy. The location may be fratty, but the bars aren't.

Stir
1363 1stAve (btwn 73rd & 74th) 212-744-7190
www.stirnyc.com/nyc-guest-bartend.html
(Upper East Side: 6 to 77th St)
Get candlelit loungy with whichever 15 friends don't feel their masculinity, butch-osity, or just plain self-respect is compromised by specialty cocktails with names like Passion, Flirt, and Trance. Sign up online to do your duty any night of the week.

CRAFT FAIRS
If you are capable of producing distinctive sock monkeys that people will pay good money for, it might be worth your while and application fee to be a vendor at one of NYC's alternative-flavored craft fairs.

March, May & December
Brooklyn Craft Market at the Brooklyn Lyceum
227 4th Ave
(btwn Union and President, Park Slope, Bklyn)
www.bkcraftcentral.com (Park Slope: R to Union St)
The Brooklyn Lyceum has started attracting all sorts of interesting events, including this one. Unfortunately, it is my sad duty to mention that the venue is far from wheelchair accessible.

May
BUST Magazine Spring Fling Craftacular
www.bust.com/Craftacular/Craftacular-Home.html
Like the Holiday Craftacular (see December, dawg) with-

out the built-in excuse to buy something.

June

Renegade Craft Fair
www.renegadecraft.com/brooklyn
We exported the Craftcular to LA and London, so I guess it's okay if we import a little of Chicago's biggie to Williamsburg's McCarren Park. Hmm. Can we get a side order of Austin's Stitch with that?

December

Indie craft fairs are as ubiquitous as Derle Farms eggnog at this time of year, so keep a sharp eye for posters on lampposts and in local businesses. The Nonsense New York list will keep you apprised of the odder ducks. Even that red and white striped tent city that springs up in Union Square has some interesting, one-of-a-kind type items amid all the gaggy Bed & Bath Works-smelling scented candles and Unemployed Philosophers Guild tchotchkes.

Holiday Craftacular
www.bust.com/craftacular
Oh, those crafty ladies of BUST magazine! From their humble, Xeroxed beginning, they have forged a glittery, four-color, girl power empire. The Holiday Craftacular brings many of their back pages advertisers and other DIY vendors to a big, noise-filled hall (used to be Warsaw, lately it's been the Metropolitan Pavilion). Past favorites have included bras made out of yamulkes, zombie ornaments, cupcakes courtesy of Amy Sedaris, a photo booth where you can have your picture snapped in a hideous reindeer sweater, and beer on tap. Janeane Garofalo bought my zine here!

Gifted
www.brownstoner.com/brooklynflea/holiday
The Brooklyn Flea's holiday craft fair provides potential gifts for everyone on your list. And it provides a much needed bump to Flea regulars who get seasonal affect disorder when their beloved weekend activity goes into hibernation for the winter.

Hearts and Crafts Fair
www.breadbykira.com/kirabirneythehea.html
You've got to be local to vend at this small Brooklyn booster, but you can be from wherever if all you want to do is shop and draw founder Kira a mermaid kitty, which she collects.

Aren't you sweet, wanting to help us out? Pretty much every annual event listed in this guide, as well as the various music, film, and book festivals would love to make use of your donated labors on the day of, so check their websites for how to sign up in advance. I don't want to start a stampede, but they may even feed you, or force you to wear an ugly t-shirt that you'll then get to take home. Here are some other worthy organizations, all richly deserving of your short-term charitable labor.

Food Not Bombs
Sundays, 1pm (serving in Tompkins Sq at 3pm)
ABC No Rio
156 Rivington St (btwn Suffolk & Clinton)
212-254-3697 ext. 27
www.abcnorio.org/affiliated/fnb.html
(LES: F/J/M/Z to Delancey-Essex)
&
Bushwick Chapter
Thursday, 10am (serving in Bushwick Park at Knickerbocker & Starr at 1pm)
Surreal Estate
15 Thames St
(btwn Bogart & Morgan St, Bushwick, Bklyn)
www.myspace.com/fnbbushwick
(Bushwick: L to Morgan)
If you're in Manhattan on Sunday, Food Not Bombs operates out of ABC No Rio. Show up to help cook great vegetarian food, then bring it out to the park to share with everyone you come across. (And don't forget to help clean up afterwards...) – Victoria Law

D TRAIN

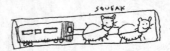

GIANT RATS PULL THE D TRAIN THROUGH THE TUNNELS.

AT THE MANHATTAN BRIDGE, A GIANT PIGEON TAKES OVER.

COCKROACHES MAKE THE CORNIEST CONDUCTORS

"STAND CLEAR OF THE CLOSING DOORS. YOU DON'T WANT TO LOSE A LEG OR SOMETHING. ME, I GOT LEGS TO SPARE, BUT YOU ONLY GOT TWO OF 'EM."

Fresh Art Sock Monkey Sewing Circle
548 Broadway, 3rdfloor (btwn Prince and Spring)
646-262-3273
www.freshartnyc.org (SoHo: R to Prince St)
Calling all Suzy and Siggy Seamsterpants! Come birth a sock monkey at one of Fresh Art's biweekly Thursday night sewing circles. Your simian's online sale will benefit programs for New York City artists with special needs.

Solidarity Center
55 W 17th St. (btwn 5th and 6th Ave) 212-633-6646
www.iacenter.org/nycactions
(Chelsea: F/L/M/ to 14th St-6th Ave)
No radical activist's visit to the Big Apple is complete without attending a demonstration, march or protest meeting. A good place to get the low-down and help organize is the Solidarity Center. This all-volunteer space hosts immigrant rights, anti-war, anti-racist, women's and queer-rights groups, especially (but not exclusively) with a Marxist bent. The Solidarity Center provides a meeting place for local coalitions and regularly makes its space available for community and cultural events at low- or no-cost. To volunteer, call or stop by Monday-Saturday between 12pm and 8 pm. – redguard

KittyKind
Petco Union Square
860 Broadway (@ 17th St) 212-726-2652
www.kittykind.org
(Union Sq: L/N/Q /R/4/5/6 to 14th St- Union Sq)
My wife and I volunteer for KittyKind, an organization providing care for the cats who are up for adoption at Petco. We clean their cages and play with them. They call it "socializing them." I call it fun. – Josh Medsker (KittyKind is connected with that Cat Art Film Fest at the Anthology! – AH)

Church of the Holy Apostles Soup Kitchen
296 9th Ave (@ W 27th St) 212-924-0167
www.holyapostlesnyc.org/haskhome.htm
(Chelsea: C/E to 23rd St)
I usually feel comfier sticking with the secular, but there's a lot to love about a church whose rector refused to cave to a request to shut down their long-running, 5-days-a-week soup kitchen operation "for security reasons" when the 2004 Republican National Convention was convening a few blocks away. There's no proselytizing of any kind, just a hell of a lot of casserole. Whether you're scooping mashed potatoes, busing tables, or refilling sugar shakers, a morning's shift will put you in contact with hundreds of hungry New Yorkers. I'm comfortable with any God Bless Yous that get bandied around. Your paper hat is yours to keep, though you can take it off for the hot staff meal everyone shares once the last guests have cleared out. Email Clyde, the guy who keeps this mighty craft on course, with the date or range of dates you're available. Give him a few days to get back to you with whether or not there's room for you on the schedule.

Bags for the People
Spacecraft
355 Bedford Ave (btwn 3rd St & 4th St) 718-599-2718
www.spacecraftbrooklyn.com
(Williamsburg: J/M/Z to Marcy Ave)
&
3rd Ward
195 Morgan Ave (btwn Meadow & Stagg) 718-715-4961
www.3rdward.com (East Williamsburg: L to Morgan Ave)
www.bagsforthepeople.org
This non-profit organization was founded by three workers at the Union Square Greenmarket who were being driven apeshit by the volume of plastic bags they saw handed out for market shoppers' organic, responsibly-farmed produce. Instead of bitching about it, they bought a heaping helping of by-the-pound thrift store clothing, cut it up, broke out the sewing machines, and restitched

the salvaged material into reusable shopping bags which they handed out free in front of the Hawthorn Valley farmstand. How's that for making friends and influencing people? Despite their messianic efforts, the demand continue to exceed the supply, so they've institutionalized a monthly Sweat Shop Social. Music, beer, and conversation...just like an old-fashioned sewing bee! If you don't know how to sew, you can seam rip by the much-chattered-about pile of cast-off duds and linens. (I live for the day I see a Greenmarket customer toting curly kale in my favorite, broke-ass pj bottoms.)

BARC
253 Wythe Ave (@ N 1st St, Williamsburg, Bklyn)
718-486-7489
www.barcshelter.org (Williamsburg: L to Bedford) Puppies! Kitties! Awww! If you're feeling homesick for your companion animal, two-time that critter by taking one of this Williamsburg no-kill-shelter's canine friends for a spin (you've got to be down with picking up poop). If you're more of a cat person, you already know how their fur is going to look all over your black sweater, so dress accordingly. The dogs go out every day from 9am to noon, and again on weekdays from 5 to 7:30. The cats entertain callers from noon to 5pm, Tuesday through Saturday. If Mom and Dad aren't with you, you should be 21.

Books Through Bars
Freebird Books & Goods
123 Columbia St (btwn Kane & Degraw, Cobble Hill, Bklyn) 718- 643-8484
www.freebirdbooks.com (Cobble Hill: F/G to Bergen)
www.abcnorio.org/affiliated/btb.hm
Books Through Bars is an all-volunteer group that sends books, zines, and other reading material to people in prison nationwide. When you arrive to volunteer, we will show you the hundreds of letters we get each month from people in prison requesting reading material. Peruse our shelves overflowing with donated books and choose items that best match each person's interests. Then you get to wrap them and get them ready for mailing! You don't need to bring anything but yourself, but if you are so inclined, we always welcome brown paper bags, wrapping paper, large re-used envelopes or anything that can act as paper to wrap packages (note: padded envelopes are not allowed in prisons), snacks, and your iPod! We'll plug it into our speakers so that we can listen to some new music! - Victoria Law

Homeless Outreach Population Estimate (HOPE)
www.nyc.gov/dhs
Every January, the NYC Department of Homeless Services enlists thousands of volunteers to cruise parks, subways, and other likely non-enclosed public spaces to try to get an accurate head count on the number of New Yorkers going roofless. If you're a night owl who's impervious to the cold, this could be a match made in heaven. Ditto if you're one of those who insist on dragging a car with you to NYC. Rather than paying a fortune to put it in a garage for the night, or getting your windows smashed on the street, you could put that sucker to good use by volunteering to drive your team of three to five around the public-transit-challenged outer borough fringes. (Official vans will handle transport for anyone you meet who's eager to get to a shelter.) Bring your warmies.

Write-A-Thon
Usually a weekend day in mid May
www.nywriterscoalition.org, 718-398-2883
It's like National Novel Writing Month divided by 30, but more social, and instead of obsessively posting your word count online, you shake friends and relatives down for pledges to help fund creative writing programs for seniors and formerly homeless, at-risk youth. The NY Writer's Coalition will keep you going with breakfast, lunch, and inspirational workshops, but you better start squeezing that executive stress ball the minute you register if you want your hands to go the near-eight-hour distance.

Feeding NYC
Tuesday before Thanksgiving
www.feedingnyc.org
If you celebrate Thanksgiving and turkey figures into it, you could earn some karmic cranberries by showing up a couple of days before the actual holiday to pack and distribute dinner with all the trimmings to families in all five boroughs. Over 2000 households will get their feast on thanks in part to your efforts.

Town - Woody Guthrie - Let's Get Rid of New

Cranksgiving
Pre-Thanksgiving
www.cranksgiving.org
Suggested for those who prefer to combine their charitable Thanksgiving acts with a cardio workout. Part alley
cat race, part one of those game shows where contestants
tear around the supermarket throwing items into their
cart, Cranksgiving sends bike messengers and other two-
wheeled enthusiasts on a mad dash tour of Manhattan
groceries, armed with a list of ingredients for a holiday
dinner. Upon crossing the finish line, all the food gets
donated to a homeless shelter.

You could go ask the people at Bluestockings Bookstore
for suggestions. They usually know wuts'up. - Fly

Try volunteering in a community garden. There are a tril-
lion on Greene Ave in Bedstuy, where I live. – Cristy Road

SHOPPING

BOOKSTORES

Bookstores that sell zines
All bookstores are special, but to paraphrase George Orwell, some bookstores are more special.

Bluestockings Books
172 Allen St (btwn Stanton & Rivington) 212-777-6028
www.bluestockings.com (LES: F to 2nd Ave)
Originally founded to fill an appalling New York City
void—the lack of a dedicated feminist bookstore—Bluestockings has morphed into something a bit more free-
form, and anarchy-flavored. They've got live events nearly
every night, a helpful, mostly volunteer staff, a hopping
location, fair trade coffee, and best of all, zines! Email
zines@bluestockings.com to get up to the minute info
on how to submit yours for consideration, or just drop a
complimentary copy off at the counter. – AH (If New York
is a small town, Bluestockings is my general store. When
I'm bored, in need of gossip or new ideas or good coffee,
I go to Bluestockings and run into everybody I know!
Manager Jeffrey Lloyd Lewis is the Oscar the Grouch of
Bluestockings. He knows everybody and is glad to see
them even if it doesn't show. – Jessica Max Stein) (Almost
every night they have some sort of educational, political,
or literary event. When I'm looking for something to do, I
check out the events calendar on their website – Amanda
Plumb) (Best. Bookstore. Ever. - Caitlin McGurk)

St. Mark's Bookstore
31 3 Ave (@ Stuyvesant Pl) 212-260-7853
www.stmarksbookshop.com (East Village: 6 to Astor Pl)
Big, graduated zine gorillas like *Bust, Bitch, Giant Robot,
Venus*, and any title with paid ads and an appearance the
general public equates with a "magazine," can be found
mid-ships, across from the info desk. On the actual info
desk, on shelves so low you'll have to squat in front of
them, you'll find a smutty sprinkling of hardcore porno
zines like *Straight to Hell: the Manhattan Review of Unnatural Acts*. Less X-rated zines camp out on a wall rack in
the way back. That's okay! At least they're selling them!
Non-barcode zines are here on consignment, as opposed
to purchased outright. If such terms are acceptable to
you, drop a copy off and fill out the index card. If you're
feeing cocky, and don't mind possibly flushing three copies down the Johnny, drop off three, because that's how
many they'll ask for, should they give you a greenlight.
Then eventually you'll get a postcard in the mail, telling
you when all three copies have been sold, with instructions
about how to claim your dough and replenish their holdings. - AH (That rack is full to bursting with titles I've
never heard of, except for *PEOPS*, which is always awesome. – Josh Medsker) (Okay, so I work there! So come
and visit. – Fly)

A comic shop that is very friendly towards zinesters. It's also right in the shadow of the Empire State Building. – Marguerite Dabaie (The best comic book store in the city! They take comics on consignment so go and talk to Nick. – Fly) (You'll get a fat discount on other merch if they agree to sell your self-published efforts here. – AH)

Desert Island Books
540 Metropolitan Ave (btwn Lorimer & Union, Williamsburg, Bklyn) 718-388-5087
www.desertislandbrooklyn.com
(Williamburg: G/L to Metropolitan-Lorimer)
A microscopic indie comic oasis in the not-so-obviously-hoppin' section of Williamsburg. Desert Island's a good place for events, despite cramped quarters. They have a really muscular selection of self-published comics, too. If you bring yours in for their consideration and never hear back, save face by blaming their lack of square footage. In the happy event that they do embrace it, there's a consignment form to download on the website.

Bergen Comics
470 Bergen St (btwn 5th Ave & Flatbush Ave, Park Slope, Bklyn) 718-230-5600, www.bergenstreetcomics.com
(Park Slope: 2/3 to Bergen St)
If I were a comics shop, I'd be this one. Besides having an excellent collection of literary, European, and mainstream comics, this store is super-friendly in courting independent/local creators! They welcome mini-comics and host signings and workshops by local comic artists. – Becky Hawkins (I dig Bergen Comics' plushy, old-fashioned gentleman's club look, complete with seating. – AH)

Forbidden Planet
840 Broadway (btwn 12th St & 13th St) 212-473-1576
www.fpnyc.com
(Union Sq: 4/5/6/L/N/Q/R to Union Square)
If you're a superhero fan, this is the place, though they're not going to shun you if you favor the more indie shelves. If you want to stretch your graphic novel dollars, start with a browse at Forbidden Planet, but don't buy anything until you've ascertained that the desired titles aren't available cheaper, used, on the second floor of the Strand, a block away.

St. Mark's Comics
11 St Mark's Pl (btwn 2nd Ave & 3rd Ave) 212-598-9439
www.stmarkscomics.com (East Village: 6 to Astor Pl)
Fanboy superhero stuff, alternative underground comix and tons of appealing keychains, lunchboxes, bendable figures, trading cards, stickers and other dust catchers.

Printed Matter
195 10th Ave (btwn 21st St & 22nd St) 212-925-0325
www. printedmatter.org (Chelsea: C/E to 23rd St)
A haven for zines that push the boundaries of artsy or artistic into the realm of actual art. They're often a little (or a lot) more expensive than your average bear, but they sure are nifty to look at, what with their ingenious bindings, cunning layouts, and carefully pasted-in color photographs. Printed Matter, in gallery-rich Chelsea, lards their shelves with a goodly helping of these. Go there to browse and shop, but don't plan on dropping off a copy of your own self-published art-zine. Their website has very specific protocols for sending in your submission by mail, which is the only way they will accept it.

Comic Shops

The Animal Farm metaphor applies to comic shops too, which is why the first three stores listed are the first three stores listed.

Jim Hanley's Universe
4 W 33rd (btwn 5th Ave & Broadway) 212-268-7088
www.jhuniverse.com
(Garment District: B/D/F/M/N/Q /R to 34th St)

Gentlemen Band • The History of Punk on the

Want to pass yourself off as an East Village rent control resident? Look around contemptuously, then announce, "Ugh, I never walk down St. Mark's Place if I can help it." That pretty much captures the staff attitude, too, even though they work there.

New Books

As an author, I probably shouldn't admit this, but I rarely buy new books for myself. If I'm at a reading, and the author is sitting behind the signing table, pen in hand, a look of panic in her eyes, and a smile pasted on her face, then, yes, because what kind of citizen does not do unto others? Between my friends and the kids' friends, I've got enough birthdays to hold my head up high in my favorite indie bookstores, which get a sizable lump of my dough. In addition to all the specialty booksellers in NYC, and St. Mark's and Bluestockings, which we heart because they sell zines, there are several notable indies that have set themselves up as dependable general practitioners.

McNally-Jackson
52 Prince St (btwn Lafayette & Mulberry) 212-274-1160
www.mcnallyjackson.com (NoHo: 6 to Spring St)
The greatest thing about this big, gracious indie is the frequent drop-in book clubs, each oriented toward a particular interest. Even more intriguing is that the Greater New York Chapter of the Betsy-Tacy Society's Violent Study Club holds its bimonthly meetings here (www.klitzner.org/BT/index.html). There's a café and floors so polished you can look up your own skirt.

Shakespeare & Co.
716 Broadway (btwn Washington & Waverly) 212-529-1330 (Greenwich Village: N/R to 8th St)
&
939 Lexington Ave (btwn 68th St & 69th St)
212-570-0201 (Upper East Side: 6 to 68th St)
&
14 Hillel Pl (btwn Campus Rd & Kenilworth Pl, Midwood, Bklyn) 718-434-5326 (Midwood: 2/5 to Flatbush)
www.shakeandco.com
It was a sad day when Shakespeare and Co's Upper West Side flagship closed. This place was the embodiment of a certain corduroy-jacketed, bearded Upper West Sider, the benevolent parent who's still living in the big but crumbling rent-stabilized, pre-war 3BR where his kids grew up. Barnes and Noble clobbered him dead. The other locations have wisely thrown in with NYU, Hunter College, and Brooklyn College, buying back textbooks and ordering professors' reading lists. They don't hold much sit-down appeal, but the Broadway location is handy if you're looking for something to read in Washington Square, and the Midwood one is a great service to the neighborhood and parrot fans.

Unoppressive Non-Imperialist Bargain Books
34 Carmine St (btwn Bleecker & Bedford) 212-229-0079
www.unoppressivebooks.blogspot.com
(Greenwich Village: A/B/C/D/E/F/M to W 4th St)
The name's probably got the musty ghosts of socialist bibliophilic New York rattling their bags of old newspapers in disgust at the stock, but not me, especially right before Xmas when the Strand's crazy crowded. Remaindered copies of Simpsons comics anthologies, coffee table *Kama Sutras*, last season's gimmicky cookbooks, and the seemingly innumerable tomes designed to extract more lettuce from the ardent R. Crumb fan—who's your discount Santa? Whoever owns it seems to love John Lennon and Shakespeare in equal measure.

Book Culture
536 W 112th St (btwn Broadway & Amsterdam)
212-865-1588, www.bookculture.com
(Morningside Hts: 1 to 110th St-Cathedral Pkwy)
You'll get smarter just walking through the door, even if you're not a Columbia student. Book Culture is one of the most focused academic bookstores I've ever seen. The selection of little magazines and journals is extremely impressive. The politics of the shop run slightly left-of-center, reflected in its Political, Philosophy, and Cultural Studies sections, and throughout the store. Between Book Culture and St. Mark's Bookshop, pomo thinkers should

Bookcourt
163 Court St (btwn Dean & Pacific, Cobble Hill, Bklyn)
718-875-3677
www.bookcourt.org (Cobble Hill: F/G to Bergen St)
A beloved, long-time independent in a neighborhood
packed with writers, readings at Bookcourt are especially
jolly whenever a Brooklyn author is featured. It's a family
operation in the best possible way. Their allegiance to
local authors is fierce. Plus, they are nice to children and
will wrap your purchases for free. A recent remodel has
expanded the children's section and created lots of light-
filled, airy space in which a couple of couches are now
installed. It's a testament to the neighborhood and the
level of service that Bookcourt provides that the big B&N
down the street can't even begin to cast a shadow. – AH
(Bookcourt is the kind of bookstore you wish was in your
neighborhood. You can tell that the buyers are brilliant.
Oh, and the poetry section is HUGE! – Heath Row)

Word
126 Franklin St (btwn Greenpoint Ave & Kent St, Greenpoint, Bklyn) 718-383-0096
www.wordbrooklyn.com (Greenpoint: G to Greenpoint Ave)
They don't have everything, but they have the best of
what you might want. They make twice-a-week special
orders so you can get any in-print book within a day or
two. The children's section is awesome and the graphic
novels section is very smart and very well represented.
They have a section dedicated to McSweeney's-related
books, which might give you a sense of the proprietor's
literary leaning. – Heath Row (A Bookslut Indie Heart-
throb, Word is small but mighty, luring tons of authors
out to Greenpoint for events in their very basement-y
basement. Upstairs everything is cute as pie, with one of
those Flintstone-looking Ikea plastic tables for the kiddies, and lots of blonde wood. If I were to pick one author
whose work sums up the spirit of this bookstore, I would
go with Kerri Smith. – AH)

In this town of fountain pen hospitals and okonomiyaki
stands, is it any wonder that some bookstores choose to
focus in on a particular subject?

Partners & Crime
44 Greenwich Ave (btwn Charles & Perry) 212-243-0440
www.crimepays.com (Greenwich Village: 1 to Christopher St)
If you're a mystery reader, this is your shop. – Heath Row
(The first Saturday of every month, they stage an old-time
mystery radio show, with live actors, an organist and a

sound effects guy. Reserve tickets for that one by calling
212-462-3027. – AH)

East West Books
78 5th Ave (btwn 13th St & 14th St) 212-243-5994
www.eastwestnyc.com/ewbooks.html
(Union Sq: L/N/Q /R/4/5/6 to 14th St- Union Sq)
It's got to be the best-smelling bookstore I've ever been in.
Why? The people. No, kidding, it's the incense. There are
books by and about spiritual leaders; books on Buddhism,
Taoism, and other Eastern philosophies; scads of books
related to yoga; texts on Christianity, including more
mystical branches; and a good selection of health, relationship, and other related books. The highlight for me
was the large shelving area devoted to esoterica. Elizabeth
Clare Prophet gets her own shelf. – Heath Row (There's a
veggie café on the mezzanine, and so many opportunities
for New Age-y personal growth, I could pull the wings off
an angel card. – AH)

Books of Wonder
18 W 18th St (btwn 5th Ave & Avenue Of The Americas)
212-989-3270, www.booksofwonder.com
(Flatiron: F/L/M to 14th St-6th Ave)
Books of Wonder gives one hope on many levels. This is
the children's bookstore to go to. It's independent and
extremely focused in what it carries. The place is all about
sharing stories and resonates with a love of reading. It's
organized for the explorer as well as the sentimental.

Rogers & Hart • New York, New York – Nina

paper, *Revolution* is $1. – Heath Row

Classic picture books are shelved separately for easy reminiscing. And youth fiction is organized by age range. It feels just awesome to see *Charlotte's Web* shelved so closely to the *Cricket in Times Square* and *Bunnicula*. And there's a café area that sells cupcakes. – Heath Row

Idlewild Books
12 W 19th St (btwn 5th Ave & Ave of the Americas) 212-414-8888
www.idlewildbooks.com (Flatiron: R to 23rd St)
Idlewild is a travel bookstore and the shtick is that all the books are arranged by country. Fiction has a place alongside guidebooks and essays. Get it? *The People's Guide to Mexico* is shelved with *Under the Volcano*, *A Field Guide to Mexican Birds*, and activist Stephanie Elizondo Griest's memoir *Mexican Enough: My Life between the Borderlines*. This system provides a good way to get some three dimensional insights into places that we rarely hear described as anything other than "war torn." You could start your NYC trip here, pick a country to focus on, and spend the rest of your visit chasing down its food, movies, artwork, and pride parades!

Revolution Books
146 W 26th St (btwn Avenue Of The Americas & 7th Ave) 212-691-3345
www.revolutionbooksnyc.org (Chelsea: 1 to 28th St)
One of many regional bookstores associated with the Revolutionary Communist Party, the New York location carries the works of RCP chairman Bob Avakian, as well as other left-leaning books, media, and periodicals, including one of my faves, *Social Anarchism*. It's also a community center of sorts, hosting an active schedule of events, including film screenings and talks. The party's weekly

Socialist Workers Party
306 W 37th St, 10th fl (btwn 8th & 9th Ave) 212-629-6649
(Garment District: A/C/E to 34th St)
This is the local space for the SWP, *The Militant* weekly newspaper, and perhaps even Pathfinder Press. It's the party's office, community center, workspace, and book store. Not really a shop you can just pop into, given that it's also their workspace, but if you're interested in socialism, labor unionism, and related political issues, it's a good place to learn about current events and issues. I'm sure they'd welcome book buyers—there's a focus on Trotsky, Lenin, and Cuba. – Heath Row

The Complete Traveler Antiquarian Bookstore
199 Madison Ave (btwn 34th St & 35th St) 212-685-9007
www.ctrarebooks.com (Murray Hill: 6 to 33rd St)
Not a used bookstore, not a travel bookstore, this is an antiquarian bookstore that traffics in travel books. They have a wonderful selection of books on New England, and their New York collection is even more extensive. If you're looking for a reading copy, you can find less expensive options elsewhere. That said, if you need a book restorer, they know someone in Nevada who does good work. – Heath Row

Drama Bookshop
250 W 40th St (btwn 7th Ave & 8th Ave) 212-944-0595
www.dramabookshop.com
(Theater District: A/C/E to 42nd St)
Even if you hate theater, I'm banking that you like wine and cheese. They give it away free here on Thursdays from 6 to 8, and they also have weekly drawings for three pairs of theater tickets. See if you can tell the theater people from the civilian boyfriends or girlfriends (usually boyfriends) dragged in against their will. On a personal note, some of y'all may know that my husband penned *Urinetown: The Musical*, but are you also aware that he also wrote *Pig Farm, Eat the Taste, The Truth About Santa*, and *An Examination of the Whole Playwright/Actor Relationship Presented as Some Kind of Cop Show Parody*? You can get the scripts for all of them right here. I'm happy to pass along your mash notes to the playwright.

Kinokuniya
1073 Ave of the Americas (btwn 40th & 41st St) 212-869-1700, www.bookweb.us.kinokuniya.co.jp
(Midtown: B/D/F/M/7 to 42nd St-Bryant Park)
Kinokuniya is a two-story Japanese bookstore/stationery supply/café. It's a great place to buy cute host/ess gifts.

Unfortunately, most everything is a little pricey, but I can normally find a decent deal if I look around. Downstairs there are cute pens, stationary, erasers, folders, and *Totoro* paraphernalia. Most of the books and magazines are written in an Asian language, but they have a great selection of cookbooks in English. Despite my inability to read them, I've found that some of the craft books and design magazines are full of great ideas (pictures don't speak any language). – Amanda Plumb

Kitchen Arts and Letters
1435 Lexington Ave (btwn 93rd & 94th) 212-876-5550
www.kitchenartsandletters.com
(Upper East Side: 6 to 96th St)
If you love to cook, you should for sure check this place out. If you can barely get your ants on a log, surely one of the 13,000 new, used, or out-of-print cookbooks in there will tell you how to.

Hue Man Bookstore & Cafe
2319 Frederick Douglass Blvd (btwn 124th and 125th St)
212-665-7400
www.huemanbookstore.com (Harlem: A/B/C/D to 125th St)
Hue Man has all the classics of African-American lit. They also carry kids' games and even dolls, and a good selection of interesting magazines. There's a book swap. Bring a book, and take a book with you. – Jerry the Mouse (Hue Man is that rare bookstore that embraces self-published work. If you're an African American author, there may be an empty shelf with your name on it! Take a copy of your book with you when you go. You have to have an ISBN # and be distributed by Ingram's. – AH)

Don't forget that NYC's museum gift shops often function as specialty bookstores in their own right! MOMA, PS1, the LES Tenement Museum, and the Museum of the Moving Image are among my favorites. I know I trash talk the New Museum, but their gift shop's small book selection is pretty great, even if their zine prices are generally way too rich for my blood.

Used Books
Heaven.

Housing Works Used Book Cafe
126 Crosby St (btwn Houston & Prince) 212-334-3324
www.housingworks.org/bookstore
(SoHo: B/D/F/M to Broadway-Lafayette)
Not every used bookstore/café keeps a fishbowl of free condoms on the counter, but then, not every used bookstore/café's revenues go toward providing services and

housing for People with HIV and AIDS, a charitable designation that pretty much guarantees every literate gay man in a 20-mile radius will unload his reading material here. A while back, Housing Works caught on with the *New Yorker* set, and suddenly, this was the place for high profile readings and events. You can also gorge on CDs, vinyl, videos, and chocolate-dipped macaroons from the volunteer-run café in back. At their twice-yearly Open Air Street Fairs, you'll find a block's worth of books priced to move at a buck apiece. – AH (If you're looking for a place to sit, get in from the cold, *use the bathroom*, browse books, do some writing, and people-watch, this is a great place. It is impossible for me to leave without buying a book from the $1 racks. – Lauren Jade Martin)

The Strand
828 Broadway (@ 12th St) 212-473-1452
www.strandbooks.com
(Union Sq: L/N/Q /R/4/5/6 to 14th St-Union Sq)
I devoted nearly an entire issue of my zine to my on-again-off-again love affair with The Strand. A combination of disorganization and infuriating staff 'tude led me to pull the plug on it for a long while. These days, we're back on, mostly because of the beefed-up graphic novel and craft book section, my long overdue discovery of the top floor Rare Books room, and what must be a new hiring practice permitting non-assholes to work there too. As an author, it's disheartening to see all the titles that wind up on their famous (everything about the Strand is famous) $1 sidewalk carts, but as a cash-conscious, compulsive reader, it's like *oh hell to the yeah*. According to the financial newspaper *Nikkei*, a Strand totebag is the #1 souvenir that Japanese tourists bring back from New York. – AH (I usually get so overwhelmed that I just leave. If you have the patience, sure. – Megan Garrity) (I think that place is gross and filled with weirdos. – Josh Saitz)

East Village Books
99 Saint Marks Pl (@ Ave. A) 212-477-8647
www.buyusedbooksnewyork.com (East Village: 6 to Astor Pl)
East Village Books carries the complete oeuvre of Charles Bukowski (new) as well as a large selection of those fringe-y and increasingly hard to find Loompanics titles.

Book-Off
49 W 45th St (btwn 5th Ave & 6th Ave), 212-685-1410
www.bookoff.co.jp/en/info/kaigai02.html
(Midtown: 7/B/D/F/M to 42nd St-5th Ave-6th Ave)
This Japanese giant has lots of previously-owned English language treats in addition to all the nifty looking titles from the land of the rising sun, everything from

My Metrocard - Le Tigre • Fuck New York - Blatz •

Books books **books** Books **BOOKS!**

YORK   HISTORY   MEMOIRS   BIOGRAPHY   ECONO

Ooh, blueberry muffins!

Special events (comedy, readings) happen over here.

Be nice to these people - they're volunteers!

I know it's tempting, but don't slide down these!

GUINNESS is good

BAR

ORIGINAL Pabst Blue Ribbon Beer POPULAR PRICE

FICTION

SALE $5.00 7-$1.00

Comic books are back here

These tables fill up with laptop-users during the day.

Housing Works Bookstore Cafe

last year's ghost-written celebrity autobiographies and priced-to-move kids' books to hard-to-find, hardcore gay anime (which, if you're in the market, who cares what language they're in?). If a 14-hour flight looms in your future, Book-Off is also a great place to score the latest English language guidebooks, as well as beautifully il-lustrated books on Japanese food, culture, architecture, and manners. No credit for trade ins, and the cash offer for your giant bag of used books won't net you more than a Lincoln, so save it for The Strand, or donate them to a good cause.

Spoonbill & Sugartown
218 Bedford Ave
(btwn 4th St & 5th St, Williamsburg, Bklyn) 718-387-7322
www.spoonbillbooks.com (Williamsburg: L to Bedford Ave)
If I loved architecture I would love Spoonbill & Sugar-town. It's not all they carry, but that subject is so promi-nently displayed, it keeps me from spending much time in the uninspired brick mini-mall that houses them.

Unnameable Books
600 Vanderbilt Ave (@ St. Mark's, Prospect Hts, Bklyn)
718-789-1534
www.unnameablebooks.net (Prospect Hts: B/Q to 7th Ave)
Their recommended shelves are smart, and they have a sizable comics and graphic novel section. New and used aren't shelved together, and the used books are priced slightly higher than I'd like. They have a pebbled event space in the yard behind the building that they use for readings. – Heath Row (Nice owner, buyback policy, and a new zine section! – Cecile Dyer)

Street Sellers
Secondhand book tables are an *al fresco* NYC DIY tradi-tion. There's even an award-winning documentary film about these all-weather tough nuts, Jason Rosette's *BookWars*. The merchandise varies from day to day, and sometimes includes little extras like incense or shea but-ter. Some reliable spots to find these guys are 6th Avenue below 8th Street, along the east wall of the Chase Bank Building just south of the Astor Place cube, and the west

side of Broadway, north of 72nd Street. – AH (You can get fine art books from hundreds of street vendors in SoHo. On the Upper East and Upper West Sides there are also dozens of street vendors who sell everything from coloring books to fine art coffee table books, all at substantial discounts. – Josh Saitz)

Salvation Army Family Day
Let's not forget that every Wednesday is Family Day at every Salvation Army in town. Forget the clothes—used books go for 50% less than they do every other day of the week!

Magazines

You know about zines by now, but have you ever of these things called magazines? They come from all over the world, and often contain pretty pictures. Then there are the ones they keep behind the counter.

Ink on A
66 Avenue A (btwn $th & 5th) 212-871-6125
(East Village: F to 2nd Ave)
Ink stocks all sorts of magazines and newspapers I've never heard of 'til I get there. (And candy, cigarettes, and gum, just like a regular newsstand.) It's a bit messy but you'll find gems in the milk crates.

Casa Magazines
22 8th Ave (btwn 12th & Jane) 212-645-1197
(Greenwich Village: A/C/E/L to 14th St-8th Ave)
This is my favorite newsstand in the city. Despite the small shop's sense of clutter, Casa, also known as Global News, has an amazing selection. – Heath Row

Union Square Magazine Shop
200 Park Ave S (btwn 17th St & 18th St) 212-598-0618
(Gramercy Park: 4/5/6/L/N/Q/R to Union Square)
Not only does Union Square stock a lot of magazines of varying sorts, they have at least three porn shelves: two of straight and at least one of non-straight. They're not the best organized shelves—they mix new issues, back issues, and value packs, but they were there, and I found what I was looking for. – Heath Row

Around The World
28 W 40th St (btwn 5th Ave & Ave Of The Americas)
212-575-8543, www.aroundtheworldnyc.com
(Midtown: B/D/F/M/7 to 42nd St-Bryant Park)
This awesome and sizable newsstand just south of Bryant Park specializes in domestic and international fashion magazines and books. They have a smallish general selection in the front window area, but upstairs and into the main part of the store, it's all fashion and design titles,

from all over, which can make for magazines on the weightier—and pricier—side. Somewhat frustrating, I know, but there is a backup plan in the very back of the store, where there are discounted back issues. Same titles, just older, dustier, sometimes pre-read, and at a substantially lower ticket price. – Heath Row

Universal News
1381 Ave of the Americas (btwn 56th St & 57th St)
212-246-4777
(Columbus Circle: A/B/C/D/1 to 59th St-Columbus Circle)
&
977 Eighth Ave (btwn 57th St & 58th St) 212-459-0932
(Midtown: 4/5/6 to 59th St)
&
676 Lexington Ave (btwn 7th & 8th Ave) 212-750-1855
(Theater District: A/C/E to 42nd St)
&
234 West 42nd St (btwn 8th & Fashion Ave) 212-221-1809
(Garment District: A/C/E to 42nd St - Port Authority)
&
1586 Broadway (btwn W 47th & W 48th St) 212-586-7205
(Theater District: N/R to 49th St)
&
29 West 35th St (btwn 5th Ave & Avenue of the Americas)
212-594-3258 (Garment District: B/D/F/N/Q/R/M to 34th St)
&

The Ramones • Moving to New York – The

50 West 23rd St (btwn 5th Ave & Avenue of the Americas) 212-647-1761 (Flatiron: R to 23rd St)
&
11 West 14th St (btwn 5th & 6th Ave) 212-627-5708 (Union Sq: F/L/M to 14th St-6th Ave)
&
270 Park Ave S (btwn 20th & 21st St) 212-674-6595 (Gramercy Park: 6 to 23rd St)
&
484 Broadway (btwn Grand & Broome) 212-965-9042 (SoHo: N/Q /R to Canal St)
www.universalnewsondemand.com

Man, I love these magazine shops! Universal's got an awe-inspiring selection. Once I was in search of political magazines and picked up current issues of *the Nation, the Progressive, Extra!*, and *Fifth Estate*, and impressive Italian hacktivist periodical *Neural*. The one on Avenue of the Americas is also a UPS store with a shipping counter in back. – Heath Row

MUSIC STORES

Our research shows that zinesters who hate to shop don't hate shopping for cds and records almost as much as they don't hate shopping for books! We've refrained from differentiating between those selling used and new, seeing as how almost all of them do both.

Downtown Music Gallery
13 Monroe Street (btwn Catherine & Market) 212-473-0043
www.downtownmusicgallery.com
(Chinatown: F to East Broadway)
They got pushed off the Bowery after being thereabouts for a long time. They support a lot of experimental and hard-to-find stuff, especially things by DIY music-makers, lots of CDs and vinyl and they'll order whatever you are on the search for. These really nice guys even manage to host shows in their uber-tiny space. I can't say enough good things about them. – Matana Roberts

Gimme Gimme Records
325 E 5th St (btwn 2nd Ave & 1st Ave) 212-475-2955
www.myspace.com/gimmerecords
(East Village: F to 2nd Ave)
Gimme Gimme is a wonderful, small, focused shop specializing in used records. Some might call it vintage vinyl, given their concentration on hip-hop, new wave, jazz, country, and other genres. Nice prices, but the proprietors know what they've got and the really good stuff is priced slightly higher. – Heath Row (It may not be the most convenient for those in town from Monday to Thursday, but you've got to admire the work ethic that

leads them to curtail their opening hours to Friday, Saturday, and Sunday evenings and afternoons. – AH)

Kim's Video and Music
124 1st Ave (btwn 7th & St. Mark's) 212-533-7390
www.mondokims.com (East Village: F to 2nd Ave)
Much has been made over the decline of Kim's once massive empire, but I actually prefer the consolidated version. There's a little more attention paid to the customer, not that the staff is conforming to anyone's preferences but their own. Employee Picks still list toward the latest releases from Pissed Jeans and CoCoComa. New or used, you can probably find it here, though know you're at high risk of spending two hours browsing. *Maximumrocknroll* and other music zines are for sale up front.

St. Mark's Sounds
20 St. Mark's Pl (btwn 2nd and 3rd Ave) 212-677-3444
(East Village: 6 to Astor Pl)
They sell a lot of promotional copies, and these are the ones you should look for first because you can get cheap, brand-new CDs that some DJ or zinester got from the record company, sometimes before it is even released to the streets. They don't have a lot of imports, singles, or rarities, they have nothing in the back, they won't order anything, they probably won't help you and may even smoke cigarettes and ignore you when you're trying to check out. – Josh Saitz

Norman's Sound
67 Cooper Sq (btwn St. Mark's Pl & 7th St) 212-473-6599
www.normanssoundandvision.com
(East Village: 6 to Astor Pl)
Norman carries everything, but especially jazz and world music. He freely admits that the stuff that's popular today is not really his bag. The easy to overlook basement is crammed full of major CD, vinyl, and DVD deals. The pickin's become psychotically cheap during Norman's frequent $1 CD sales. They also have a smattering of used books, almost as if they discovered a couple of titles at the bottom of a milkcrate full of CDs and thought, "Oh, what the hell, maybe someone'll buy them too."

Bleecker Street Records
239 Bleecker St (btwn Carmine & Leroy) 212-255-7899
www.bleeckerstreetrecords.com
(Greenwich Village: AB/C/D/E/F/M to W 4th St)
Bleecker Street Records is a tad on the pricey side. But for what they've got, one really can't complain. Not only do they stock classic genre comps such as *Frolic Diner*, but they've got practically the full-run of the *Stompin'* comp

series on CD and lesser-known rarities. I scored several CDs of raw Harlem soul. – Heath Row

Bleecker Bob's
118 W 3rd St (btwn Ave of the Americas & Macdougal) 212-475-9677, www.myspace.com/bleeckerbobs (Greenwich Village: AB/C/D/E/F/M to W 4th St)
This is my all-time favorite record store in all of NYC. It's been around forever and is open until 4am! Their reggae/ska section isn't as big as I wish, but what it has is certainly a full line of *gems*. They have a giant rock section, with punk, powerpop, metal, psychedelic, and garage sub-sections—really. Behind the counter are a bunch of little boxes with rare and out-of-print 7"s! They are all separated by genre and each box is decorated accordingly. I've spent many hours listening to the entire contents of the 2-tone ska box. – Cristy Road

Generation Records
210 Thompson St (btwn Bleecker & W 3rd St) 212-254-1100 www.generationrecords.com (Greenwich Village: AB/C/D/E/F/M to W 4th St)
This was the first record store I visited here, and had heard of it even in Florida. They have a massive room full of vinyl, and pretty insane/extensive rock and soul sections. They also buy your used stuff. – Cristy Road (There is nowhere else in the city where you can find two dozen Beastie Boys live or rare CDs, right near bootleg concert videos, rare vinyl, and stickers, and in the basement, there are posters and used CDs up the wazoo. Each of the bootlegs is around $22 and the quality is usually very good. They also have a lot of unofficial releases, singles, b-sides, and promo-only stuff. They basically sell all the

shit that is against the law, but they seem to get away with it. – Josh Saitz) (They will always be close to my heart, but they've become a tad pricey! – Caitlin McGurk)

Other Music
15 E 4th St (btwn Lafayette & Broadway) 212-477-8150 www.othermusic.com (NoHo: B/D/F/M to Broadway-Lafayette)
If you want to find cool CDs, weird shit from all over the world, and talk to smart, friendly, informed people, the best store in the city is Other Music. They have lots of music zines as well. When Robyn Hitchcock puts out a vinyl-only collection of b-sides, they have a dozen copies. When all my online searching for a new Boo Radleys record proves fruitless, they'll have ten copies of their new CD. They also have a shitload of flyers for clubs, shows and other happenings. Their prices are reasonable. They even have used crap and some things that you won't find anywhere else in America. – Josh Saitz

Academy Records
12 W 18th St (btwn 5th Ave & 6th Ave) 212-242-3000 (Flatiron: R to 23rd St)
&
415 E 12 St (btwn 1st Ave and Ave A) 212-780-9166 (East Village: L to 1st Ave)
&
96 N 6th St (btwn Berry & Wythe, Williamsburg, Bklyn) 718-218-8200 (Williamsburg: L to Bedford Ave) www.academy-records.com
The Williamsburg Academy is my favorite new-ish record store in NYC. They not only buy used stuff, they bought *all* of my used stuff. It employs a bunch of the rad people I see around at shows. I could sit in front of the new arrivals section for hours. Seriously, I once found the Mr. T Experience's cover album of the Ramones' *Road to Ruin*, the Zombies' *S/T*, and *Steppin Out* by Joe Jackson *all at once*. Used and affordable. They have an amazing Latin/Caribbean section, and vast rock and soul sections, and a pretty killer punk section. – Cristy Road

Jazz Record Center
236 W 26th St Room 804 (btwn 7th & 8th Ave) 212-675-4480 www.jazzrecordcenter.com (Chelsea: 1 to 28th St)
It's on the eighth floor of a building without a doorman. Buzz up from the street, and they'll ring you in or send someone down to get you. They've got an impressive collection of LPs and CDs as well as a bunch of books, all of which appear to be shelf copies. It'd make an awesome research library. Feels more like a store for targeted

Man Who Sold the World – Nirvana • Balloon

searches, knowing what you want when you go in rather than for browsing. Proprietor Fred Cohen seems to really know his stuff. – Heath Row

Colony Records
1619 Broadway (btwn 49th & 50th St) 212-265-2050
www.colonymusic.com (Theater District: 1 to 50th St)
This place strikes me as a slice of a life that's largely gone. Sure, it panders to the high school musical, band geek, and Broadway groupie sets, but Colony is somewhat about democratizing the performance of music, which is worthy. I've bought sheet music for my mom, sheet music for my sax, a book of George Formby uke music for my boss, and a book on listening to jazz. – Heath Row (They also have a totally sick section of karaoke tracks and hardware. – AH)

Rincon Musical
1936 3rd Ave (btwn 106th & 107th) 212-828-8604
(East Harlem: 6 to 103rd St)
&
80 Graham Ave (@ Moore, Williamsburg, Bklyn)
718-388-0803 (Williamsburg: J/M to Flushing Ave)
&
398 Knickerbocker Ave (@ Himrod St, Bushwick, Bklyn)
718-574-0621 (Bushwick: M to Knickerbocker Ave)
&
7814 Roosevelt Ave (btwn 78th & 79th St, Jackson Heights, Queens) 718-651-9310
(Jackson Heights: 7 to 82nd St-Jackson Hts)
&
968 Southern Boulevard (btwn Aldus & 163rd St, Longwood, Bronx) 718-861-4506 (Longwood: 6 to Hunts Pt Ave)
www.rinconmusical.com
Rincon is a great source for Latin music, staffed by friendly people who would be delighted to help you find some new tunes if you're unfamiliar with most of the artists in their cd bins. They also do a mean business in drums and other musical instruments, sheet music, and decals to help make your love of various Spanish-speaking cultures and locales a matter of public record.

Sound Fix
44 Berry St (btwn N 11th St & N 12th St, Williamsburg Bklyn) 718-388-8090
www.soundfixrecords.com (Williamsburg: L to Bedford Ave)
The staff recommendation cards at Sound Fix are a great way to discover new, and especially local, music. Given space limitations both the new and used selections have a carefully considered, hand-picked feel. Music-related zines and DVDs are next to the listening station. Every

now and then, they'll have an in-store show, though escalating noise beefs with the neighbors have caused them to go all-acoustic. – AH

Passout Records
131 Grand (btwn Bedford & Berry, Williamsburg, Bklyn)
718-384-7273
www.passoutrecordshop.com (Williamsburg: L to Bedford)
Passout specializes in punk, hardcore, garage, and soul. If your ears can't take it, pop in some plugs and go for the band names. They frequently schedule live performances, and it's just as sweaty and mosh pitted out as you would expect. They even rent practice rooms for $15 an hour.

Greek Music & Video Superstore
2550 31st St (@ 28th Ave, Astoria, Queens) 718-932-8400
(Astoria: N to Astoria Blvd)
Not much to say about it, except that in my opinion everyone should listen to Savina Yannatou every day. And Aleka Kannelidou. The other biggie is the Athens Music & Video Superstore at 3097 31st Street. – Jerry the Mouse

The stores below predate the resurgence of vinyl releases. We thank them for having kept the dream alive.

Permanent Records
181 Franklin St (btwn Green & Huron, Greenpoint, Bklyn)
718-383-4083, www.permanentrecords.info
(Greenpoint: G to Greenpoint Ave)
This shop is a mecca of affordably-priced used and new CDs, records, music DVDs, and obscure compilations. Marjorie runs a tight ship. Orders come in when they say they will. The staff is friendly and helpful. It's a comfortable and smartly-organized atmosphere, and they even put on in-house shows during the summer! – Caitlin McGurk

The Thing
1001 Manhattan Ave
(btwn Huron & Greene, Greenpoint, Bklyn) 718-349-8234
(Greenpoint: G to Greenpoint Ave)
Be prepared to tie your hankie around your face, or come prepared with a dust mask like the hardcore record hounds do. Compared to the chaotic ground floor, a veritable Grey Gardens of used books, photographs, and some seriously nasty-ass clothing, the basement where records are shelved floor-to-ceiling is a model of orderliness. The owner has decreed that everything costs a flat $2, even if you happen to pan up some gold.

The Vortex
222 Montrose Ave (btwn Bushwick & Humboldt, Bushwick, Bklyn) 718-609-6066
www.myspace.com/vortexnyc (Bushwick: L to Montrose)
The Thing's little cousin, the Vortex, offers less of an overwhelming selection (and less dust), but is still well worth a dig. – AH

I'm partial to the CD-Rs sold by my favorite street buskers, and merch tables at shows. – Kate Black

I like the Pakistani shops along Brooklyn's Coney Island Avenue twixt Newkirk and Avenue H for two dollah cassettes of Nusrat Fateh Ali Khan and the like. – David Goren

Events for Music Collectors
The WFMU Record Fair
One weekend in late October
www.wfmu.org/recfair
If there's an audible equivalent to the zine universe, WFMU (91.1 FM or WFMU.org) is it. For over 50 years they've delighted in dousing the local airwaves with a mighty clamorous clang from their studios in Jersey City. The annual WFMU record fair in NYC is a crucial fundraising event for the listener supported station. The heart of the event is the dozens of dealers of vintage records and CDs of every musical flavor. Paw through raw material before it gets to the dealer at WFMU's own holdings near the entrance, including thousands of vinyl records and CDs priced to move at $1-3 bucks. The icing on the cake is the live performance stage. There's also an A/V lounge featuring quirky films and videos, and an album cover defacing station complete with crayons, glue and buckets of glitter. – David Goren (You can volunteer by calling 201-521-1416 x228. – AH)

The ARChive of Contemporary Music's twice yearly sale
54 White St (btwn Broadway & Church) 212-226-6967
www.arcmusic.org (Tribeca: J/N/Q /R/Z/6 to Canal St)
The ARChive of Contemporary Music is a not-for-profit devoted to preserving popular music of all cultures and races throughout the world from 1950 to the present. Their research and consultation rates keep out most would-be gatecrashers, except for these sales, when the archive unleashes oodles of triplicates from the collection as well as brand new CDs donated by philanthropic-type record companies.

Musical Instruments
You like to listen to it. Perhaps you like to play it too!

Main Squeeze
19 Essex St (btwn Hester & Canal) 212-614-3109
www.mainsqueeze-nyc.com (LES: F to East Broadway)
Tiny, but the tag line "for all your accordion needs" sums it up, if you're seeking lessons or if you're an already accomplished player looking for sheet music, straps, or tuxedo studs shaped like your instrument. The owner, Walter Kuhr, founded the world's only 14-piece all-female, all-accordion orchestra. (Because he saw it in a dream.)

Matt Umanov Guitars
273 Bleecker St (btwn Jones & Morton) 212-675-2157
www.umanovguitars.com
(Greenwich Village: A/B/C/D/E/F/M to W 4th St)
Half the dads in my neighborhood are musicians, so I took the opportunity when we were all hanging out on the playground one day to ask one of them what the best music store in New York is. He immediately suggested Matt Umanov, even though he himself is a piano player. "That's right," another piano-playing father chimed in. "That's where all the guitar guys go." A third rolled up. "You talking about Matt Umanov?" he asked. And thus the three of them spent the rest of our time together happily chattering about Martins, Fenders, hot hollowbodied Gibsons, and what the third one's wife was going to do with the kids while he was off being a rockstar for three weeks.

Music Inn World Instruments
169 W 4th St (btwn 6th and 7th Ave) (212) 243-5715
(Greenwich Village: A/C/E/B/D/F/M to W 4th St)
If you're looking to pick up a sitar, some sleigh bells, a previously owned trombone, and a banjo made out of a wooden cigar box, you've come to the right place! Mind your head or risk a concussion courtesy of the many world instruments slung from the ceiling like so many streamers and party balloons.

Papaya – Bugout Society • Detachable Penis –

Drummers World
151 W 46th St, 3rd fl (btwn 6th Ave & 7th Ave) 212-840-3057
www.drummersworld.com
(Theater District: N/R to 49th St)
Those same piano-playing daddies who told me about
Matt Umanov said if they were drummers, they'd go to
Drummers World.

Steinway Hall
109 W 57th St (@ 6th Ave) 212-246-1100
www.steinwayhall.com (Midtown: F to 57th St)
As long as you're polite, clean-fingered and take care to
caress the keys with more finesse than your average chim-
panzee, you're entitled to tickle a few high class ivories
here. Keep your ears open—you may hear something others pay good money for! And don't feel intimidated! For
all its worldwide reputation and rich history, Steinway
Hall is just another goofball Libra with a Myspace page
(www.myspace.com/steinwayhall).

Keur Djembe
568 Union St (@ 3rd Ave, Gowanus, Bklyn) 718-825-4638
www.keurdjembe.net (Gowanus: F/G to Carroll St)
For $20, take a two hour lesson in learning to play a keur
djembe, the tall Senegalese drum that gives this West African instrument shop its name. Don't split the goat skin
or that loaner's gonna cost you a lot more than $3.

ART AND OFFICE SUPPLIES
Who is immune from the lure of such items?

MANHATTAN

Pearl Paint
308 Canal (btwn Broadway & Mercer St) 212-431-7932
www.pearlpaint.com (TriBeCa: J/M/Z/N/Q /R/6 to Canal St)
Seems like you either love or hate this five-story art supply emporium. Some of the staff can be a little world-
wearier than thou. You have to pay for your purchases
before leaving every floor. There's a firetrap elevator—the
alternative is a creaky, dusty staircase that I kind of like
when not schlepping 20 sketchpads in an overheating
winter coat. My only real quibble is the cornucopia-like
abundance of the stock, which I guess puts me in the
love-it category. A whole floor of pens! Heaven! I like the
way it smells, too. Teachers and students get a discount,
so bring that ID. – AH (That place is too claustrophobic
for me. – Melissa Bastian)

Oriental Books & Stationery Arts
29 East Broadway (btwn Catherine & Market) 212-962-3634
(Chinatown: F to East Broadway)
You can get calligraphy practice books, brushes and ink
for under $5 total. – Jerry the Mouse

Blick Art Materials
1-5 Bond St (btwn Lafayette & Broadway) 212-533-2444
www.dickblick.com/stores/newyork/newyork
(NoHo: 6 to Bleecker St)
Dick Blick is my favorite place for art supplies. People
always say Pearl, but Blick, oh...wide open and spacious,
with at least half an aisle of whatever it is you can think
of: pens, markers, pastels, gorgeous papers, stationeries,
cheap-o frames to make your bar napkin doodle look like
a masterpiece, screenprinting supplies, sculpting tools,
more acrylic paint than you can shake a stick at, and
the biggest selection of stretched canvas I've ever seen.
They also carry plenty of kitschy, gifty stuff. – Melissa
Bastian (They don't abuse you like they do at Pearl. – Amy
Burchenal)

JC Casey Design Rubber Stamps
322 E 11th St (btwn 1st Ave & 2nd Ave) 917-669-4151
www.caseyrubberstamps.com (East Village: 6 to Astor Pl)
Head to this East Village boite for some outside-the-norm
images. If you've got time, they'll make one from your own
design, thus allowing postal employees and cover-charge-
paying bar patrons to share in your joy. Ask to the see the
documentation of other customers' unique images.

Utrecht Art Supplies
111 4th Ave (@ E 12th St) 212-777-5353
www.utrechtart.com (East Village: 6 to Astor Pl)
Utrecht is just a few doors away from my post office, the
Cooper Union on the corner of 4th Avenue and 11th Street
and that is seriously the best post office in the city! – Fly (I
shop at Utrecht too, but never again during the first week
of NYU's fall semester, when the incoming freshman do
everything but strip the bark off the shelves. – AH)

New York Central Art Supply
62 Third Ave (@ 11th St) 212-477-0400
www.nycentralart.com (East Village: L to 3rd Ave)
You can't go in without finding a whole new section.
Upstairs, the paper area is one of the foremost art paper
suppliers in the world. I'm not kidding—they're written up in Fine Paper books, and the specialists up there
give talks on the history of paper all around town. They
also are working with the government to create a Paper
Museum. They're unionized, and have their own framing

store a few blocks away. – Jerry the Mouse (They also carry obscure Japanese supplies, like screentone and G-pen nibs. – Marguerite Dabaie)

Jam Paper & Envelopes
135 3rd Ave (btwn 14th and 15th St) 212-473-6666
www.jampaper.com (Gramercy: L to 3rd Ave)
Brightly colored envelopes from Jam's Close-Out department (25 for $2) have been a hallmark of *East Village Inky* quality since issue #2. No better way to mail a greeting card sized project. They also have an entire wall of fluorescent plastic envelopes in sizes ranging from business card to legal, the very thing to keep your precious originals unbesmirched should there be some sort of liquid accident in your bag.

Greenwich Letter Press
39 Christopher St (btwn W 4th St & Waverly Pl)
212-989-7464, www.greenwichletterpress.com
(Greenwich Village: 1 to Christopher St)
Correspondence-wise, I'm a big recycler of manila envelopes, the front half of greeting cards, and the ten million flyers my kids drag home from school. This is not only good for the environment, it keeps me from blowing the monthly food budget on the sort of tantalizing stationery porn that passes muster in this small Village shop. Fortunately, it's free to look. I think of it as a miniature museum. If you, too, fetishize rubber stamps, vintage typesetting, certain types of card stock, and invitations to parties you'll never throw away, make sure your hands are clean and check it out.

Murray's Cheese Shop
254 Bleecker St (btwn Cornelia & Leroy) 212-243-3289
www.murrayscheese.com
(Greenwich Village: A/C/E/B/D/F/M to W 4th St)
In addition to their range of cheeses and antipasti, Murray's sells special cheese wrapping paper. Plastic wrap encourages cheeses to mold, and they can't breathe in there. So that's where Murray's waxed paper (printed with the store logo, and a variety of cheese wedges) comes in. I mostly use it for the intended purpose of dairy storage, but like much ephemera that finds its way to my home, I've also incorporated it into books. The printed pattern makes it a no-brainer for making gifts for cheese-obsessed friends, and the waxy finish comes in handy in my personal sketchbooks, where I use it as a palette for glue and paint. – Kate Black

The Ink Pad
22 8th Ave (btwn 12th St & Jane) 212-463-9876
www.theinkpadnyc.com
(Greenwich Village: A/C/E/L to 14th St-8th Ave)
I have very specific rubberstamping needs. I need ink pads! I have ink pads at home, but none at work. I want several colors in both places. Am I a dork or what? – Heath Row

Typewriters & Things
56 8th Ave (btwn 13th St & Horatio) 212-255-5252
(Greenwich Village: A/C/E/L to 14th St)
Notebook and pen fetishists will love T&T. They carry almost the full line of Rhodia and Moleskine notebooks and they have an impressive selection of writing implements. If you buy five pens, the sixth one is free—but you can't mix and match pen styles, just colors within the same kind of pen. They have rubber stamps for filing, ledger books, and a small selection of other office supplies, including cables. Tiny, tidy, terrific. – Heath Row

Adorama
42 W 18th St (btwn 5th Ave & Ave of the Americas)
212-741-0052
www.adorama.com (Flatiron: F/M/L to 14th St-6th Ave)
Adorama is a user-friendly photography shop with good prices and a mix of new and used equipment. They also do printing for digital photographers. I became a convert to Adorama when I was looking for an alternative to a more well-known photography supply shop that treats women like crap. I don't want to give them press, but there's an

Halloween Parade – Lou Reed • I Guess the Lord

ampersand in their name. – Kate Black

17th Street Photo
34 W 17th St, 3rd fl
(Btwn 5th Ave & Avenue Of The Americas) 212-366-9870
www.17photo.com (Flatiron: F/M/L to 14th St-6th Ave)
I can also recommend the service at 17th Street Photo. It
has a limited selection of camera equipment but is great
for film. The scary elevator has soft spots in the floor, so
take the stairs. – Kate Black

DaVinci Artist Supply
132 W 21st St (btwn 6th & 7th Ave) 212-871-0220
(Chelsea: N/R to 23rd St)
&
137 E 23rd St (btwn Lexington & 3rd Ave) 212-982-8607
(Gramercy Park: 6 to 23rd St)
www.davinciartistsupply.com
The people at DaVinci are very helpful and not at all
snotty like I thought art store people might be. I was looking for erasers, pens, sketching paper, and "something to
make squares" and ended up having a long conversation
with one of the guys about comics. – Josh Medsker

B&H Photo-Video-Pro Audio
420 9th Ave (btwn 33rd St & 34th St) 866-265-7999
www.bhphotovideo.com
(Garment District: A/C/E to 34th St)
B&H is a massive operation that takes up an entire city
block. It's staffed in large part by Orthodox Jews, so don't
go on Saturday. They stock everything from humble, used
point 'n' shoots to top of the line professional monsters
capable of withstanding Himalayan temperature drops
and oceanic pressure. Before I ventured in to B&H, I had
no idea this much camera paraphernalia could exist in
the world, let alone New York. I enjoy skulking from floor
to floor, nibbling on the free hard candy they've got sitting out everywhere.

Talas
330 Morgan Ave (btwn Metropolitan & Sharon, East Williamsburg, Bklyn) 212-219-0770
www.talasonline.com (Williamsburg: L to Grand St)
Talas is a fine bookbinding supplier. Hobbyists may find
themselves a bit out of their league, but archivists and
serious binders will feel right at home. They carry exotic
marbled papers, book cloth in a variety of fiber types,
presses, sewing frames, needles, book leather (much thin-
ner than garment leather) and artisanal tools. It's not the
most browsing-friendly experience, but it's easy to order
online and pick up your goods in person. – Kate Black

Barclay School Supplies
166 Livingston St (btwn Gallatin & Smith, Bklyn)
718-875-2424, www.barclayschoolsupplies.com
(Downtown Bklyn: A/C/F to Jay St-Borough Hall)
Barclay isn't something you just stumble upon while
you're out browsing. Take the elevator to the basement of
this ugly office building. Once there, you can totally play
Teacher in this wonderland of felt boards, magnetic letters, plastic food in an impressive array of ethnic configu-
rations, cardboard decorations for holidays I didn't even
know we're supposed to celebrate, and enough Good Job
stickers to choke a Chancellor. I'm always circling around
the library pockets, which I've seen used to great effect in
other zines. Here they're available in fluorescent colors,
economy packs, you name it.

KC Arts
252 Court St (@ Kane St, Cobble Hill, Bklyn) 718-852-1271
(Cobble Hill: F/G to Bergen St)
KC Arts is an inexpensive, independently-owned
neighborhood-staple, and the staff is incredibly helpful.
– Caitlin McGurk (They have several racks of beautiful
greeting cards and a healthy selection of kids' supplies
and kits. – AH)

Materials For The Arts
3300 Northern Blvd (@ 33rd St, Long Island City, Queens)
718-729-3001
www.mfta.org (LIC: N to 39th Ave)
Materials For The Arts is a bad-ass warehouse full of
great, donated fabric, paint, office supplies, and such
in Long Island City, Queens, but you need to a) make an
appointment and b) be affiliated with an approved arts
organization or non-profit. – Matana Roberts (If you've
got a pal in the pipeline, it's worth it to get your name on
their organization's list ahead of time, so you too can don
one of Materials For the Arts' hardhats for a dive in their
officially sanctioned dumpster. If that fails, they recently
started holding evening craft workshops that are free and
open to the public! – AH)

The streets themselves are cornucopias of ephemera. But
as with all trashpicking, the joy has been mitigated by the
rise of bedbug infestations. I recommend carrying reseal-
able plastic bags, and keeping new finds in a freezer for at
least one month to kill off bloodsucking pests. – Kate Black

Must Be in New York City - Harry Nilsson • Sheena

Craft Supplies

As seductive as art and office supplies! Twice as likely to attract ravens. Three times as likely to gather dust on my shelves!

The Wall Street Humidor Corporation
18 Warren St (btwn Broadway & Church) 212-96-CIGAR
(Tribeca: R to City Hall-Broadway)
Come here to buy wooden cigar boxes before they become extinct. The aroma is a shock, now that we've all grown used to the ban on smoking in NYC bars and restaurants.

Canal Rubber Supply
329 Canal St (btwn Greene St & Mercer St) 212-226-7339
www.canalrubber.com (Tribeca: J/N/Q /R/Z/6 to Canal St)
A pity rubber isn't more breathable, or my Mermaid Parade costume would be pulled together with bright fluorescent tubing, flexible sheeting, and "extruded parts" from this most utilitarian and longstanding of suppliers. I don't think they get too many casual browsers, which is why people like me get such a warm welcome.

Canal Plastics Center
345 Canal St (btwn Wooster St & Greene St) 212-925-1717
www.canalplasticscenter.com
(Tribeca: J/N/Q /R/Z/6 to Canal St)
Name one thing that couldn't stand to be souped-up with adhesive-backed, reflective plastic cut-outs of dolphins, cherries, skull 'n' crossbones, and sexy mud flap ladies! Pimp your bike. Pimp your lunch box.

M & J Trimming
1000 6th Ave (@ 37th St) 212-391-6200
www.mjtrim.com
(Garment District: B/D/F/M/N/R/Q to 34th St)
You can wear those tattered rags forever if you tart them up with silk-covered buttons. Choose from hundreds of crowd-pleasing designs, from Boticelli's *Venus* to disturbing-countenanced rabbits in vintage Easter bonnets.

Toho Shoji
990 6th Ave (btwn 36th and 37th St) 212-668-7465
www.tohoshoji-ny.com
(Garment District: B/D/F/M/N/R/Q to 34th St)
Hot bead-on-bead action. They've got all the things you need to get them on your ears and around your neck: jump hoops, earring wires, how-to books, and trays upon which you can calculate your design. How I would have loved the tubes upon tubes of itsy bitsy seed beads when I was a kid.

Tender Buttons
143 E 62nd St (btwn 3rd Ave & Lexington Ave) 212-758-7004
(Upper East Side: F to 63rd St-Lexington Ave)
Yes, that was Gertrude Stein's pet name for Alice B Toklas' nipples. The service can be a little harsh here. Funny. But they do have nipples, I mean buttons, and lots of them. I've heard tell they even have buttons from George Washington's inauguration suit that cost thousands of dollars.

Junk
197 N 9th St (btwn Bedford & Driggs, Williamsburg, Bklyn)
718-640-6299 (Williamsburg: L to Bedford Ave)
&
214 Franklin St (btwn Green & Huron, Greenpoint, Bklyn)
(718) 383-3751 (Greenpoint: G to Greenpoint Ave)
www.myspace.com/brooklynjunk
These guys truck mainly in vintage housewares, some of which will have you resenting Grandma for letting those metallic ice tea glasses and wooden shoeshine boxes go for pennies at her long-ago yard sales. Once you get that out of your system, have at the baskets of old craft mags someone's granny traded for a magic bean sometime in the '70s. They always seem to have a lot of old Polaroids, slide projectors, and recording equipment, if you're one of those who prefers your technology big 'n' clunky.

The Painted Pot
339 Smith St (btwn President & Carroll, Carroll Gardens, Bklyn) 718-222-0334
(Carroll Gardens: F/G to Carroll)
&
8009 Third Ave (btwn 80th St & 81st St, Bay Ridge,Bklyn)
718-491-6411
(Bay Ridge: R to 77th St)
www.paintedpot.com
At first the Painted Pot seems kind of cheesy, but it's a pleasant time and you can BYOB at night. You pay for whatever piece you select ($20 for a big mug, less for soy sauce dishes and ornaments, more for mixing bowls and platters), and then another $8 or so for studio time (though you can sit as long as you like, and there are frequent deals—Ladies' Night, Guys' Night Out, Two-for-the-Price-of-One, etc). It takes them about a week to fire your piece, but they can ship it to you.

Brooklyn General
128 Union St (btwn Columbia St & Hicks St, Carroll Gardens, Bklyn) 718-237-7753
www.brooklyngeneral.com (Carroll Gardens: F/G to Carroll St)
Catherine, my former midwife, runs this beautifully-equipped yarn store. Hooray for labors of love that are

is a Punk Rocker - The Ramones • New York, New

also successful, independently-owned businesses. She sells fabric and all the relevant craft books too. It's a bit of a hike from the subway, so if I were you, I'd keep my energy up with lunch at Ferdinando's Focacceria and a bit of a poke around Yesterday's News.

Yesterday's News
428 Court St (btwn 2nd Pl & 3rd Pl, Carroll Gardens, Bklyn) 917-375-1361
www.brownstonetreasures.com
(Carroll Gardens: F/G to Carroll St)
If I owned this store, I'd apply for non-profit status and run it as a museum. Vintage recipe pamphlets, old photos, maps, postcards, pulp fiction, and *Playboys*... They have a big tin of vintage stamps, so beautiful, ten for a dollar.

Sav-a-Thon
824 Flatbush Ave (btwn Caton & Linden, Flatbush, Bklyn) 718-282-9100 (Flatbush: Q to Parkside)
&
Save-a-Thon
2452 Flatbush Ave (btwn 53rd St & Avenue T, Marine Park, Bklyn) 718-258-8500
&
5733 Myrtle Ave (@ Weirfield, Flushing, Queens) 718-497-0100
&
9 E Fordham Rd (btwn Morris & Jerome, Fordham, Bronx) 718-295-6070
If you need to add a little dazzle to your duds before marching off wherever, this joint has all the cheap sequined fabric, feathers, lace, pom-poms, iron-on letters, First Communion tiara-forms, jingle bells, rosettes, tiny plastic babies, and die-cut Styrofoam shapes you need to make the day special. I favor the location on Flatbush near Caton because of its rejection of the silent e and its convenience to all manner of cheap and delicious Caribbean food. NYC recently got its very first Michael's (on Columbus btwn 97th & 100th), which may be the death knell for Sav-a-Thons.

Materials Resource Center
2111D Lakeland Ave (Ronkonkoma, Long Island) 631-580-7290
www.materialresourcecenter.org
Oh, how I wish I could write that this place was in, say, Bushwick, which is geographically daunting enough for most people. Obviously we're none of us going to make this pilgrimage without a car (and someone who knows how to drive the damn thing). I can understand not wanting to pay Union Square rents, when you're a not-for-profit, open-to-the-public recycling center selling donated craft supplies by the pound. To the public! No membership or proof of non-profit status required. They've got everything from file cabinets, fabric and fancy paper to plastic swans, sequin punch rolls and doll wigs.

99¢ STORES

New BJ99¢
15 Pike St (btwn East Broadway & Henry) 212-964-6869
(Chinatown: F to East Broadway)
A 99¢ paradise awaits beneath the clouds of incense from the Buddhist temple just up a flight of Fontainebleau-ish outer stairs. I have picked up everything from umbrellas to killer plastic swords to the long-in-front-short-in-back rain ponchos favored by bicycle delivery boys. The biggest draws are the Korean pencil cases, stationery, and small, sloppily-printed notebooks featuring such uncommon-domain legends as Spiderman, Winnie the Pooh, and Barbie, spouting slogans like "I Ate You."

JS99¢
113 Eldridge St (btwn Broome & Grand) 212-966-8728
(LES: B/D to Grand St)
Santa's stuffed a few stockings with the Chinatown-type souvenirs here. And I've slapped down for some surprisingly beautiful kites, in season. What keeps me coming back time and again are the flexible rubber puzzles of the human digestive tract. I got my rainbow-ribbon-wrapped, adult-size, weighted hula hoop here. It cost $8, which is no 99¢, but still a bargain.

Teng Fei Grocery
329 Grand St (@ Ludlow) 212-431-9520
(LES: F/J/M/Z to Delancey-Essex)
This tiny Lower East Side hybrid is pure Chinatown, and
scores big with me for stocking beer alongside its less-
than-a-buck bicycle bells, off-brand Tiger Balm, and the
Chenglish stationery supplies I so crave. Classy!

Jack's 99¢ Stores
110 W 32nd St (btwn 6th & 7th Ave) 212-268-9962
(Garment District: B/D/F/M/N/Q /R to 34th St)
Even if you won't be stocking a pantry on this trip, Jack's
first floor is worth it for the educational overview of low budge
interpretations of better-known snack and cereal brands. Upstairs the prices are higher, and the goods less desperate.

99¢ City
31 Hoyt St (btwn Livingston & Fulton, Downtown Bklyn)
718-855-8831 (Downtown Bklyn: 2/3 to Hoyt St)
If an approaching holiday's got you in the mood to put
the big pot in the little, as my father would say, the wall
to the left of the bag check has garlands, deely bobbers,
and ornaments galore. I wouldn't want 'em in my home,
but they can sure dress up a bike. There's also a keen stash
of rubber baby dolls, organza goodie bags, and satin rosettes. My children's earliest video viewing can be sourced
back to the DVD rack back between the cashier and the
kitchen department, which helped us tube up to such
greats as Felix the Cat, Shirley Temple, Godzilla, Betty
Boop, and the Fleischer brothers' feature-length *Gulliver's
Travels*. – AH

Williamsburg 99¢ Bonanza!
I like the stores on Grand Avenue in Williamsburg, Bklyn.
Cheap! You can buy 99-cent wooden bead bracelets and
NYC keychains for your homies back home. They'll never
know you cared so little! – Dear Drunk Girl
Greenpoint 99¢ Mecca!
Kinetic sculptor Dr. Gerbo (www.gerbomatic.com) turned
me on to this strip of prime 99-cent pickins along Manhattan Avenue between the G line's Nassau Avenue and
Greenpoint Avenue stops in Greenpoint, Brooklyn. These
include Super Deal 99¢ (#662), NYC Super Store (#679),
99¢ And Up (#799) and Bang for the Buck (#852). Worth
your while? I think so. A recent survey yielded borscht
mix, fake boogers, a whole host of Korean stationery and
pencil cases, an oversized wooden mouse trap that totally
belongs in MOMA's design galleries, a martial arts double
feature DVD and some Sheerly Touch-y brand little boys'
A-line undershirts.

Bedford-Stuyvesant 99¢ Cornucopia!
Fulton is the usual drag where I get all my home needs.
Although it's not entirely 99¢, Fulton between New York
Avenue and the Fulton Street Mall is *full of treasures*. My
entire house has been decorated by the fine emporiums
on this drag. Many stores with the word "bargain" in their
name = always a plus. – Cristy Road

Banzai 99¢ Plus
Flushing Mall, 133-31 39th Ave (btwn Union & Main,
Flushing, Queens) 718-445-0940
(Flushing: 7 to Main St)
&
136-90 Roosevelt Ave (btwn Union & Main, Flushing,
Queens) 718-321-0202 (Flushing: 7 to Main St)
&
156-17 Northern Blvd (btwn 156th & 157th, East Flushing,
Queens) 718-445-4300 (East Flushing: Q15 to 41 Ave-150 St)
www.banzai99.com
Banzai is a lovely way to exercise your 100-yen store jones
without flying all the way to Tokyo. The quality of the
merch is much higher than your average 99-centporium.
All you crafty beavs will get off on the unbelievably
low priced bamboo knitting and crochet needles, while
beauty kings and queens can load up on makeup, cosmetics brushes, and tiny razors well suited to shaving things
besides just eyebrows. If you're foot-sore and luggage-
light, invest eight bucks in a pair of Dr. Scholl-ish wooden
reflexology sandals. I believe this is where I got my pink
Cherry Rabbit: I never want to lose the innocence in my heart
soap case.

ABC Superstore
2127 31st St (btwn 21st Ave & Ditmars Blvd, Astoria,
Queens) 718-278-2076 (Astoria: N to Astoria-Ditmars Blvd)
& several bazillion other locations too numerous to list
ABC has TP, soap, and all the essentials, and helps cut
down on the bills, dig? Also, a great place to get soda and
a corkscrew in a pinch! – Josh Medsker (There's a ton of
these suckers in exactly the sort of locations where you
might expect to find a big discount store selling off-brand
baby powder, fugly shower curtains, flimsy cooking
implements, and those snap front house dresses favored
by hardy, female seniors. – AH)

Just go to Queens. They're everywhere. – Melissa Bastian

CLOTHING
NYC has the strange power to make visitors who are
normally satisfied with their sense of style or lack thereof
suddenly feel about as fetching as a dump truck.

Used

Manhattan has several streets beloved by those who love thrift shops, though you'd better hurry; a bunch of my faves have folded of late.

If you're thrifting with a vengeance, you'll appreciate the comparatively high concentrations on:
23rd st btwn 2nd & 3rd Ave
3rd Ave btwn 81st & 84th with detours down 81st btwn 1st & 3rd, and 84th btwn 2nd & 3rd
and then, just for old times sake, 17th St btwn 6th & 7th Ave

Salvation Army
Every Wednesday is Family Day at *every* Salvation Army in NYC! All clothing, shoes, and books are half price. Bring on the men's cashmere sweaters for $1.99 a pop! You want a challenge? Hit every Sal' in at least two boroughs on Family Day, buy an item of clothing in each, and send me a photo of yourself wearing all of your purchases at once! You do that, and I'll send you an *East Village Inky* fun pack, provided you don't make me look up the cross streets and phone numbers. I'll leave it to you to plot your route:

Manhattan:
536 West 46th St, Midtown
220 E. 23rd St, Gramercy Park
112 4th Ave, East Village
41 West 8th, Greenwich Village
26 E. 125th St, Harlem
208 8th Ave, Chelsea
268 W. 96th St, Upper West Side

Brooklyn:
981 Manhattan Ave Greenpoint, Bklyn
176 Bedford Ave Williamsburg, Bklyn
6822 3rd Ave, Bay Ridge, Bklyn
3718 Nostrand Ave, Sheepshead Bay, Bklyn
436 Atlantic Ave, Boerum Hill Bklyn
22 Quincy St, Bedford-Stuyvesant Bklyn
239 Flatbush Ave, Fort Greene, Bklyn

Queens:
34-02 Steinway St Astoria, Queens
148-15 Archer Ave Jamaica, Queens
39-11 61st St Woodside, Queens

The Bronx:
4109 Park Ave, Tremont, Bronx
2359 Jerome Ave, Morris Heights, Bronx
1294 Southern Blvd, Morrisania, Bronx

2582 3rd Ave, Mott Haven, Bronx

Staten Island:
1442 Castleton Ave, Port Richmond, Staten Island
2052 Clove Rd, Concord, Staten Island

Stoop Sales

Bless the residents of Brooklyn neighborhoods Park Slope, Boerum Hill, and Carroll Gardens! How they love to throw stoop sales on the weekends! Good stuff ? Let's just say, some of these folk own their own brownstones. Expect a lot of books and kids' clothes. Try taking the F to Bergen Street, Carroll Street, or 7th Avenue on any non-rainy Saturday from April to October. Survey the lamp-posts for likely looking signs. These same neighborhoods are often hotbeds of lemonade-stand-related activity, and their ties to the stoop sales are both suspicious and overt.

Charity Thrift Stores

Housing Works Thrift Shop
143 W 17th St (btwn 6th & 7th Ave) 212-366-0820
(Chelsea: 1 to 18th St)
&
157 E 23rd St (btwn 2nd & 3rd Ave) 212-529-5955
(Gramercy: 6 to 23rd St)
&
130 Crosby St (@ Jersey St) 646-786-1200

(SoHo: B/D/F/M to Broadway-Lafayette)
&
119 Chambers St (btwn W Broadway & Church)
212-732-0584 (Tribeca: 1/2/3 to Chambers St)
&
1730 2nd Ave (@ E 90th St) 212-722-8306
(Yorkville: 4/5/6 to 86th St)
&
245 W 10th St (btwn Hudson & Bleecker St) 212-352-1618
(Greenwich Village: 1 to Christopher St)
&
202 E 77th St (btwn 2nd & 3rd Ave) 212-772-8461
(Upper East Side: 6 to 77th St)
&
306 Columbus Ave (btwn W 74th & W 75th St)
212-579-7566 (Upper West Side: 1/2/3 to 72nd St)
&
122 Montague St (@ Henry St, Brooklyn Heights, Bklyn)
718-237-0521 (Brooklyn Hts: M/R to Court St-Borough Hall)
 www.housingworks.org/social-enterprise/thrift-shops
Housing Works is totally taking over these days, which
is great news for both thrift store shoppers and people in
need of homes who are living with HIV/AIDS. Given that
the latter group benefits every time the register rings up
a sale, the former group will please refrain from bitching
about the higher-than-Goodwill prices. Every NYC gay
man of a certain age with stuff to throw at a charity shop
drops his donation off here, which makes for a fascinating composite portrait, a rich selection of menswear, and
the occasional pair of pumps in a size you won't find at
Payless. Housing Works is also a darling of designers,
which can at times translate to a whole lot of ugly, as well
as a special room at the 17th Street location to which the
particularly label-conscious are admitted by request.
Even though Housing Works has a dedicated Used Book
Café in SoHo, all these locations have books and CDs in
addition to clothing and housewares. Look on the website
to see which store is doing what to make things themati-
cally fun and/or cheap. That's also a good place to find out
about their Long Island City warehouse sales. – AH (They
aren't slap-me-I-must-be-dreaming cheap, but they're
definitely nice. – Marguerite Dabaie)

Angel Street Thrift Shop
118 W 17th St (btwn 6th & 7th Ave) 212-229-0546
www.angelthriftshop.org (Chelsea: 1 to 18th St)
Angel Street can save you a lot of trouble with their
stringently-adhered-to ROYGBIV rack policy. Heaven help
you if you misfile a green non-keeper on the purple rack.
I get the sense that the all-volunteer workers really enjoy
fancying up the store in this way. They often have dressy

special-occasion-type things, because they too get merch
straight off the runway and the designers' misfire racks.
The purchase of your fancy pants will help fund programs
for New Yorkers with substance abuse problems, mental
illness, and HIV/AIDS.

Vintage Stores

Monk
165 Ave A (btwn E 10th & E 11th) 917-534-0511
(East Village: L to 1st Ave)
&
183 Ave B (btwn E 10th & E 11th) 212-673-5961
(East Village: L to 1st Ave)
&
177 Ave C (@ E 11th) 212-505-7309
(East Village: L to 1st Ave)
&
175 MacDougal St (btwn W 8th St & Washington Sq N)
212-533-0553
(Greenwich Village: A/B/C/D/E/F/M to W 4th St)
&
579 5th Ave (@ 16th St, Windsor Terrace, Bklyn) 718-788-2950
(Windsor Terrace: B/D/F/M to 47th-50th St)
The best one is definitely on Avenue A, and if you don't
find anything you like there, it's a short distance to the
ones on B and C. All three seem to have an inside line
on cowboy boots. Monk is definitely not as upscale in
presentation as some of its similarly priced ($10 for a pair
of jeans) East Village brethren, but that helps keep the
junkier—in all senses of the word—Avenue A of days
gone by alive for me.

Tokio 7
83 E 7th St (btwn 1st Ave & 2nd Ave) 212-353-8443
(East Village: 6 to Astor Pl)
Are those glamorous Manhattan-dwelling clotheshorses
making you feel dumpy and ill turned out? Don't let it
ruin your visit. You may have to suck in your gut because
most of the ultra cool threads at this pricey but possibly
worth it secondhand store were consigned by the Dex-
edrine and lettuce crowd. Even if you don't find anything
you like in a size that fits, you can still score kewpie dolls
in a variety of colors and dimensions ranging from key-
chain to newborn.

Search & Destroy
25 St. Mark's Pl (btwn 2nd and 3rd Ave) 212-358-1120
(East Village: 6 to Astor Pl)
Search & Destroy's prices seem a wee bit inflated until
you fall head over heels with some whacked out, buy-

Lou Reed • People Who Died - Jim Carroll •

now-or-bid-adieu-forever item in a decidedly non-clothing-like print. That's when it begins seeming like a bargain, especially for NYC. Even if you don't buy anything, it's awfully fun to look. Visit in the cooler months for hairy sweaters and a history of outerwear. There's a bouquet of *lucha libre* masks for sale near the $5 t-shirt rack. More valuable t's are arranged alphabetically by band name. Speaking of which, they've got a Kiss pinball machine.

Atomic Passion

430 E 9th St (btwn 1st Ave & Ave A) 212-533-0718
www.myspace.com/atomicpassion (East Village: L to 1st Ave)
I left the flowered 1950s bathing suit I got at this crammed East Village emporium in a rice and beans place on Avenue C a few summers ago, after a trip to the Dry Dock pool, and I'd like to get around to replacing it. Maybe I'll just go for a girdle and a bullet bra instead.

Tokyo Joe

334 E 11th St (btwn 1st & 2nd Ave) 212-473-0724
(East Village: L to 1st Ave)
Good thing they don't sell china here because I'd be the bull who knocks it over. Maybe Tokyo Joe keeps the square footage small as a way of deterring eager-to-consign *gaijin* from coming in with fourteen ripped shopping bags stuffed full of pilly, stretched-out sweaters. Their extreme selectiveness is a side-effect of their exquisite taste.

Buffalo Exchange

332 E 11th St (btwn 2nd Ave & 1st Ave) 212-260-9340
(East Village: L to 1st Ave)
&
504 Driggs Ave (btwn N 9th St & N 10th St, Williamsburg, Bklyn) 718-384-6901 (Williamsburg: L to Bedford)
www.buffaloexchange.com
I was almost sad when I learned that this vintage chain was opening an outpost in NYC, because it robs me of the touristic thrill of going there when I'm in Berkeley, LA, or Austin. Except not really, because the NYC stuff is just as good. Apparently there are no geographic boundaries when it comes to young actors and college students buying more clothes than they can possibly wear, until it gets so bad, they have to cash in a hundred pounds worth to make room for more. I cannot speak highly enough of the buyers' bedside manner. They reject pretty much everything I drag in, but do so with an attitude of wistful regret, as if the only reason they aren't taking it is some sort of seasonal overload. – AH (It's pretty much like Buffalo Exchange everywhere, but they still have '50s retro shirts. – Josh Medsker)

HORACE GREELY

No Relation

204 1st Ave (btwn 12th St & 13th St) 212-228-5201
novintage.wordpress.com (East Village: L to 1st Ave)
Moving up the food chain, No Relation is clean, bright, and packed to its hipster gills with racks upon racks of well-organized variety. Apres-ski? Pin monkey? Square dancing? Boogie Nights? What mood are we in today? I bought my favorite cowboy shirt here for ten bucks. There's a little room filled with just shoes, and another that's all leather coats. The salesmen claim they get all their neat stuff at estate sales, possibly to underline their policy of not giving cash or credit to customers rolling up with old clothes.

Rags a Go Go

218 W 14th St (btwn 7th & 8th Ave) 646-486-4011
www.joshuasuzanne.com (Chelsea: A/C/E/L to 14th St-8th Ave)
This is a unisex emporium, where NYU frat boys come to deck themselves out in fashion trends created by (and looking much hotter on) butch lesbians. Think trucker hats and My Little Pony t-shirts. It does a body good to see the stuffed animals stapled up as decorations. Get a discount for answering the Question of the Day, posted on the store's Twitter account (reachable via owner Joshua Suzanne's website).

Reminiscence
50 W 23rd St (btwn 5th & 6th Ave) 212-243-2292
www.reminiscence.com (Flat Iron: F to 23rd St)
Back in the day, I used to go here for their signature
baggy, canvas overalls, which I wore when in lieu of ma-
ternity clothes. They also have plenty of low budge costume jewelry, cigarette cases, and other such gew gaws.
My most pleasurable find of recent years was the kid-size
marching band jacket that completed my daughter's cigarette girl costume one Halloween. Reminiscence is also
a reliable East Coast supplier of *Simpsons* ephemera and
the Archie Mcphee catalog's line of boxing nun puppets,
bacon band-aids, Librarian action figures, etc, etc.

Beacons Closet
88 N 11th (btwn Berry & Wythe, Williamsburg, Bklyn)
718-486-0816 (Williamsburg: L to Bedford Ave)
&
92 5th Ave (@ Warren St, Park Slope, Bklyn) 718-230-1630
(Park Slope: 2/3 to Bergen St)
www.beaconscloset.com
I shop at Beacons Closet in Billysburg, Brooklyn partly
because every now and then you'll run across some art-
student-wanna-be-ironic-hipster's fashion ridiculous-
ness for cheapo. – Matana Roberts (Play hooky and go on
a weekday though—it gets mobbed on weekends. – Dear
Drunk Girl)

Shop the Ops (*aka* Thames & Bocker)
96 Knickerbocker Ave (btwn Thames and Grattan, Bushwick, Bklyn) 718-497-1331 (Bushwick: L to Morgan)
The *ropa usada* here is a bit unusual in that it's got tags
and is 100% pit-stain free. Why? Because it's not *usada*
at all! It's brand spankin' new! The labels invariably lead
back to Old Navy, Target, Delia's...but even those whose
greatest sartorial fear is being mistaken for a member
of the mainstream can strike it rich here. Cash only, so
bring a wad or suffer the ATM fees at the bodega across
the street.

The Urban Jungle Vintage/Thrift Warehouse
120 Knickerbocker Ave (btwn Flushing and Thames,
Bushwick, Bklyn) 718-497-1331
www.urbanjunglevintage.com (Bushwick: L to Morgan Ave)
I will give you a lifetime subscription to my zine if you
can convince one of the employees of this massive, wonderful thrift store to scale the walls for the Ask Me About
My Hiney t-shirt they've put up as "decoration." I've asked
three times, and every time the response is negatory. If
you can't make it all the way out to Bushwick, comfort
yourself at its Manhattan cousin, No Relation.

Re/Dress NYC - Vintage & Resale Boutique
109 Boerum Pl (btwn Dean and Pacific, Boerum Hill,
Bklyn) 718-522-7962
www.redressnyc.com (Boerum Hill: F/G to Bergen St)
This plus-size vintage palace is the new kid on the shopping block, but already it's my number one favorite
clothing store in NYC. The proprietress Miss Deb and her
incredible staff cherry pick only the best stuff brought
in for cash or store credit by their fatshionista clientele,
and then resell it at super reasonable prices. – Emily Rems
(The staff's gracious about letting ladies with skimpier
proportions nibble on giraffe-print ankle boots, arresting
chapeaux and femme fatale bags. They sell *Fatshionista*,
a clothes positive, size positive zine. One of the editors
works here! They host occasional events like craft fairs
and fitness classes. – AH)

Church ladies thrift (no real name)
On the corner of Marcus Garvey and Putnam in Bedford-
Stuyvesant, Bklyn
(Bed-Stuy: C to Kingston-Throop Aves)
There's no real name for this place. When I inquired they
looked at me kind of funny, so I guess it's a secret. Really
nice things here though, kind of like an old-school ladies'
bazaar, and it's right down the street from my favorite
Bed-Stuy café, Food 4 Thought. Bed-Stuy's motto used to
be Bed-Stuy, Do Or Die, but now it's more like Bed-Stuy,
Do & Thrive! – Matana Roberts

Thrift Stores

Ditmars Thrift Shop Donation Corp
3120 Ditmars Blvd (@32nd St, Astoria, Queens)
718-545-2529 (Astoria: N to Ditmars Blvd)
Ditmars Thrift Shop is amazing. They have cheap, fun
t-shirts, and lotsa records! I just got a mess of vinyl for a
buck-fifty each! We got Poison, some Mahler, Schubert,
and...(wait for it) *Phantasmagoria* by The Damned. Hell to
the yeah. – Josh Medsker

Cabrini Thrift Store
520 Main St (north of the subway & tramway, Roosevelt
Island) 212-486-8958
(Roosevelt Island: F to Roosevelt Island)
NYC thrift stores tend to be overpriced and picked
through, but this one is like a thrift store in another city,
cheap, with a feeling that people like you haven't already
been there and gotten the things you'd want. – Esther Smith

Flash & the Furious Five • Avenue B – Gogol Bordello

Score!
www.scoredatscore.com
But enough of these tiresome monetary transactions!
Score is a roving pop-up swap event, a chance to cash in
on someone else's misfires, while simultaneously ridding
yourself of yours. After you've ponied up your $3 entry fee
and dropped any donations you may have schlepped with
you at the receiving table, you're free to gambol through
the various "departments," helping yourself to whatever
happens to catch your eye. If you're shy about digging
in, music and libations should get you in the mood.
Rock and Wrap It Up, an anti-poverty "think tank" that
distributes donations to worthy non-profits throughout the city, will make sure even the most misfit of this
event's leftover goods lands in a good home. There's neither obligation nor financial incentive to donating castoffs
of your own, but for those with a well-developed sense of
self worth, it can be pretty amusing to eavesdrop on the
comments as your stuff mulches to the top of the pile.

New Clothes
Don't worry, we're not going to put you on a bus to the
outlet mall.

Century 21
2 Cortlandt St (btwn Broadway & Church) 212-227-9092
(Financial District: A/C/J/Z/2/3/4/5 to Fulton St-Broadway-
Nassau)
&
472 86th St (btwn 4th Ave & 5th Ave, Bay Ridge, Bklyn)
718-748-3266, www.c21stores.com (Bay Ridge: R to 86th St)
I would say I average a visit here once every four years,
when I need a bathing suit that will make me feel toler-
ably foxy from a minimum of three angles. Which is to
say an expensive one, but c'mon, I'm not going to pay a
hundred bucks! So I go to Century 21, and marvel anew
at all the designer clothes and all the foreign tourists
weighed down with more packages than they can possibly
pack onto an airplane. I bought my last watch here for
5.99 and it is still ticking.

CFG Boutique
129 Walker St (btwn Baxter & Centre St) 917-237-0688
www.cfgboutique.com
(Chinatown: J/N/Q /R/Z/6 to Canal St)
I have nothing in my life to justify the purchase of a sequined Suzie Wong-style *cheongsam* featuring the Manhattan skyline, but perhaps you do. I would love it if someone I
knew actually bought and wore such a garment.

New Era Factory Outlet
63 Orchard St (@ Grand) 800-875-4959
www.newdresssuits.com (LES: B/D to Grand)
If I were a man in the market for some natty threads, I
would totally go here instead of Brooks Brothers. Doesn't
a lifetime of drab plumage seem like the kind of thing
that could bum you out on your deathbed? Besides,
nothing commands respect more than the confident
sporting of a banana colored suit with matching fedora
and contrasting pocket square. A bright purple, double-
breasted dress suit goes for about $60 here, a matching
bowler takes the ensemble up to an even Benjamin,
and long-coated zoot suits, which come with vests, are
around $130. You can find many retailers offering this
sort of eye-popping menswear along Brooklyn's Fulton
Mall (take the 2/3 to Hoyt St), but New Era offers the sort
of attentive, small-shop-type service a gentleman such as
yourself deserves.

Moo Shoes
78 Orchard St (btwn Broome & Grand) 212-254-6512
www.mooshoes.com (LES: F/J/M/Z to Delancey-Essex)
Vegans are no longer the red-headed step-children of New
York city's over-the-top shoe shopping! They have high
heels even, everything but leather and the slaughterhouse
glue that's been known to bind entirely innocent-looking
canvas to seemingly virtuous rubber! Hopefully, your
love of animals extends to cats, because they've got some
on premises.

Orchard Corset Center
157 Orchard St (btwn Rivington St & Stanton St)
212-674-0786
www.orchardcorset.com (LES: F/J/M/Z to Delancey-Essex)
If your girls swing low, the three of you should go on a
date with the no-nonsense staff of the Orthodox-owned
Orchard Corset Center. They'll size you up with a glance,
rummage around in the bins behind the counter, then
herd you into the stock room with a couple of serious-
looking bras. A couple of minutes later, one of the experts
will be back to yank on your straps, criticize your hook
setting, and show you how to adjust your nipples to keep
both headlights trained on the road. Truly, this is one of
the most womanly experiences you can have in New York
City, even if your purchase is rung up by a bearded Orthodox man in glasses and a white long-sleeved shirt. The
price ($25? $30?) may be higher than you're accustomed
to paying for your bras, but it is worth it for the experience and for the integrity of your rack.

Live Fast
57 Clinton St (btwn Stanton & Rivington) 212-228-8863
www.livefastnyc.com (LES: F/J/M/Z to Delancey-Essex)
If you like punk/skater type clothes... – Victoria Law

Trash and Vaudeville
4 St Marks Pl (btwn 2nd Ave & 3rd Ave) 212-982-3590
(East Village: 6 to Astor Pl)
Knee-high stilettos with built-in riding crop holsters?
Purple net petticoats, vinyl Merry Widows, Adam Ant
jackets, and gauntlets? Low-rise tartan bondage trousers?
They've got it all. Definitely enlist the help of dandyish,
bone thin salesman Jimmy, once the subject of a *New
Yorker* profile. Jimmy is a New York treasure!

The Sock Man
27 St. Mark's Pl (btwn 2nd and 3rd Ave) 212-529-0300
www.thesockman.com (East Village: 6 to Astor Pl)
You can get the striped socks favored by Trixie the *Dead-
wood* hooker and myself at cheap chains like Strawberry
and Forever 21, but there's a certain Zen symmetry to
buying socks from a vendor who sells nothing but. (I'm
willing to overlook the handful of garter belts and fetishy
vinyl items in back.) The guy manning the *al fresco* counter fronting the shop is unfailingly jolly, whatever the
weather, but you've got to plumb the climate-controlled
interior for specialty stuff like tattoo print hosiery, bow-
trimmed thigh highs, and split toe *tabi* socks.

Enz's
125 2nd Ave (btwn 7th St & St Mark's Pl) 917-841-5989
www.enzsnyc.com (East Village: 6 to Astor Pl)
Enz's is a tiny little shop that turns 21st century women
into hot '50s tomatoes and their male counterparts into
the sort of tough monkeys who've got exactly that sort of
gal tattooed on their forearms. The only thing is, Enz's
marks their goods up like 50 bucks. And I hear the owner
gets wicked pissed if you try things on in her store, then
sneak off to your computer to buy it elsewhere. Maybe
time it for the end of the season and hit the sale rack.

Jillery
88 E. 10th St (btwn 3rd & 4th Ave) 212-674-9383
www.jillery.com (East Village: 6 to Astor Pl)
I've got to applaud owner Jill Fagan for making a go of it
by chopping up and reassembling costume jewelry on one
of the East Village's least inspiring blocks, but her website
does not do justice to the store. At all. If you're done playing dress up with the unstrung, broken clasped junk at
the bottom of your jewelry box, make an appointment to
sell it to Jill. Use the proceeds to buy something up-cycled
and one-of-a-kind.

Content • Crack Rock Steady • Choking Victim •

Vampire Freaks
189 Ave A (btwn 11th and 12th St) 212-505-VAMP
www.vampirefreaks.com (East Village: L to 1st Ave)
The people who work here are the sweetest salesclerks
ever, and I don't think they'd mind me saying so! Surrounded by skulls and spikes, they're given to say things
like "the weatherman said that there's snow coming" and
"I ate the best caramel turtle ever when I went to New
Jersey last weekend!" I love them. I also love their striped
socks, steam punk goggles, and this shiny vinyl miniskirt
attached via a network of straps to animalistic craft fur
leggings. As a community hub for the local goth/industri-
al scene, they carry music and magazines from as far off
as Australia. It's my go to spot whenever I need goggles
for my author photo.

Tokyo Rebel
170 Ave B (btwn 10th St & 11th St)
www.tokyorebel.com (East Village: L to 1st Ave)
So tiny, it could just about fit in the doll-sized purse
dangling from a Gothic Lolly's beribboned, lace-trimmed
wrist. If you're going for the full-on look, better search
the consignment rack in the back, because this shit ain't
cheap. It is fascinating, though. Even the brand names...
Angelic Pretty, Atelier-Pierrot, Innocent World, SEX POT
ReVeNGe...The owners pride themselves on carrying the
real Harajuku deal, straight from Japan. For a further eyeful, pick up a copy of KERA, the Japanese fashion monthly
that inspired the Gothic & Lolita Bible.

Halloween Adventure
104 4th Ave (btwn 11th & 12th St) 212-673-4546
www.newyorkcostumes.com
(East Village: L/N/Q /R/4/5/6 to Union Square)
Beware the crowds in October and the ghoulier-than-thou
staff, but as far as your dress-up needs go, Halloween
Adventure's got you covered year-round. For those too
anemic to toddle the six or so blocks to Religious Sex on
St Mark's Place, Gothic Renaissance right next door has a
good supply of velvet cloaks, lurid thigh highs, and those
bondage-y evening gowns favored by the undead.

Girl Props
153 Prince St (btwn Broadway & Thompson) 212-505-7615
www.girlprops.com (SoHo: C/E to Spring St)
I don't "like" shopping but it's fun to think of this place
blowing some kid's mind. Besides, there's always some
switchblade-carrying neo-burlesque accessory to be
found among the feather boas, ice cube-sized cocktail
rings, rhinestone chokers, and Plexiglass bangles. When
Inky got her ears pierced, I treated her to some dirt cheap

earrings shaped like subway tokens and the Statue of
Liberty's torch hand.

Shoe shopping on W 8th St
(Greenwich Village: A/B/C/D/E/F/M to W 4th St)
The Village boasts some of the best shoe shopping in the
world along 8th Street. The main drag of shoe shops runs
between Broadway and Sixth Avenue, with the highest
concentration coming as you approach Sixth Avenue.
I've been buying shoes here since I was 14, I've gradually
learned that the better the prices, the worse the selection
and vice versa. – Josh Saitz

H&M
111 5th Ave (@ 18th St) 212-539-1741
(Union Square: L/N/Q /R/4/5/6 to Union Sq)
&
125 W 125th St (btwn 7th Ave & Lenox) 212-665-8300
Harlem: A/C/B/D/2/3 to 125th St
&
1328 Broadway (@34th St) 646-473-1165
(Garment District: B/D/F/M/N/Q /R to 34th St)
&
150 E. 86th St (@ Lexington Ave) 212-289-1724
(Upper East Side: 4/5/6 to 86th St)
&
435 7th Ave (@34th St) 212-643-6955
(Garment District: 1/2/3 to 34th St)
&
505 5th Ave (@ 42nd St) 212-661-7012
(Midtown: S/4/5/6/7 to 42nd St-Grand Central)
&
640 5th Ave (@ 51st Street) 212-489-0390
(Midtown: B/D/F/M to 47-50th St-Rockefeller Center)
&
731 Lexington Ave (@ 59th St) 212-935 6781
(Midtown: N/R/4/5/6 to 59th St-Lexington Ave)
&
558 Broadway (Btwn Prince St & Spring St) 212-343-2722
(SoHo: R to Prince St)
&
515 Broadway (btwn Spring and Broome) 212-965-8975
(SoHo: R to Prince St)
www.hm.com/us
Yeah, it's a chain, but it's a Swedish chain, and besides,
I'd be a pantyfree hypocrite were I to leave it out. If the
clothes that looked so cool on home soil betrayed themselves as hayseeds upon NYC splashdown, a trendy, inexpensive, poorly-sewn garment may be the quick fix you
need. Also good to hit if you've forgotten your mittens.

Peachfrog
136 N 10th St (btwn Bedford & Barry, Williamsburg, Bklyn)
718-387-3224
www.peachfrog.com (Williamsburg: L to Bedford Ave)
Not a restaurant as Monty Python would have us think.
It's more of an indie TJ Maxx, prescreened for the non-scruffy Billysburg bargain-hunter, and placed in a non-mallish, Beacon's Closet-y setting. The friendly owner makes it a point to welcome everyone with his fashion-conscious dog, who sports a different daily accessory. Men's and women's offerings include dress shirts in funky colors, fancy shoes, cashmere sweaters, and glamorous, colorful bras displayed like bon-bons, for $10 bucks a pop.

Zapteria Mexico
4505 5th Ave Brooklyn, 718-851-4074
And here I thought I'd have to haul it all the way to Austin Texas for cowboy boots. Be sure and grab some Mexican food while you're in the neighborhood.

CANDY STORES
The fistfuls of lemon drops we fling at the Mermaid Parade crowds come from the 99¢ store. The trick or treaters of brownstone Brooklyn get fun-size whatevers from the drugstore. But there's a certain charm to buying candy from an actual candy store.

Aji Ichiban
37 Mott Street (btwn Mosco & Pell) 212-233-7650
(Chinatown: J/N/Q /R/Z/6 to Canal St)
&
23 E Broadway (btwn Market & Catherine) 212-571-3755
(Chinatown: F to East Broadway)
&
167 Hester St (btwn Elizabeth & Mott) 212-925-1133
(Little Italy: B/D to Grand St)
Several Tokyo-born friends scoff that this Hong Kong based chain is doing a lame job of trying to pass themselves off as Japanese, but you could've fooled me. A lot of the thrill here is in the packaging, which is never the same from visit to visit.

Economy Candy
145 Rivington (btwn Essex & Ludlow) 800-352-4544
www.economycandy.com (LES: F/J/M/Z to Delancey-Essex St)
I dig Economy for being one of those tough New York City places that sells things dear to children without fawning all over them. It's packed to the rafters and claustrophobic as hell. You'll likely knock a tub of Chupa Chups on your neighbor's head when you go up on tiptoe to reach

that giant Homer Simpson Pez dispenser. Don't think that fumbling in your wallet is going to earn you an understanding smile from the grouch waiting to take your money. Licorice connoisseurs will fall to their knees from the sheer variety displayed behind the counter. – AH

Raul Candy Store
205 Ave B (@ E 13th St) (East Village: L to 1stAve)
Raul's has a somewhat intimidating, not-entirely-open-to-the-public vibe. Once you get past the Xeroxed warnings about bad batches of crack cocaine posted in the window, and the random paperbacks and other secondhand flotsam placed stoop sale style on the sidewalk, there's shockingly little to buy except candy and gum, sold the old-fashioned way, one piece at a time from a Plexiglas honeycomb. You tell the shopkeeper what you want and he gets it for you.

Dylan's Candy Bar
1011 3rdAve (@60thSt) 646)-735-0078
www.dylanscandybar.com
(Upper East Side: N/R/4/5/6 to 59thSt-Lexington Ave)
I'm not feeling it. It's all a bit too self-consciously precious and Willy Wonka for me. Light-up plastic stairs encasing actual candy, arranged to spell out a sweet motto or two? Autographed, Plexiglas boxes in which celebrities place their favorites? Dolled-up, sugar-crazed 5 year olds swinging $50 goodie bags as they exit the private party room? No thank YOU! Still, Dylan, who, dish, dish, just happens to be Ralph Lauren's daughter, does stock pretty much every still-available confection that an American child might conceivably have fixated upon in the last 50 years, including gummi bras and edible posing pouches made from the same pastel beads they use in candy necklaces. It's a fun place to lay in supplies before a matinee at the Big Cinemas, though the nearby Duane Reade is guaranteed cheaper.

KITCHEN SINK

You don't have to drop so much as a Coney Island batting cage token at the following stores. It's fun enough just to browse.

Hua Mei Imports and Exports
120 East Broadway (@ Pike St) 212-748-1278
(Chinatown: F to East Broadway)
It's hard to get past the sidewalk display of stone ball-spinning, dry ice-spilling, bonsai and bridge trimmed fountains. When you feel you can, drag your eyeballs inside where there are unbelievably cheap, unbelievably

Officer Munn (aka Lurch is a Bastard) by Sewage

thumping workout at Great New York Noodletown to the specialty griddles that would enable a home chef to make the tiny cakes available from nearby street carts (though, why, when they come 20 to the dollar in a little wax paper sack?)

Babeland
94 Rivington (btwn Essex & Orchard) 212-375-1701
(LES: F/J/M/Z to Delancey-Essex)
&
43 Mercer (btwn Broome St & Grand St) 212-966-2120
(Park Slope: 2/3/4 to Bergen)
&
462 Bergen St (btwn 5th Ave & Flatbush Ave, Park Slope, Bklyn) 718-638-3820
(Park Slope: 2/3/4/5/M/N/Q/R/B/D to Atlantic Ave-Pacific Ave)
www.babeland.com
If you need something a touch more heavy duty than the rotating lollypop holders available at nearby Economy Candy, head to this woman-owned sex toy emporium, where the staff is much more customer service oriented. They've test driven pretty much every vibrating wang dang doodle on the market, and can tell you what's appropriate for use in the hot tub vs. the airplane bathroom. They also stock slippery stuff, batteries, videos, books, and condoms (including the jet black ones one of the owners recommends as an economical way to give your favorite non-human phallus a "butch, fetish-y" makeover.

Make Up Mania
182 Allen St (btwn Houston & Stanton) 212-533-5900
www.makeupmania.com (LES: F to 2nd Ave)
I'm too lazy and inconsistent for make-up, but I've a nose-to-the-window fondness for this subway-car-shaped storefront, whose front wall is basically all window. It seems like shopping here would be an improvement on grabbing a tube of Maybelline off a rack at Rite-Aid. Certainly better than navigating the bewildering gauntlet that is Macy's cosmetics floor. I particularly like gazing in from the sidewalk after sunset, when the reflection of the cabs and buses heading north on Allen takes my breath away.

Exit 9
64 Ave A (btwn 4th St & 5th St) 212-228-0145
(East Village: F to 2nd Ave)
&
127 Smith St (btwn Pacific & Dean, Boerum Hill, Bklyn) 718-422-7720 (Boerum Hill: F/G to Bergen St)
www.shopexit9.com
Nothing here is overtly hand-made but you can tell the owners swing that way, given all the crafty books. They

tiny figurines to further accessorize the tasteful insanity of your fountain. Taped birdsong provides a subliminal sales pitch for ornate bamboo birdcages, not too much more expensive than the paper lanterns next to which they hang. Pretty much any time you go, you can count on some guy with a bunch of little cartons spread out on newspaper, eating lunch on the selling floor. During Chinese New Year celebrations, Hua Mei's sidewalk area is a prime spot for vendors selling tissue paper cannons and sawdust-packed street poppers for half of what they're going for in the more touristic Western sector.

Hung Chong Imports
14 Bowery (bwtn Pell & Doyers St) 212-349-1463
(Chinatown: B/D to Grand St)
I have a weakness for restaurant supplies. They're all over the Bowery and Chinatown, but I'm particularly partial to Hung Chong, because the staff is really nice about letting non-pros browse, and they have everything from the serious cleavers and cutting boards getting a constant

ON THE Q-TRAIN,
IT'S TOUGH TO DECIDE:
SHOULD YOU LOOK UP AT
THE JET PLANES OR DOWN
AT THE ROW HOUSES?

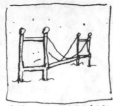

THE MANHATTAN
BRIDGE FEELS
LEFT OUT.

THE OLD McGRAW-
HILL BLDG. EATS
TWO POWDERED
DONUTS!

WHEN NO
ONE ELSE
IS GLAD
TO SEE
YOU, THE
WOOLWORTH
BLDG. IS!

THE CITICORP
BLDG. KEEPS
SHOWING UP IN
SKATER
BOYS'
DREAMS.

ACTUALLY, THE TWIN
TOWERS GET
ALONG REALLY WELL.

fit right in with the children's paint sets from Europe, all the cunning cards and stationery, and the home décor tchotchkes I'm always hoping people who feel obliged to give me a present but don't know me very well will give me. Among their Archie McPhee-generated items is the Avenging Unicorn Playset my son is so obsessed with (it comes with a skewer-able mime).

Sustainable NYC
139 Ave A (btwn St Mark's Pl & 9th St) 212-254-5400
www.sustainable-nyc.com (East Village: 6 to Astor Pl)
The greenest people I know aren't necessarily springing for organic cotton linens and those bamboo picnic plates that cost more than the entire picnic. Who's buying this stuff? Go to Brownsville or Crown Heights, and tell me how many boutiques are doing a brisk business in whimsical hemp baby toys shaped like rain forest animals. Know what I mean? Rant aside, it does seem that Sustainable NYC's heart's in the right place. I really am all for inner tubes, Metrocards, junk mail, and drink pouches going to the ball as jewelry, wallets, i-Pod cases, and lip balm, I guess I just fantasize that we'll all find the time, inclination, and creativity to upcycle them ourselves, for you know, pennies. (Sustainable NYC hosts monthly classes toward that end.) The morning shift people at the café in back have always been perfectly lovely to me at 8am, when few other East Village businesses are open, much less with free wifi.

Toy Tokyo
91 2nd Ave (btwn 5th & 6th St) 212-673-5424
www.toytokyo.com (East Village: F to 2nd Ave)
Every time I go in here, I regret my failure to buy the *Simpsons* bathtub plug and chicken nuggets shaped like Bart's head that I ran across overseas. Fool that I was, I prided myself on not loading up on souvenirs I didn't need. Now they would be collectible! Toy Tokyo is a clearing house for Wallace and Grommit...Snoopy...Astro Boy...the little goth guys from *The Nightmare Before Christmas*...and other highly valued characters, some of whom are little known on our shores. Some of the rarer items can ratchet up the ol' wallet, but someone has kindly (and wisely) decided to stock a bunch of items that punch in well below the $10 mark, too. Blind boxes galore! Hooray!

A Repeat Performance
156 1st Ave (btwn 9th & 10th St) 212-529-0832
www.repeatperformancenyc.com
(East Village: L to 1st Ave.)
An East Village mainstay for over 25 years, this tiny antiques store is crammed with endlessly fascinating ephemera from days gone by. Truly there is no better place to nab a to-die-for retro lamp, a deliciously dated typewriter, or a musical instrument that looks like it's clocked some hours on the road. But usually, I just stop by to browse and chat with the store's delightful boss ladies Sharon Jane Smith and Beverly Bronson, two rockin' women who, for the last decade, have been using proceeds from the store to support Ghar Sita Mutu, a

entire Rent soundtrack • Crazy Rhythms (the

home Beverly founded for abandoned children in Nepal. – Emily Rems

Surprise, Surprise
91 3rd Ave (@12th St) 212-777-0990
www.surprisesurprise.com (East Village: L to 3rd Ave)
Those of you who aren't staying on the floor of a friend's luxurious Ave C studio walk-up may have yet to figure out how *anyone* can survive in a 340-square foot apartment, let alone someone with roommates or more than one child. This store sheds some light on how we manage. Most of us may not have the funds or inclination to spring for a folding dish rack that looks like it's part of the US space program, but it is kind of nifty to get a gander at how these cunningly-equipped things double as magnetic bulletin boards or i-Pod docks. I bought the world's skinniest trashcan here, once upon a time.

Pearl River Mart
477 Broadway (btwn Grand and Broome) 212-431-4770
www.pearlriver.com (SoHo: J/N/Q /R/Z/6 to Canal St)
The uber Chinese tchotchke store! – David Goren (Browse through the bizarre household product section or the fantastic figurine and toy sections. – Robyn Jordan) (Upstairs it's all hardwood floors, high ceilings, embroidered baby shoes, fancy tea sets, beautiful floral fabric, and Suzie Wong. The downstairs comes nearer to the cluttered feel of the old Canal Street location, and is where you'll find flimsy undershirts, Hell Bank Notes, novelty alarm clocks, paper parasols, Bee & Flower Brand soap, cheap dishes, and the Double Horse Brand wadded silk comforter I give thanks for nightly. – AH) (I find lots of cute kitchen-y things that no one really needs but everyone really wants, like a red metal thermos with a hot pink flower or a set of stacking lunch tins. – Amanda Plumb)

Evolution
120 Spring St (btwn Greene and Mercer), 212-343-1114
www.theevolutionstore.com (SoHo: R to Prince St)
Quit whining, or Mommy's going to take you to the store that has real skulls, taxidermy animals, and lollipops with scorpions and worms trapped in them! – AH (If you need a raccoon penis bone, you can get it here. – Kate Black)

Kiosk
95 Spring St, 2nd fl (btwn Broadway & Mercer)
212-226-8601, www.kioskkiosk.com (SoHo: R to Prince St)
It's hidden upstairs and around a corner, with little or no outdoor signage. You have to know it's there. The owners curate a small and interesting collection of goods from a chosen region, and each display model on the floor has a tag explaining what's so special about that item. The region changes. The first time I went here, their theme was Florida, and everything they featured was made in Florida, from artist-made objects to orange-flavored penny candy. – Kate Black

The Village Chess Shop
230 Thompson St (btwn 3rd St & Bleecker)
212-475-9580, www.chess-shop.com
(Greenwich Village: A/B/C/D/E/F/M to W 4th St)
Want to immerse yourself in a small slice of Greenwich Village past? Go to the Village Chess Shop. It's been here since 1972 and it still doesn't have air-conditioning. You can buy chess sets here, yes, but the primary objective is not to sell you some novelty board with pieces painted like *American Idol* contestants or world leaders. Come here with time to kill. You can play pick-up for $2 an hour or just hang around watching the ones in progress. (No cussing—they'll fine you nearly twice the hourly rate!) They don't spurn beginners—chess has honed their patience. Many of the regulars have been coming for decades.

Flight 001
96 Greenwich Ave (btwn 12th St & Jane St) 212-989-0001
(Greenwich Village: A/C/E/L to 14th St-8th Ave)
&
132 Smith St (btwn Dean & Bergen, Boerum Hill, Bklyn)
718-243-0001
(Boerum Hill: F/G to Bergen St)
www.flight001.com
I can't imagine myself ever paying for a luggage tag. I also have a natural suspicion of any store that looks like a conference room of the *Starship Enterprise*, but I do get a bang out of inspecting all the latest travel gadgets here. I would only ever buy gifts here—my friend Karen got a bright orange piece of plastic that folds out into a cereal bowl.

Tah-Poozie
50 Greenwich Ave (btwn Perry & Charles) 212-647-0668
(Greenwich Village: 1/2/3 to 14th St)
Tah-Poozie is the place for crazy wind-up toys, Slinkys, and goofy pretty things. – Jessica Max Stein (I just turned to the internets to confirm Tah-Poozie's coordinates, and discovered that the name means to "masturbate to orgasm, while pooping at the same time." Uh...they have an abundant supply of greeting cards, too. – AH)

C.O. Bigelow Pharmacy
414 Ave of the Americas (btwn 8th & 9th St) 212-533-2700
www.bigelowchemists.com
(Greenwich Village: A/B/C/D/E/F/M to West 4th St)

Downstairs is a historic, hideously expensive pharmacy specializing in the sorts of beautifully packaged toiletries that keep European women and babies so timelessly chic and sun damage free. Upstairs is a frill-free bonanza of nifty items to ease a traveler's life. Just think how convenient it would be to have a leak-proof disposable urinal in your backpack the next time nature calls. Don't forget the no rinse shampoo, gel inserts, blister kits, and Velcro strap buggy hooks to hang all over your bike. (The door to the much less historic-looking upstairs is out on the sidewalk, just north of the fancy pharm. Ring to be let up. If you can't figure it out, go ask the pharmacist downstairs.)

New York Cake and Baking Distributors
56 W 22nd (btwn 5th Ave & Avenue Of The Americas) 212-675-2253, www.nycake.com (Chelsea: F to 23rd St)
Just because our kitchens are the size of your bathtub doesn't mean we're not drawn to the creative possibilities of crystallized violets, IV bags full of lurid frosting, and the Bar Mitzvah Boy with Torah lollipop mold—a steal at $2.50!

Butala Emporium
108 East 28th St (btwn Lexington & Park Ave)
212-684-4447 (Gramercy Park: R to 28th St)
&
37-46 74th St (btwn 37th Ave & 37th Rd, Jackson Heights, Queens) 718-899-5590
(Jackson Hts: E/F/M/R/7 to 74th St-Roosevelt Ave)
www.indousplaza.com
When I get a yen to go back to India, I head for Jackson Heights. After a snack, I'm ready to hit up Butala and just wander around looking at all the stuff they sell, some ordinary, some exotic. Some dhoop sticks, a CD, or a postcard of Hanuman is usually souvenir enough for me.

The Compleat Strategist
11 E 33rd St (btwn Madison & 5th Ave) 212-685-3880
www.thecompleatstrategist.com
(Murray Hill: 6 to 33rd St)
A solid game store that has a full range of recent role-playing games and magazines as well as any other kind of game you could think of, including a great selection of military strategy games and adult (not erotic) card games. The store's a little cluttered, so if you're looking for something or have a question, ask. Most nights they're only open until 6pm, but Thursday is game night, when folks gather to play various games in the back room or basement until 9pm. The spirit of gaming is alive and well. – Heath Row

Ricky's
375 Broadway (btwn Franklin & White) 212-925-5490 (Year round costume superstore)
(Tribeca: J/N/Q /R/Z/6 to Canal St)
&
590 Broadway (btwn Houston & Prince) 212-226-5552
(SoHo: R to Prince St)
&
44 E. 8th St (btwn Greene & University Pl) 212-254-5247
(Greenwich Village: R to 8th St)
&
466 Avenue of the Americas (btwn 11 th & 12 th St) 212-924-3401 (Greenwich Village: A/C/E/B/D/F/M to W 4th St)
&
111 3rd Ave (btwn 13 th & 14 th St) 212-674-9640
(East Village: L to 3rd Ave)
&
Other locations too numerous to list here. Look 'em up!
www.rickys-nyc.com
My favorite hair supply store is Ricky's. They sell grooming accessories, sex toys, and dozens of dye colors, and they also have the most expensive and diverse collection of hair-care products in the city. If you need to spend

about NYC but it feels like a time capsule of

$25 for a little tub of some weird foreign gunk, this is the store for you. – Josh Saitz (Ricky's has everything the make-up and hair pros haul to the film set, as well as the tackle boxes they use to schlep it all there. They stock every shade of nail polish and lipstick ever invented, and sparkle encrusted, inch-long false eyelashes in an astonishing array of configurations. They have a side business in the raunchy crap Spencer Gifts was famous for in the late '70s and early '80s. Also your source for boob tape and those little silicone bean bag things you're supposed to stuff in your bra.

KCDC Skateshop
90 N 11th St (btwn Berry & Wythe, Williamsburg, Bklyn)
718-387-9006
www.kcdcskateshop.com (Williamsburg: L to Bedford Ave)
KCDC is the largest skateshop in NYC. Housed in this massive warehouse are a large selection of shoes, skateboard decks, clothing and a five-foot mini ramp. The staff skates and the space occasionally holds art shows. It is one of the few places to pick up a copy of the ever-awesome *Elk* zine, written by sometimes NYC resident and skate historian Jocko Weyland. – Jon Bocksel

FUEGO 718
249 Grand Street (btwn Driggs & Roebling, Williamsburg, Bklyn) 718-302-2913
www.fuego718.com (Williamsburg: L to Bedford Ave)
The owner, Alex, is the nicest man in Brooklyn and a joyous supporter of local artisans. There's something here for shoppers at every price point, from $1 postcards to handmade bags and sculptures upwards of several hundred. Most items hover in the $20-40 range. Jewelry, books, *Dia de los Muertos* sculptures, bamboo curtains, and the most extensive *milagro* selection in all five boroughs all have a home here. – Kate Black (Fuego 718 is my source for the embroidered patches I use to combat and cover any unsavory logos on my children's thrift store clothing. –AH)

Whisk
231 Bedford Ave (btwn N 3rd St & N 4th St, Williamsburg, Bklyn) 718-302-2913
www.whisknyc.com (Williamsburg: L to Bedford Ave)
Whisk is an incredibly well-stocked kitchen supply store geared toward enthusiastic home cooks. They sell a full range of Lodge cast iron cookware, one of the few brands still made in the USA. They also carry my favorite brands of French presses, hermetically sealed bottles (for homemade liqueurs), and a variety of small, useful tools, like candy thermometers and silicone basting brushes. The staff here is knowledgeable and friendly. Come here instead of Williams-Sonoma. Unless you're a professional, in which case the industrial kitchen shops on the Bowery are a better bet. – Kate Black

Kill Devil Hill
170 Franklin St (btwn Java St & Kent St, Greenpoint, Bklyn) 347-534-3088
www.myspace.com/killdevilhillny
(Greenpoint: G to Greenpoint)
Okay, so there are probably 30 other places in NYC where you can get mustache wax, old briefcases and vintage cowboy kitsch, but when I asked for a business card, the owner wrote the address on the back of a black and white snapshot, and had to look up his own store's phone number on his cell phone. That alone makes it one-of-a-kind, not to mention endearing!

The perfumed oil stores of Atlantic Avenue
From 4th Ave to Hoyt St, Boerum Hill, Bklyn
(Boerum Hill: B/D/M/N/R Q /2/3/4/5 to Atlantic Ave-Pacific St)
I'm intrigued as to why the majority of Middle Eastern groceries and restaurants wound up west of Court Street, while pretty much all of the stores that sell shea butter, black soap, perfumed oils, and the over the top fancy containers in which to store them are here by Target and the big mosque. I'm drawn to some of their auxiliary products, like Arabic alphabet charts and a big many-faced clock that helps you keep track of prayer times throughout the day. Start at the 4th Avenue end of things and wander down past Court to end the expedition at Sahadi's or the Yemen Café (though be forewarned that the barber next door is not allowed to cut ladies' hair). Stops on the way should include the Black Seed (#576), the Fertile Crescent (#570), Madina (#568 – for all your fancy fountain needs), Makka (#564), Al-Agsaq Inc (#556), Al Firdous (#490) Dar Es Salam (#486) and Anwaar (#354)

The Brooklyn Superhero Supply Company
372 5th Ave (btwn 5th St & 6th St, Park Slope, Bklyn)
718-499-9884
www.superherosupplies.com (Park Slope: F/G to 4th Ave)
Don't tell the Green Hornet, but it's really a front for 826NYC, a tuition-free writing center for kids (and teenagers who yearn to spend their summers writing novels). It's also the only place in the five boroughs where you can get cans of Matter, Anti-Matter, Invisibility, and Chaos, as well as grappling hooks, Gigantor gloves, and other items you may have noticed being marketed somewhat differently in the plumbing parts aisle of Home Depot. Leave

the city.)

yourself at least a half hour to read the hilarious signage, and be prepared to recite the Superhero Pledge to the volunteer salesclerk when making a purchase.

Brooklyn Homebrew
163 8th St (btwn 3rd & 4th Ave, Gowanus, Bklyn)
718-230-7600
www.brooklyn-homebrew.com (Gowanus: F/G to 4th Ave)
I'm so glad these guys got an actual store. I'd imagine selling hops, mash paddles, and carbonaters to the public out of your living room could take its toll on a marriage, and that's what they'd been doing. Danielle and Benjamin are trained chefs who turned their time-consuming hobby into a business when the restaurant where they'd both been working went belly up. They can talk you through the process or amp you up with supplies to take it to the next level.

Film Biz Recycling
43-26 12th St, 2nd fl (btwn 43rd Rd &43rd Ave, Long Island City, Queens) 718-392-3304
www.filmbizrecycling.org (LIC: E/M/G to LIC-Court Sq)
Film Biz Recycling is a nonprofit whose aim is reducing the waste, overconsumption, and ecologically unsound practices that are an unfortunate, and unnecessary byproduct of making movies, commercials, and the like. This mission is partly financed by having a shop set up to sell donated props, costumes, and set dressing to civilians like you and me. Make 'em an offer! Arrange a rental if you're a non-materialistic creative type whose only want is to use it in a film of your own.

The Little Soap Shop
2207 36th St (@ Ditmars Blvd, Astoria, Queens)
718-704-4408
www.thelittlesoapshop.net (Astoria: N to Ditmars Blvd)
The Little Soap Shop is a local gem. The owner, Vivian is hyper-friendly, and makes all organic soaps and bath products. My fave is the Eucalyptus bath soak. She also carries shaving kits. Go in to smell the goodness, and take a small sample. – Josh Medsker (Everything's vegan and bunny 'buse free! – AH)

FLEA MARKET
Like Macy's but previously owned, al fresco, and no Thanksgiving parades.

Antiques Garage
112 W 25th St (btwn 6th & 7th Ave) 212-243-5343
www.hellskitchenfleamarket.com (Chelsea: F/M to 23rd St)

Saturday & Sunday, year round
Head for this indoor parking garage when the weather turns foul. (Later, you can hop the $1 shuttle bus to Hell's Kitchen, to save your umbrella from turning inside out when you face into the wind). Things here are not as cheap as I have been trained to believe they should be but as my fleamarketeering is primarily of a museum-going nature, I don't mind. Besides, there's always some tattered old photo or comic within my price range. My apartment looks at me funny if I come home with anything much bigger than that.

Hell's Kitchen Flea Market
39th St (btwn 9th Ave & 10th Ave) 212-243-5343
www.hellskitchenfleamarket.com
(Hell's Kitchen: A/C/E to 42nd St)
Saturday & Sunday, year round
Like the Antiques Garage, the Hell's Kitchen Flea Market rose from the ashes of the famous flea market on 26th St. You can probably identify who are the designers assistants and *Vogue* staffers rooting around, looking for inspiration. I wait for the day a vintage flour sack will find its way onto a runway.

GreenFlea
The playground of MS 44
Columbus Ave between 76th & 77th St, 212-239-3025
www.greenfleamarkets.com (Upper West Side: B/C to 81st St)
Sundays year round
This is one of the oldest fleas in NYC. It's been holding down the same middle school playground for a quarter century, and prides itself on not letting little things like windchill and snow get in the way. It's got a good, old Upper West Side feel, possibly because there are plenty of neighbors for whom a poke around is a long-standing weekly tradition. The GreenFlea also hosts a small farmer's market, in case you need some cucumbers to go with those vintage canning jars you bought.

Artists & Fleas
125 & 129 N 6th St (btwn Bedford & Berry, Williamsburg, Bklyn)
Saturday & Sunday
&
Northwest corner of McCarren Park, Berry & N 12th
Saturday (seasonally)
www.artistsandfleas.com
(Williamsburg: L to Bedford Ave)
Unfortunately, the guy who used to make letterpress business cards on the blank side of used cereal box cardboard hasn't been seen in these parts for quite some time, but you can salve that heartbreak with some jewelry made

Bonus Animal Safari! NYC is crawling

out of old typewriter keys. I also like vendor Epoch Beads' vintage and vintage-looking selection. In the clothing department, modification seems to be the watchword. Actually, most of it's not my kind of ugly to begin with. Like the Brooklyn Flea, it's possible to throw your online hat into the vendor ring, if only for a day.

Brooklyn Flea
Bishop Loughlin Memorial High School
176 Lafayette Ave (@ Clermont, Fort Greene, Bklyn)
718-935-1052
(Fort Greene: C/G to Clinton-Washington Ave)
Saturday
&
The Williamsburg Savings Bank
1 Hanson Pl (@ Flatbush) 718-935-1052
(Fort Greene: B/D/M/N/Q /R/2/3/4/5 to Atlantic /Pacific)
Sunday
www.brooklynflea.com
Financially speaking, the best deal here is probably a plate of pupusas from the Red Hook Vendor's truck. Even if you end up keeping your wallet in your pants, it's fun to browse the racks of vintage clothing, handicrafts, and such locally-grown delicacies as Rick's Picks pickles, Mast Brothers chocolate, and Brooklyn Brew Shop homebrew kits. Every week, the Flea posts photos of a couple of vendor items on their website. If you're the lucky cuss who finds that vintage record or Scottie-shaped ceramic planter in the giant haystack of vendors' tables, it's yours to keep. The Flea accepts vendors on a daily basis, but you have to apply well in advance. Sunday's indoor Flea transpires inside a really cool (and phallic!) NYC landmark.

Brooklyn Indie Market
Smith Street @ Union St (Carroll Gardens, Bklyn)
718-499-3105, www.brooklynindicmarkct.com
(Carroll Gardens: F/G to Carroll St)
Saturdays: April – July, September-December
Sundays: April, May September-December
As a crafter, this is my favorite place to sell, hands down. The cooperative owners and all the other vendors are great. A lot of new folks get their start there. I always spend money there even when I don't earn any. I'm always open for a trade. – Andria Alefhi (I know the conventional wisdom is to hit these things early, but these vendors don't want to deprive themselves of brunch. Don't go before 11am.)

SOUVENIRS
We heart you and want you to get something better than a Statue of Liberty pencil sharpener.

New York City Store
Manhattan Municipal Building, 1 Center St (@Chambers)
212-NEW-YORK, www.a856-citystore.nyc.gov
(Financial District: 4/5/6 to Brooklyn Bridge-City Hall)
If you're getting hitched at the Manhattan Marriage Bureau, or playing Law & Order on the steps of the state Supreme Court, pop over to City Hall for some truly inventive New York City souvenirs, including a fine selection of NYCentric children's books, and a wide variety of Greek coffee cup and subway kitsch.

Lower East Side Tenement Museum Shop
108 Orchard St (@ Delancey) 212-982-8420
www.tenement.org/shop.html
(LES: F/J/M/Z to Delancey-Essex)
May we cut to the chase and declare the Lower East Side Tenement Museum t-shirt the best official Museum t-shirt in the history of Museum t-shirts? Based on a price list a cop fished from the pocket of a NYC tough over a hundred years ago, the front features a nose-bandaged sad sack and, splayed across the back, extremely reasonable fees for such acts as "stab" and "ear chawed off." This triumph of museum giftshoppery is rounded out with the usual compliment of subway and taxi gear. There's also a healthy selection of books focusing on NYC, the LES, and all the immigrant populations that have made their mark on the neighborhood over the years.

Fish's Eddy
889 Broadway (at 19th St.), 212-420-9020
www.fishseddy.com (Flatiron: R to 23rd St)
This crockery hot spot gained notice as a place to buy nifty dishes previously owned by airlines, hotels, executive dining rooms, and the like. A few barrels of that stuff remain, but their own Manhattan Blue Plate Special pat-

tern proved such a moneymaker they've beefed up their original product line with more such crowd pleasers. The skylines of Manhattan and Brooklyn. Architectural floor plans ranging from penthouse to studio. Urban "pedestrians," one of whom is a bicyclist. – AH (They also can ship anywhere in the world, so if you find something you like, have it sent to your home. Even if you can't go, you should check out their stuff. – Josh Saitz)

NYU Health Sciences bookstore
333 E 29th St (btwn 1st and 2nd Ave) 212-998-9990
www.bookstores.nyu.edu (Hill: M to 28th St)
Excuse me, doctor, but I'd be much more willing to let you proceed with the examination if you were wearing a surgical logo implying that you actually attended medical school. From what I hear, NYU is one of the best in the country. This branch stocks all sorts of fun props, too, like stuffed animal-shaped stethoscope sheaths, and pocket-sized cheat books to help get you through that emergency appendectomy.

NYPL gift shop
The New York Public Library Stephen A. Schwarzman Building (5th Ave & 42nd St) 212-930-0641, www.thelibraryshop.org
(Midtown: B/D/F/M/7 to 42nd St-Bryant Park)
There are lots of books here of course (maybe even this one!), as well as some classy vintage imagery of the Empire State building, the Chrysler building, and other such icons. You can bet your sweet bippy they're pimping those damn lions out on everything from mugs to paperweights to cufflinks and ties.

Video Cafe
697 9th Ave (between 44th &45th St) 212 765-6165
(Hell's Kitchen: C/E to 50th St-8th Ave)
This video store in Hell's Kitchen has an unaffiliated counter selling both Irish shamrock-trimmed and Puerto Rican-graffiti-tinged Hell's Kitchen hats and t-shirts as a favor to the owner's friend at KoolKat productions. Also shirts that say "Midtown." Now that is about as unfashionable a statement as it's possible to make in this town. I hope he sells a million of 'em!

Brooklyn Tattoo
99 Smith St (btwn Atlantic Ave and Pacific St) 718-643-1610
www.Brooklyntattoo.com (Boerum Hill: F/G to Bergen St)
Not so long ago, Artez'n, a little shop on Atlantic Avenue, was my wedding present hook up. Give 'em a Brooklyn Love martini shaker and a House of Dentention pint glass, and that union is sure to last! It was a sad day when Artez'n closed, but the blow was softened by the

knowledge that ZG2NYC contributor Adam Suerte has assumed responsibility for the Brooklyn landmark pint glasses, with plans to put out new editions to join the likes of Ebbets Field, the Parachute Jump, and of course, the Brooklyn Bridge. You can also call upon Adam for the sort of permanent souvenir that doesn't wash off in the shower, but the pint glasses are a good option for the anti-ink and needle averse.

Lola Starr
Coney Island Boardwalk (btwn 12th St and Stilwell Ave, Coney Island, Bklyn) 800-362-5116
&
Inside the Stillwell Ave subway station
(Coney Island: D/F/N/Q to Stillwell Ave)
www.lolastar.com
(Coney Island: D/F/N/Q to Coney Island-Stillwell Ave)
Lola Starr is a real live Coney Island Baby. If she puts the Cyclone, the Elephant Hotel or that sinister mascot head (his name is Tillie) on a t-shirt, it's more than fashion. She's got a soul connection to the place. As is true of so many Coney Island lovers, she also has a thing for mermaids, pirates, and cartoon bluebirds of the sort who populate vintage tattoos. If you're not into t-shirts, tributes to Lola's spiritual homeland are also available in belt buckle, mug, and mouse pad form. She takes the winter off.

I (Heart) NY But I'm Not In (Heart) With NY stickers
www.sorrynewyork.com
Send for your free souvenirs in the mail. I'm not sure how Drew can afford to give these stickers away, but spiffing up your bike, laptop, or guitar case with one is guaranteed to start a conversation sooner or later.

Free NYC condoms at the LGBT Community Center (208 W 13th St, 212-620-7310) – redguard (These are available in other locations as well, like Housing Works Used Book Café. To find more locations, or set your NYC business or event up as a distribution point, call 311 or visit www.nyc.gov/html/doh/html/condoms/condoms.shtml.)

The best NYC souvenir would be the one you find on the street. There is amazing stuff to be found there! Just keep your eyes open! I have this really great necklace that I made out of a huge old, handmade nail that I pulled out of the rubble in my building. I attached it with wire to one of those sink stopper chains that you can get for pennies at the hardware store. That is my kind of souvenir! Or there is this guy who makes really cool stuff out of matchbooks that he sells on the street in the Lower East Side

& award you 2 points for Patience &

for $1. You can find some cool stuff in SoHo. Matthew Courtney, who used to run the open mic at ABC No Rio back in the late '80s now sells his paintings and drawings there. You can usually find him on Prince Street, just east of the Apple Store, usually on the north side of the street. He will sell you original drawings that are amazing for as cheap as $10. You can also get a Lower East Side Girl's Club t-shirt at the Girl's Club, or a Bluestockings Bookstore t-shirt (and lots of other t's) at Bluestockings Books. A Times Up! t-shirt would make a really great souvenir (especially my design!). – Fly

TATTOO

For those seeking a more permanent souvenir:

NY Hardcore Tattoos
127 Stanton St (btwn Essex and Norfolk) 212-979-0350
www.hardcorenyc.com (LES: F/J/M/Z to Delancey-Essex)
I highly recommend Tasha Rubinow from NY Hardcore Tattoos on the Lower East Side. She tattooed me at a music festival in Park Slope last summer and did a really nice job. – Eric Nelson

Andromeda
33 St Marks Pl (btwn 2nd & 3rd Ave) 212-505-9408
www.andromeda-nyc.com (East Village: 6 to Astor Pl)
Andromeda is great and the first tattoo/piercing place I visited on St. Marx, upon my first visit to NYC. I've gotten all of my facial piercings there, and the woman who took care of business was awesome and comforting—made me very eager to stick metal through my face. The interior

is beautiful and covered in art and bizarre sculptures. – Cristy Road

Hand of Glory Tattoo
429 7th Ave (btwn 14th and 15th St, Park Slope, Bklyn)
718-832-5020
www.handofglorytattoo.com (Park Slope: F/G to 7th Ave)
Park Slope's Hand of Glory is the friendliest tattoo shop I've ever been in. They don't do walk-ins, but they are super polite, listen to what you have to say, play tight jams while you get work done, give you good advice on tattoo care and safety and are people that you would want to be friends with! I felt totally comfortable and Jonah Ellis did such an awesome job on my tattoo. It *ruled*. – Cecile Dyer
(This place is awesome, covered in beautiful paintings, and my favorite tattoo spot in Park Slope. The artists are great. I got my work done by Jonah. He is no longer full-time at HOG, but Craig Rodriguez is another artist here and he makes some sick shit. – Cristy Road)

Saved
426 Union Ave (@ Devoe, Williamsburg, Bklyn)
718-486-0580, www.savedtattoo.com
(Williamsburg: G/L to Lorimer-Metropolitan)
This is where I've gotten most of my work done, by Dan Trocchio. The artists here are awesome, and two of my other favorites, who I hope to get work done by someday, also work here: JK5 and Michelle Tarantelli. The environment is less like a tattoo shop, and more like a beautiful gallery with lots of room to breath. – Cristy Road

Twelve 28
28 Marcy Ave, 2nd floor (btwn Hope & Metropolitan, Williamsburg, Bklyn) 347-602-2560, www.1228tattoo.com (Williamsburg: G/L to Lorimer-Metropolitan)
Joy Rumore does incredible bright color work. The house specialty is animal/pet portraits, but she's equally good at vivid, traditional style. – Kate Black

Brooklyn Tattoo
99 Smith St (btwn Atlantic Ave and Pacific St) 718-643-1610
www.brooklyntattoo.com (Boerum Hill: F/G to Bergen St)
Most definitely go to Adam Suerte. – Fly (As featured in the ZG2NYC! And while you're at it, pick up *Aprendiz*, Adam's four-part, full-color comic about the long, oft humiliating road that led to his becoming a full-fledged tattoo artist with a shop of his own. A fascinating look at the profession. – AH)

Another amazing tattooist is Nico de Gaillo, the front woman for Lower East Side punk rock superheros the Star Fucking Hipsters. When she is not living the rock star life on tour you can find her working at various tattoo shops in the LES. Lately she has been working in a shop on St Mark's Place. – Fly

Stick and pokes at varying house shows—if you fancy that sort of thing. – Cristy Road

I got mine in jail. – David Goren

SPLURGE
ZG2NYC contributors were polled as to what they'd be willing to blow a significant chunk of dough on here in NYC. Following their lead will run you anywhere from $5 to the entire month's grocery budget.

Russian Turkish Baths
268 E 10th st (btwn 1st Ave & Ave A) 212-674-9250
www.russianturkishbaths.com (East Village: L to 1st Ave)
The 10th Street baths are so worth a huuuge splurge! Last time I was there I could stay as long as I wanted, at least until closing. The whole block smells amazing because of them and they have masseuses so you can spend a little extra to get even more relaxed. – Fly (The staff is kind of rude, and the cleanliness ethic there is not for the weak, but for 30 bucks you get unlimited towels, robes, and heat, as well as lounging rights to an outdoor deck and access to amazing scrubs and massages. If you're planning on going more than once, you can get cheaper entrance by buying a pass. Ladies only on Wednesdays from 10am to 2pm. – Mantana Roberts) (I wouldn't spring for another cursory, untrained Russian Turkish Baths massage. I wouldn't expect too much from a "happy ending" here either, though allegedly gentlemen, and some ladies, don't even have to ask to get one. – AH)

Spa 88 (formerly known as the Wall Street Baths)
88 Fulton St (btwn Gold & William) 212-766-8600
www.wallstreetbath.com (Financial District: A/C/J/Z/2/3/4/5 to Fulton St-Broadway-Nassau)
$32.50 (Arrive with a friend between 11am & 1:30pm, Monday through Friday and the second admission is half off.) BYOFlip-flops in addition to your bathing suit if you're worried that the creepy rubber loaners might melt to your feet in this Russian *banya*'s Turkish sauna, the hottest in town. It's a madhouse on the weekends. Go on a less-crowded weekday and alternate steaming with plunging into an Arctic dunk-tank. (There's a trash barrel of ice by the shower if you're too wimpy for the full polar bear.) Bundles of oak leaves are for sale at the counter for friends interested in beating each other with a DIY *platza*—if you're unsure what to do, just hang out in the sauna, and watch how the big bellied muscle men do. There's also a low-lit area with screened platforms for stretching out and dozing off. Also check out the billiards room, attached restaurant, and pool.

Yi-Pak
10 W 32nd St (btwn 5th Ave & Broadway) 212-594-1025
www.yipakspa.com Garment District: B/D/F/M/N/Q /R to 34th St)
$100 + tip
Sorry, boys, this one's ladies-only. (There's a men's spa upstairs but I don't know what goes on there.) Female attendants in sopping, supportive undergarments administer body-scrubs with economy brand soaps and baby oil in a communal treatment room, heaving their clients' legs around like joysticks, completely disregarding any personal modesty you may have left. I appreciate the frankness of the Korean staff, most of whom are a long way from calling English their second language. A harassed mama friend I brought along once commented that having a body scrub (with sauna, steambath, shampoo, and face pack) at Yi-Pak was like being a baby again, washed by an experienced, slightly rough grandma. It's totally true.

Spa Castle
131-10 11th Ave (@ 131st St, College Point, Queens
www.nyspacastle.com (College Point: 7 to Main St-Flush-

AHH, THE TATTOO CUSTOMER . . .

ing, then a free shuttle bus)
$35 weekday. $45 weekend. Under 3-feet-tall: $20 weekday, $25 weekend. Under 2: Free

Unbelievable. Don't waste cash on any massages—the many saunas, jet pools, nap chairs, etc. will treat you like royalty. This is a day-trip destination. – Robyn Jordan (It's way, way out in College Point, Queens. You take the 7 train to the end, then their shuttle bus comes to the nearby Municipal Parking lot every half hour. You have probably never seen anything like it. They have like ten different saunas and three floors of outdoor pools, indoor pools (not for swimming but more lounging), hot tubs, etc, plus a full Korean restaurant and also other kinds of food plus fresh juices and bubble tea all for purchase. Your $35 includes a towel. – Andria Alefi) (It's birthday suits only on the gender segregated ground floor, but when you hit the upper floors where the food, sauna igloos, and out-door pools are, you'll be sporting the latest in hilariously unflattering short legged spa scrubs, blue for men, pink for women, and high visibility yellow for the kiddies. Bring a bathing suit for underneath, because the outdoor pools are amazing, especially in January. Be sure to factor in a nap on the heated floor of the resting area, though you may want to bring earplugs if chattering neighbors or the antics of galloping kids bum you out. Or head for the recliners of the kid-free TV lounge. Both more crowded and more expensive during the weekend. – AH)

The Tui Na massage places in Chinatown
Starts at less than a buck a minute, and gets cheaper the longer you stay. About $45 for an hour plus tip. I've been to more than one of these and it's been worth the splurge every time. – Robyn Jordan (Here's a few in Chinatown to get you started. If you don't speak Manda-rin, your conversation is likely to be conducted primarily

in grunts. Squeal if the pressure gets to be too much. For real, I've noticed that most people think the practitioner knows best, but you're the only one who can say for sure how your body feels. – AH)
Yaoshen Cai, LIC
221 Canal St Ste 515 (btwn Mulberry & Baxter) 212-966-0565 Chinatown: J/N/Q /R/Z/6 to Canal)
&
Fishion Herb Center
107 Mott St (btwn Canal & Hester) 212-966-8771
(Chinatown: J/N/Q /R/Z/6 to Canal)
&
Wu Lim Qi Gong Master
179 Grand St (btwn Mulberry & Baxter) 212-925-1276
(Chinatown: J/N/Q /R/Z/6 to Canal)
&
Foot Heaven
16 Pell St (btwn Bowery & Doyers) 212- 962-6588
(Chinatown:B/D to Grand St)
&
88 Chinese Qi Gong Tui-Na
329 Bowery, Basement Level (btwn 2nd St & 3rd St, 212-260-7829
(East Village: B/D/F/M to Broadway-Lafayette)

Acupuncture with Margarita Alcantara
www.alcantaraacupuncture.com
malcantara.lac@gmail.com
Traveling ain't always a bed of roses. Likely as not, your knee's been hurting since Knoxville, you've been feeling down since Louisville, and that headache isn't anything to write home about either. Enter Margarita Alcantara, a.k.a. Sabrina Margarita, editress of *Bamboo Girl* zine (www.bamboogirl.com) for 10 glorious years. She flipped butterfly knives with the best of them, promoted the

You've got to keep track after that. Hint:

empowerment of ladies, especially those of mixed blood descent, and has recently earned a Masters degree in acupuncture from Pacific College of Oriental Medicine. Her specialty is treating emotional disorders and various physical body pains, both acute and chronic. Her initial appointment is a 3-figure affair, but because she is one of the kindest people you'll meet in NYC, she's offering a little ZG2NYC break.

Coney Island Cyclone, Wonder Wheel, and Luna Park
834 Surf Ave (@ 10th St, Coney Island, Bklyn) 718-265-2100
www.coneyislandcyclone.com
(Coney Island: D/F/N/Q to Stillwell Ave)
$8, www.wonderwheel.com
The Cyclone is the famous old-fashioned wooden roller coaster in Coney Island. It's hard to decide which is the scariest part of the ride—the fear that it could fall apart at any minute or the fear that your neck will be irreversibly damaged from the constant jostling. Either way, it's very scary. Be sure to secure your valuables; better yet, leave them with the ride operators. Your first trip on the Cyclone is $8, and then they'll let you ride again for $5. It's not cheap, but it's a must-do. You should take your date for a ride on the Wonder Wheel. It is the epitome of romance. It's more than your everyday, run-of-the-mill Ferris wheel because some of the carts move on their own track. There's something a little unsettling about moving around a Ferris wheel and suddenly racing forward—a great excuse to cozy up to your date. Tickets are $6. And you want to get on a swinging car. – Amanda Plumb (I deeply regret not springing for one of the photos that are automatically taken of each car as they come around after the first Cyclone plunge. As bummed as I was when Astroland was razed, I must admit the rides at the new Luna Park are both photogenic and fun. Assume you'll want to try them all and spring for the unlimited armband. Kiddie rides are cheaper, but not by much, especially when you consider that all they're really doing is going around and around in a circle. – AH)

The Village Vanguard
178 7th Ave S (btwn 11th St & 7th Ave) 212-255-4037
www.villagevanguard.com (Greenwich Village: 1/2/3 to 14th St)
$35
In 1935 impresario Max Gordon opened this basement jazz club, and his widow Lorraine continues to book the most important players, famous or not. At $35 per set (includes one mandatory drink) it ain't cheap, but the vibe is one of serious listening, and the room reeks with history, unlike other newer clubs like Birdland that trades on the name of a defunct historic club with all the cachet of a motel

lobby. Ask your wait person to point out the lamp that a disgruntled Charles Mingus smashed. – David Goren

DIA:Beacon
3 Beekman St (Beacon, NY) 845-440-0100
www.diabeacon.org (Beacon NY: Metra North to Beacon)
Train from Grand Central or Harlem-125th + Museum
$29.50. Seniors: $23. Students: $27.50. Ages 11 to 5: $1.50.
Under 4: Free
Okay, so technically, it's two hours away from New York City, but if MOMA leaves you hankering for more MA, it's a scenic ride up along the Hudson to this former Nabisco Factory/current art mecca. There are so many great conceptual pieces here, I once mistook the spackled screw holes from a temporarily-removed Donald Judd for a particularly sly work of art. The grounds are picturesque, the bookstore's got plenty to trigger your drool reflex, and the proximity to the Culinary Institute of America can make for a pretty spectacular feed in the museum café. – AH (Get the MTA North Dia:Beacon package to get rail fare and admission for one low price. Bring a picnic lunch! – Linn Edwards & Brian Bell)

Shoe Shine at Grand Central Station
42nd St (@ Park Ave) 212-340-2345
www.grandcentralterminal.com
(Midtown: S/4/5/6/7 to Grand Central)
$4
One of the best splurges, especially for a traveler on a tight budget who has to look nice for a special occasion is to get your shoes shined at one of the stands outside of Grand Central Station. It'll only cost you a few dollars, but seeing your shoes come to life really puts a spring in your step. Shoe shine guys in New York have been doing their jobs for years and really know their stuff. – Eric Nelson

Circle Line Boat Tours.
Pier 83 (W 42nd St @ 12th Ave) 212-563-3200
www.circleline42.com (Hell's Kitchen: A/C/E to 42nd St)
The Circle Line takes you on a bit of a cruise around the island of Manhattan (bottom half or all the way around, depending on what you pick). Occupies several hours. You get to be on a boat. It's beautiful. You get to really see the unique physical geography of the islands. If the announcer person is good you get to learn some history, and you can take plenty of pictures that your friends won't believe aren't postcards. – Melissa Bastian (Highlights include the Statue of Liberty, Governors Island, the abandoned sanitarium on Ward's Island, and the stretch up by Spuyten Duyvil. There's a cafe stand on board, but they don't serve alcoholic beverages all the time. The machine-

if you don't see any at eye level, look

made latte is actually quite tasty. Sit on the back deck. It's the best place to be. – Heath Row)

MOMA

11 W 53rd St (btwn 5th & 6th Ave) 212-708-9400
www.moma.org
$20. Seniors: $16. Students: $12. Under 16: Free
If you *really* enjoy art and spending the entire day at a museum, MOMA is worth the $20 admission. It's far less crowded on a weekday, and you can just sit and stare at, say, your favorite Picasso. If you're not dedicated to the cause, though, wait until it's free. – Melissa Bastian
(Those Fridays after 4pm when it's Free at MoMA? The crowds are enough to inspire agoraphobia in the most outgoing. – Kate Black)

The National Club

273 Brighton Beach Ave (btwn Brighton 2nd St & Brighton 3rd St, Brighton Beach, Bklyn) 718-646-1225
www.come2national.com
(Brighton Beach: B/Q to Brighton Beach)
For an all-out experience, hit the National Club in Brighton Beach. It's like attending an elaborate Russian wedding. Food all night long, bring-your-own-vodka, and constant entertainment. Words cannot describe. – Amy Burchenal

Cocktails at Death & Company

433 E 6th St (btwn 1st Ave & Ave A) 212-388-0882
www.deathandcompany.com (East Village: F to 2nd Ave)
I'm going to totally flout the preference for cheap bars and suggest Death & Company, which serves up $12 to $15 cocktails. Truly spectacular classics and memorable house specialties. I would rather have one excellent drink than several cheap, shitty ones. – Kate Black

The Ted and Amy Supper Club

tedandamysupperclub.com
$35
Were you to splash out on a high-end meal in a NYC restaurant, you'd probably not make friendly with anyone but the waiter. A couple of glasses of wine alone would run you what it costs to wine *and* dine in this secret restaurant in a Fort Greene apartment. (It's actually by donation, but let's remember our manners and help our hostess break even by kicking in the suggested $35.) The restaurant seats 12 once every two weeks or so. Not vegetarian, though accommodations can be made. The online reservation form jumpstarts the icebreaking with a couple of questions about what you like to do with your life, where you live, and your favorite restaurant in NYC. (Congee Village!) Assuming there's room left at the table,

you'll be sent a paypal link and some conversation-kindling information about your dining companions.

Dinner at Anthony Bourdain's restaurant, Les Halles
411 Park Ave S (btwn 28th & 29th St) 212-679-4111
www.leshalles.net (Gramercy Park: 6 to 28th St)
It's not even that expensive. My wife and I can get two steaks with frites and wine plus tip and get out under a hundred dollars. – Josh Medsker

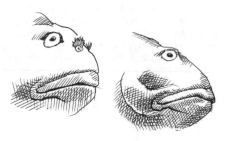

Omakase at Taro Sushi
446 Dean St (btwn 5th Ave & Flatbush Ave, Park Slope, Bklyn) 718-398-0872
(Park Slope: 2/3 to Bergen St)
If like me you've squandered...could it be *thousands* of dollars on indifferently assembled tuna rolls over the years, it's high time to get pennywise to Taro's $50 *omakase* or chef's choice. Those who haven't spent much time in Japan will be introduced to fish and flavors they never knew existed. If you're paying that much for dinner, you'll also want to pay attention, so sit at the bar and watch your meal come together. God knows what you'd pay for this in some fancy-pants Manhattan sushi temple. I not only prefer Taro's humble surroundings, I trust them!

Ichi Umi
6 E 32nd St (btwn 5th Ave & Madison Ave) 212-725-1333
www.ichiumi.com (Murray Hill: B/D/F/N/R/Q /M to 34th St)
M-Th $18.95 lunch, $28.95 dinner. F-Sun $21.95 lunch, $31.95 dinner
Loosen your drawstring pants, partner. Ichi Umi's all-you-can-eat, serve-thyself bar runs for nearly an entire block, a good part of it devoted to sushi that rises far above the bodega quality for which I'd been bracing. If you don't do raw fish, there's lovely veggies, yakitori, shumai, fresh fruit, a made-to-order noodle station, and foofy little desserts. If you have sushi-loving children under 4 1/2 feet tall, they're half price!

up. Don't forget to jot where you saw

Triad Theater
158 W 72nd St, 2nd fl(btwn Broadway & Columbus)
212-362-2590, www.celebrityautobiography.com
(Upper West Side: 1/2/3 to 72nd St)
One Monday per month, 7:30pm, $35 - $60 + 2 drink minimum and ticket agency surcharge
Celebrity autobiographies read verbatim by a revolving cast of celebrities. Past brilliance featured Will Forte reading Tommy Lee, Scott Adsit reading Kenny Loggins, Rachel Dratch treating us to a little Joan Lunden, Kristen Johnson shocking us with Mr. T, and Richard Kind's heartfelt performance of Vanna Speaks by Vanna White. You'll see stars from SNL, Broadway, film and TV making a room full of people laugh at other stars' expense. It won some sort of Drama Desk award, and ticket prices reflect that, but it's worth it. – Ed Herbstman & Melanie Hoopes

OUTDOORS

PARKS AND GREEN SPACES

New Yorkers have a special relationship with their parks, especially those of us dwelling in one-closet apartments the size of suburban laundry rooms with three other people and a cat. For many of us, the parks are as close as we'll ever come to having a back-yard.

Central Park
From 59th St to 110th, btwn 5th Ave & Central Park W (ie 8th Ave) 212-310-6600
www.centralparknyc.org (South End: A/B/C/D/N/R/Q /1; North End: B/C/2/3; West Side: B/C, East Side: 4/5/6 but the hike's the same as getting off on the West Side)
There are plenty of New Yorkers who've yet to make it to the Statue of Liberty or the top of the Empire State Building, but outside of Chinatown, you'll be hard pressed to find one who doesn't have some sort of personal relationship with the sprawling yet orderly, bucolic yet urban, uber-famous, aptly named Central Park. It used to have a scary reputation, but these days it's pretty rare to discover an unresponsive body lying just a few feet from a well-traveled foot path. There are so many awesome spots here. I'll just throw a bunch of my favorites against the wall and you see what sticks:

The Delacorte Clock
Between the Children's Zoo and the Wildlife Center, just west of 5th Ave and south of 65th St
(Upper East Side: N/R to 5th Ave)
Just past the gauntlet of jugglers, balloon twisters, and

caricaturists hanging out on the path leading to the Children's Zoo is the archway topped by the Delacorte Clock. In this techno age, you've got to love anything that can draw huge, expectant crowds with some wholesome, lo-fi, musical animal action. Every hour and half hour from 8am to 5pm these bronze figures twirl (arthritically) to some seriously Ding Dong School numbers. It's very sweet.

The Friedsam Carousel
Midpark @ 64th St, 212-879-0244
www.centralparkcarousel.com
(A/B/C/D/1/9 to 59th St-Columbus Circle)
Year round (weekends only January-March)
$2
That damn calliope starts pumping out "Sing (Sing a Song)" from Sesame Street and I bawl on cue. You can gaze out at the park, but I prefer to direct my glance inward, toward the excellent monkey and Martian figurines.

The Conservatory Water and the Delacorte Sculpture
East Side from 72nd to 75th St
www.cpmyc.org (Upper East Side: 6 to 68th St)
Sailboat Rental: Starts at $10/hr
If you're feeling flush, an attendant will rent you a Stuart Little sized remote control yacht so you can race the pampered pants off some Park Avenue swell-in-training. A short skip away from the Conservatory Water is the giant, climbable, much-photographed mushroom on which a version of the Mad Tea Party is permanently taking place. It's not really a playground, but it will be swarming with kids. If you thought the toy sailboat pond was anachronistic, get a load of the uniformed nannies! They're rare, but this is the likeliest place to find them.

Strawberry Fields
West Side btwn 71st & 74th (Upper West Side: B/C to 72nd St)
If cameras were divining rods, they'd seek not water, but the Imagine mosaic, the centerpiece of Yoko Ono's tribute to her late husband, John, who, you may have heard, was assassinated by a crazed fan just outside the Dakota (it's that big gabled one looming on the corner of 72nd and CPW). There are always a few moony acolytes garnishing it with Gerbera daisies and votive candles. Down the hill is the lake, and if you follow that around to the north, you'll come to a big mother rock that makes for a fine waterside picnic spot.

Bethesda Fountain
Midpark @ 72nd St (Upper West Side: B/C to 72nd St)
The fountain's neoclassical seraphim is not only the first

them in the margins, for later reference

major public work in NYC to be commissioned from a female artist, she's also the inspiration for the angel who—spoiler alert—comes crashing through the ceiling at the end of the first part of *Angels In America: A Gay Fantasia on National Themes*. If tranquility and theater history aren't sufficient draw, there are weekend drum circles and, more recently, this mellow guy on the terrace who lets kids and people like you use his hula hoops and bubble guns.

Belvedere Castle and the Delacorte Theater
Midpark @ 80th St (Upper West Side: B/C to 81st St)
Now that Meryl Streep stars in every other production of Shakespeare in the Park, getting in's even harder, though don't let me dissuade you from getting on that free ticket line a couple of hours before sunrise. You may make it to the box office before they pull the shutters down. If you get shut out, or you're traveling in a non-Shakespearean season, you can get a bird's eye view of the wood-walled arena where the magic happens by climbing up to Belvedere Castle, which totally looks the part, even if it's just a weather station.

Conservatory Garden
5th Ave & 105th St (East Harlem: 6 to 103rd St)
Less rich with broken glass and ciggie butts than other areas of the park. The manicured lawns by the fountain attract bridal parties on the weekend. Due south is a pretty, formal garden perfect for pacing while you contemplate your dangerous liaisons.

Non-Central Parks

MANHATTAN

Tompkins Square
From E 7th St to E 10th St (btwn Ave A & Ave B)
www.nycgovparks.org/parks/tompkinssquarepark
(East Village: 6 to Astor Pl)
For an eyewitness account of the famous riots of 1988, when the escalating clash between squatters and the police sent to evict them turned bloody, read Fly's *Dog Dayz* zine. – AH (What can I say? I've been here over 20 years, squatting and rebuilding a gutted tenement building, holding off the city—the police—surviving for years without heat and often with no electricity or plumbing. Some memorable moments have been in the midst of riots at Cooper Union and Tompkins Square Park. – Fly) (These days, the park is a placid—mostly—neighborhood gathering spot, a place to chill out, and get some fresh air. If you're a pooch, you'll be hanging out in the dog run, sniffing butts, and taking names. If you're a little kid, the main playground at 9th and Avenue A is the hoppingest place to be. I'd like to put in a plug for the adults who frequent that place, who are among the friendliest, least neurotic, most diverse parent bodies I have encountered anywhere. If you're an addict, recovering or unreconstructed, you'll find you're not alone—cruise the benches to get a feel for where you'll fit in best. Maybe I'm sentimental, but I also find Tompkins Square to be the loveliest park in the city. The Temperance Fountain in the rain or the snow, shortly after the street lights come on, never fails to take my breath away. If you want to get on really intimate terms with a forgotten bit of New York history, listen to David Rakoff's second act monologue in episode 194 of *This American Life*'s online archive. Maybe because this one's played the most central role in my life, it's the park I think of when I think of New Yorkers living theirs in public. – AH) (Brilliant people-watching spots depend on what kind of people you want to watch, but Tompkins Square Park is always good, especially when there are big shows happening, like the HOWL fest or the Riot Reunion. Look for Eak the Geek, one of my favorite New Yorkers, the bald, fully-tattooed poet hanging out on

LIONS " (← that's a 2, not an eleven,

the benches. – Fly)

Abe Lebewohl Triangle
Northwest corner of E 10th St & 2nd Ave
www.evpcnyc.org/lebewohl (East Village: 6 to Astor Pl)
Please go visit Abe Lebewohl Triangle. Since you probably
aren't aware of him, Abe Lebewohl was a very well-loved
Ukrainian immigrant, who opened the 2nd Avenue Deli,
which grew over the decades to become a Jewish mecca
for all kinds of traditional food. The restaurant was across
the intersection from the triangle. Abe himself was a
Holocaust survivor and sadly, he was murdered in a rob-
bery near the restaurant. So the city decided to dedicate
the area to his memory and it's become a safe haven for all
kinds of pigeons, though the city discourages you from
feeding them. It's a nice peaceful place to sit and reflect
on the fragility of life and stare at some charming boka
boka chickens. – Josh Saitz

The High Line
Gansevoort St to 20th St...eventually 34th St, btwn 10th
Ave & 11th Ave, 212-500-6035
www.thehighline.org
(Meatpacking District: A/C/E/L to 14th St-8th Ave;
Chelsea: C/E to 23rd Street & 8th Avenue)
Steer clear on the weekends, when pastoral getaway is
trumped by excessive crowds, ambling shoulder to shoulder down this old elevated railway line-cum-park. There's
no place to spread out, through there are some very nice
built-in wooden chaise lounges. Expect delays on either
side of the Standard Hotel, which was specifically designed to straddle the High Line. Its windows earned high
marks from photographers and amateur porn lovers as
showcases for exhibitionistic guests getting it on with the
drapes wide open. Even though it's died down, I suspect
the Standard will always reward the High Line patient
with a sliver of gratuitous nudity. Even if it doesn't, the
legend will never die. It's our Loch Ness monster. (There
are plenty of other things to look at from the High Line,
of course—native flowers, New Jersey...) On certain summer evenings when the party lanterns on an adjoining
20th Street fire escape are a-light, the Renegade Cabaret is
gearing up for another show. This DIY refreshment-free
nightspot is programmed by former punk scene photog-
rapher Patty Heffley, who, not so incidentally, has lived
in the apartment attached to that fire escape for over 30
years. (www.renegadecabaret.com)

Union Square
From 14th St to 17th St, btwn University Pl & Broadway
www.unionsquarenyc.org
(L/N/Q /R/4/5/6 to 14th St-Union Square)
You'll notice lots of squirrel houses high up in the trees
and dozens of squirrels walking around on the ground.
They're all quite tame and if you're gentle and careful, you
can feed them by hand. They'll climb trees, fences, even
your pants leg in a cute quest to get some fresh peanuts!
It's all fun! When you're done, make sure to use a Handi
Wipe, says my wife. – Josh Saitz (With regard to photo
ops, please, please do NOT take photos of squirrels! Seriously! You do NOT need a photo of a fckn squirrel! They
are like rats. You do NOT need this. If you take photos
of squirrels then people will know that you are a clueless tourist and they will mug you. Do NOT take photos
of squirrels! (Or pigeons—c'mon people! Please!) – Fly)
(Uh... squirrels aside, Union Square was the site of the
first Labor Day celebration. It has a sculpture of Gandhi
and a giant famous Greenmarket every Monday, Wednesday, Friday, and Saturday. – AH)

ya cheatah.) MONKEYS _____ BEARS _____

Madison Square Park
From 26th to 23rd St, btwn Broadway & Madison Ave,
212-538-1814
www.madisonsquarepark.org (Flatiron: R to 23rd St)
There are great parks all over the place, but this one usually has the perfect balance of being somewhat-bustling
but not unable-to-find-a-seat bustling, especially if you
go before or after the lunch rush. – Marguerite Dabaie (It
tends to get overlooked, but it is nice because it doesn't
have the idiot tourist factor that Central Park does. It's
also very compact. There is a dog run, so you can watch
neat dogs. There is also the Shake Shack at the southeast
corner of the park, if you want to stand in line watching
people as you wait for your grease-bomb burger. – Josh
Medsker) (I like to loiter in the morning to see the beautiful light gilding the gray business-attire-clad hordes
streaming ever eastward on their way to work. Madison
Square Conservancy funds some nifty public art type
stuff, too. – AH) (Right across from the Flatiron building,
it's very scenic and nice and it's near a lot of other stuff,
including transportation. – Josh Saitz)

The Church of the Transfiguration
("The Little Church Around the Corner")
One E 29th St (btwn 5th Ave & Madison Ave) 212-684-6770
www.littlechurch.org (Flatiron: R to 28th St)
Madison Square isn't too far away, but what with the
infernal lunch buzz surrounding the Shake Shack, I
sometimes prefer the gardenly peace and quiet this
church makes available to even fallen angels like myself.
Keep your eyes peeled and you'll find plenty of open-to-
the-public gardens and seating-equipped terraces in the
shadow of NYC's churches, post-war apartment com-
plexes and office buildings.

John Jay Park
76th St to 78th St, btwn Cherokee Pl & FDR Drive
www.nycgovparks.org/parks/johnjaypark
(Upper East Side: 6 to 77th St)
They have handball courts, lots of playgrounds, basketball, and a bunch of public pools, and it's not often
crowded. – Josh Saitz

Carl Schurz Park
From 84th St to 90th St (btwn East End Ave & the East River)
www.carlschurzparknyc.org (Upper East Side: 4/5/6 to 86th St)
Excellent views, nice people, friendly dogs in the dog run,
and since it's not in any guidebooks (Ho, ho! – AH), it
will be filled with locals and their children. It's also a nice
place to just sit on a bench and relax, but be sure to take
the path toward Gracie Mansion where the mayor lives

and check it out for yourself. Bloomberg is so rich that
this mansion in a public park, right on the river, would be
a step down for him, so he lives in his own townhouse on
Park Avenue. – Josh Saitz

BROOKLYN

McCarren Park
From Bedford to Bayard, btwn N 12th & Leonard, Wil-
liamsburg/Greenpoint, Brooklyn
www.nycgovparks.org/parks/mccarrenpark
(Williamsburg: L to Bedford Ave & Greenpoint: G to Nassau Ave)
This is exactly what a community park should be. Sporty
teenagers playing tennis, old men running track and using the built-in exercise equipment, Hispanic families
kicking the soccer ball around at BBQ birthday parties,
hip twenty-somethings playing in the summer kickball
league, little kids running rampant on the slides and
swings and through the sandbox, people of all kinds just
hanging out on the grass on a beautiful spring day; Mc-
Carren Park is always packed and it always seems like
everyone's having the greatest time. Throw in the occasional craft fair or community event, the rock shows at
the reopened McCarren Park Pool, and the proximity to
the food and drink on Bedford, and you've got yourself an
all-in-one destination for all-day fun. – Megan Gerrity

Monsignor McGolrick Park
From Driggs to Nassau, btwn Monitor & Russell, Greenpoint, Brooklyn
www.nycgovparks.org/parks/B114
(Greenpoint: G to Nassau Ave)
McGolrick Park is a small, family-friendly park stuck
between Driggs Avenue, Nassau Avenue, Russell Street,
and Monitor Street. It's got this strange sort of majestic
feel to it—always nearly empty, not yet overrun by hip
sters (and stay out!) and despite its size accommodates a
number of statues, a beautiful pavilion (with bathrooms),
a dog park, children's play area, and rows of benches.
Great place for drawing or picnicking, though it is known
to be an occasional hotspot for old and (relatively well-
behaved) drunks. – Caitlin McGurk

Von King Park (originally known as Tompkins Park)
From Lafayette to Greene, btwn Marcy & Tompkins,
Bedford-Stuyvesant, Brooklyn
www.nycgovparks.org/parks/herbertvonking
(Bed-Stuy: G to Bedford/Nostrand)
Von King in Bed-Stuy has a big baseball diamond, great
trees, big field, and kind of scuzzy dog run – Robyn Jordan

Empire Fulton Ferry State Park
From Washington St to New Dock St, btwn Water St and the NY Harbor, DUMBO, Brooklyn, 718-802-0603 www.brooklynbridgepark.org (DUMBO: A/C to High St)
Enjoy the same view as DUMBO swells who paid millions to live in Civil War-era spice warehouses, though admittedly, they're at less risk of getting goose poop in their hair should they decide to do a spontaneous headstand. Buttressed between the Manhattan and Brooklyn Bridges, this small park boasts a fine grassy knoll from which to view the comings and goings of the Staten Island ferries, water taxis, tug boats, and garbage barges. There are picnic tables in one corner, a playground equipped with a semi-abstract pirate ship to the south, a summer film festival, bathrooms, and best of all (except for when you're about to be busted for climbing a tree), an actual park ranger in one of those brown uniforms that comes with a Smokey the Bear hat. Only thing is the whole shebang's scheduled to go into hibernation until the spring of 2011, so the Conservancy can put in lights, irrigation tanks, and a beautiful, old carousel. Don't let this keep you away though. The adjacent Fulton Ferry Landing, where all the

Chinese bridal parties roll up in their limos on Sunday, is still a lovely place to drink in the view, and Piers 1 and 6 are scheduled to open as public space/part of the Brooklyn Bridge Conservancy's blueprint for green domination.

Valentino Pier in Louis Valentino Jr. Park
From Coffey to VanDyke, btwn Ferris St & the New York Harbor, Red Hook, Brooklyn
www.nycgovparks.org/parks/B418 (Red Hook: B61 bus to Coffey & Van Brunt or IKEA water taxi)
I predict that it won't be long before Red Hook's Valentino Pier replaces the Brooklyn Heights Promenade as the best loved movie view of New York harbor. The only way to beat this view of the Statue of Liberty is to board a boat. It's also a great place to find out what if anything is bitin', though I'm not sure I'd be up for ingesting anything hauled from those waters. Parkwise, there's not much in the way of acreage here, but it makes up for it with some of the lushest, longest, non-private grass in Brooklyn. My children think of the skaggy little stone beach as an Aladdin's cave of beach glass, possibly because they're the only ones who go looking for it there, and they're not too picky with regard to jagged edges. You may see—or be—a Red Hook boater paddling around on a complimentary kayak or canoe trip.

Prospect Park
Shaped like a house in the heart of Brooklyn, let us think of it as a crumpled diamond. The boundaries are formed by Washington Avenue and Eastern Parkway in Prospect Heights, then down Ocean Avenue in Lefferts Gardens, across Parkside Avenue at the bottom, then up Prospect Park Southwest in Kensington and Windsor Terrace, and on up through Prospect Park West in Park Slope (to orient you, if Park Slope had a 9th Avenue, this would be it.) The cherry on top is Grand Army Plaza. It's much easier to find than I just made it sound. It's the Central Park of Brooklyn. On weekends, a little trolley makes the circuit, and will get you to all the greatest hits for free. (Starting at Grand Army Plaza and going clockwise, the closest subway stops are: 2/3 to Grand Army Plaza, B/Q /S to Prospect Park, Q to Parkside, F to Fort Hamilton Pkway, F to 15th St and F/G to 7th Ave)
www.prospectpark.org, 718-965-8951
There is more to Prospect Park than the great kite-watching in Long Meadow. Best dog watching: The Nethermead. Best bird-watching: Way back in the trees. Pretend you're not even in New York! – Jessica Max Stein (Best place to shoot an impromptu zombie movie: the creepy, crumbly Oriental Pavilion. Best place to miss seeing Goren Bregovic for $3 because it's raining: Celebrate

(no, real ones do not count)

Brooklyn at the 9th Street Bandshell. I also look forward to spring, when the swans who hang around outside the Audubon Center hatch their adorable, fuzzy, little cygnets. Like Central Park, Prospect Park was designed by Frederick Olmstead. Everyone uses them both, but Prospect's location makes for a greater diversity of neighborhood flavor in the settled areas butting up against it.– AH)

Brooklyn Botanic Garden
Eastern Pkwy to Empire Blvd, btwn Washington & Flatbush, Prospect Heights, Brooklyn, 718-623-7200
(Northern Gate: 2/3 to Eastern Parkway-Brooklyn Museum & Southern Gate: B/Q /S to Prospect Park)
www.bbg.org
$8. Seniors/ Students: $4. Under 12: Free
Free all day Tuesday & before noon Saturday (except during big festival events)
A gracious oasis that's worth it even when you have to pay to get in—though why would you, knowing there are times when they'll let you in for free? There's a big old greenhouse to keep things tropical year-round, but the point is to go when things are blooming in the great outdoors, as they do from April to October-ish. I'm particularly fond of the Shakespeare garden, the Japanese garden, and the Fragrance garden. There's also a lovely cherry blossom esplanade, best viewed close to, but not actually during, the crowded annual Sakura Matsuri (i.e., cherry blossom festival). Another favorite garden pastime is reading the names of all the different types of water lilies growing in the murky ornamental pool, and checking out the mighty koi swimming below.

QUEENS

Gantry Plaza State Park
From 47th Rd to 49th Ave, btwn Center Blvd & the East River, Long Island City, Queens 718-786-6385
www.nysparks.state.ny.us/parks/149/details.aspx
(LIC: 7 to Vernon-Jackson Ave)
Gantry Plaza State Park on the southwestern coast of Queens is spacious and well-planned; there's plenty of lush grass, and there's the iconic old Pepsi-Cola sign. It's a lovely, long stretch along the river, perfect for a romantic stroll in the day or evening. There are a variety of chairs to lounge in, and the whole setup is very well-maintained. It's easy to get to, just a couple of blocks from the subway.
– Melissa Bastian

COMMUNITY GARDENS

Green Thumb
www.greenthumbnyc.org
GreenThumb is the umbrella organization for the city's community gardens, most of them started in abandoned lots (that unfortunately started looking a lot more attractive to developers once they greened up). The website has a comprehensive garden locater that will give you both coordinates and open-to-the-public hours, as well as listings for free activities and events.

The Liz Christy Garden
Houston @ Bowery, northeast corner
www.evpcnyc.org/lizchristy (East Village: F to 2nd Ave)
NYC's first community garden, named for its late founder, an artist and original Green Guerrilla. I get perverse enjoyment from the crazy traffic barreling on the other side of the wrought iron fence. Unlike the other community gardens this one does not have a tucked-away feel. The resident turtle knows he's got it good, and does not try to escape. Saturdays are the most dependable day for year-round entry, as well as Tuesday evenings in summer.

6th and B
6th St @ Ave B, southwest corner
www.66bgarden.org (East Village: F to 2nd Ave)
This one's always been my favorite community garden
on the Lower East Side. It began the greening process in
1983 and for over 20 years enjoyed notoriety as the place
with the tower of two-by-fours, abused-looking stuffed
animals, busted Big Wheels, and other curbside refuse.
The tower (it eventually hit 65 feet) and its creator Eddie
Boros, both of them polarizing East Village originals, are
no longer with us but the garden thrives, funky as a weed.
I really appreciate its crazy quilt nature. Like any long-
term communal effort, it's seen its share of squabbles and
stand offs, but the gardeners are pretty much free to do as
they like with their plots, which always makes it interesting to stroll around before picking a pleasant place to sit
and read. Like all community gardens, it has open-to-
the-public hours (currently on the weekend) and is also
accessible at other times, whenever a garden member is
in there working. It has a stage and a gazebo for frequent
slideshows, lectures, workshops, and concerts.

La Plaza Cultural de Armando Perez
9th St @ Ave C, southwest corner
www.laplazacultural.org (East Village: L to 1st Ave)
I'm a sucker for willow trees and La Plaza has a huge one,
grown from seed! It's got a great stage made out of old railroad ties, that every September plays host to the Loisaida
Cortos Latino Film Festival (love that $3 suggested admis-
sion). Saturday afternoons are the surest bet for visitors.

WATERFRONT FUN

Islands

Governors Island
www.govisland.com, 212-440-2200
Manhattan Ferry: 10 South St (btwn Whitehall & Broad)
(Financial District: 1 to South Ferry Station)
Brooklyn Ferry: Saturdays and Sundays only from Pier
6 in Brooklyn Bridge Park (Atlantic Avenue at the river)
(Brooklyn Hts: R/2/3/4/5 to Court St-Borough Hall)
The island recently opened and the ferry is free. Go in the
summer and bring a big bag of your own food and you
can make a day of it, though you won't see it all. There
is a lot to see and do there, from art exhibits to open-air
concerts to painting and sculpture for the kids, most all
of it free. – Josh Saitz (Governor's Island hosts the lushest,
greenest, tenderest expanse of open-to-the-public-but-
still-convenient New York City grass on record. On Friday
evenings, rental bikes are available for free, and once

during the Figment Festival I was so filled with holiday
spirit that I shelled out for one of those goofy, canopied,
impossible-to-turn six-seaters. In other disporting news,
it seems that the mini-golf course that started as an art
installation is now a perennial. Also keep your ears peeled
for Punk Island, Fly's favorite event. (www.myspace.com/
mmnypunkisland) – AH)

Roosevelt Island
212-308-6608
www.rioc.com (Roosevelt Island: F to Roosevelt Island...
though, really, you should take the N/R to 59th-Lexington
Avenue, so you can take the tram from 59th Street and
2nd Avenue. (Or at least take it back!)
For all of its bizarre history, Roosevelt Island is actually
quite beautiful. With a swipe of a Metrocard you can ride
the tram—which is super fun—over the east river, and
then walk along the water until you find the perfect spot
for a picnic. The far northern tip is home to a cool little
lighthouse, but it's pretty windy up there. Stay along the
western coast of the island, as the eastern coast, which
faces Queens instead of Manhattan, isn't nearly as nice. –
Melissa Bastian (Roosevelt Island is a sort of middle-class
Truman Show-esque enclave. The views from the tram are
amazing. There is also a very nice playground and basketball court on the eastern side of the island. Take the ride
over, have a picnic on the other side and then come back.
The tram leaves very frequently. – Josh Saitz) (There's a
little red bus that'll take you around the island from the
tram stop for 25¢. – AH)

Marina

79th Street Boat Basin in Riverside Park
Hudson River @ 79th St, 212-496-2105
www.nycgovparks.org/facilities/marinas/10
(Upper West Side: 1 to 79th St)
A whole 'nother category of New York City real estate.
Many of the houseboats docked here seem to be in it for
the duration. It's fun to speculate about the far-outside-
the-mold lives going on below decks. The arched area that
is HQ for the seasonal café (expensive beer, unappetizing
food) used to shelter a population of peaceable, homeless
alcoholics. Back in 1997, accessing the Boat Basin from
79th Street, rather than a point higher up or lower down
in Riverside Park always felt kind of dicey, like I was barging into a stranger's living room without invitation. Their
lost world is documented in a very interesting chapter of
Jennifer Toth's *The Mole People: Life in the Tunnels Beneath
New York City*.

Beaches

Coney Island
Btwn Surf Ave & the Atlantic Ocean, Brooklyn – navigate by the Wonder Wheel and you'll find it!
Technically it runs from Corbin Pl to W 37th St, but 12th St is the sweet spot.
www.coneyisland.com (Coney Island: D/F/N/Q to Stillwell Ave)
I love the Coney boardwalk, any time of year. It has a certain desolate beauty in the wintertime. Walk out towards Brighton Beach, have your picnic, and then visit the aquarium! But bundle up if you do brave it in winter—it WILL be colder there than in the city. – Melissa Bastian (I love Coney Island in any season. *Time Out New York* screws the pooch annually by featuring scrawny, overwhelmingly white, young models in its swimsuit issue, ignoring the real life banquet of body types, skin tones and swimming costume interpretations, free for the taking in on Coney Island every summer weekend. – AH) (Coney Island is less about the beach, than it is about everything else—the rides, the hot dogs, the Mermaid Parade, the Cyclone, and the Sideshow. Historically the working-class vacation getaway, it's not too different today. The Hamptons and their less posh neighbors attract professionals and wealthy folks who have the money and time to spend weekends, if not summers, at the shore. Brighton Beach and Coney Island attract a diverse crowd of families just in for the day. – Amanda Plumb) (See the Splurge section for inducement to hop on the expensive, don't-miss rides. – AH)

Manhattan Beach
From Ocean Ave to Oriental St, btwn Oriental Blvd & the Atlantic Ocean, Brooklyn
www.nycgovparks.org/parks/manhattanbeachpark
(B/Q to Sheepshead Bay, then the B49)
The beach itself is clean, and the view of Far Rockaway spectacular. Take the B49 to the end of the line... – David Goren

Brighton Beach
Boardwalk from Ocean Pkwy to Brighton-14th St, Brooklyn, 718-934-1908, www.brightonbeach.com
(Brighton Beach: B/Q to Brighton Beach)
Brighton Beach is slightly closer and tends to be less crowded than Coney Island. The neighborhood is Russian, nicknamed "Little Odessa." There are bountiful fruit stands and grocery stores where I can't decipher any of the product names. It's always an adventure to bite into a crepe bundle, hoping it's stuffed with cheese or fruit and not meat. – Amanda Plumb (In addition to the "ice cold beer" touted by guerrilla vendors, as at Coney Island, you can get pirogies and peacock feather fans without having to leave your towel. – AH)

CEMETERIES

The Green-Wood Cemetery
500 25th St, Sunset Park, Bklyn 718-768-7300
Main Entrance: 5th Ave and 25th St
www.green-wood.com (Sunset Park: R to 25th St)
Another hotbed of goose poop, this cemetery may not have much dead rockstar cache, but it's still *Pere LaChaise* huge. Permanent residents include Leonard Bernstein, hundreds of Civil War troops in the process of being identified, and an actress who witnessed the assassination of Abraham Lincoln. (Too bad they've no way of taking advantage of the abundance of delicious, cheap *y muy authentico* Mexican food a mere stone's throw from the 5th Avenue gates.) The absolutely best time to pay them a call is during Open House New York Weekend (usually the first weekend in October) when the grounds come to

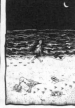

life (ha ha!) with a free event called Angels and Accordions, ethereal dancers in white wilting against the crypts while somber accordion players in Victorian funeral garb stalk nearby. The chapel hosts year-round performance events that can get pretty lively. The resident historian, a man who clearly loves his job, leads zesty, anecdote-filled walking tours that only get better the closer one gets to Halloween. If you're pooped, there are trolley tours every Wednesday. Don't forget to check out the wild parrots squatting in the gothic spires of the main entrance.

Woodlawn Cemetery
Melrose, The Bronx, 718-920-0500
Main Entrance: Webster Ave & E. 233rd St
(also Jerome Ave @ Bainbridge Ave)
www.thewoodlawncemetery.org
(Melrose: 4 to Woodlawn)
Cemetery equals romance if you are a sentimental bloke like me. Some of my favorite musicians, who made some of the most romantic music ever, are buried in there— Duke Ellington, Miles Davis, Coleman Hawkins, WC Handy... – Matana Roberts

And then there's...

The Earth Room
141 Wooster St (btwn Prince and Houston) 212-989-5566
www.earthroom.org (SoHo: R to Prince St)
Wednesday-Sunday, 12-3pm & 3:30- 6pm. Free
Technically not a green space. It's more of a brown indoor space. It's been there for over 30 years, and weighs 280,000 lbs. Even if the public's not allowed to sprawl on it (or even touch it), it's still possible to commune with it via the olfactory organs. Even the most country-phobic city slicker can appreciate art that smells like a freshly-tilled field minus the associated manures. I also love that it's eating up an entire SoHo loft.

The Staten Island Ship Graveyard
2453 Arthur Kill Rd, Staten Island, 718-984-4100
www.donjon.com/ctx.htm
(Staten Island: S74 Bus to Rossville Ave)
This is the best place ever if you have a car, a camera, and an up-to-date tetanus shot! I braved the rusty ships without one. Use discretion when climbing the ancient mariners. It's down a mile or two from Bavaria House, a quaint German pub and grub. – Dear Drunk Girl (Go here after getting off the ferry on your romantic date – Cristy Road)

WILDLIFE
Don't go feeling sorry for us because there are no deer and rabbits devouring the container gardens on our windowsills. We have plenty of fauna without Bambi and Thumper.

Rats
Log even a small amount of time in New York City and you, too, will have a gnarly rat story on which to dine out. As you may have heard, we grow 'em big here. When the subway trains are running slow, and you've forgotten your book, they'll make the time go faster by scampering up and down the tracks, seemingly impervious to the third rail. (I've found the ratspotting to be particularly good at the East Broadway stop on the F.) If you'd like to learn more about our Rattus Norwegius friends, check out *Rats: Observations on the History and Habitat of the City's Most Unwanted Inhabitants* by Brooklyn author Robert Sullivan. – AH (The rats that scamper across the west end of the L platform at Union Square really like grapes. – Kate Black)

Pigeons
Also known as sky rats. The spikes you see bristling from the sills of any window above street level are an attempt to keep those dirty birds at bay. Sometimes I think we might do better to install a couple of spikes on the benches where senior citizens park themselves to feed their feathered friends bread crumbs, croutons, fried rice... thus attracting the kind of rats who don't have wings. Socrates Sculpture Park contains a particularly apt tribute to these hideous creatures. It's called The Dump. At first glance, it appears to be a monument to the noble rat. But who should be riding that giant cement rat's back but a slightly-larger-than-life-size, realistically colored pigeon. Look closer and you'll notice streaks of white cascading down to the plinth.

Owls
When I first moved here, I spent a lot of time on the Upper West Side wondering what was up with all those plastic great horned owls on pre-war windowsills. Were they the cosmopolitan equivalent of lawn flamingos? A secret signal? Masons? Brothels too discreet to advertise in the back of the *Village Voice*? Turns out they're there to fool the pigeons into thinking they're real.

Wild Parrots
www.brooklynparrots.com
Legend has it that in the 1960s a shipment of Quaker parrots escaped from the tarmac of JFK (possibly because some mob guys jimmied open the crate looking for

something else), and the ones squatting in the gothic spires of Greenwood Cemetery's main entrance are their descendants. It does feel rather special to find a pretty green and pink feather in the wilds of Brooklyn. Parrots have also been spotted in the residential neighborhoods near Brooklyn College. Steve Baldwin, who maintains the parrots' website leads free safaris every now and then.

Canada Geese

For transient creatures traveling on such short-term visas, they sure manage to shit up our green spaces. There's a reason those of us who live here don't express our carefree sense of fun by rolling down that hill in Empire Park. Better not let me catch *you* pooping all over the place!

Chihuahuas

Mastiffs, pits, and French bulldogs stroll the city streets *en masse*, but the canines that have made the biggest NYC impression on me are these quivering, bug-eyed souls. Until moving here, I'd had limited exposure to the breed. They are often in their owners' arms, and seem to dress up more for Halloween, probably due to their inability to mount much in the way of resistance. Their best-known representative is Reverend Jen Jr., the beloved companion of Lower East Side Art Star, author and Anti-Slam host, Reverend Jen.

Hua Mei Fighting Thrushes
Hua Mei Bird Garden
Sara Delano Roosevelt Park
Broome St (btwn Forsyth & Chrystie)
(LES: J/M to Bowery)
Daily 8am – 10:30am-ish

Want to hear something pretty? Get up early and come to the Hua Mei Bird Garden, just north of the Pit where the bike polo matches take place. Every morning Chinese retirees gather to hang out, drink tea and show off their song birds in fancy bamboo cages hung from hooks installed for this purpose. There are hardcore daily regulars,

and weekend warriors swell the chorus to about 50 on Saturdays and Sundays. Most of them live in the neighborhood, but there are guys who travel over a hundred blocks to participate. Think of that the next time you don't feel up to walking a 1/4 mile in the rain. The birdies themselves are cute little fuggers with markings that look like eyebrows, but their golden throats are their sexiest feature, particularly when there's a lady bird caged next door.

Cats

Cats can put a serious crimp in the short-term sublettor pool. I'm still waiting for someone to design a space saving litterbox that will perfectly compliment the rest of my décor. They do look picturesque perched in the window. The cat pee smell in certain less-than-upscale grocery stores indicates the presence of feline census takers monitoring the basement rat population. My cat, who was born in a dumpster, but, like Rapunzel, has spent very little time outside the confines of his Ivory tower, is always very interested in plastic bags from Met Food, regardless of what food may be in there.

Cotton top Tamarin

Central Park Children's Zoo

830 5th Avenue, 212-439-6500
www.centralparkzoo.com
(Upper East Side: N/R to 5th Ave-59th St)
Although the Central Park Children's Zoo is very small, they have a lot of interesting animals and environments to see. For you trivia dorks out there, it's the oldest zoo in the United States. In addition to a huge building that simulates a rainforest, they also have snow monkeys, sea lions, and lots of other animals. You can visit Gus the polar bear, along with his two main chicks, Lily and Ida. I don't feel bad that they're in this zoo because all three polar bears were born at other zoos and weren't well-cared for. My favorite thing in all of Central Park is the Penguin House, located at the north end of the zoo. Inside they have a little land mass and a huge tank. Within the freezing display are dozens of penguins, both Chinstrap and Gentoo, and they swim and dance and play in the water and on the land. They're so delightful to watch and they're so well cared for that just thinking about it now has calmed me. The keepers simulate the penguins' natural conditions, even though all were born in captivity. The light is low and sets early, the air is frigid, and the fish are tasty. They swim back and forth, launch themselves up onto the rocks, poop, eat, and if you go in the spring, you can see them mating, making nests out of rocks, and raising their young. – Josh Saitz (The small admission charge includes the outpost a bit northeast of the main area, where a quarter in the goat chow dispenser will buy you at least one ticklish, unsanitary friendship. – AH)

Prospect Park Zoo

450 Flatbush Ave (btwn Empire Blvd & Lake Dr, Prospect Hts, Bklyn) 718-399-7312, www.prospectparkzoo.com
(Prospect Hts: B/Q /S to Prospect Park)
I'm a softie for this place, which inspired my first kid's book, *Always Lots of Heinies at the Zoo*. It's a favorite Sunday outing for the Hasidim of nearby Borough Park. Not the most comprehensive zoo in New York, but its proximity to other attractions within the park (it's on the free weekend trolley's route) makes it a pleasant enough spot to spend an hour or two. The prairie dog exhibit is fixed up so visiting kids can pop up beside the burrows in plastic domes that would be see-through if they weren't so thoroughly smudged up with little hand and noseprints.

Bronx Zoo

2300 Southern Blvd (btwn E 183rd & Grote St, East Tremont, Bronx) 718-220-5103, www.bronxzoo.com
(East Tremont: 2/5 to E. Tremont Ave-West Farms Square) $15. Seniors: $13. Ages 3-12: $11. Wednesday: Pay-what-you-wish
Bronx is home to some big gorillas and multitudes of other fragrant, dangerous, non-native, big ticket creatures beloved by junior naturalists. Lately they've taken to acting like an airline, making the public pay a la carte. Actually seeing the aforementioned gorillas is going to cost you an extra three bucks (unless you spring for the all-access Total Experience, which nearly doubles the prices listed above). Avoid those sirloin admission fees by joining the masses on Wednesday, which used to be a very-straight-up free, and is now a suggested admission. The Congo exhibit is nifty, especially if a zoo baby favors you by pressing palms with you through the glass. (I'm thinking one-way mirror?) It's a hike from the nearest subway, and the grounds sprawl, so save your Manolos for the *Sex and the City* tour.

The New York Aquarium

Surf Ave & W 8th St (Coney Island, Bklyn) 718-265-FISH
www.nyaquarium.com (Coney Island: F/Q to W. 8th St) $13. Seniors: $10. Ages 3 – 12: $9. Friday after 3pm: Pay-what-you-wish
A 365-days-a-year pillar of science tucked in one cup of Coney Island's mermaid-loving, freak-shooting, honkytonk brassiere. Don't be intimidated by the big, loud school groups. They'll thunder past soon enough, leaving you alone with such inscrutable (and fishy smelling!) beauties as the jellyfish, seahorses, and stingrays. Things get a tad Coney Islandier in the open air coliseum where dolphins and sea lions are encouraged to pull all sorts of unscientific stunts in return for prizes.

BIKING IN NYC

A helmet, light, and lock are essential for a safe cycling experience in NYC. I also recommend a sense of humility and plenty of time to reach your destination, so you don't succumb to the urge to swing out in front of a cab. Bike lanes are proliferating. Use them whenever possible, but stay alert so you don't get doored. Here are some of our favorite bike shops, most of which have rentals available in case you didn't BYO.

Bike Shops

Recycle-a-Bicycle
75 Avenue C (btwn 5th & 6th St) 212-475-1655
(East Village: F to 2nd Ave)
&
35 Pearl St (@ Plymouth, DUMBO Bklyn) 718-858-2972

(DUMBO: F to York St)
www.recycleabicycle.org
$30 day/$100 week
Tandem: $16 hour / $70 day
Recycle-a-Bicycle is a community-based organization
that not only does its bit for the environment by making
Frankenbikes available to the non-bike-building public,
it runs bike mechanic electives in several NYC public
schools. Youth who drop in after school can get hands
on experience and earn volunteer points toward a bike
of their own. Support the cause by renting one of their
orange Sun Kruisers, which come with a lock, a rarity in
the NYC bike rental biz.

Spokesman Cycles
34 Irving Pl (btwn 16th & 17th) 212-995-0450
(Union Square: L/N/Q /R/4/5/6 to 14th St-Union Sq)
&
49-04 Vernon Blvd (btwn 49th Ave & 50th Ave, Long Island City, Queens) 718-433-0450
(LIC: 7 to Vernon-Jackson Ave)

www.spokesmancycles.com
$6 hour/$30 day/$35 24 hours/$100 week
Tandem: $15 hour / $50 day
The people here are very friendly and helpful. They have a
big selection of gear and clothing. You get the sense that
they actually bike. – Josh Medsker (They also rent helmets, babyseats, and toddler trailers. – AH)

Landmark Vintage
136 E 3rd St (btwn 1st Ave & Ave A) 212-674-2343
www.landmarkbicycles.com (East Village: F to 2nd Ave)
$35 24 hours
I find that vintage models are the bikes best suited to my
abilities, posture, and reluctance to haul such an item
up three flights of stairs to my already overstuffed apartment. Newer bikes have been stolen off the street sign
that I consider my semi-private parking space, but the
worst thing that ever happens to my 1948 Robin Hood is
someone leaves a crumpled tissue in the basket. This is
the sort of bicycle Landmark restores, rents, and acces-
sorizes with all the bells and wicker baskets you need to
get your Gulch on.

Al's Cycle Solutions
693 10th Ave (btwn 47th & 48th St) 212-247-3300
www.alscyclesolutions.com
(Hell's Kitchen: C/E to 50th St)
$10 hour / $40 a day
The nice thing about renting one of Al's Cannondale
mountain or hybrid bikes is that you're right by Central
Park and the car-free Hudson River Greenway, and the helmet's included. The bad thing is Al doesn't rent locks, so you'll
be chained to that puppy for the duration of your rental.

MODSquad Cycles
2119 Frederick Douglass Blvd (btwn 114th & 115th St)
212-865-5050
www.modsquadcycles.com (Harlem: B/C to 116th St)
$8 hour / $40 day
MODSquad is a nice, new, family-owned addition to the
neighborhood. The owner has competed in several fancy
European races, biked in places I'd like to know more
about, and treats customers with such a high level of
diplomatic grace that he could probably make a go of it in
public office, should the bike shop thing fail to work out.
His rentals come with locks. Helmets are $5 extra. The
store has an explicit policy barring their rental vehicles
from participation in organized group events, so this is
not the place to go if you're fixing to hop on some pick-up
bike polo. (Temporary ownership via Salvation Army is
probably your best bet for that one   you can donate the

Museum of Natural History)

carcass to Recycle-a-Bicycle when you're done.)

Bicycle Station
171 Park Ave (btwn Carlton and Adelphi, Fort Greene,
Bklyn) 718-638-0300, www.bicyclestationbrooklyn.com
(Fort Greene: G to Clinton-Washington)
Bicycle Station, located right under the BQE, is hands-
down my shop of choice in Brooklyn. The prices are fair,
the mechanics know their stuff and go out of their way
to explain everything they're doing, with tips on how
to do it yourself! The whole place has an unintimidating
and no-bullshit air that leaves you feeling comfortable and
confident when handing over your precious ride. No rentals.
– Caitlin McGurk

King-Kog Bike Emporium
455 Graham Ave (@ Herbert, Greenpoint, Bklyn)
347-689-2299
www.kingkog.com (Greenpoint: L to Graham Ave)
King-Kog is a girl-owned and run, feminist bike shop
specializing in high-end fixed-gears and a sweet variety
of accessories. If you're looking to make any ol' bike purchase this probably isn't the shop for you, but for good
quality handmade parts and adornment, not to mention
inexpensive repairs, King-Kog is well worth checking out.
No rentals. – Caitlin McGurk

There are plenty more places to rent bikes in NYC. Bike
New York maintains a list of likely suspects for its annual
5 Boro Ride, but the information is good year round. It's
always a good idea to reserve ahead to ensure that the
equipment you're planning to pedal away on will be there
when you show up. Don't forget to inquire about helmets and locks. www.bikenewyork.org/resources/local/
shops_rentals.html

Where to Ride

Critical Mass
The last Friday of the month, 7pm
www.times-up.org/index.php?page=critical-mass
The basics: the ride starts at 7pm in Union Square Park,
the north end, when construction allows—rain, snow,
or holiday. The Halloween and New Year's rides are very
lively. We don't typically take off until 7:30 or even later,
sometimes in small groups when it's advisable to confuse
or distract New York's Finest. The police do ticket riders
for all kinds of bullshit infractions, including some that
are not illegal. However, I have heard of very few tickets
that stand up in traffic court. (See www.cmtickets.com
for more info.) They have stopped—for the most part—

arresting people. Rollerbladers and skateboarders are
represented, as are people on tall bikes, folding bikes, and
whatever tricked out non-motorized wheeled vehicles
people want to bring. Occasionally we're joined by political celebrities like Reverend Al Sharpton or City Council
Member Rosie Mendez. – Jenna Freedman

Riverside Park on Manhattan's West Side is a great park
with many public artworks. You can ride from the north
end at 125th Street down to the south end at 72nd Street,
and then get onto the Hudson River Greenway which
goes all the way down to the southern tip of Manhattan.
It's a great bike ride. – Andy Singer

Roosevelt Island is pretty cool and you can access it from
the backside of Astoria, Queens if you don't feel like
hopping on a train or taking the tram thing. – Mantana
Roberts

Governors Island in the summertime. You don't even have
to bring your own—you can rent one for a few bucks once
you get there on the free ferry. Yet another NYC surround-

CRABS   COWS

ing island with a bizarre history, Governors Island for decades served as a home for visiting dignitaries. – Melissa Bastian (Just a little yawp to the Governors Island Powers that Be—please continue the practice of free Friday evenings bike rentals! Much appreciated! – AH)

Ocean Ave in Brooklyn has a bike path to Brighton Beach. – Linn Edwards & Brian Bell (This ride's human interest factor doubles on Jewish holidays if you're passing by just after the synagogues let out, when the parishioners are out in force, strolling and visiting with friends, families and neighbors. – AH)

Over the Manhattan and Willie B Bridges. – John Mejias

Past all the awesome graffiti on Wythe Avenue in Williamsburg, Brooklyn – Eric Nelson

Bed-Stuy! – Jon Bocksel

Over any bridge, down Wythe or Kent Ave, the bike lane by the Westside highway, to Coney Island on Ocean Avenue...all of NYC, I guess. I take different routes each time, depending on where I am going. Side streets are a plus. Avoid Flushing. – Cristy Road

My favorite bike ride is along Shore Parkway in Brooklyn. It is a car-free path along the harbor, leading you from Bay Ridge, underneath the Verrazano Bridge, and to Coney Island (well, the last leg is a bit off the path and in the streets, just follow the little green signs). Start on the 69th Street pier in Bay Ridge and go until you hit the beach! – Lauren Jade Martin

Weirdly, across the bridges. You don't have to deal with the cars, you get your own lane (unless pedestrians are stupidly ignoring the "walk direction" signage, and the view is amazing. – Megan Garrity, *Scribble Faster*

Red Hook at night for the view. Flushing Meadows for the weird remnants of the World's Fair. Brooklyn's Dead Horse Bay for its weird collection of trash from the '30s and '40s. Also it's fun to take your bike on the Staten Island Ferry and bike along the shore to the historic fort. – Cecile Dyer

Riding your bike in NYC kind of sucks, but that's part of the fun/challenge. Take the streets. – Jenna Freedman

Queens seems to have a shitload of bike lanes, and there is one area, up by the Fort Totten area, where you can ride along by the water. – Josh Medsker

There is a bike path that pretty much circles the entire island of Manhattan with a few detours. I used to skate this path almost every day. You can pretty much bike the whole thing in a day. You'll have a very sore butt. Riding anywhere in the city in the midst of traffic can be intense if you are not from NYC, and I strongly suggest that people wear a helmet! This is coming from someone who has experienced extreme physical damage. Seriously, wear a fckn helmet! If you are skating, then wear the helmet and the wrist guards! Don't say I didn't warn you! - Fly

Across the George Washington Bridge, into Fort Lee, NJ. – Jerry the Mouse

NOT anywhere near Atlantic Avenue or Flatbush Avenue in Brooklyn. Super aggressive drivers in these areas. Also, NOT on sidewalks. Pedestrians have as much justified anger at asshole cyclists as cyclists have at asshole drivers. – Kate Black

The bike paths in Central Park or Brooklyn's Prospect Park. I am too scared to ride a bike on the streets of Manhattan, though I have often rollerbladed through the streets. No, I am happily married, but thanks for the offer. – Josh Saitz.

Bike Resources & Events

Times Up!
www.times-up.org, 212-802-8222
From Critical Mass and the Bicycle Clown Brigade's liberation of the bike lanes, to the Doggie Pedal Parade, and the Moonlight Rides in Central and Prospect Parks, Times Up! is your prime news source for group cycling events in NYC. They'll teach you how to maintain your steed for free. Their volunteers are out to save the world by clearing the streets of automobile traffic. Bike parking and bike lanes for all!

Transportation Alternatives
www.transalt.org, 212-629-6036
Transportation Alternatives shares Times Up!'s vision of car-free streets. They've become best known as the folks behind the Tour de's—Tour de Brooklyn, Tour de Bronx, Tour de Queens, and the New York Century—a choose-your-own-distance (up to 100 miles) five borough adventure. Their resource section has links to a ton of downloadable maps of interest for two wheelers ready to take on the city and surrounding countryside (www.

transalt.org/resources). This same section has good info on the various rules for taking your bike on the subway, ferries, Metro North, the Long Island Railroad, and New Jersey Transit. They've compiled a big list of NYC bike and skate shops offering discounts to their members—a good way to find a repair or rental shop in your hour of need.

Ghost bikes
www.ghostbikes.org/new-york-city
That all-white Ghost Bike you see chained to a street lamp is both tribute to a person who's not here anymore and a reminder that a cyclist was fatally wounded in this location. My travels frequently lead me past the one honoring 28-year-old Liz Padilla on Brooklyn's 5th Avenue, killed by a delivery truck in broad daylight and the child-sized one for Alexander Toulouse just south of Cadman Plaza. Every January the Street Memorial Project sponsors a ride to visit the bikes and raise public awareness about the need for more (and safer) bike lanes. If you would like to make your own tour of the ghost bikes, and learn more about the people whose lives they acknowledge, the website has a map with the bikes' locations and some biographical sketches. Be vigilant and ride safely!

Bike Month NYC – May
www.bikemonthnyc.org
For a lot of New Yorkers, every day is Bike Day NYC, but in May, if you swing by a NYC grocery to pick up the freebie neighborhood paper, you'll no doubt see an article about that borough's president cycling—very publicly—to work. It's also when all of Transportation Alternative's Tour de's take place.

My Bike Lane NYC
www.nyc.mybikelane.com
Cars, trucks, and vans that double park in the bike lane fill me with the same rage as guys who allow their wide open thighs to take up two seats on the subway. I try not to mind when the drivers have their hands full escorting an enfeebled older person or sleeping baby. It allows me to channel more rage toward those who really have no excuse. Rather than go ricocheting out into traffic, it's better to come to a full stop, whip out your camera and snap a photo of the offending vehicle with its license plate showing. Your vigilance may not earn the driver a parking ticket, but you get the option to call them nasty names when you upload the evidence to the Internet.

NYC Bike Jumble
www.nybikejumble.com
The periodic Bike Jumbles in Brooklyn and Manhattan are a chance to pick up everything from beaters to luxury vehicles, as well as a ton of information from fellow city biking enthusiasts, both organized and individual. You can also pick up enough handcrafted chain jewelry and tube wallets to cover everyone on your gift list for the next decade or so.

Bike Polo
The Pit in Sara D. Roosevelt Park
Chrystie & Broome St (LES: B/D to Grand St)
www.nycbikepolo.com
Sunday 12pm / Tuesday & Thursday 6pm
If you've got a bike and you can steer with one hand while swinging a mallet with the other, get in the Pit for some pick-up bike polo! If your polo mallet got lost with the rest of your luggage, the regular players can loan you a spare, but it's BYObicycle. And for god's sake, wear a helmet! If you're scared of getting hurt, there's no shame in just watching.

PARTICIPATORY SPORTS
If that bicycle seat's beginning to rub, NYC does offer some other options for getting a little exercise and showing off your physical prowess.

GOATS/SHEEP

Yoga to the People
Power Vinyasa
12 St Marks Place, #2R (btwn 2nd & 3rd Ave)
(East Village: 6 to Astor Pl)
&
Traditional Hot Yoga
115 W 27th St, 3rd fl (btwn 6th Ave & 7th Ave)
(Chelsea: N/R to 28th St)
&
Hot Power Vinyasa
1017 6th Ave, 3rd fl (@ 38th St)
(Garment District: B/D/F/M/N/Q /R to 34th St)
917-573-YOGA , www.yogatothepeople.com
Pay-what-you-can
Your downward facing dog needn't stretch far to put you
on intimate terms with the butt of the mutt one mat in
front of you. The crazy crowds are more than offset by the
pay-what-you-can price, which you donate into a Kleenex
box at the end of class. The St Marks Place location is less
infernally overheated than the others.

ComeUnity Yoga at the 6th Street Community Center
638 E 6th St (btwn Ave B & C) 212 677 1863
(East Village: F to 2nd Ave)
$7 donation
The absolute best yoga class in the city is the ComeUnity
weekly yoga class with Pahztrami aka Ananda-B aka
BlackJack. It's on Wednesdays from 7pm–9pm. There's a
$7 donation and it is recommended that you do not eat or
drink for two hours before class. - Fly

Hosh Yoga at Otom Gym
169 Calyer St (btwn Manhattan and Lorimer, Greenpoint,
Bklyn) www.hoshyoga.org (Greenpoint: G to Nassau)
Pay-what-you-can
The instructors of Hosh are disciples from Yoga to the
People's instructor-school. It's run totally independently
from YTP, though it seems they've borrowed the business
model. The teachers are in fact magnificent, and as this is
a fairly new institution the classes are always very small
(though maybe not by the time this book comes out!),
often six or seven people, and they could use some well-
deserved support. You do not need a gym membership to
take this class. – AH

Punk Rope
14th Street Y
344 E. 14th St (btwn 1st & 2nd Ave) 212-780-0800
(East Village: L to 1st Ave)
Mondays 7pm, $12

&
Long Island City Y
32-23 Queens Blvd (btwn 33rd St & 32nd Pl, LIC, Queens)
718-392-9401
(LIC: subway)
Tuesday 7:30pm, Friday 5:30 Free trial class! Then $15
&
Greenpoint Y
99 Meserole (btwn Manhattan Ave and Lorimer, Greenpoint Bklyn) 718-389-3700
(Greenpoint: G to Nassau Ave)
Wednesday, 7:30pm, $15
www.punkrope.com
Punk rope is a serious workout—wear your most supportive footgear and bra. I particularly like how the
instructors take the themes in dead earnest, with bits of
costume and thoughtfully constructed playlists. I have
fond memories of the Oktoberfest when instructor Shana
(aka Pippi) had us clasp our ropes behind our backs, bend
at the waist, and lead with our noses, like boars searching
for truffles in the Black Forest. A couple of times a month,
punk ropers replenish their lost calories with après-class
drink specials in sympathetic Greenpoint and East Village bars.

Downtown Dodgeball
La Salle Academy
44 E. 2nd St (btwn 1st and 2nd Ave)
www.downtowndodgeball.com
Not every dodgeball game has to play out like a scene
from Freaks and Geeks. For $8, you can join a co-ed pick-
up game organized by league veterans from teams with
names like the Money Shots and Balls Incorporated. These
Olympians are more interested in picking up new friends
than creaming the less athletically gifted, so it's true
what they say about all skill levels being welcome. The
leagues play on Tuesday nights. Check the website for the
pick-up schedule when a Lincoln will get you two hours
of dodgeball mayhem and a bar that's expecting you later
in the evening.

Circle Rules Football
Long Meadow, in the heart of Prospect Park in the heart of
Brooklyn (www.prospectpark.org/longmeadow)
www.circlerulesfederation.com (Park Slope: F/G to 7th Ave)
Sunday, April-November
Circle Rules has done a lot to heal the scars of those
chronically picked last in gym. It helps that it's played
with a big, goofy physio ball, and that its founder, Greg,
an NYU experimental theater wing alumnus, is committed to the idea of it being an inclusive team game, a hybrid

of art and competitive sports. Basically, you lollop around in a circle, trying to knock the ball through a wiggly goal post set up in the center. (It's made out of white PVC pipe and falls apart pretty easily.) It's a great, sweaty time. The more experienced players may be fitter than you, but they'll make sure you feel welcome and even send the ball your way. There's a pick-up game every Sunday from April—November in Prospect Park, after which you can stick around to watch the league players play a higher stakes match. Games start at 2pm. Play once, and you'll be burning to start a league in your town.

Sixth Street Pilates
525 E. 6th St. (btwn Avenues A & B) 212-677-5545
www.sixthstreetpilatesny.com
(East Village: F to 2nd Ave)
$14 + $1 mat rental
The drop-in price is a pretty good deal for NYC. If you're going to be here a while, you can get ten classes for $120. The studio is a cute ground floor apartment in Alphabet City. The instructors are all nice, and learn your name by your second class. If you can make it during the day, the 12:30 classes are rarely crowded, so you can stretch your arms out without disturbing anyone. – Jenna Freedman

Hudson River Park Skate Park
West St, just north of W. 30th St
Saturday & Sunday from Memorial Day to Labor Day, 11-6,
(Garment District: A/C/E to 34th St)
Free
Don't go here if you're one of those fools who worries that your helmet makes you look unsexy. We don't want your brains splashed all over our riverfront property, and besides they won't let you in without one. Ditto a waiver, which must be signed by your parents if you're under 18. They've got a bowl, a mini-half pipe, and a view that might take your eyes off the road.

Hula Hoop lessons with Miss Saturn
www.misssaturn.com
www.schoolofburlesque.com/hulahoop.html
Jenny McGowan, aka Miss Saturn, aka Saturnova, Russian diva and hula hoop artiste, can spin 75 hoops simultaneously, and surely she can get you to the point where you can keep a measly one of them from crashing to the floor with every swivel of your uncoordinated hips. She's so busy hooping, she doesn't always have time to update her website, so give her a yawp, or check in with the School of Burlesque, under whose auspices she frequently teaches.

Inwood Canoe Club
Dyckman St & the Hudson River (look for the red, stilted boathouse about 100 yards south of the Dyckman (Tubbyhook) marina) www.inwoodcanoeclub.org
(Inwood: A to Dyckman/200th St)
Sunday, Memorial Day – Labor Day
You can go kayaking and canoeing with the Inwood Canoe Club, a very old establishment that offers you a free kayak and lesson. They'll take you in a group down the Hudson and back up, from an Inwood pier. – Jerry the Mouse

Nature hike in Palisades Park
Start at the George Washington Bridge
Pedestrian entrance at the SW corner of Cabrini Blvd and W. 178th St)
(Washington Hts: A to 175th St)
www.njpalisades.org
Cross the George Washington Bridge on foot or bike from Inwood and you will be in Fort Lee, NJ. The town has a good park to your left as you exit the bridge, but the bridge exit is also on the bottom edge of Palisades Park, a long strip of wilderness along the coast deemed to remain wild in perpetuity thanks to the Rockefellers. The great result is that from Ft. Tryon Park in Manhattan, across the river, you see undeveloped wilderness on the opposite shore, very beautiful; and if you walk across the bridge you can wander up the Hudson shoreline through thickets and woods with deer, rabbits, and squirrels. If you want to follow a path, you can take one of the hikes offered by the Park; there is some difficult climbing as you go north, and you will hit large boulders when you are most tired, but it's totally worth it. Climb out of the park at the very end, and take a quick bus into Nyack, NY, a multi-culti little arts enclave right outside the city. Refuel at the venerable Skylark Diner, which has awesome old decor, original wood paneling, what looks like original diner checkerboard flooring, an enormously long counter and great pasta. Any place that gives you a hot pastrami sandwich *plus* a cup of soup for $6.99 just cannot be bad.
– Jerry the Mouse

Urban Park Rangers Astronomy Nights, Hawk Watches, and Owl Prowls
www.nycgovparks.org
Inwood Hill Nature Center
Enter park at W. 218th St and Indian Rd, 212-304-3401
www.nycgovparks.org/parks/inwoodhillpark
(Inwood: A to 207th St)
Check out the NYC Parks website for a list of days and nights throughout the year when the Urban Park Rangers

EYES OF DR TJ ECKLEBERG • 60-89 = FRIEND

guide you through the skies and around the waterfronts and grassy fields of New York City. Inwood Hill Park is an especially active center if you'd like to do some stargazing, owl watching, hawking, or learn about the bald eagle re-introduction project. – Jerry the Mouse (Apparently, winter is prime owl spotting time, with most of the action centering around Pelham Bay Park's Bartow-Pell Mansion in the Bronx. The Ranger's schedule is so active, you could spend your entire trip tracking scat, identifying fungus, and early birding. You'll find woodsy type goings on in all five boroughs by clicking Nature in the Events by Interest section of the Park's Dept homepage. – AH)

Melody Lanes

461 37th St (btwn 4th Ave & 5th Ave, Sunset Park, Bklyn) 718-499-3848, www.melodylanesny.com
(Sunset Park: D/M/N/R to 36th St)
I hate bowling. I'm clumsy and I loathe even the idea of wearing someone else's shoes, disinfected or not. I've been "forced" into bowling only twice (other times I've more happily sat on the sidelines, drinking and watching). One of those real bowling times was at Melody Lanes. I can say this: It's cheap. It's full of bowling league types. It's kind of dirty. It's probably never been renovated. I don't think they stick to their posted hours of operation. And don't even think of asking them for a band-aid if you need one. But if you insist on bowling, I guess this place is okay. – Shayna Marchese

Handball

www.handballcity.com/locations_to_play.htm
This proud New York City tradition is kept alive at hundreds of courts all over the place, in playgrounds and parks. Basically any public space where adults shoot hoops or do chin-ups will have a handball wall. Some of my favorite locations are Sara Roosevelt Park at Houston and Chrystie, the northeast corner of Tompkins Square, and Vesuvio Playground in SoHo at Thompson and Spring. The website above lists many, many more. You can buy pinkies at any corner bodega. What's that? You don't know how to play? Ah jeez, go watch a video on YouTube or something. It ain't brain surgery!

Lotus Music & Dance

109 West 27th St, 8th fl (btwn Ave of the Americas & 7th Ave) 212-627-1076
www.lotusmusicanddance.org (Chelsea: R to 28th St)
$19 drop in class
Bollywood Fusion, *Bhangra*, Japanese Folk Dance, Men's Hula, belly dancing...you can drop into pretty much any beginning or mixed level class, though be forewarned that there are some *personalities* amongst the dance teachers. (Just like in the movies. You can handle it.) They're in it to snag new students, so play along by showing up half an hour early to fill out the paperwork. When you're snooping around, it's a good idea to see how deep into the session the class is, and whether you're supposed to supply your own long skirt, or some fruit to wear on your head, or something.

Mark Morris Dance Group Classes

3 Lafayette Ave (btwn Ashland Pl & Rockwell Pl, Fort Greene, Bklyn) 718-624-8400
www.markmorrisdancegroup.org/the_school
(Fort Greene: B/D/M/N/R Q /2/3/4/5 to Atlantic Ave-Pacific St)
$13 drop in class
African dance is one form where I don't give a damn what or who I look like, partly because I get the sense that the other, more practiced participants don't either. Even at the end of class, when we form a ring, and each take a turn crossing it, tails in the air. Who gives a hell? I pretend I'm picking pumpkins to those *djembe* drums! I have yet to sample the 18th Century Dance Classes taught by members of the New York Baroque Dance Company the first Saturday of every month. There's live music there, too, but you need special shoes. The facility where all this takes place is beautiful and airy. If the terrace is open, go out on it to feast your eyes on Brooklyn.

Parks and Recreation Public Pools
www.nycgovparks.org/facilities/pools, 718-760-6969
Almost as popular as a jimmied fire hydrant in combatting July and August's oppressive heat are the Department of Parks & Rec's 54 public pools. The changing facilities may be battered and bare, and there's a laundry list of rules, but swimming is swimming. Bring a lock, a towel and an actual bathing suit, as opposed to cut offs and a sports bra. Don't bring a stroller, pool toys, newspapers, food, or any cover up that isn't a plain white t-shirt. Our favorites include the comparatively tiny Tony Dapolito Pool at Clarkson & 7th Ave in Greenwich Village (it has a Keith Haring mural and appears in the movie KIDS; 212-242-5228), the giant Red Hook Pool at Bay & Henry in Brooklyn (on weekends, vendors sell fantastic *comida Latino* and the announcements over the loudspeakers are the stuff of legend; 718-722-3211), and the equally huge Astoria Park Pool at 19th St & 23rd Drive in Astoria, Queens (awesome East River view and great sprinklers; 718-626-8620).

NYC Swim
www.nycswim.org, 1-888-NYC-SWIM
April - October
The New York City Department of Environmental Protection doesn't want you jumping in the rivers unless they're watching. There are several races from May to October, but entry ain't cheap, and even the least expensive 1.3 mile jaunt down the Hudson from Christopher Street to Battery Park will require some fairly involved, official proof that you're no sinker.

Macro-Sea Dumpster pools
www.macro-sea.com 212.533.1200
July? August? Who knows! Bring your bathing suit, just in case! This is one country club I'd like to join. Actually, I want more of them, and I want them to be made available to all. These underground DIY pools caused quite a stir when word of the first one got out, but because one can only crowd so many guests into a water-filled Dumpster, the public never wound up being invited. Charges of exclusivity hurt the project developers' feelings. I guess no good deed goes unpunished. Macro-Sea secured the necessary city documents to let everyone in on the fun in dumpster pools set up outside Grand Central and the Park Avenue Viaduct for one glorious August day in 2010.

Grace Bar pool at Grace Hotel
125 W 45th St (btwn Ave of the Americas & 7th Ave)
212-380-2822, www.room-matehotels.com/eng/nuevayork-hotel/gracehotel/gracehotel.php
(Theater District: N/Q /R/S/1/2/3/7 to 42nd St-Times Sq)
$10 entry for non-guests
I shouldn't let this one out, but there's a bar in the Grace Hotel (formerly known as Hotel QT) that has a *pool in it*. The drink prices are steep as all hell, but there's no charge for swimming. And you're not only in a bar that has a pool in it, but the bar is in the pool. Really. – Caitlin McGurk (It has a steam room and sauna too. – AH)

Big City Fishing in Hudson River Park
Pier 46, Hudson River near Charles St
(Greenwich Village: 1/2 to Christopher St)
&
Pier 84, Hudson River near 44th St
(Hell's Kitchen: A/C/E to 42nd St)
Saturday & Sunday, Memorial Day to Labor Day/Tuesday-Sunday in July & August, 10am-4:30pm
www.hudsonriverpark.org/education/big_city_fishing.asp
Free
Borrow all the tackle and bait you want, but better bring your insurance card in a bucket if you plan on eating anything you happen to catch. Just kidding. They're not going to let you. If you're really serious about supplementing your daily toxin intake with the catch of the day, you're better off bringing your own gear to dangle off Red Hook's Valentino pier, where the non-recreational anglers go.

Red Hook Boaters
Valentino Pier (off Coffey Street in Red Hook, Bklyn)
www.redhookboaters.org 917-676-6458
(Red Hook: B61 bus to Coffey & Van Brunt or IKEA water taxi)
Free
Mid May – Mid September, Sunday 1-5pm & Mid June –

ZINESTER MAILBAG ... in which our nonNYC-

Mid August, Thursday 6-8pm
The Red Hook Boaters will take you paddling in their kayaks and canoes, launching from the Valentino Pier Thursday evenings and Sunday afternoons. You'll have about 20 minutes out on the water to drink in that Statue of Liberty view before you'll be called back to admire it from shore so another eager participant gets a chance to splash around. You'll also experience the thrill of mandatory good citizenship. The Red Hook Boaters believe in leaving the beach cleaner than they found it and they don't believe in shirkers.

Tide and Current Taxi
www.marielorenz.com/tideandcurrenttaxi.php
Free (year round, depending on weather & availability)
Marie Lorenz builds wooden boats and takes people day-tripping on them for free. In return for taxi-ing you around the watery NYC destination of your choice (hopefully one she's yet to explore fully herself), she gets to publish the story of your voyage on her website, illustrated with lots of action shots. Some of the trips are mission based, like planting a peach tree on North Brother Island in memory of Typhoid Mary, a cook famed for her peach ice cream, among other things. Others have a more open-ended, see-what-happens feel. Marie's trip reports remind me of Maira Kalman's illustrated historical reportage in *The Times*—educational, moving, and observant. If your cabby's got time in her schedule, she'll consult her charts and calculate when you'll be setting out. She gets more fare requests than she can possibly handle, so if it wasn't meant to be this visit, please don't hold it against her. If the trip's a go, be a sport and bring a lunch for both of you!

Shoot the Freak
Btwn Surf Ave & the Boardwalk Coney Island, Brooklyn
www.coneyislandfunguide.com/Attraction/Shoot-the-Freak.htm (Coney Island: D/F/N/Q to Stillwell Ave)
Shoot the Freak is to be avoided at all costs. It brings out the worst in humanity, charging folks to shoot a paintball gun at a human target. – Amanda Plumb (According to the man who runs the concession, the freak is the only guy in Brooklyn who won't shoot back. – AH)

Fake your way to a gym bunny work out!
Crunch, 1-888-2-CRUNCH
www.crunch.com/en/Locations/New York City.aspx
&
Equinox, 212-774-6363
www.equinox.com
&

New York Sports Club, 1-800-301-1231
www.mysportsclubs.com/regions/NYSC.htm
Crunch and sometimes Equinox and New York Sports Club offer free passes on their websites. Some may be for locals only, but in this case I strongly advise you to bring a passport instead of a driver's license and lie your ass off by saying you just moved here. If you know someone that lives in NY, it should be easy for them to get friends guest passes to their gym. Whenever a houseguest of mine wants to go to Equinox, I always ask for passes and get them. – Josh Saitz (Crunch is the only one who makes it easy to find that free pass on their website. I like the one on Lafayette, across the Public Theater. – AH)

Forest Equine Center
8811 70th Rd (@Sybilla St, Forest Hills, Queens)
718-263-3500, www.forestequinecenter.com
(Forest Hills: E/F/R to 71st & Continental Ave)
Forest Equine Center is awesome. They take you through Forest Park in Forest Hills, Queens. Pretty great, horseback riding in New York City! It's about $30 and it's so worth it. – Josh Medsker

Ice Skating in Prospect Park's Wollman Rink
Ocean Ave & Parkside Ave (Lefferts Gardens, Bklyn)
718-965-8999
www.prospectpark.org/visit/activities/ice_skating
(Lefferts Gardens: B/S/Q to Prospect Park)
$5. Seniors & Under 14: $3. $6.50 skate rental
Late November to Mid-March
Central Park has the romance, and the Pond in Bryant Park has the press because it's free (free to stand in line forever for the privilege of rumbling like sardines over a surface that's roughly equivalent in size and texture to a corduroy bathmat...) I like skating in Prospect Park best. If you want to be really cheesy, go before 10am Monday morning, when you can do your Hamill Camels to ballroom music. Michael Jackson's passing brought on a mania for the soundtrack skate. There's one pretty much every weekend. I can do without the Disney Tunes, but Bruce Springsteen is going on my calendar right now.

Adult-sized Monkey Bars!
Columbus Park Playground
Mulberry St (btwn Bayard & Mosco)
www.newyorkled.com/columbuspk.htm
(Chinatown: J/N/Q /R/Z/6 to Canal St)
Need I say more?

Pick Up Basketball at The Cage
West 4th St & Ave of the Americas
www.insidehoops.com/west-4th-street-basketball.shtml
(Greenwich Village: A/B/C/D/E/F/M to West 4th St)
You may think you got game, but try it on here, and you
may find that all you are is tall. This kind of elbow-to-the-
breadbasket street ball makes mince meat out of genteel
notions of sportsmanship. That's why it's so fun to watch,
and why new players should resist the urge to whine that
they were fouled. Yeah, so? Why don't you go cry about it
to your mama? I know a lot of guys who make a habit of
NYC pick-up basketball, but few who claim to have done
it here. I respect them for knowing their limits. Tompkins
Square is tough enough. Don't let us scare you out of it
though. Here's a link where you can search for pick-up
games that proceed at something closer to tea party
speed: www.nofouls.com/map/10115/New_York-N.Y

Old Man with Peach Catch & Release
Chinatown
Shou Xing (aka Shou Hsing, Nan Ji Xian Weng, Shou Lao)
is the Chinese God of Longevity, a cheerful old chrome
dome with flowing beard and robes. He hangs out with a
deer, a bat, and a crane, and carries a peach. Hit one of the
big Chinatown groceries to buy (or otherwise document)
all the products bearing his likeness. (Hint: start with the
Longevity Noodles. For extra credit, keep track of every
brand that boosts its sales with the lucky number 88.

St. Mark's Place T-shirt Safari
East Village
I don't do t-shirts but I get an anthropological thrill out of
the ones in the windows of the trashy tourist shops on St.
Mark's between 2nd and 3rd. Divide the street in half. You
write down the slogans on display in half of these stores,
while a friend records the rest. Then meet back to see
who has captured the most witless vulgarity. If you need
a tiebreaker, the one who has written the word "fuck" the
most wins (triple points awarded for any slogan managing to use it three times on a single shirt.)

Grand Central Peeper
Take the time to really see Grand Central Station—play
in the shops; hang out in the main hall watching crowds
go by, staring at the constellations in the ceiling—can
you find the lighted stars? Can you find the bricks they
didn't clean? Peruse the latest exhibit at the Transit Museum. Walk the long hall of the Market and marvel at the
beautiful tree "chandelier" at the street end; have lunch or
dinner downstairs in one of the sit-down restaurants; find
the whispering hall. Find out why there are oak leaves and
acorns carved into the marble. There's really so much to
do there. – Melissa Bastian

Rubber Safari
It's not what you're thinking. C'mon, that would be gross,
and not nearly as easy as it once was. Equip yourself with
some crayons (strip the wrappers off, so you can use them
on their sides) and a tablet of newsprint, and see what
raised surfaces are there for the rubbing. I find it interesting that the majority of NYC manhole covers are made in
India. Feel extra important if your last name is Harrison
or Campbell, as those words are embossed on at least half
the sewers in the East Village. - AH (Manholes make great
rubbings, but beware in the summer. They might explode
on you. Actually, any time of year you could get elec-
trocuted by a Con-Ed manhole, so ummm...good luck!
There's lots of other stuff you can use for rubbings. – Fly)

LES Peeper
Bring a sketchpad and walk through the Lower East
Side—sketch as many different examples of typefaces
as you can find. Look at existing signage, but also look
around for evidence of old signage or words built into the
architecture. – Robyn Jordan

7 Safari
Take the 7 train to its furthest stop all the way out in
Queens. Along the way you'll see all kinds of stuff, includ-
ing that big famous stadium where people play baseball.

to know where it's at : IS THE LESBIAN HERSTORY

When you arrive at the last stop, get off and walk through the grounds where the US Opens happen every year. You'll cross over a train yard where you can see several old "redbirds"—the old red subway cars that are so super awesome. Keep walking and you'll walk through the grounds of the 1964 World's Fair; you'll see where they buried time capsules in the ground and read what they put in them, and see that giant globe and the "flying saucers" that are so iconic. Then spend an hour or two at the Queens Museum of Art. It's never too crowded, admission is low or free, the exhibits are always interesting and relevant to New York and current times, and they've got that enormous scale model of NYC! It is so much fun to find things on that model. If you're really adventurous, finish up the day by having dinner in Flushing's Chinatown! – Melissa Bastian

The Joey Ramone Pilgrimage
Walk from Joey Ramone's home in Queens (he attended Forest Hills High School, 6701 110th St) to CBGB's (315 Bowery). This will take you all day and will be a great insight to the city. – Fly (I think it's important to celebrate Joey Ramone until we die. Let's get real, if it weren't for him there would be no pop-punk, no Green Day, no Muffs, no bridge between punk and powerpop. Maybe there would be, but it wouldn't be half as good. – Cristy Road)

Deliberate Inconvenience
If you have to run an errand, let's say the bank, or the post office, look up a distant location, and walk there. If it's too far, take a bus halfway. Not to discount the ever-so-scenic above ground F, Q, J, M, and Z trains, but it's nice to take a bus. You can use hopstop.com to figure out your route. I guess you can also do this and deliberately go somewhere exciting, as opposed to running an errand, but the point

of this is to make daily life exciting. Errands will take on a new meaning. In the process, make sure to pick up cheap pizza. – Cristy Road

SoHo Peeper
Walk through SoHo and look for patterns in the street art—do you start seeing installations/tags/posters that appear to be by the same person or people? – Robyn Jordan

International Chef
Go to the Strand and browse cookbooks featuring the cuisine of a country other than your own. Buy it. Choose a recipe. Make a shopping list. Go to the NYC neighborhood where you'll be able to find the ingredients. Have lunch. Hit the grocery. Go to a bakery or sweet shop and buy the weirdest looking sweet you can find. If the counterperson speaks English, ask if you may interview him or her. If not, ask if you may take their picture for an "article" you're writing. Ask for a business card. Go home. Use your ingredients to cook the recipe you selected back back in NYC. Have a party where you serve this dish to at least six friends. Make a zine about the experience, starting with the Strand, and ending with your friends' reviews of what they've just eaten. Make sure you send a copy to your new friends in the bakery. Don't forget to include a personal note.

Gallery Peeper
Chelsea / Williamsburg / Bushwick
Find the art openings. Wear exciting clothes to them. Drink the free wine, eat the free fruit, and laugh (internally) at the free art or enjoy it, should it happen to be good. – Melissa Bastian

Do It To It
Attend a rally or demonstration! There is something going on here every day. – redguard.

NYC Free For All
Try spending a day here without spending any $ whatsoever. Seriously, not one single penny. Eat out of the garbage. Sleep on the street. Hop the trains. Whatever, try it. Believe me, it is possible. Just one day out of your life—one single day—24 hours... consider that this is how many people survive every day. – Fly

Manhattan circa 1609
Much of subterranean NYC is actually natural streams. They've now been diverted/re-channeled by urban planners for hundreds of years. Use the Mannahatta Project (www.themannahattaproject.org) interactive map to cre-

ate your own tour of Manhattan's natural history, dating back to 1609. – Ling Teo

Get to the Alice Austen House using only public transport. – Amy Burchenal

Locate and then travel to (and try to get a peek at, if you can do so legally!) all of the abandoned subway stations in the five boroughs. Try to figure out: Why did the city stop using these stations? – Melissa Bastian

ODDS & ENDS

ROMANCE

Crushing on someone? Allow our contributors to play Cupid.

Take advantage of the views! I suggest DUMBO's waterfront. – Marguerite Dabaie

The Staten Island Ferry. No joke, bring a flask and take-out and stand outside by the railing for a gorgeous, waterfront ride at sunset. – Robyn Jordan

Take long walks through Fort Tryon and Prospect Park. – John Mejias

Ride the 6 train to its southern terminus, City Hall. Make sure the conductor's message says, "The next stop on this train is City Hall, Uptown Platform." Stay on the train. You will take a tour, fast though it may be, through the abandoned original City Hall station—once called the crown jewel of the subway system. Don't tell your special someone what's happening until you're in the secluded dark tunnel. It'll go by fast, so be prepared. Do some research in advance so you can bust out the knowledge. If you're lucky, the train will move slow. Once you've gone through, keep going north and see if you can spot the next abandoned station on the line at 18th street. Then take him/her out to dinner. You're in like Flynn. – Melissa Bastian

Just pick a 'hood you haven't been to and start exploring. – Megan Garrity

Once you're teetering on that edge of Greenpoint, you'll have the water just a few blocks from you in two directions. I suggest sneaking down to the little industrial dead end of Huron Street, where the sparkling East River practically hits the pavement and some punks have built

a skate ramp. I've had a number of romantic moments as well as creepy ones down over there. Not at the same time, of course. – Caitlin McGurk

A Brooklyn seaside stroll. Start at Brighton Beach, and walk down to Coney Island. Hold hands, breathe the sea air, gaze at the freighters off shore as they head toward port in New Jersey. Dodge the ubiquitous Russian metal detector guys. – David Goren

Trader Joe's wine, movies rented from Videology on Bedford, to-go margaritas from the Turkey's Nest and a picnic in McCarren Park. Or borrow a car for a trek out to Staten Island to climb around and take pics at the rusty Ship Graveyard. – Dear Drunk Girl

Stroll around the Lower East Side, grazing for snacks, for example, nachos at San Loco, then walk across the Brooklyn Bridge to the Brooklyn Ice Cream Factory for delicious ice cream and a lovely, preferably sunset, view of Manhattan. – Becky Hawkins

Hotels are expensive, so date someone who lives in the city. Preferably, someone without roommates. Also, pretty, monochromatic tulip bouquets are about $6 at damn near every bodega in the city. Take advantage. – Kate Black

Climb the cables of the Brooklyn Bridge. You risk arrest, but it is an amazing date (trust me). – Fly

GETTING HITCHED IN NYC

Eloping? Mazel Tov!

If it's a male plug, female outlet situation, you go to the Marriage Bureau for a marriage license. Same sex couples register as domestic partners in the same place, after which, I am sorry to say, you'll have to take it elsewhere. As of this writing, only couples with unlike tackleboxes get to before a city employee to say "I do." Maybe we should all just grab our papers and Universal Life it in the park. Or at least French kiss on the stairs.

If you want to make it legal and/or official, grab your intended and appear together in person at one of the Marriage Bureaus:
Manhattan: 141 Worth St (btwn Centre and Baxter)
212-669-2400
&
Bronx: 851 Grand Concourse, Room B131 (btwn 158th St & 161st St) 718-590-5307

Chantel Guidry, "Poet-in-the-Box", Lawrence, KS

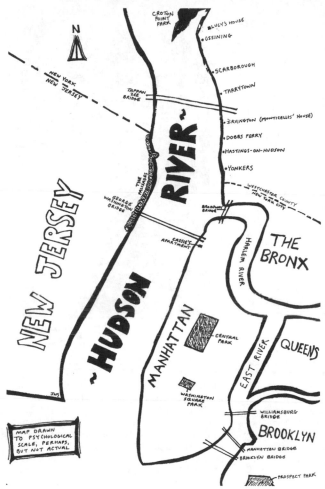

Fill out an application, basically not all that different than if you were applying to work at Burger King. You'll need a money order in the amount of $35 (payable to "City Clerk of New York"), proof of your identities, and proof of your ages, particularly if one of you appears to be jailbait. Blood tests, like rabbit tests, are cinematic, but also unnecessary, a thing of the past. Your marriage license is good for 60 days, but you have to wait 24 hours from the time of issuance to use it. Get a hotel or something. Yes, you can marry your cousin. Domestic partnerships go into effect immediately, so bring some rice.

The days of getting married at City Hall are over. They souped up the new Manhattan Marriage Bureau with big mirrors in the restrooms, a bouquet concession and a photo studio where you can pose in front of a back drop of City Hall. It's not quite Vegas, but if you load some Elvis singing "Hawaiian Wedding Song" on your iPod, they'll play it for all to hear. The cost of a civil ceremony is $25 (payable by credit card or money order). Arrive no later than 3:15 pm. If you're under 18, you've got to bring your folks. If all you need is a witness, email me and I'll try to make it. Remind me to bring my driver's license and my camera.

If I had it to do over again I would get married in Housing Works Used Book Café (www.housingworks.org/social-enterprise/the-works-catering/weddings2/) or the Freak Bar at Coney Island (718-372-5159). The Hungry March Band would play (www.hungrymarchband.com), the Red Hook vendors would cater (www.myspace.com/redhookfoodvendors), and my friends would kindly refrain from getting my groom seriously over-liquored up at Café Noir after the festivities (www.cafenoirny.com).

&

Brooklyn: 210 Joralemon, Room 205 (btwn Court & Adams) 718-802-3585

&

Queens: 120-55 Queens Blvd, Room X001 (btwn 82nd Ave & 80th Rd) 718-286-2829

&

Staten Island: 10 Richmond Terrace, Room 301 (conveniently located right by that romantic ferry) 718-816-2290
www.cityclerk.nyc.gov/html/home/home.shtml

a: Sure! Just call 718·768·DYKE before hopping

Take them to Chinatown. Take them to MOMA, and every other museum in the ZG2NYC except the Museum of Sex and Bodies: The Exhibition. So what if they might have a meltdown? Bagels were invented to buck up whining children. There are playgrounds all over the place, not just in Tompkins Square. (If it's summer, bring a plastic bag and a bathing suit, or at least a pair of dry underpants for after they run through the sprinkler.) Take them to Santa at ABC Carpet and Home, on 19th and Broadway. Take them to Coney Fucking Island! Please! I know you Hip Mamas and Rad Dads know that NYC is a child's oyster too. That said:

Children's Museum of the Arts
182 Lafayette St (btwn Broome & Grand) 212-941-9198
www.cmany.org (SoHo: 6 to Spring St)
$10 (yes, even if you just turned one)
Pay as You Wish Thursday 4-6pm
This is the only Manhattan children's museum I can handle. (The one on the Upper West Side is like McDonald's, one corporate character promotion after another and way more expensive than you would imagine!) Lots of art supplies that the kids probably don't get to use with impunity at home: staplers, scissors, messy paints, clay and computers.

Sunshine Cinema Rattle & Reel
143 E Houston St (btwn 2nd Ave & Chrystie St) 212-330-8182
www.landmarktheatres.com/Market/NewYork/Sunshine-Cinema.htm (East Village: F to 2nd Ave)
I remember wishing my kids were babies again so I could partake. Every Wednesday at 11am, the Sunshine picks one of their current grown-up releases to screen for infants, and more importantly their caregivers. The grown-ups pay full price. The babies are free, as babies and—credit to Dr. Seuss—maybe all creatures should be.

Big Movies for Little Kids
Cobble Hill Cinema
265 Court St (@ Butler, Cobble Hill, Bklyn) 718-596-9113
www.bigmoviesforlittlekids.blogspot.com
(Cobble Hill: F/G to Bergen St)
Every other Monday at 4pm, $6.50
So much better than watching the damn Disney channel, and a lot rowdier than staying home with a video, the biweekly Big Movies for Little Kids after-school matinée rarely screens dreck. The fare's usually classic—Buster Keaton, Pingu, Lucille Ball. If your kid's audience manners start heading south, you won't be alone. Lap passengers don't ride free for this one.

Puppetworks
338 6th Ave (@ 4th St, Park Slope, Bklyn) 718-965-3391
www.puppetworks.org (Park Slope: F/G to 7th Ave)
Adults: $8, Children $7
Calling David Lynch! I don't wanna tell you where to shoot your next movie, but um, here. This storefront was long ago transformed into a marionette theater, where children sit on carpet samples, and any mom or dad whose leash is long enough retires to the benches ringing the room to eye the creepy, dangling stars of past shows, a storage solution as disturbing as it is decorative. Nicolas Coppola, the impresario of this anachronism, has great taste in source material: Peter and the Wolf, The Firebird, The Snow Queen and none of these modern updates!

The New York Hall of Science
47-01 111th St (@ 47th Ave , Corona, Queens, 718-699-0005
www.nysci.org (Corona: 7 to 111th St)
My kids' dad is usually the one to haul the feral young to this interactive and allegedly scientific wonderland, because I get skeeved out by the noise and the overpow-

the (F) to 15th st to find out what their hours are,

ering reek of jacked-up child sweat. The only thing of personal appeal to me is the expansive *al fresco* Science Playground, a timed entry fantasia that's only open in clement weather. Don't wear flip-flops, feed offsite unless you don't mind junky suckateria crap, and keep a sharp eye on that clock.

New York International Children's Film Festival
www.gkids.com, 212-349-0330
This festival gives us Americans a rare chance to see how countries other than Japan go about entertaining their young. Wow. People die. They make sex jokes. People are naked. Fart jokes are actually funny. The organizers pack 100 films (some short, some animated, many defying description) into several late February/early March weekends, then spend the rest of the year reheating the tastiest leftovers, usually at the IFC Center or Symphony Space. The gentle funny bunny stuff that goes down so well with the preschool demographic is balanced by darker, more twisted features for young teens. And because the festival understands that it's setting you up to regard 90 percent of what passes for mainstream children's entertainment even more dimly than you did before, it maintains a vast archive of its favorite shorts, viewable for free online. My children recommend starting with *Fuggy Fuggy* or *Frog*.

Madame Alexander Heritage Gallery
615 W 131st St (btwn Broadway and Riverside Dr W) 212-283-5900
www.madamealexander.com/heritage_gallery
(Harlem: 1/9 to 125th St)
Free
Tour 85 years worth of fancy dolls where they're made.

Forbes Collection at the Forbes Magazine Galleries
62 5th Ave (@ 12th St) 212-206-5548
www.forbescollection.com
(Greenwich Village: L/N/Q /R/4/5/6 to 14th St-Union Sq)
They've got 10,000 tin soldiers, from big names like Alexander the Great and George Washington to many, many handfuls of anonymous sword and cannon fodder. Also enough toy boats to make you wonder what was going on in Malcolm's bathtub.

New York Public Library's Children's Center at 42nd St
Stephen A. Schwarzman Building
5th Ave @42nd St, Ground Floor, Room 84, 212-621-0208
www.nypl.org/locations/schwarzman/childrens-center-42nd-street (Midtown: B/D/F/M to 42nd St-Bryant Park)
In addition to all the books, events, and cozy oversized pillows that make a mockery of my branch library's rick-

ety chairs and lice-ridden stuffed animals, they've got the original Winnie the Pooh and friends. They might underwhelm kids who prefer the cuted-up Disney version, but I think you'll enjoy the bittersweet reality of the real thing. If you're lucky enough to be sharing child-wrangling duties with another adult, you can take turns exploring the big library or maybe sneak off to the Children's Literary Café, an adults-only, one-Saturday-per-month conversation.

Jane's Exchange
191 E. 3rd St (btwn Ave A & B) 212-677-0380
www.janesexchangenyc.com (East Village: F to 2nd Ave)
Parents who've been on the receiving end of a clerk's stink eye for such offenses as nursing in a commercial establishment, or asking if a crotch-clutching, hopping toddler can use a store's bathroom will feel a sensation akin to sinking into a warm bath when visiting this source for child-sized clothing, furnishings, toys, and other sundry gear, all previously-owned, though given the nature of babies and baby showers, not necessarily always worn. This is where the clothes-conscious, downtown Euro-mamas unload their *petits choufleurs'* too smalls.

& whether any special events are brewing.

There are so many wonderful, independently-owned businesses in New York City, it'd be a shame to throw money at an indifferent corporate behemoth whose national executive offices probably occupy several hundred acres of former farmland near a Midwestern airport. Boo! On the other hand, there's plenty of business to get done there that doesn't involve making a purchase.

Bathrooms

Whole Foods bathrooms are spacious and, at least in the ladies' room, feature lavender-scented liquid hand soap much nicer than their cheap-o store brand.

Barnes & Noble bathrooms are usually located near the children's book department and have been known to feature tinkle-sprinkled seats and indignant toddlers writhing on the fold-down diaper decks.

New York City Starbucks bathrooms are the Waterloo where corporate identity breaks down utterly. Certain locations have all-but admitted they're no match for gang graffiti, broken locks, and homeless people who hold court on the pot for hours. Coffee being a diuretic, you may be in for a long wait. But any port in a storm...

Views & Relaxation

If you need to get off your pins for a while, it might be worth buying a can of something you won't have to tip a waitress for, provided it comes with a view. Or hell, don't buy anything. Just look like you're taking a brief time-out before continuing with your shopping. This usually works best if you're not up against the lunch rush.

Whole Foods is the hands-down winner in this department. The one on Houston between 2nd and 3rd Avenue has both squishy chairs and table seating from which to peer out their massive floor-to-ceiling second-story glass windows. The upper-level seating in the one on 14th Street between Broadway and University Place looks north across Union Square to the Empire State Building. Gorgeous! Particularly if it's raining or snowing out!

The Astor Place K-Mart's second-story café has a beautiful, semicircular window looking toward the East Village. Keep an eye on the Cube sculpture. As funny as it is seeing a group of punk kids trying to spin it when you're on the ground, it's even more amusing viewed from on high.

The Target on the second-story of Brooklyn's Atlantic Center Mall looks out on one of the most fucked-up, perilous intersections in New York. Be glad you're not navigating those waters in a car!

I think Barnes & Noble actually encourages people to hang around and read books. It's highly unusual for a retail outfit to say, "Listen, you can buy our wares and take them home or NOT buy them and sit on this comfortable couch and enjoy them for free. If you don't finish, come back again tomorrow, you can even pick up a new copy." No wonder print is dying. – Josh Saitz

Internet

I recommend going to an Apple Store location to use the internet for free. The one on 5th Avenue is open 24 hours! – Robyn Jordan

Souvenir Photos

All of the Apple Stores' computers have built-in iSight cameras, so go in, launch the PhotoBooth app, take a few snapshots, then log into your e-mail account and send them to yourself. You can even do special effects and backgrounds. – Josh Saitz

Air Conditioning

They've got it. You want it!

Banking

Don't pay a service fee for making a withdrawal from an ATM outside of your bank's network. Rite-Aid and CVS will give you cash back if you use your debit card to make a purchase. The limit at CVS is $35. Rite-Aid will give you up to $100, but probably won't be able to first thing in the morning. The post office can also serve as an ATM if you need stamps for postcards to the folks back home. CVS: 1-800-746-7287, Rite Aid: 1-800-748-3243

They're at 484 14th St in Park Slope. Q: "WHERE

Oatmeal

I have to say it, if only so I can take it off my taxes. Early in the morning, Whole Foods stations a big pot of oatmeal where the soup usually is, and the price is fixed based on container size, so you can weight her down with raisins and dried cranberries, and provided you're discreet and a dab hand with a lid, some fruit from the salad bar and maybe a strip or two of bacon! Don't forget those views.

Picnicking in the Park

You can avoid the long lines and high prices of Central Park's hot dog, pretzel, and Dove Bar vendors by standing in the long lines and paying the high prices of the Time Warner Center's Whole Foods, across the street from the park's southwestern corner.

A few corporate behemoth addresses:
Whole Foods
270 Greenwich St, Tribeca (btwn Warren & Murray)
&
95 E Houston (btwn 2nd & 3rd Ave, LES)
&
250 7th Ave (between 24th St & 25th St, Chelsea)
&
808 Columbus Ave (between 97th St & 100th St, UWS)

Apple Store
401 W 14th St (@ 9th Ave, Meatpacking District)
&
767 5th Ave (btwn 58th & 59th, Midtown East)
&
103 Prince St (@ Greene St, SoHo)
&
1981 Broadway (btwn 67th & 68th, UWS)

Barnes and Nobles and Starbucks are so numerous, and formatting all these addresses has sapped our strength so badly, we can't even think about listing them all. If the hairs on your arm start to stand on end, it's probably a good bet that you're near one.

PHOTOCOPYING
We can't say goodbye until we tell you where to copy your zine.

Wholesale Copies
1 E 28th Street, 4th Floor (@ 5th Ave) 212-779-4065
www.wholesalecopies.com (Flatiron: R to 28th St)
I love these guys for exuding a perfect mix of profession-alism and looks-like-the-circus-is-back-in-town gaiety every time I come banging through their bulletproof door

with the latest ish of *The East Village Inky*. They've had the gig since Issue 2. (The first one was an illegal, self-service job at a friend's workplace, held together with rubber bands.) The bulk of their work seems to be printing legal briefs, which makes me doubly appreciative of their good humored willingness to help out the occasional nutjob. Depending on the size of your run, your job could run you as little as 3 1/2¢ a side.

King's Copies
45 E 7th St (btwn 2nd & 3rd Ave) 212-673-8481
www.kingscopiesny.com (East Village: 6 to Astor Pl)
My favorite spot is King's Copies, this little copy shop run by a bunch of East Asian guys who always get my orders totally wrong and are incredibly nosy about my work but I like their machines. They are nice folks and there is something about the environment that is just heartwarming and strangely homey. – Matana Roberts

Source Unlimited
331 E 9th St (btwn 1st & 2nd Ave) 212-473-7833
www.thesourceunltd.com (East Village: L to 1st Ave)
I used to work as an overnight manager at Kinko's and did a lot of zine copying then. After that I had a few free copy connections but I soon learned that to get decent copies without owing something (other than $$), I have to spend a few bucks, so now if I have to copy stuff I go to the Source. This is a great Lower East Side business to support, a very small neighborhood place with great quality and great prices, run by Santo and his partner. Tell them Fly sent you! There's not really room to do cutting and pasting, and there are no self-serve machines, but you

STILL IN THE "NEW MOMMY" PHASE

SOMETIMES I LOVE SITTING AND JUST **LOOKING** AT ITS LITTLE **STAPLES.**

Becky Hawkins–2008

will get great service and great quality. You can even email them stuff to print out or take a disk or whatever! They also publish a monthly local newsletter and collect cans for the food drive. – Fly (I am a big fan. They are fast and really reliable. I also suspect the owner is an artist and an East Villager from the old, pre-overpriced gentrification days, and even though that's before my time, I tend to get a bit overly sentimental about those times of artsy fartsy yore. – Matana Roberts)

East Side Copy
15 E 13th St (btwn University Pl and 5th Ave) 212-807-0465
www.eastsidecopy.com (Greenwich Village: L/N/Q/R/4/5/6 to 14th St-Union Square)
Having a zine printed, folded, and staple-bound at East Side Copy cost about the same as just printing it at Staples. Doing everything myself was more work, but I had more control over the product. – Robyn Jordan

Copy Com
70A Greenwich Ave (btwn 6th & 7th Ave) 212-924-4180
www.rentmailbox.com
(Greenwich Village: F/L/M to 14th St-6th Ave)
A low-key, dingy place that did a good, fast job when I came in needing 190 copies of a four-page, standard-sized half-black-and-white and half-color zine. The guy working the counter was helpful, and it took 16 minutes from entrance to exit. Had I done all black and white, they would have collated and stapled for free! In the end, I ended up paying about eight cents a copy. For me, their primary appeal is that they're independent, and that they've been in business since 1982. – Heath Row

Graphicolor Digital Copy Center
121 5th Ave (btwn Sterling Pl & St John's Pl, Park Slope, Bklyn) 718-398-8745
(Park Slope: 2/3/4 to Bergen St)
I used to work in a print shop in Florida and expected every NY print shop worker to be twice as grumpy as my work self, *but* these guys are friendly and relaxed. No self-service though. – Cecile Dyer

5¢ Copy Machines – an endangered species!
Ten years ago, it was nothing to bang out a few copies in a bodega or drugstore for a nickel apiece. A few brave merchants struggle to keep the 5¢ copy dream alive. That dream usually ends once their elderly machines croak. Keep your eyes peeled for those distinctive yellow 5¢ signs, though by the time you arrive, the 10¢ trend may have taken over entirely. One practical newsstand owner on East 14th is splitting the diff at 7 1/2¢. Call before you go, to ensure that these holdouts' machines have not gone to toner heaven:

Alphabet Deli
89-97 Avenue C (@6th St), 212-777-7055

Neighborhood Convenience Store
222 1st Ave (btwn 13th & 14th) 212-673-5203

Bio Med Drugs & Surgical Supply
48 3rd Ave (btwn 10th & 11th) 212-388-0346

P & P Candy Store
790 Manhattan Ave (btwn Messerole & Calyer, Greenpoint, Bklyn) 718-389-2823

King's Pharmacy
241 Bedford Ave (btwn N. 3rd & N. 4th, Williamsburg, Bklyn) 718-782-1000

Gowanus Pharmacy
236 Hoyt St (btwn Butler & Douglass, Boerum Hill, Bklyn) 718-747-3637

Scenic Views

Out the windows of the Roosevelt Island Tram

The Williamsburg Bridge

Atop any given roof

Bowstern, "Xtra Tuf", Portland, OR Ⓐ At the

When the Manhattan skyline comes into view as you're driving back from New England.

From a high hill in Fort Tryon Park.

Lying down on the beach at Coney Island so that my head is directly aligned with the Wonder Wheel.

Watching the traffic lights changing simultaneously at dusk all the way down Avenue B

The back view of the children at the feet of Henry Ward Beecher sculpture, just south of the Brooklyn General Post Office

The Temperance fountain in Tompkins Square

The beach at Coney Island seen from the top of the Wonder Wheel, or alternatively, the Cyclone, as you're being cranked up that first hill

All the daffodils that the Netherlands gave to NYC after 9/11 starting to bloom

The Statue of Liberty seen from the Valentino Pier in Red Hook

Parked in a comfy chair by the floor to ceiling windows overlooking 2nd Avenue from the 2nd story of the Whole Foods on Houston St.

The intersection of Columbia and Union in Red Hook

Out the left side window of any Stillwell Ave-bound train, when the Cyclone and the Wonder Wheel loom into view

From Sunset Park

Looking down on any major street from any high building to see streams of yellow cabs looking like matchbox cars.

The Peace Fountain at the Cathedral of St. John the Divine

The windows of The Standard Hotel, as viewed from the High Line

The Union Square Greenmarket before 8:30 am, when all the chefs with their white jackets, checked pants and rubber clogs, push rubber wheelbarrows full of produce destined for that night's menu

Brooklyn's Williamsburg Savings Bank tower, dubbed the "most phallic building in New York City" by writer Jonathan Ames

From the Staten Island Ferry

From Smith and 9th on the F and G trains, the highest subway stop in the system - you can see the Statue of Liberty, the Empire State and Chrysler buildings... and, you know, Gowanus

From the N and Q trains going over the Manhattan Bridge either to or from Brooklyn

From Red Hook behind the Fairway

new Fulton Fish Market Cooperative, inconveniently

Peeking into the long windows of Washington Square North's fancy row housing on a Saturday night in December, when the holiday parties are in full swing. It's a bit Little Matchgirl, but glamorous and exciting

From the Manhattan Bridge or Empire State Park in Brooklyn, from which you can see both Manhattan and the Manhattan Bridge

Empire State from the 11th Floor or higher

The unobstructed view of the Empire State Building from 21st and Broadway

Top of the Rock view is pretty cool

From the lawn at the Alice Austen House in Staten Island

The Brooklyn Heights Promenade at Sunset

42nd Street from the east side is neat because it's on a hill.

The Lower East Side has become something different than what it was, but there is still some grit left if you look for it.

Queensboro Bridge gets overlooked, but it gives a full view of the city, and also a chance to look in people's windows as you leave Manhattan. It's hilarious.

Don't go to the hole in the ground where the WTC used to be. You can re-enact what thousands of people did on 9/11, walk across the bridge and think about all the people that made it out.

Old School B&W photobooth strips have been an integral part of the East Village Inky's cover design since Issue 1, though with the exception of Lakeside Lounge, all those booths have disappeared, along with the establishments they occupied. Spring for a photobooth strip any time you get the chance, especially when traveling. Even on a bad day, there are enough of them in the East Village to do a photobooth crawl, but don't get belligerent if they're not working. It's not the bartender's fault, and you should've phoned ahead to check. Speaking of the bartender, don't forget that you should tip, even if you're a tea totaller who'll only be there for as long as it takes the booth to spit out your strip.

B&W Photobooths

East Village
Lakeside Lounge, 162 Avenue B
Otto's Shrunken Head, 538 E. 14th St, 212-228-2240
Niagara, 112 Avenue A
Vazacs Horseshoe Bar (aka 7B), 108 Avenue B, 212-473-8840
Whiskey Town, 29 E 3rd St, 212-505-7344
The Smith, 55 3rd Ave, 212-420-9800

LES
The Living Room, 154 Ludlow St, 212-533-7235

NoHo
Bleecker Street Bar, 58 Bleecker St

Tribeca
Bubby's Pie Company, 120 Hudson St

Chelsea
Ace Hotel, 20 West 29th St
Trailer Park, 271 W. 23rd St

Hell's Kitchen
9th Ave Saloon 656 9th Ave, 212-307-1503

Brooklyn
Bubby's Brooklyn, 1 Main St, DUMBO, Bklyn
Bushwick Country Club, 618 Grand St, Bushwick Bklyn 718-388-2114
Union Pool, 484 Union Ave, Williamsburg Bklyn, 718-609-0484
Bar 4, 444 7th Ave, Windsor Terrace, Bklyn, 718-832-9800

relocated to Hunts Point in the Bronx. It's open

New Fangled Color Photobooths

East Village
K Mart Astor Place, 770 Broadway, 212-673-1540

Garment District
Daffy's Herald Square, 1311 Broadway 4th fl

Brooklyn
Deno's Wonder Wheel, 3059 W 12th St, Coney Island,

Bklyn, 718-372-2592
The Bell House, 149 7th St, Gowanus, Bklyn
PINBALL

Down with the tyranny of Big Buck Hunter! If I wanted to shoot a gun at animals, I could've stayed in Indiana. Give me some flippers and a silver ball any day. These are a few of the places where you can keep the noble tradition of pinball alive. Many have the added attraction of being dive bars, which enhances the pinball experience, makes one play better, and one has more quarters to burn.

If you're a fanatic, you should check out the NYC Pinball League's website for a listings of what machine is where, and user-submitted reviews of how they're playing. (www.nycpinball.org)

East Village
Ace Bar, 531 E. 5th St, 212-979-8476
Reciprocal Skateboards, 402 E. 11th St
Double Down Saloon, 14 Ave. A
Niagara, 112 Ave. A, 212-420-9517
Fat Black Pussycat, 130 W. 3rd St, 212-533-4790
Vazacs Horseshoe Bar (aka 7B) 108 Avenue B
Otto's Shrunken Head, 538 E. 14th St
Lucy's, 135 Ave A
Amsterdam Billiards, 110 E 11th St, 212-995-0333

Chelsea
McKenna's Pub, 245 W 14th St
Barracuda, 275 w 22nd St

LES
Max Fish, 178 Ludlow, 212-529-3959

Brooklyn
Mug's Ale House, 125 Bedford Ave, Williamsburg
Satellite Lounge, 134 Havemeyer St, Williamsburg
Enid's, 560 Manhattan Ave, Williamsburg 718-349-3859
Brooklyn Icehouse, 318 Van Brunt, Red Hook
Red Hook Bait and Tackle, 320 Van Brunt, Red Hook
Bar Great Harry, 280 Smith St, Carroll Gardens, 718-222-1103
The Bell House, 149 7th St, Gowanus
Southpaw, 125 5th Ave, Park Slope
The Freak Bar, 1208 Surf Ave, Coney Island, 718-372-5159

Queens
Racks Billiards, 19-26 Steinway St, Astoria
Steinway Billiards, 35-25 Steinway St, Astoria

WHERE TO GO IN A SNOWSTORM

Sheeps Meadow in Central Park
Inwood Hills Park
Fort Greene Park
Café Ost at 12th and Ave A
Tompkins Square
Brooklyn Botanical Garden's greenhouses
City Bakery, get a "hot chocolate shot" and watch the
storm through the big windows
Someplace dark that serves hot toddies.
The sledding hill in Prospect Park's Long Meadow
Angel's Share Bar
Any residential street in the far West Village
Down the center of the street!
Owls Head Park has great sledding.
The Brooklyn Botanical Garden greenhouses
The Temple of Dendur in the Metropolitan Museum of
Art
Somewhere high.
Wherever there is a mass exodus of my friends.
Not an airport, that's for sure.

If it is a huge snowstorm, the best place to be is building
snow forts on Broadway! In '95 there was this massive
blizzard that shut down the city. They had to bring in the
National Guard. There was no traffic allowed in the city
and yes, there were snow forts & snowball fights happening on Broadway! There where cross-country skiers on all
of the major avenues! – Fly (I remember that! I was sublet-
ting a big apartment on the corner of 79th and West End
Ave, and when it really started coming now, my brand
new husband and our friend, Bill, decided that this was
the ideal time to take the air conditioner out of the window. Our other friend, Little MoMo and I were huddled
on the bed, under a mountain of comforters, screaming

with laughter as Greg and Bill staggered under the weight
of that thing, snow howling in through the window like
something out of a Dudley Do-Right cartoon. – AH)

WHERE TO GO IN A HEAT WAVE

The Red Hook Pool
The McCarren Pool
Any public pool
The sprinkler park at the top of Tompkins Square
The Wonder Wheel at Coney Island
Bloomingdales
Any public library
Barnes and Noble
The movies
Metropolitan Museum. It's enough to see for hours, and
you pay-what-you-wish
Art galleries in Chelsea, ducking in and out quickly to
minimize the time outside
The subway trains (particularly refreshing after the hell-
ish platforms)
The non-frequented parts & wildlife refuge areas of Fire
Island
The World Financial Center's Winter Garden
Grand Central
The nearest Mister Softee truck
The Cake Shop
Madison Square Park. Not as crowded as Union Square
Park, copious amounts of shade trees, large enough to
catch a breeze.
The west side piers in the evening, when overhead sun
isn't a concern
Under FDR Drive just north of South Side Seaport is al-
ways several degrees cooler than anywhere else in the city
& if you walk even further south to around Wall St, there
is this parking garage that is FREEZING!!!!
St Marks Bookshop's zine rack & anarchist section
Get the hell out of town!!!
Jones Beach
The Jersey Shore
Go to the mountains!!
Failing that you could go to Coney Island...what is left
of it.
Just try not to go into the water for too long
Upstate.
The Tenement Museum, as a reminder to be glad we no
longer have to sleep on the fire escape to cool off on a hot
night.

need wheels & 5 bucks to park 'em. A field

MEMORABLE GRAFFITI
of bathrooms and elsewhere

Hungarian Pastry Shop

Kenka on St. Mark's

The Nuyorican poets café

The PIT theater (backstage)

Mars Bar

Community Bookstore on 7th Ave. in Park Slope

Kate's Joint

The Foodswings bathroom in Williamsburg is pretty nuts.

Mercer St. Think Coffee

Geido Sushi on Flatbush

Decibel Sake Bar

Washington Square's public bathroom - grout writers anonymous

ABC No Rio

Barnes and Noble in Union Square

The Cock (formerly The Hole)

The CBGB bathroom was by far the best, a thing of infamy, but now it's a John Varvatos store. (Irony or sad? You decide)

ROYALTY

Lemon Ice King of Corona
Bruno the Ravioli King
Antonio the Parzmigiana King
Vinnie the Tampon Case King
Barney Greengrass the Sturgeon King
Papaya King
New Beef King
King of Falafel and Shawarma
Noodle King
Potato King
Tasty King
King Wok
Food King
Dumpling King
Taco Tortillas King
Smoothie King
Health King
Laundry King
King of Plasma
Best Space King
Value King of 3rd Avenue
King Taxi
Egg Custard King

Taco King 1
King Taco Supreme
Schnitzel King
Tortillas King
The Pizza King
Kleener King
Closet King
Floor King
Barbeque King
Royal Fried Chicken King
Beeper King
Aquarium King
Pita King
The Hero King
Cellular King
Sneaker King
5th Ave Baby King
Tony Crab King
Plastic King
Ninety Nine Cents King
Gyro King
Gas King
CD King
Sewer King
Tuxedo King
Go-Go Souvlaki-King
PC Repair King

Queen of Steinway
Filter Queen of New York
Premier Laundry Queen
The Jewelry Queen
Bathroom Queen
Havana Sandwich Queen #2
Weave Queen
Ices Queen
Maureen the Cleaning Queen

Island Pressure King
The King of Radiators
King Kog
Pastrami Queen
Lipstick Queen
Diamond Queen
Velma Queen of Illusion
Absolute Copier Queen
99 Cents Queen

GROSSEST

The ZG2NYC is proud to present a disgusting pastiche of some of the grossest things our resident correspondents have borne witness to in NYC:

Stepped over a dead guy on 81st street my first night living in the city. Got spooged on in a packed 4/5 train between Grand Central and 14th St. – Amy Burchenal

Some people love them but I despise the smell of those nut vendors. It's so sickly sweet and gross. Human feces are also pretty foul, and that's happened a few times. – Megan Garrity

A stiff dead cat laid to rest in its own unemptied litterbox, atop a stinking, overflowing dumpster. - AH

About a dozen open garbage cans full of rotting meat, behind the Food Bazaar in Bushwick. I still have trouble gripping the fact that this wasn't a nightmare. – Catilin McGurk

Pigeons eagerly feasting on a puddle of fresh vomit. - AH

The lidless, outgoing toilets contractors place on the curb when they are renovating apartment bathrooms. - AH

Half a squashed rat. - AH

Men jerking off in the subway are pretty consistently revolting. Unfortunately, I'm way past seeing just one of them. – Kate Black

An abandoned speedboat filled to the gunwales with trash on a desolate strip in the East Williamsburg Industrial Zone. - AH

A plastic spoon stuck in a dollop of excrement. (Poor man's pudding!) - AH

That militant banshee woman who used to hang out in front of the Astor Place Starbucks, brandishing blow ups of graphic, painful-looking bondage porn, screaming at any woman who declined to make a donation. Once she yelled after me to stop breeding. I thought she said, "Stop breathing!" - AH

A homeless woman having a bowel movement in a plastic shopping bag on 6th Ave in the teens on a most frigid day. - Genevieve Texeira

Vomit on the subway stairwell, vomit in the train. – Cristy Road

At three in the morning, I was on my way to open the Starbucks in Times Square. I swear to god, I saw a woman in a hooded coat who I'm pretty sure had leprosy. She bumped into me coming down the stairs in the train station on 42nd street, and I saw her face. It was so hideous, I jumped back. She had what looked like a sweet potato hanging from her face, and you could barely see the rest of her face for all of the lumps. I felt awful for my reaction. But it was freaky. – Josh Medsker

That day when the grey and yellow snow begins to melt and all the dog do is revealed. - AH

Trash day in the summer. – Mantana Roberts

Fish markets in the summer, any of them. – Dear Drunk Girl

Garbage trucks on Van Brunt St in Red Hook and the live

Q: "SINCE I AM EVIL, I MIGHT LIKE A LIST OF INFAMOUS

chicken market on Richardson St. – John Mejias

Those disgusting putrid puddles in the summer. – L. Nichols

Subway car - human turd and other bodily fluids in the summer, possibly not even in the summer. – Ling Teo

Times Square on New Year's Eve. – Andria Alefhi

The last time there was a garbage strike and the streets were covered with rotting garbage in the sun. – Josh Saitz

#1) Piles of human feces in the Canal St. Station. #2) A woman on a subway train I was riding took her shoes off when she reached Canal St. and proceeded to walk around the station barefoot. Why?! – Marguerite Dabaie

Gowanus Canal! Super Fund site. – Linn Edwards & Brian Bell

The contents of Christmas tree stand's leaky Port-a-Potty seeping out onto the sidewalk in front of St Mark's Church, where it mingled with the trunks of all those beautiful, fresh-cut evergreens, who no doubt lapped it up like water. - AI I

Rotting rats/mice inside walls. I smelled this in a store for the first time. I knew this is what it was because my boyfriend worked there. Now I recognize the same smell in other places occasionally... – Robyn Jordan

Dead bodies, yeah, sorry, but lots of dead bodies; shot, drowned, stabbed. the sight & the smell is not nice. Also when I broke my back in the spring of 1997 and I was in the ER and they stuck me in the hall screaming in pain for hours and someone next to me took a shit in their pants and I was strapped down on one of those spinal boards so I could not turn my head to see who the hell it was or what the hell was happening. that was a disgusting smell. I had to smell it for a really long time! Oh! And also when people puke (or shit) in front of you on the sidewalk, that fuckin sucks! Sorry! That might be too disgusting to include, but it happens! It is a serious reality in many of the not so posh neighborhood. – Fly

Shit. - Cecile Dyer

STOPS ON THE **OLFACTORY TOUR** OF NEW YORK CITY

HOSTESS PRESENT

You can keep your fancy jams! If you're looking for a small token to express your appreciation for letting you crash on the couch of our 340-square-foot apartment, get us a hostess present:

An original pesto slice from Ray's on Prince St. – Jon Bocksel

Clearly I am cheap and like artsy things and boozy things—you can't go wrong! – Dear Drunk Girl

Any vegan food item from Mee Wah on Hester Street or a bag of Vietnamese coffee from the Vietnamese deli on Broome St. – Victoria Law

Metromint bottled water – Andria Alefhi

A bottle from Astor Place Wines – Linn Edwards and Brian Bell

A 6-pack of beer from the local deli. – L. Nichols

A bag of frozen dumplings from the dumpling house on Eldridge and Broome. – Matana Roberts

Martin's Pretzels, the Amish-made crispy treats that

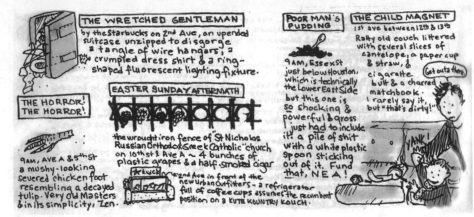

THE WRETCHED GENTLEMAN
by the Starbucks on 2nd Ave, an upended suitcase unzipped to disgorge a tangle of wire hangers, a crumpled dress shirt & a ring-shaped fluorescent lighting fixture.

THE HORROR! THE HORROR!

9AM, AVE A & 5th St
a mushy-looking severed chicken foot resembling a decayed tulip. Very old Masters-ish in its simplicity, Zen.

EASTER SUNDAY AFTERMATH
the wrought iron fence of St Nicholas Russian Orthodox Greek Catholic "church on 10th st & Ave A ~ 4 bunches of plastic grapes & a half-smoked cigar

2nd Ave in front of the new Urban Outfitters - a refrigerator full of coffee cups assumes the recumbent position on a KUTE KOUNTRY KOUCH.

POOR MAN'S PUDDING
9AM, Essex St just below Houston, which is technically the Lower East Side but this one is so shocking & powerful & gross I just had to include it: a pile of shit with a white plastic spoon sticking out of it. Fund that, N E A!

THE CHILD MAGNET
1st ave between 12th & 13th
Ratty old couch littered with several slices of cantelope, a paper cup & straw, a cigarette butt & a charred matchbook. I rarely say it, but "that's dirty!"

Get outa there.
YANK!

are the Beluga caviar of the pretzel world. They are sold every day of the week at one of the NYC Greenmarkets, including Union Square. The best deal is to buy a bag of brokens. – David Goren

Get me a dozen bagels from H&H or Ess-A-Bagel. Not plain, not garlic, but include some multi-grain and salt. – Josh Saitz

Cheese, always appreciated. East Village Cheese Shop is the place. Or what about knitted finger puppets that can be found at lots of summer street fairs or street-corner vending tables? They're usually a couple of bucks per puppet, with discounts if you buy in bulk. – Robyn Jordan

Burritos! Brunch! I want to be paid in delicious NYC food. – Megan Garrity, Scribble Faster

Coffee from Guerilla Coffee on 5th Avenue in Brooklyn, nice bread from Amy's Bread in the Village or a nice note. In NYC you always have people visiting and I would feel bad if they all felt like they should leave gifts. – Cecile Dyer

Mondel's chocolate from their shop at 115th & Broadway. – Jerry the Mouse

If you get it from Fish's Eddy, I will like it. Please note: I think the ceramic hands are kind of weird and Liz already got me the carnival pint glasses. – Amanda Plumb

Pretty chopsticks from Pearl River Mart. – Melissa Bastian

I don't know any NYCer who wants more stuff. Astor Wines (399 Lafayette St) has affordable spirits. Murray's Cheese shop (254 Bleecker) and Porto Rico Coffee (201 Bleecker, or 40 1/2 Saint Marks Pl, among other locations) are also good bets. I prefer light roasts—they have more caffeine. – Kate Black

Something Coney Island-related—anything corny, or something from 1 Schubert Alley, the Broadway musicals store in Times Square. I guess not everyone is a nut for Broadway Musicals, but I am and I can hardly afford them. – Cristy Road

Spend an hour at the Painted Pot, glazing the highlight of your visit onto a tiny soy sauce dish (or Chopstick Bowl, if you're feeling flush). It'll take them a week to fire it, but as long as it's your treat, I'm more than happy to pick it up! Every time I use it, I'll think of you. Aren't you glad it's dishwasher safe? Also I would appreciate it if my female guests would refrain from flushing tampons down the toilet, as a hostess gift to my very patient landlady. - AH

I always want plants from either the Grand Army Plaza Farmer's Market or the one at Union Square. – Jessica Max Stein

A bag of weed. – Amy Burchenal

CREDITS

CONTRIBUTORS
...and their zines!

Andria Alefhi
315 E 5th St # 6C
NY NY 10003
www.neverhaveparis.blogspot.com
neverhaveparis@gmail.com
We'll Never Have Paris (Twice yearly, $4, submissions are welcome of narrative nonfiction of 1000 words or less on the theme of things never meant to be)

Liz Baillie
www.lizbaillie.com
www.freewheelcomics.com
liz@lizbaillie.com
My Brain Hurts (Available as a 2-volume anthology, $12 each + $3 S&H)
Freewheel
did illustrations on pages 8, 78, 87, 117, 124, 133, 160, 165, 172, 235

Melissa Bastian
PO Box 2340
New York, NY 10009
www.toomanycombined.blogspot.com
www.brightdesign.etsy.com
bastian613@gmail.com
blank the plague (five issues plus a best-of compilation, no longer publishing, still printing/distributing, $1.50 per copy)
Anywhere I lay my head (one-issue zine about my experiences with Hurricane Katrina, $4.00 per copy which includes a $1 donation to Common Ground Collective in NOLA)
The Plague Project (one-issue zine about living with the chronic pain of fibromyalgia, $7.00)

Vegetable Vegetable Mineral (quarterly zine about the food industry, by a vegan, for everyone, $1.50)

Lola Batling
144 Old Bergen Rd, # C3
Jersey City, NJ 07305
www.inkigirl.com
theferalmuse@yahoo.com
Nepenthe ($5 quarterly or $15 for a year)

Kate Black
PO Box 1415, Cooper Station
New York, NY 10276
www.kateblack.com
kate@badbuttons.com
TTV NYC (Through The Viewfinder New York City, $2.75, full color, 2-4 times yearly, online transactions preferred)

Jon Bocksel
www.jonbocksel.info
jonbocksel@gmail.com
Eye Sludge
Long Haired Freaky People
High Archy's
Jesus Loves Me
(contact Jon for ordering info)
did illustrations on pages 58, 123, 232

Bill Brown
www.heybillbrown.com
dreamwhip@gmail.com
Dreamwhip (price varies, email Bill, or order from Microcosm)
did illustrations on pages 46, 151, 161, 190, 242

Lynn Brown
www.freefallnyc.org
faller@msn.com
Lynn creates low-tech, high-concept dance theater with FreeFall, of which he is a founding member.

Amy Burchenal
www.amybphoto.com
www.etsy.com/shop/zburch
zburch@mindspring.com
Somewhere South of Roanoke ($10)
Jazz of the City ($10)
Ode ($10)
I Went to Coney Island ($10)
NYC Texture Vol. 1 ($10)

Marguerite Dabaie
1416 Ditmas Ave
Brooklyn, NY 11226
www.margoyle.net
margoyle@margoyle.net
The Hookah Girl ($6)
Starfish ($3)

Cecile Dyer
573 Sackett St 2R
Brooklyn, NY11217
www.wooloo.org/ceciledyer
cecile.dyer@gmail.com
I Live in Brooklyn
HEY YOU (written and illustrated with Ian Hart)

Linn Edwards & Brian Bell
270 Rutland Rd
Brooklyn NY 11225
www.lefthandedpublishing.com
contact@lefthandedpublishing.com
Goodbye Summer
Private Domain
Daily Situations
($6 - $30, contact us for prices)

FLY
www.peops.org
www.Flyspage.com
fly@peops.org
PEOPs
Dog Dayz
FLY (maggot-zine)
(Fly has been at it for over 20 years, publishing zines
with all different titles. Please order them from www.
microcosmpublishing.com. She's also in the band Zero
Content)
did illustrations on pages 25, 39, 153, 162, 213, 223

Jenna Freedman
203 Rivington St., #3C
NYC, NY10002
jenna.openflows.com
leslzine@gmail.com
Lower East Side Librarian Winter Solstice Shout-out, annual
since 2001 ($2)
Lower East Side Librarian Reading Log, separate from *Shout-
out* since 2007 ($1)
unsolicited trades only from library workers
co-editor, *Zine Librarian Zine* #3, "DIY-IYL: Do It Yourself
in Your Library" (donation)

Sharon Furgason
P.O. Box 5735
Astoria, NY 11105
www.inkylagoon.com
www.adistantmemory.com
sharon@inkylagoon.com
archipelago
Nina the Librarian
did illustrations on pages 29, 69, 120, 143, 170

Megan Gerrity
1407 W Erie St, #2R
Chicago IL 606042
meggerrity@gmail.com
Scribble Faster ($3, published irregularly, back issues available.)

Adam Gnade
c/o Microcosm Publishing
222 S. Rogers
Bloomington, IN 47404
www.adamgnade.com
did illustrations on pages 95

David Goren
723 E. 18th St
Brooklyn, NY 11230
www.shortwaveology.com
shortwaveology@mac.com
Shortwaveology (published semi-irregularly...email for
details)

Alisa Harris
www.alisaharris.com
alisamharris@hotmail.com
Urban Nomad ($5)
Counter Attack ($2)
did illustrations on pages 21, 103, 104, 111, 129, 167, 189, 211,
220, 233

Becky Hawkins
486 Brooklyn Ave. #E19
Brooklyn, NY 11225
www.frenchtoastcomix.com
hawkins.becky@gmail.com
French Toast Comix (ranges from $1- $3, publication is currently irregular)
did illustrations on pages 13, 45, 75, 76, 119, 125, 148, 157,
195, 229

My Small Diary, Birmingham, AL @ John

Leslie Henkel (*a.k.a* Dear Drunk Girl)
57 Thames St #3L
Brooklyn, NY 11237
www.deardrunkgirl.etsy.com
www.deardrunkgirl.com
tightpantsydrew@gmail.com
L Hath No Fury: A Tight Pantsy Drew Mystery #1 ($3)
D.I.Y. or Die: A Tight Pantsy Drew Mystery #2 ($3)
Flickred Out : A Tight Pantsy Drew Mystery #3 ($3)
Fixed Fear : A Tight Pantsy Drew Mystery #4 ($3)
did illustrations on pages 81, 126, 159, 186, 206, 214, 227, 235

Ed Herbstman & Melanie Hoopes
Magnet Theater
254 West 29th Street
New York, NY 10001-5290
www.magnettheater.com
ed@magnettheater.com
Ed and Melanie teach improv and make comedy at the Magnet Theater. Melanie is also Brooklyn's premier hypocritical advice columnist at:
www.psreader.com/hypocrites_almanac

gracie janove
RadicalFood@gmail.com
herstory of the three month long laugh: poems ($3)

Jerry the Mouse
www.jerise.com
www.jerise.etsy.com
jerise@jerise.com
Subway People
Greek Travel Sketchbook

Robyn Jordan / Naptime Press
www.robynjordan.com
robyn@robynjordan.com
Getting There ($3)
Hot Town ($3)
Stop Touching That ($3)
(...and many more fine zines, so inquire!)
did illustrations on pages 66, 145, 163

Victoria Law
PO Box 20388
Tompkins Square Station
NY NY 10009
www.resistancebehindbars.org
VikkiML@yahoo.com

Tenacious ($3)
Don't Leave Your Friends Behind ($3, or 2-for-$5)
Enter the 90s: Punks and Poets at ABC No Rio ($3)
Nefarious Doings in Revisionist Tourist Attractions: A Mother-Daughter Photo Zine (trade)
Tell Me About the First Time You Came to ABC No Rio (free, but you have to pick it up from the ABC No Rio Zine Library!)
Mama Sez No War (out of print, but available for perusal at Barnard & ABC No Rio zine libraries)

Shayna Marchese
www.voidscomic.com
info@shaynamarchese.com
Pieces / Voids
did illustrations on pages 15, 63, 73, 144, 147, 192, 219

Lauren Jade Martin
laurenjademartin@gmail.com
Quantify (no longer publishing)

Kelly McClure
BUST Magazine Associate Music Editor
P.O Box 1016 - Cooper Station
New York, NY 10276
kellymcclurewritesstuff@gmail.com

Caitlin McGurk
57 Grove St, # 1B
Brooklyn NY 11221
www.goodmorningyou.net
Goodmorningyou@gmail.com
Good Morning You (trade me by mail!)
did illustrations on pages 31, 52, 164

Carrie McNinch
PO Box 49403
Los Angeles, CA 90049
www.myspace.com/carriemcninch
cmcninch@gmail.com
You Don't Get There From Here (quarterly, $3)
did illustrations on pages 91, 108, 141, 231

Josh Medsker
29-21 21st Ave. #A4
Astoria, NY 11105
www.blogspot.com/twentyfourhourszine
JoshMedsker@gmail.com
Teach (free, comes out irregularly)
Twenty-four Hours (free online, updated monthly)

Rosemary's fates led to The Dakota @ 72nd &

John Mejias
www.paping.org
papingzine@gmail.com
Paping (price varies per issue, see website for specifics)
did illustrations on pages 35, 57, 60, 107, 185, 228, 249

Anthony Meloro
www.comics.goldmineanthology.com
goldmineanthology@gmail.com
Goldmine Anthology
did illustration on pages 43

Eric Nelson
Queens, NY
www.cupandsaucerpress.tumblr.com
ericnelson82@gmail.com
Cup and Saucer Chronicles ($2)

L. Nichols
www.dirtbetweenmytoes.com
wormulus@gmail.com
Jumbly Junkery (3 to 4 times a year, $5)

did illustrations on pages 113

Amanda Plumb
1264 McPherson Rd SE
Atlanta GA 30316
amandaeplumb@gmail.com
I (Heart) NYC, Not Really But I'm Trying ($2)

redguard
PO Box 1568
NY NY 10276
www.absent-cause.org
redguard@gmail.com
Absent Cause (2 issues annually, $3)

Emily Rems
BUST Magazine, Managing Editor
P.O Box 1016 - Cooper Station
New York, NY 10276
www.myspace.com/royalpinkrocks
emilyrems@bust.com
Emily drums for the all girl power pop band, Royal Pink.

Cristy C. Road
PO Box 20229
NY, NY 10009-9991
www.croadcore.org
croadcore@yahoo.com

Address for zine orders: www.microcosmpublishing.com,
www.akpress.org
Green zine (on indefinite hiatus, though Cristy's working
on some comics to be published as zines)
Indestructible (book)
Bad Habits (book)
did illustrations on pages 131, 137, 207, 230

Matana Roberts
545 8th Avenue #401
New York, NY 10018
www.matanaroberts.com
matanaroberts@yahoo.com
Fat Ragged (quarterly, $5 or trades/barter/gift economy for
those who really need it! no back issues)

Bill Roundy
www.billroundy.com
bill@billroundy.com
The Amazing Adventures of Bill (free, weekly)
Man Enough: a queer romance
Yes Master: a horrible romance
Bill's Bartending Guide
did illustrations on pages 82, 84, 169

Heath Row
438 N. Stanley Ave.
Los Angeles, CA 90036

1.

2.

3.

4.

5.

6.

Central Park West (8 because you're evil you

www.mediadiet.net
kalel@well.com
Karma Lapel, Hedge Trimmings, Jungle Radio, Snow Poster City, Snow Poster Township, Faculae & Filigree, Wild Analyst, The National Fantasy Fan, Blue Moon Special, Papernet Gazet, .zap!!, Media Diet ($3 or The Usual. Requests for specific titles will get the most recent issue of that title still in print.)

Ashley Rowe
fatbottombakers@gmail.com
Barefoot & in the Kitchen #1-4 ($3 each)
Fat Bottom Bakery in Oakland, CA
did illustrations on pages 245, 247

Kenan Rubenstein
www.underthehaystack.net
boyblue@boyblueproductions.com
The Oubliette
did illustrations on pages 65, 71, 115, 166, 203

Jøsh Saitz
P.O. Box 12, Lenox Hill Station
New York, NY 10021
www.negcap.com
josh@negcap.com
Negative Capability: A paper zine where narcissism meets misanthropy
I also do a joke site about famous but uglier siblings at www.donswayze.com.
did illustration on pages 239

Andy Singer
2103 Berkeley Avenue
Saint Paul, MN 55105
www.andysinger.com
andy@andysinger.com
Comics for Vegetables
No Exit
did illustrations on pages 11, 17, 23, 101, 116, 181, 201, 204, 233, 237

Esther Smith
Purgatory Pie Press
19 Hudson St #403
NY, NY 10013
www.purgatorypiepress.com
esther@purgatorypiepress.com

Jessica Max Stein
www.jessicamaxstein.com
gaymuppeteer@gmail.com

The Rainbow Connection: Richard Hunt, Gay Muppeteer ($7)
The Long Walk Back to Myself ($3)
did illustrations on pages 216, 225

Adam Suerte
Brooklyn Tattoo
99 Smith St
Brooklyn, NY 11201
www.adamsuerte.com
adam@adamsuerte.com
Aprendiz 1- 4 ($3.95 each)
did illustrations on pages 27, 51, 176, 197, 199, 234

Ling Teo
305 E 91st St, # 5B
New York NY 10128
www.etsy.com/longtailedcomets
lingette@gmail.com
Summer Rain At the Boathouse ($2)
Fall Haiku in Central Park ($2)
Winter Haiku in Central Park ($2)
Spring Haiku in Central Park ($2)
Yonkers Power Station Zine ($5)

Genevieve Texeira
1909 Quentin Rd, 5B
Brooklyn NY 11229
www.myspace.com/going_native_nyc
going.native.nyc@gmail.com
Going Native NYC (3 issues annually, $3)

Acknowledgments
As a collaborative effort, the Zinester's Guide to NYC owes its very existence to the expert and uncomplaining volunteer efforts of Joe Biel, Adam Gnade, Matt Gauck, Rio Safari, Kate Savage, Ally the Intern, and all of the contributors. I would also like to thank Moe Bowstern, Elly Blue, Rachel Fershleiser, Dave Awl, Jim Glenn, Nate Beaty, the late great Rocketship, Bluestockings, St. Mark's Bookshop, Housing Works Used Book Café, Jane's Exchange, Quimby's, Women and Children First, Reading Frenzy, Powell's, Atomic Books, Monkey Wrench, City Lights, Toronto Womens Bookstore, Parcell Press, Microcosm, all the Facebook friends and members of We Make Zines who helped out with questions, suggestions, and titles, the subscribers of *The East Village Inky* and all citizens, past and present, of New York Fuckin' City, especially Greg, India and Milo Kotis.

Ayun Halliday, ZG2NYC
PO Box 22754
Brooklyn NY 11202
Ayun@AyunHalliday.com
did illustrations on pages
19, 37, 41, 49, 54, 89, 93,
97, 99, 105, 135, 139, 154,
174, 179, 183, 211, 222, 226,
238, 241

INDEX

board rejected an application from KISS's

245

terrorize all of NYC, even though he

Staten Island) I have a hunch you're not

Little Paper icee cups

Maps

For those of you without global positioning systems on your dang phone, enter any subway station by the main entrance and you should find a map to the neighborhood. Study it long enough and someone will come up and pick your pocket or ask if you need help finding someplace. If you're ever turned around, duck below ground. Chances are that neighborhood map will get you straightened out.

To get you started we've included our own (patented!) very basic overview of Manhattan, with supplemental maps for neighborhoods like Chinatown and Williamsburg, both of which defy the grid-like, oft numeric-based layout of the rest of the city. Yes, we know that Williamsburg isn't in Manhattan. We were just checking to see if you did too. The reason these maps don't fold out is we don't want you to look like a tourist.

NYC & Co.
www.nycgo.com/?event=view.maps#
NYC & Co is an official governmental office charged with promoting arts and culture. Its website has downloadable maps of bike routes, parks, the subway, and a handful of featured neighborhoods.

These maps are in reverse order with the backside of the book moving away from central Manhattan.

in Gravesend or Forest Hills, so may I

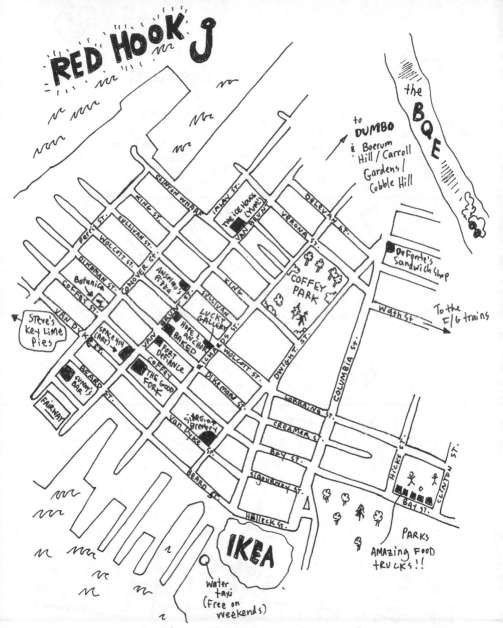

RED HOOK

the BQE

to DUMBO
& Boerum Hill / Carroll Gardens / Cobble Hill

CLINTON WHARF
KING ST.
SULLIVAN ST.
WOLCOTT ST.
DIKEMAN ST.
CONOVER ST.
PIER ST.
COFFEY ST.
VAN DYKE ST.
BEARD ST.
VAN DYKE ST.
BEARD ST.
VAN BRUNT
IMLAY ST.
KING
SULLIVAN ST.
VAN BRUNT
RICHARDS ST.
WOLCOTT ST.
DIKEMAN ST.
DWIGHT ST.
LORRAINE ST.
CREAMER ST.
BAY ST.
SIGOURNEY ST.
HALLECK ST.
BEARD ST.
DELEVAN ST.
VERONA ST.
COLUMBIA ST.
HICKS ST.
CLINTON ST.

The ice house (YUM!)
DeFonte's Sandwich Shop
COFFEY PARK
W 9th st. → To the F/G trains

Botanica
Anselmo's Pizza
LUCKY GALLERY
HOPE & ANCHOR
BAKED
Space 414 (ART)
FORT DEFIANCE
THE GOOD FORK
COFFEY
Sunny's Bar
FAIRWAY
SIXPOINT Brewery

← Steve's Key Lime Pies

BAY ST.
PARKS
AMAZING FOOD TRUCKS!!

IKEA

Water taxi (Free on weekends)

recommend the Chelsea Hotel @ 222 W. 23 251

And read The Post & The Daily News ~ maybe

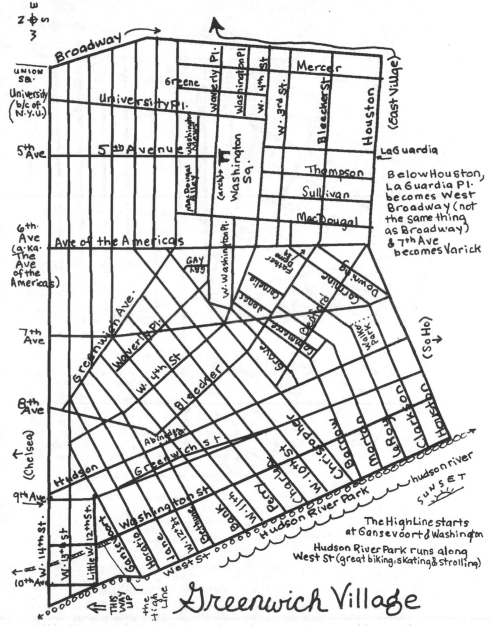

Greenwich Village

TRIBECA
(△ Below Canal)
Hudson River Park
runs all along West St.

viewed from above, the nightmare
traffic patterns of the Holland
Tunnel bear an uncanny resemblance
to an alien. especially if one is inclined
to add nostrils & eyes

X CITY HALL
(& probably
the crew
from Law
& Order)

crime scene before the yellow police

Little Italy, Lower East Side & Chinatown

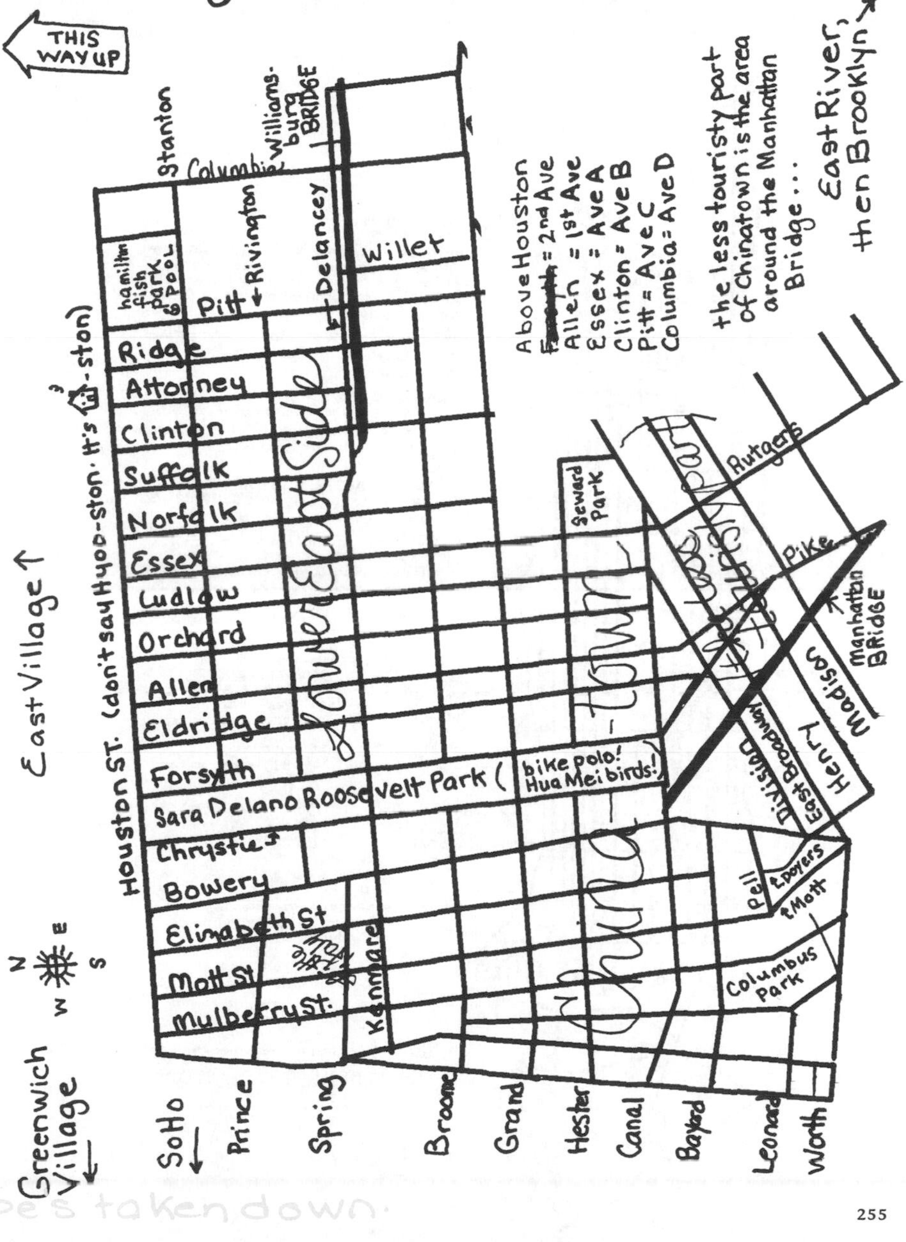

THIS WAY UP

East River, then Brooklyn →

Above Houston
Forsyth = 2nd Ave
Allen = 1st Ave
Essex = Ave A
Clinton = Ave B
Pitt = Ave C
Columbia = Ave D

...the less touristy part of Chinatown is the area around the Manhattan Bridge...

Stanton
Columbia
Williamsburg BRIDGE
Rivington
Delancey
Willet
Hamilton Fish Park & Pool
Pitt
Ridge
Attorney
Clinton
Suffolk
Norfolk
Essex
Ludlow
Orchard
Allen
Eldridge
Forsyth
Sara Delano Roosevelt Park (bike polo! Hua Mei birds!
Chrystie
Bowery
Elizabeth St
Mott St
Mulberry St.
Kenmare

Lower East Side

East Village ↑

Houston ST. (don't say Hyoo-ston. It's Hâ-ston)

Greenwich Village ↓

N E S W (compass)

SoHo ↓
Prince
Spring
Broome
Grand
Hester
Canal
Bayard
Leonard
Worth

China-town

Seward Park
Rutgers
Pike
Madison
Manhattan BRIDGE
Henry
East Broadway
Division
Pell
Doyers & Mott
Columbus Park

tape's taken down.

255

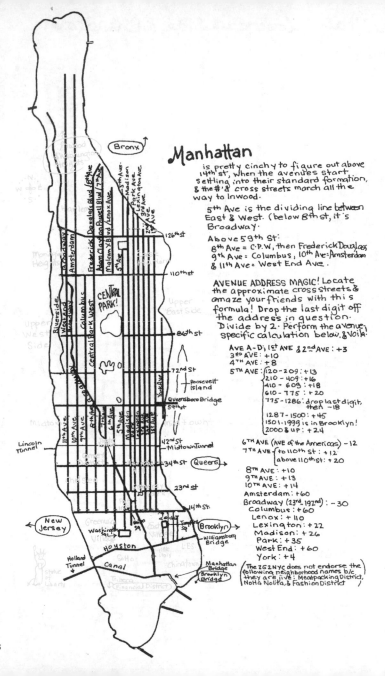

Manhattan

is pretty cinchy to figure out above 14th St, when the avenues start settling into their standard formation, & the #'d cross streets march all the way to Inwood.

5th Ave is the dividing line between East & West. (below 8th St, it's Broadway).

Above 59th St:
8th Ave = C.P.W., then Frederick Douglass
9th Ave = Columbus, 10th Ave = Amsterdam
& 11th Ave = West End Ave.

AVENUE ADDRESS MAGIC! Locate the approximate cross streets & amaze your friends with this formula! Drop the last digit off the address in question. Divide by 2. Perform the avenue specific calculation below, & voila!

AVE A–D, 1st AVE & 2nd AVE : +3
3rd AVE : +10
4th AVE : +8
5th AVE : { 120–209 : +13
210–409 : +16
410–609 : +18
610–775 : +20
775–1286 : drop last digit, then −18
1287–1500 : +45
1501–1999 is in Brooklyn!
2000 & UP : +24

6th AVE (AVE of the Americas) −12
7th AVE { to 110th St : +12
above 110th St : +20

8th AVE : +10
9th AVE : +13
10th AVE : +14
Amsterdam : +60
Broadway (23rd–192nd) : −30
Columbus : +60
Lenox : +110
Lexington : +22
Madison : +26
Park : +35
West End : +60
York : +4

(The 2G2NYC does not endorse the following neighborhood names b/c they are jive: Meatpacking District, NoHa Nolita, & Fashion District)

Bronx

Inwood
Washington
Heights

Harlem

Morningside
Heights

126th St

110th St

Upper
East Side

Upper
West
Side

CENTRAL PARK!

Riverside
West End
Broadway
Columbus
Amsterdam
Central Park West

Frederick Douglass Blvd / 8th Ave
Adam Clayton Powell Blvd / 7th Ave
Malcolm X Blvd / Lenox Ave
5th Ave

Madison
Park Ave
Lexington Ave
3rd Ave
2nd Ave
1st Ave

86th St

72nd St
Roosevelt Island

Queensboro Bridge
59th St

York Ave

42nd St
Midtown Tunnel

34th St   Queens

23rd St

14th St

Midtown

11th Ave
10th Ave
9th Ave
8th Ave
7th Ave
6th Ave
5th Ave
Madison
Park
Lexington
3rd Ave
2nd Ave
1st Ave

Lincoln Tunnel

New Jersey

Greenwich Village
Washington Sq.

Houston

Canal

Holland Tunnel

SoHo

Little Italy

Chinatown

Statue of Liberty

East Village
9th St
St. Mark's

Brooklyn
Williamsburg Bridge

L.E.S.

Manhattan Bridge

Brooklyn Bridge

Financial District